MEMOIRS

OF THE

AMERICAN ACADEMY IN ROME

VOLUME XXXVII

AMERICAN ACADEMY IN ROME
1993

COSA III

THE BUILDINGS OF THE FORUM

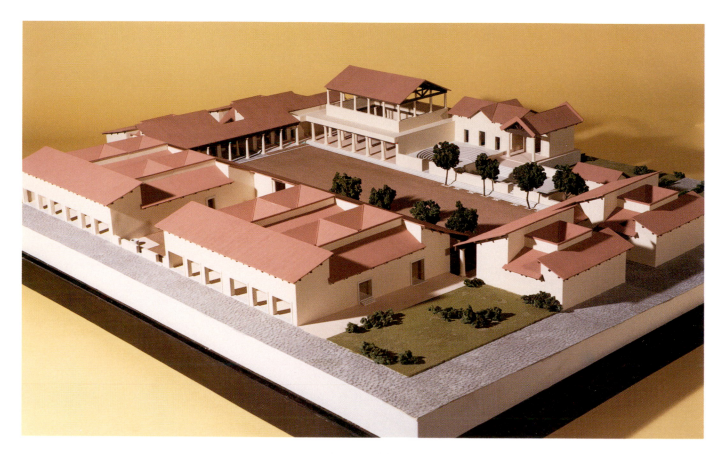

The Forum of Cosa about 150 B.C. This model, created for the "Year of the Etruscans" in Italy by Studio RomaTre, Rome, formed part of the exhibition "La Romanizzazione dell'Etruria: Il Territorio di Vulci," housed in the Polveriera Guzman in Orbetello (GR), 24 May–20 October 1985. Professor Andrea Carandini (University of Pisa) was project director. Architect Marco Travaglini directs the work of Studio RomaTre.

COSA III

THE BUILDINGS OF THE FORUM

Colony, Municipium, and Village

BY

†FRANK EDWARD BROWN
EMELINE HILL RICHARDSON
L. RICHARDSON, jr

PUBLISHED FOR THE AMERICAN ACADEMY IN ROME
by
The Pennsylvania State University Press
University Park, Pennsylvania
1993

Library of Congress Cataloging-in-Publication Data

Brown, Frank Edward, 1908–1988
   Cosa III : the buildings of the forum : colony, municipium, and
village / Frank Edward Brown, Emeline Hill Richardson, L.
Richardson.

      p.   cm.—(Memoirs of the American Academy in Rome ; v. 37)
   Includes bibliographical references.
   ISBN 0-271-00825-3
   1. Cosa (Extinct city)   2. Excavations (Archaeology)—Italy.
3. Architecture, Roman—Italy.   I. Richardson, Emeline Hill.
II. Richardson, Lawrence.   III.
DG12.A575   vol.37
[DG70.C63]
700 s—dc20
[937'.5]

92-20337
CIP

It is the policy of The Pennsylvania State University Press to use acid-free paper for the first
printing of all clothbound books. Publications on uncoated stock satisfy the minimum requirements of American National Standard for Information Sciences—Permanence of Paper for
Printed Library Materials, ANSI Z39.48–1984.

THE COSA PUBLICATIONS

Cosa I, History and Topography, by Frank E. Brown, *MAAR* 20 (1951) 5–113

La centuriazione di Cosa, by Ferdinando Castagnoli, *MAAR* 24 (1956) 149–65

Cosa: Black-Glaze Pottery, by Doris Mae Taylor, *MAAR* 25 (1957) 65–193

Cosa II, The Temples of the Arx, by Frank Edward Brown, Emeline Hill Richardson, and L. Richardson, jr, *MAAR* 26 (1960)

The Roman Thin Walled Pottery from Cosa (1948–54), by Maria Teresa Marabini Moevs, *MAAR* 32 (1973)

Cosa: The Utilitarian Pottery, by Stephen L. Dyson, *MAAR* 33 (1976)

Cosa: The Coins, by T. V. Buttrey, *MAAR* 34 (1980) 11–153

Italo-Megarian Ware at Cosa, by Maria Teresa Marabini Moevs, *MAAR* 34 (1980) 161–227

Aco in Northern Etruria: The Workshop of Cusonius at Cosa, by Maria Teresa Marabini Moevs, *MAAR* 34 (1980) 231–80

Cosa IV, The Houses, by Vincent J. Bruno and Russell T. Scott, *MAAR* 38 (1993)

The following studies of archaeological material from the excavations at Cosa are in progress and will be published in due course: *The Lamps* by Cleo Rickman Fitch and Norma Goldman, *Inscriptions on Stone and Brick-Stamps* by Edward Jan Bace,

The Sculpture and Furniture in Stone by Jacquelyn Collins-Clinton, *The Glass* by David Grose, *The Arretine Pottery, The Italic and Gaulish Sigillata* by Maria Teresa Marabini Moevs, *Black-Glaze Pottery Studies* by Ann Reynolds Scott, *The Storage Ware* by Elizabeth Lyding Will, and supplementary studies of the Arx by Ann Reynolds Scott, Russell T. Scott, Elizabeth Fentress, Michelle Hobart, and Teresa Clay.

From other publishers:

A Late Antique Shrine of Liber Pater at Cosa, by Jacquelyn Collins-Clinton (Études préliminaires aux religions orientales dans l'empire romain, edited by M. J. Vermaseren, volume 64), Leiden (E. J. Brill) 1977

The Roman Port and Fishery of Cosa, by Anna Marguerite McCann, Joanne Bourgeois, Elaine K. Gazda, John Peter Oleson, and Elizabeth Lyding Will, Princeton, New Jersey (Princeton University Press) 1987

Cosa, The Making of a Roman Town, by Frank E. Brown (Jerome Lectures, 13th series), Ann Arbor, Michigan (The University of Michigan Press) 1980

CONTENTS

List of Illustrations   xi

    Plans   xi

    Figures   xii

    Plates   xiv

Foreword   xxiii

Abbreviations   xxvii

    I.   276?–273 B.C.   3

    II.   273–241 B.C.   11

    III.   241–209 B.C.   31

    IV.   209–197 B.C.   51

    V.   197–180 B.C.   57

    VI.   180–175 B.C.   107

    VII.   175–150 B.C.   139

        Addendum 1: Temple B, Tiles and Terracotta Revetments   154

        Addendum 2: Terracotta Sculpture from Temple B   167

    VIII.   150–140 B.C.   207

    IX.   40/30 B.C.–A.D. 265/275   237

X.   A.D. 330–415   247
      Appendix 1: Paestum, "Teatro Circolare"   253
      Appendix 2: The Pottery Evidence from the "Teatro Circolare,"
         Paestum, 1955   264
      Appendix 3: Faunal Material from Forum SW/SE Cistern   295
Plates   299

LIST OF ILLUSTRATIONS

Frontispiece: The Forum in the mid-second century B.C., a model at the scale of 1:100.

Plans

    I.   Town plan
   II.   Plan of Forum
  III.   Plan of Comitium
  IV.   Plan of E buildings
   V.   Atrium Buildings I/II
  VI.   Atrium Buildings VII/VIII
 VII.   Atrium Buildings III/IV
VIII.   Atrium Buildings V/VI
  IX.   Southwest Annex
   X.   Plan of Basilica

Figures

1. Scheme of layout
2. Hill and town as planned
3. Basilica, sounding in Nave-3
4. Forum, restored plan (A), as of 241 B.C.
5. Comitium/Curia, NE and NW sections
6. Curia, SW and NE sections
7. Comitium, sounding in N corner
8. Comitium, NE sounding, potsherds
9. Comitium/Curia, restored plan and sections
10. Forum, restored NE elevation, as of 241 B.C.
11. Forum, restored plan (B), as of 209 B.C.
12. Sections of Plan IV
13. Carcer, sections, actual state and restored
14. Hypothetical bracing of posts, axonometric
15. Forum, restored NE elevation (B), as of 209 B.C.
16. Forum, restored plan (C), as of 197 B.C.
17. Forum, restored NE elevation (C), as of 197 B.C.
18. Forum, perspective, looking N (C), as of 197 B.C.
19. Forum, restored plan (D), as of 180 B.C.
20. AB I, plan, sections, and elevations, restored, first phase
21. AB I, sections A–E
22. AB I, Compluvium tiles
23. AB I, Room 18, basin
24. AB I, doorsills of Rooms 7, 1, and 12
25. AB I, Taberna 2, doorsill
26. AB I, Taberna 2, Fauces 4, and Taberna 5, sections
27. AB I, Fauces 4, "Tuscan" capital
28. AB II, plan, schematic reconstruction, first phase
29. AB II, SE façade, soundings
30. AB VII, plan, conjectural reconstruction
31. AB VII, section, center, looking NE
32. AB VII, section, Taberna 3, looking SW; AB VI, NE and NW sections; AB IV, SE Taberna, SE section
33. AB III, section, S sounding, looking SE
34. AB V/VI, axonometric, cross walls, facing W
35. Forum Annex, sections, bicolumnar monument, well-curb
36. Forum, as of 180 B.C., elevations and sections, NE, SW, and SE
37. N corner plot, sections F, G
38. N corner plot, Tabernae 25 and 24/26, I
39. Street O, sidewalk before Taberna 25, rim of puteal, presumably from Taberna 26

40. Forum, restored plan, as of 180 B.C.
41. Comitium/Curia, phase 2, restored plan and sections
42. NW cistern and settling basin, cross section
43. NW gutter, settling basin, and conduit, cross sections
44. Forum Reservoir and surroundings, plan, actual state
45. (A) Forum Reservoir, section, actual state, looking NE
    (B) Forum Reservoir, section, restored, looking SE
46. Main sewer under Street O, section at Street 6
47. Fornices, SW half, standing in A.D. 1793
48. Fornices, NW face, assembled and restored
49. Forum, as of 175 B.C., elevation and section, looking NW
50. Forum, restored plan, as of 140 B.C.
51. Forum Square, SW center along apron and sockets, restored plan and elevation
52. Forum, as of 175 B.C., elevation and section, looking SW
53. NW entranceway, *suggestus,* plans, sections, and axonometrics
54. NW entranceway, Tuscan capitals
55. N corner plot, Areas 11, 16, 21, 22 and NW Porticus Annex
56. Temple B, plan and SW and SE elevations
57. Temple B, comparison in plan and elevation with other similar temples
58. Forum, as of 150 B.C., elevations and sections, NE/SE
59. Basilica, sections as excavated
60. Basilica, N sounding, SE section
61. Basilica, E sounding, SE section
62. Basilica, plinths of columns of three types
63. Basilica, columns: shafts, bases, and capitals
64. Basilica, slabs of Vulci tufa steps of two sizes
65. Basilica, Ionic capital of Vulci tufa
66. Basilica, plaster of painted Masonry Style, restored
67. Basilica, base molding of a pedestal for a single statue
68. Basilica, well-curb of cistern
69. Basilica, restored plan
70. Basilica, restored sections
71. First basilica in Rome and Basilica Fulvia-Aemilia, partial plans, restored
72. First basilica in Rome and Basilica Fulvia-Aemilia, sections, restored
73. Forum, as of 140 B.C., elevations and sections, NW/NE
74. Basilica, new settling basin, N corner of square
75. Forum, as of 140 B.C., elevation and section looking SE
76. Forum, restored plan, 40/30 B.C.–A.D. 265/275
77. Odeum, restored section (G. C. Izenour)

78. Cosa and Succosa
79. Forum, restored plan, A.D. 330–415
80. Paestum, "Teatro Circolare," plan, actual state
81. Paestum, "Teatro Circolare," sections, actual state
82. Paestum, "Teatro Circolare," restored plan
83. Paestum, "Teatro Circolare," restored section, looking N
84. Paestum, "Teatro Circolare," pottery from trench in SW corner, center room of Curia building, first level
85. Paestum, "Teatro Circolare," pottery from trench in SW corner, center room of Curia building, second level
86. Paestum, "Teatro Circolare," pottery from trench in SW corner, center room of Curia building, second level (nos. 37–43) and apron wall (rostra) fill (nos. 53–65)
87. Paestum, "Teatro Circolare," pottery from apron wall (rostra) fill

Plates

1. SE cistern on NE side
2. NW cistern on SW side
3. Planting pit #0
4. Comitium and Curia, air view
5. Comitium, NE retaining wall, exterior
6. Unfinished planting pit, #4
7. Comitium, NE retaining wall, exterior plaster
8. Comitium, SW retaining wall, exterior plaster
9. Comitium, amphitheater center, circle step, and drain
10. Comitium, SE steps
11. Comitium, NW retaining wall/Basilica SE wall
12. Comitium, sounding in N corner
13. Curia, floor and base of pillar
14. Curia, fragments of wall decoration
15. Comitium, sounding in NE quadrant
16. Forum, E corner, air view
17. E corner enclosure, silting tank, reveal block, looking SW
18. Cistern enclosure, sounding in N corner
19. Precinct and Carcer, looking SE
20. Carcer, looking N
21. Carcer, cross wall
22. Carcer, doorway, looking NE
23. Forum Square, planting pits and post holes, NE side

24. Forum Square, Post Hole #5, NE side
25. Cistern enclosure, stair to Comitium
26. Cistern enclosure, floor and immured drum, looking E
27. Forum Square, NE retaining wall, looking E
28. Templum Beta, dry-laid NW wall
29. Templum Beta, NE wall, exterior
30. Templum Beta, NE wall, interior
31. Inscription, C72.129
32. Forum, SE cistern, SE end
33. Forum, SE cistern, NW end
34. Forum, E corner, Street Q, open drain
35. Templum Beta, forecourt, E corner
36. Templum Beta, forecourt, pavement covering the abandoned silting tank
37. Forum Square, E corner, looking N
38. AB I, balloon photograph (Whittlesey)
39. AB I, looking E
40. AB I, Impluvium, cistern vault and drains, looking E
41. AB I, Atrium, cistern drawshaft
42. AB I, Room 18, doorsill
43. AB I, Room 7, looking NE
44. AB I, Entryway 1, looking NE
45. AB I, Entryway 12, looking SW
46. AB I, Entryway 4, looking E
47. AB I, Taberna 2, doorsill, reused
48. AB I, Taberna 2, Entryway 1, Room 7, looking SE
49. AB I, Taberna 5, E corner
50. AB I, Taberna 19, soak-away pit vault
51. AB I, Taberna 15, looking NE
52. AB II, NE façade (between and beneath late walls), looking S
53. AB II, SE façade and sounding (SW wall of entryway and blocked opening of SW taberna), looking W
54. AB VII, NE façade and partition walls of Spaces 10, 8, and 6, looking NW
55. AB VII, SW wall of Taberna 3, looking NW
56. AB VII, Impluvium in 12, drain and cistern, looking N
57. AB VII, cistern in 12, looking NE
58. AB VII, gutter and steps of passageway, looking N
59. SE entranceway (Shrine of Liber Pater), "Tuscan" capital
60. Square, AB III/IV, Annex, AB V/VI, balloon photograph (Whittlesey)
61. AB III and II, juncture corners, looking W
62. AB III/IV, party wall and quoins, looking NW

63. AB III, NW façade and Reservoir, looking SW
64. AB III, NW wall, reveal, and doorsill in partition wall, looking NW
65. AB III, NW wall and opening to Reservoir, sounding with passageway and pier, looking SW
66. AB III, SE party wall, SW end and sounding, looking S
67. AB V, NE façade and portico, looking W
68. AB VI, sounding, NW taberna, looking NW
69. AB V/VI, SW wall and S corner on Streets 5 and Q, looking NW
70. AB VI, SE well, engaged half-column, looking SE
71. Forum Annex, SE column base, looking E
72. Forum Annex, SW end, stairs and exedrae, looking W
73. N corner plot, Taberna 25, looking S
74. N corner plot, Taberna 24/26, looking S
75. Street O, sidewalk before Taberna 26, "Tuscan" capital
76. Curia, SE side of podium, looking SW
77. Curia, N corner, basin and vault, looking NE
78. Forum Square, double trench, central, looking NE
79. Forum SW Porticus, looking SE
80. Forum gutter and W settling basin, looking NW
81. Forum Reservoir, looking E
82. Forum Reservoir, looking N
83. Forum Reservoir, central pier and sounding, looking N
84. Forum Square, SE end, post holes of one square, looking SE
85. Forum Square, SE end, post hole with lid and ring
86. Forum Square, SE end, post hole, eccentric
87. Streets O and 6, looking NE
88. Street 5, sewer, looking SE
89. SE entranceway, sounding, looking W
90. NW Porticus and entranceway, looking SW
91. NW Porticus, drum and column, looking S
92. SW Porticus, capital of column
93. Antefix with head of goddess (C69.203)
94. Fornices, looking S
95. Fornices, SW unit, looking SW
96. Fornices, NE unit, looking NE
97. Forum Square, SW center, apron of slabs and sockets, looking SE
98. Forum Square, SW center, apron of slabs and sockets, looking E
99. NW entranceway, centered remains of *suggestus*, looking SE
100. NW end of SW retaining wall along Street 7, looking SE
101. Curia III, NW wall as later rebuilt, interior
102. Curia III, SE wall, interior of upper part
103. Curia III, NE wall with buttresses, view looking NW

104. Temple B, NE wall
105. Temple B, SE flank
106. Temple B, N corner and passage between Temple B and Curia III
107. Temple B, cella, interior with pit of clandestine diggers
108. Temple B, column capital found in Comitium
109. Temple B, shell antefix with a head of Silenus
110. Temple B, shell antefix with the head of a maenad (head)
111. Temple B, shell antefix with the head of a maenad (shell)
112. Temple B, raking cornice
113. Temple B, tile for the setting of the raking cornice
114. Temple B, open cresting A
115. Temple B, open cresting B
116. Temple B, revetment plaque with a design of crossed ribbons
117. Temple B, repair of the decoration, antefix shell
118. Temple B, repair of the decoration, open cresting
119. Temple B, repair of the decoration, revetment plaque of serpentine design
120. Temple B, pedimental sculpture I i 1
121. Temple B, pedimental sculpture I i 2
122. Temple B, pedimental sculpture I i 13a, profile to right
123. Temple B, pedimental sculpture I i 13a, full face
124. Temple B, pedimental sculpture I i 13a, three-quarters view
125. Temple B, pedimental sculpture I i 13b
126. Temple B, pedimental sculpture I i 13c
127. Temple B, pedimental sculpture I i 14a
128. Temple B, pedimental sculpture I i 14b
129. Temple B, pedimental sculpture I i 15a
130. Temple B, pedimental sculpture I i 15b
131. Temple B, pedimental sculpture I i 15c
132. Temple B, pedimental sculpture I i 16a
133. Temple B, pedimental sculpture I i 16b
134. Temple B, pedimental sculpture I i 17
135. Temple B, pedimental sculpture I i 18
136. Temple B, pedimental sculpture I i 19, front view
137. Temple B, pedimental sculpture I i 19, side view
138. Temple B, pedimental sculpture I i 20
139. Temple B, pedimental sculpture I i 21
140. Temple B, pedimental sculpture I i 22, interior of arm
141. Temple B, pedimental sculpture I i 22, exterior of arm
142. Temple B, pedimental sculpture I i 23
143. Temple B, pedimental sculpture I i 24a
144. Temple B, pedimental sculpture I i 24c
145. Temple B, pedimental sculpture I i 25

146.   Temple B, pedimental sculpture I i 26
147.   Temple B, pedimental sculpture I i 27
148.   Temple B, pedimental sculpture I i 28
149.   Etruscan ash-urn, Volterra, Museo Guarnacci, no. 223
150.   Etruscan ash-urn, Volterra, Museo Guarnacci, no. 221
151.   Etruscan ash-urn, Paris, Bibliothèque Nationale
152.   Etruscan ash-urn, Volterra, Museo Guarnacci, no. 238
153.   Etruscan ash-urn, Volterra, Museo Guarnacci, no. 236
154.   Etruscan ash-urn, Volterra, Tomba Inghirami
155.   Temple B, frieze I ii 1
156.   Temple B, frieze I ii 2
157.   Temple B, frieze I ii 3
158.   Temple B, frieze I ii 4
159.   Temple B, frieze I ii 5
160.   Temple B, frieze I ii 6
161.   Temple B, frieze I ii 7
162.   Temple B, fragments of life-size statuary I iii 1a
163.   Temple B, fragments of life-size statuary I iii 1b
164.   Temple B, fragments of life-size statuary I iii 1c
165.   Temple B, fragments of life-size statuary I iii 1d
166.   Temple B, fragments of life-size statuary I iii 1e
167.   Temple B, fragments of life-size statuary I iii 1l
168.   Temple B, fragments of life-size statuary I iii 1m
169.   Temple B, fragments of life-size statuary I iii 2a
170.   Temple B, fragments of life-size statuary I iii 2b
171.   Temple B, fragments of life-size statuary I iii 2c
172.   Temple B, fragments of life-size statuary I iii 2d
173.   Temple B, fragments of life-size statuary I iii 2e
174.   Temple B, fragments of life-size statuary I iii 2f
175.   Temple B, fragments of life-size statuary I iii 2g
176.   Temple B, fragments of life-size statuary I iii 3a
177.   Temple B, fragments of life-size statuary I iii 3b
178.   Temple B, fragments of life-size statuary I iii 3c
179.   Temple B, fragments of life-size statuary I iii 3e
180.   Temple B, fragments of life-size statuary I iii 4a
181.   Temple B, fragments of life-size statuary I iii 4b
182.   Temple B, fragments of life-size statuary I iii 4c
183.   Temple B, fragments of life-size statuary I iii 4d
184.   Temple B, fragments of life-size statuary I iii 4e
185.   Temple B, fragments of life-size statuary I iii 5a
186.   Temple B, fragments of life-size statuary I iii 5b
187.   Temple B, fragments of life-size statuary I iii 5c
188.   Temple B, fragments of life-size statuary I iii 5d

189. Temple B, fragments of life-size statuary I iii 6a
190. Temple B, fragments of life-size statuary I iii 6c
191. Temple B, bases I iv 1
192. Temple B, bases I iv 2
193. Temple B, bases I iv 3
194. Temple B, bases I iv 4a
195. Temple B, bases I iv 4b
196. Temple B, bases I iv 8a
197. Temple B, bases I iv 8b
198. Temple B, ex-votos, Red Group II i 1a
199. Temple B, ex-votos, Red Group II i 1b
200. Temple B, ex-votos, Red Group II i 1c
201. Temple B, ex-votos, Red Group II i 1d
202. Temple B, ex-votos, Red Group II i 1e
203. Temple B, ex-votos, Red Group II i 1f
204. Temple B, ex-votos, Red Group II i 1g
205. Temple B, ex-votos, Red Group II i 1h
206. Temple B, ex-votos, Red Group II i 1i
207. Temple B, ex-votos, Red Group II i 2a
208. Temple B, ex-votos, Red Group II i 2b
209. Temple B, ex-votos, Red Group II i 3a
210. Temple B, ex-votos, Red Group II i 4
211. Temple B, ex-votos, Red Group II i 5a
212. Temple B, ex-votos, Red Group II i 5b
213. Temple B, ex-votos, Red Group II i 6
214. Temple B, ex-votos, Red Group II i 7, front
215. Temple B, ex-votos, Red Group II i 7, side
216. Temple B, ex-votos, Red Group II i 7, back
217. Temple B, ex-votos, Red Group II i 8
218. Temple B, ex-votos, Red Group II i 9
219. Temple B, ex-votos, White Group II ii 1a
220. Temple B, ex-votos, White Group II ii 1b
221. Temple B, ex-votos, White Group II ii 1c
222. Temple B, ex-votos, White Group II ii 1d
223. Temple B, ex-votos, White Group II ii 1e
224. Temple B, ex-votos, White Group II ii 1f
225. Temple B, ex-votos, White Group II ii 2
226. Basilica and surroundings, balloon photograph (Whittlesey)
227. Basilica and surroundings, looking E
228. Basilica, NE foundations and tribunal, looking S
229. Basilica, tribunal and vault, looking WNW
230. Basilica, second cistern, looking SE
231. Basilica, SE wall with putlog holes, looking ESE

232. Basilica, NE wall of tribunal with window, looking N
233. Basilica, column base of lower tier
234. Basilica, column capital of lower tier
235. Basilica, column capital of upper tier
236. Basilica, slabs of Vulci tufa, reused
237. Basilica, Ionic capital of Vulci tufa, reused
238. Basilica, block of travertine fitted to a plinth of a column
239. Basilica, stair to the platform above the ambulatory, base in the NW cellar of the Curia
240. Basilica, stair to the platform above the ambulatory, print on the NW wall of Curia III
241. Steps along the NE side of the Square, SE section, looking NW
242. Steps along the NE side of the Square, NW section, looking E
243. AB IV, house, once taberna on Square, doubled walls
244. AB IV, house, once taberna on Square, raised floor
245. AB V, house, once taberna on Square, mosaic floor
246. AB VI, barnyard, SE wall
247. AB VI, barnyard, mangers
248. Basilica, collapsed NW wall
249. Odeum, fallen pillars beside standing one
250. Odeum, remaining piers, ramped vaults, and steps, looking NE
251. Odeum, pillar and floor of scaena
252. Odeum, inscription of Nero and Claudius
253. Odeum, stair from Street 7
254. Comitium, remains of second flooring, looking E
255. Curia, NW buttress
256. Curia, SE basement, Mithraeum, looking NE
257. Curia, SE basement, Mithraeum, parts of square pillar
258. Curia, SE basement, Mithraeum, marble leg with strut
259. Base of kiln for firing earthen vessels
260. Basilica, church in NE aisle, NW court and entrance
261. Basilica, church in NE aisle, SE apse and altar
262. Basilica, taberna with two ovens in S corner, looking S
263. Basilica, second taberna in S corner, looking S
264. Comitium, late wall and new threshing floor, looking S
265. Basilica, tabernae in S corner, statue built into party wall
266. Basilica, tabernae in S corner, statues extracted and mounted
267. Shrine of Liber Pater, central room, looking SE
268. Shrine of Liber Pater, statue of Bacchus
269. Paestum, "Teatro Circolare," imported pottery, second half of the sixth century B.C.: Corinthian: Cipriani/Avagliano 1, 17, 45, 47, 48, 49, 50; Attic Black Figure: Cipriani/Avagliano 18

270. Paestum, "Teatro Circolare," Paestan Red Figure and Black-Glaze, late fourth century: Cipriani/Avagliano 4, 88

271. Paestum, "Teatro Circolare," Paestan Black-Glaze with superimposed color, second half of the fourth century: Cipriani/ Avagliano 5, 6; Black-Glaze, first half of the fifth century: Cipriani/Avagliano 67

272. Paestum, "Teatro Circolare," headless terracotta figurine, third century B.C.: Cipriani/Avagliano 16

273. Paestum, "Teatro Circolare," fabbrica coloniale di tradizione Ionica, mid-sixth century: Cipriani/Avagliano 21, 22

274. Paestum, "Teatro Circolare," Black-Glaze, fifth century B.C.: Cipriani/Avagliano 25; Paestan Red Figure, second half of the fourth century B.C.: Cipriani/Avagliano 28

275. Paestum, "Teatro Circolare," Black-Glaze, fifth century B.C.: Cipriani/Avagliano 27

276. Paestum, "Teatro Circolare," Paestan Black-Glaze with superimposed color, end of the fourth and early third century B.C.: Cipriani/Avagliano 29, 30, 70, 71, 72, 73, 74

277. Paestum, "Teatro Circolare," gray cooking ware with white decoration, fourth to third century B.C.: Cipriani/Avagliano 39a and b

278. Paestum, "Teatro Circolare," fragments of terracotta figurines, last decades of the fourth century B.C.: Cipriani/Avagliano 44

279. Paestum, "Teatro Circolare," miscellaneous pottery: Corinthian, beginning of the fifth century B.C.: Cipriani/Avagliano 46; Paestan Red Figure, second half of the fourth century B.C.: Cipriani/ Avagliano 69

280. Paestum, "Teatro Circolare," Attic pottery, fifth century B.C.: Cipriani/Avagliano 51, 52

281. Paestum, "Teatro Circolare," Black-Glaze pottery, probably Paestan, mid-fifth century B.C.: Cipriani/Avagliano 68

282. Paestum, "Teatro Circolare," miscellaneous pottery: coloniale di tradizione Ionica, mid-sixth century B.C.: Cipriani/Avagliano 56

283. Paestum, "Teatro Circolare," miscellaneous finds: Paestan miniature oenochoe, sixth to fourth century B.C. (?): Cipriani/ Avagliano 89; Loomweights; fragment of a bronze pin

FOREWORD

This volume presents the results of the campaigns of excavation conducted by the American Academy in Rome in the forum of ancient Cosa during the months of May and June of the years 1950–54 and 1967–72. It is the authors' pleasant duty to renew the expression of their gratitude to the authorities of the Directorate General of Archaeology and Fine Arts of the Republic of Italy and, above all, to the Superintendents of the Antiquities of Etruria who fostered our work at Cosa at those times, Giacomo Caputo and Guglielmo Maetzke. Nor could it have gone forward without the constant interest and generosity of the late Marchesa Maria Rita Guglielmi, on whose land the ruins of Cosa lie.

Cosa could not have been unearthed and studied without the initiative of the American Academy in Rome and the support of its directors, Laurance P. Roberts, Richard A. Kimball, and Bartlett Hayes, during the excavations, and Henry Millon and John H. D'Arms in the period of subsequent study and research. The support of many benefactors and collaborators in the United States is likewise gratefully acknowledged: Columbia University, the State University of New York at Binghamton, Wesleyan University, the Bollingen and Old Dominion Foundations, the Samuel H. Kress Foundation, and the National Endowment for the Humanities.

The excavations were directed by F. E. Brown (1950–52, 1967–71), L. Richardson, jr (1953–54), and R. T. Scott (1972). Architects on the staff were H. A. Detweiler (1954), J. Guthrie and F. Heinsius (1967), F. Adams and D. White (1968), G. Andres, R. Diaz, and C. Morrison (1969), R. Diaz (1970), J. Guthrie and J. Stubbs (1971), and R. Gibbons, J. Guthrie, and B. R. Kelley (1972). The photographers were E. H. Richardson (1950–54), V. Brown (1967), B. B. Bini (1968–71), and K. Werner (1972). G. Tozzi, from the Sopraintendenza alle Antichità dell'Etruria, served as ceramicist (1950–54, 1967–69) and Ivo Picciolini as foreman (1950–52, 1967–72). The trench masters were P. MacKendrick (1950), G. Doria, E. Hill, and H. E. Russell (1951), M. Hoffman, E. H. Richardson, and L. Richardson, jr (1952), E. C. Baade, K. S. Falk, M. Hoffman, E. H. Richardson, L. Richardson, jr, and D. M. Taylor (1953), K. S. Falk, J. A. Hanson, E. H. Richardson, and L. Richardson, jr (1954), D. Cast, J. Collins, B. Frier, T. Pandiri, and A. Reynolds (1967), J. Collins, M. K. Gamel, G. Houston, A. Laidlaw, and A. R. Scott (1968), M. Bell, J. Collins, J. Keith, R. Kenworthy, and F. Kleiner (1969), and F. Kleiner, D. Parrish, and A. R. Scott (1970).

In the production of this volume of reports, F. E. Brown was responsible for the parts on the general design and overall history of the Forum, the Atrium Buildings, the Southwest Annex, and the Basilica. L. Richardson, jr, has contributed the reports on the buildings excavated during his years as director: the Comitium/Curia complex, Temple B and its revetments, the Carcer, and the East Corner of the Forum. He also wrote the report of the 1955 cleaning and examination of the "Teatro Circolare" at Paestum. E. H. Richardson contributed the chapter on the terracotta sculpture from Temple B. Dottoressa Marina Cipriani and Dottore Giovanni Avagliano of the Sopraintendenza alle Antichità di Salerno contributed a special study of the pottery from the "Teatro Circolare" at Paestum, and Kathy Gruspier and Dottore Salvatore Scali (Museo dell'Arte Orientale, Rome) a study of the faunal material from the cistern in the Southwest Annex.

The Richardsons' chapters were originally written more than thirty years ago, shortly after the excavations of those areas were finished. But because the plan of the northeast side of the Forum of Cosa is an intricate and interlocking one, it was decided to wait until the plan of the Forum as a whole was clearer before publishing them. Over the years in between considerable new evidence that demanded modification of the original views came to light, as well as important material for comparison at other sites. Since by the time excavations at Cosa were resumed in 1965 the Richardsons were in Italy only at intervals, as work progressed it was then not always possible to discuss at length the implications of what was emerging and to reach complete harmony on the interpretation of the archaeological picture, and on those occasions when all three authors assembled to discuss the problems of the Forum of Cosa, it was difficult to recall to mind all the factors involved in a decision. It was not until a short time ago, when this report was being put into final shape, that the whole historical picture as envisaged by Brown became clearly visible. There was some disagreement on certain details of the sequence of events, their interpretation and precise dates, but by that time Brown's failing health made it impossible to settle such questions to everyone's satisfaction.

So far as possible, we have attempted to achieve unanimity in the editing of the reports. In the few cases where that proved impossible we have allowed the excavator to have the stronger voice. A very attentive reader will find minor discrepancies and omissions due to the distance between the date of composition and the date of publication, but we have tried to produce a smooth text and to include consideration of at least the major advances in our knowledge since the first draft was written.

Emeline Hill Richardson
L. Richardson, jr
Ann R. Scott
Russell T. Scott

ABBREVIATIONS

The abbreviations of titles of periodicals and standard reference works used in this book are those approved by the *American Journal of Archaeology* and the *Oxford Classical Dictionary,* plus the following short titles:

Andrén
: A. Andrén, *Architectural Terracottas from Etrusco-Italic Temples,* 2 vols. (Lund/Leipzig, 1939)

Brown 1951
: F. E. Brown, *Cosa I, History and Topography* (*MAAR* 20 [1951] 5–113)

Brown 1960
: F. E. Brown, *Cosa II, The Temples of the Arx: The Architecture* (*MAAR* 26 [1960], 7–147)

Brown 1980
: F. E. Brown, *Cosa, The Making of a Roman Town* (Ann Arbor, Michigan, 1980)

Brunn-Körte
: H. von Brunn, *I rilievi delle urne etrusche* 1 (Rome, 1870); G. Körte, *I rilievi delle urne etrusche* 2.1 (Berlin, 1890), 2.2 (Berlin, 1896)

Buttrey 1980
: T. V. Buttrey, *Cosa: The Coins* (*MAAR* 34 [1980]), 11–153

Crawford 1974
: M. H. Crawford, *Roman Republican Coinage,* 2 vols. (Cambridge, 1974)

Dyson 1976
: S. L. Dyson, *Cosa, The Utilitarian Pottery* (*MAAR* 33 [1976])

Giglioli
: G. Q. Giglioli, *L'arte etrusca* (Milan, 1935)

Lamboglia 1952
: N. Lamboglia, *Per una classificazione preliminare della ceramica campana* (Bordighera, 1952)

Massa-Pairault
: F.-H. Massa-Pairault, "Recherches sur l'art et l'artisanat etrusco-

	italique à l'époque hellénistique," *Bibliothèque des Écoles Françaises d'Athènes et de Rome* 257 (1985)
McClean	S. W. Grose, *Catalogue of the McClean Collection of Greek Coins* (Cambridge, 1923–29)
Mercando 1963	L. Mercando, "Area sacra di S. Omobono, esplorazione delle fase repubblicane e saggi di scavo sulla platea dei templi gemelli," *BullCom* 79 (1963/64), 35–67
Morel 1963	J.-P. Morel, "Notes sur la céramique etrusco-campanienne, vases à vernis noir de Sardaigne et d'Arezzo," *MélRome* 75 (1963), 7–58
Morel 1965	J.-P. Morel, "Céramique à vernis noir du Forum Romain et du Palatin," *MélRome*, Supp. 3 (1965)
Morel 1969	J.-P. Morel, "Études de céramique campanienne, I, L'atelier des petites estampilles," *MélRome* 81 (1969), 59–117
Overbeck-Mau	J. Overbeck and A. Mau, *Pompeji in seinen Gebäuden Alterthümern und Kunstwerken* (Leipzig, 1884)
Pergamum	*Altertümer von Pergamon, herausgegeben im Auftrage des königlich preussischen Ministers der geistlichen unterrichts- und medizinal-Angelegenheiten* (Berlin, 1885–)
E. H. Richardson 1960	E. H. Richardson, *Cosa II, The Temples of the Arx: The Terracotta Sculpture* (*MAAR* 26 [1960], 301–80)
L. Richardson 1960	L. Richardson, jr, *Cosa II, The Temples of the Arx: The Architectural Terracottas* (*MAAR* 26 [1960], 149–300)
Salmon 1969	E. T. Salmon, *Roman Colonization under the Republic* (London, 1969)
Taylor 1957	D. M. Taylor, *Cosa: Black-Glaze Pottery* (*MAAR* 25 [1957], 65–193)

Abbreviations of Journal and Series Titles

AA	Archäologischer Anzeiger
AIRRS	Acta Instituti Romani Regni Sueciae (=*SkrRom*)
AJA	American Journal of Archaeology
AJP	American Journal of Philology
AnalRom	Analecta romana Instituti Danici
ArchClass	Archeologia classica
ArchEspArq	Archivo español de arqueología
AttiCStR	Atti del . . . Congresso nazionale di studi romani
BABesch	Bulletin antieke beschaving. Annual Papers on Classical Archaeology
BibEFAR	Bibliothèque des Écoles françaises d'Athènes et de Rome
BonnJbb	Bonner Jahrbücher des Rheinischen Landesmuseums in Bonn und des Vereins von Altertumsfreunden im Rheinlande
BStM	Bollettino dell'Associazione internazionale degli studi mediterranei
BullCom	Bullettino della Commissione archeologica comunale di Roma
Chiron	Chiron. Mitteilungen der Kommission für alte Geschichte und Epigraphik des Deutschen Archäologischen Instituts
CIL	Corpus Inscriptionum Latinarum
DarSag	C. Daremberg and E. Saglio, *Dictionnaire des antiquités grecques et romaines*

Délos	Exploration archéologique de Délos faite par l'École française d'Athènes
DialArch	Dialoghi di archeologia
EAA	*Enciclopedia dell'arte antica, classica e orientale*
EPROER	Études préliminaires aux religions orientales dans l'empire romain
JdI	Jahrbuch des Deutschen Archäologischen Instituts
JFA	Journal of Field Archaeology
JRS	The Journal of Roman Studies
MAAR	Memoirs of the American Academy in Rome
MEFARSupp (MEFAR)	Mélanges de l'École française de Rome. Supplement
MélRome	Mélanges de l'École française de Rome
MemLinc	Memorie. Atti della Accademia nazionale dei Lincei. Classe di scienze morali, storiche e filologiche
MonPiot	Monuments et mémoires. Fondation E. Piot
NSc	Notizie degli scavi di antichità
OpusArch	Opuscula archaeologica
PAAR	American Academy in Rome. Papers and Monographs
PBSR	Papers of the British School at Rome
PdP	La parola del passato
QAL	Quaderni di archeologia della Libia
RAAN	Rendiconti dell'Accademia di archeologia, lettere e belle arti, Napoli
RE	Pauly-Wissowa, *Real-Encyclopädie der klassischen Altertumswissenschaft*
RendPontAcc	Atti della Pontificia Accademia romana di archeologia. Rendiconti
RivIstArch	Rivista dell'Istituto nazionale d'archeologia e storia dell'arte
RömMitt	Mitteilungen des Deutschen Archäologischen Instituts. Römische Abteilung
RömQ	Römische Quartalschrift für christliche Altertumskunde und Kirchengeschichte
RStLig	Rivista di studi liguri
SkrRom	Skrifter utgivna av Svenska Institutet i Rom
StEtr	Studi etruschi
TAPA	Transactions of the American Philological Association
TLL	Thesaurus linguae latinae

COSA III
THE BUILDINGS OF THE
FORUM

I. 276?–273 B.C.

(Plans I, II; Figs. 1–3)

The planners of the colonial town of Cosa set aside for the Forum and the buildings that would eventually surround it an ample rectangular area in the eastern quadrant of the town-site. The area was delimited by four streets, now designated O and 5, R and 7. Streets O and 5 were important thoroughfares, leading to the NE and SE gates of the town, whence roads descended to the eastern half of the colonial territory and to the lagoon and anchorage at the foot of the hill, which were the nearest sources of food from the sea and goods from abroad. Street R was a processional avenue, mounting to the eastern height of the city, as yet little explored, while Street 7 was a minor roadway, included in the plan primarily as a boundary. It lay exactly 300 p.R. (88.80 m) from Street 5, did not continue northwestward beyond Street O, and in the course of time was overrun by buildings extending across it.[1]

A sounding (Fig. 3) down to its pavement and SW sidewalk under the floors of the Basilica brought to light a boundary stone, presumably one of a series. This is a squared block of limestone, uninscribed, 0.30 m on a side and 0.40 m high, set upright on the inner edge of the sidewalk, a third of the way between Streets O and Q. Below, on the pavement, was the corner of a mortar bedding for another

1. Brown 1951, 23–27, 71; Brown 1980, 18–21, 37–38.

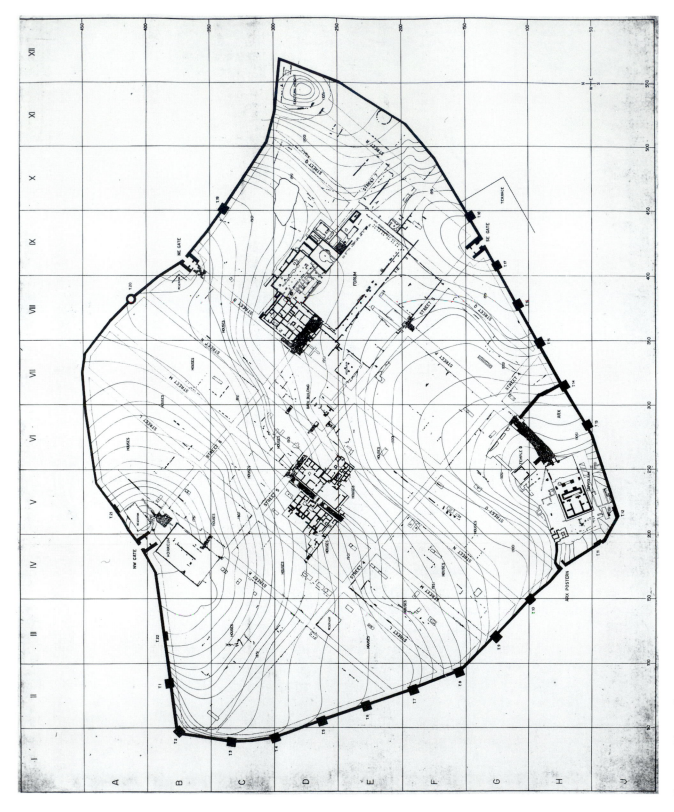

PLAN 1. Town plan

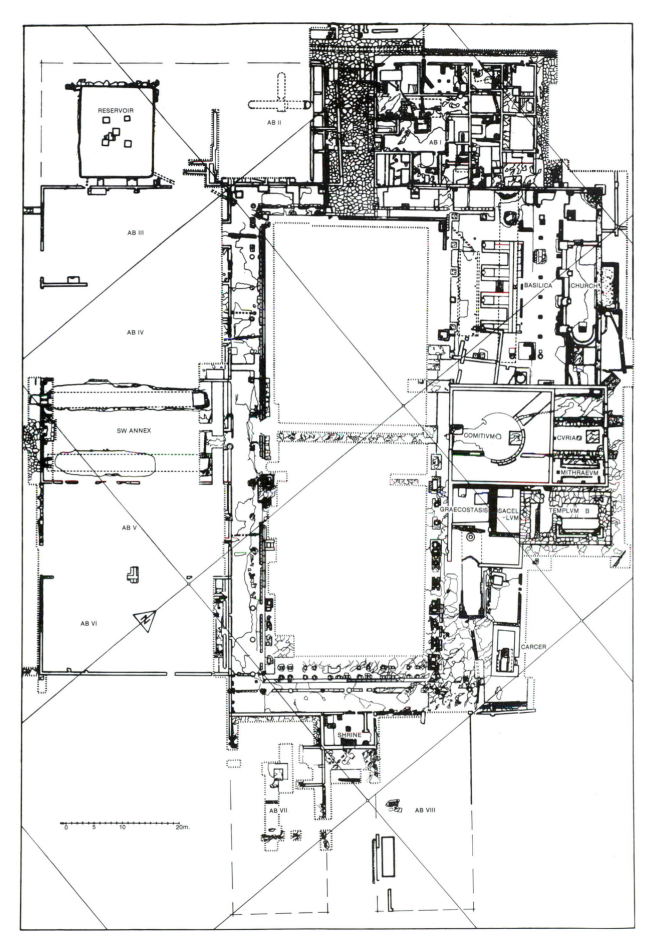

RESERVOIR

AB II

AB I

D

AB III

BASILICA

CHURCH

AB IV

SW ANNEX

COMITIVM

CVRIA

MITHRAEVM

GRAECOSTASIS SACEL -LVM

TEMPLVM B

AB V

AB VI

N

CARCER

SHRINE

0 5 10 20m.

AB VII

AB VIII

Plan ii. Plan of Forum

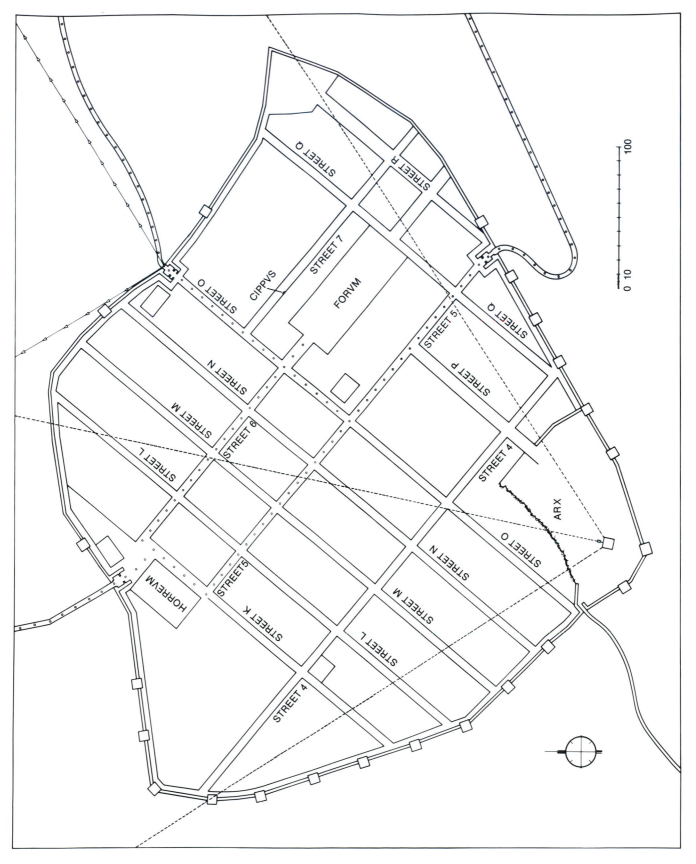

STREET Q

STREET R

STREET 7

CIPPVS

FORVM

STREET O

STREET N

STREET M

STREET 6

STREET L

STREET 5

STREET 5

STREET K

HORREVM

STREET 4

STREET L

STREET M

STREET N

STREET O

STREET 4

ARX

STREET P

STREET Q

STREET 5

100

0   10

Fig. 1. Scheme of layout

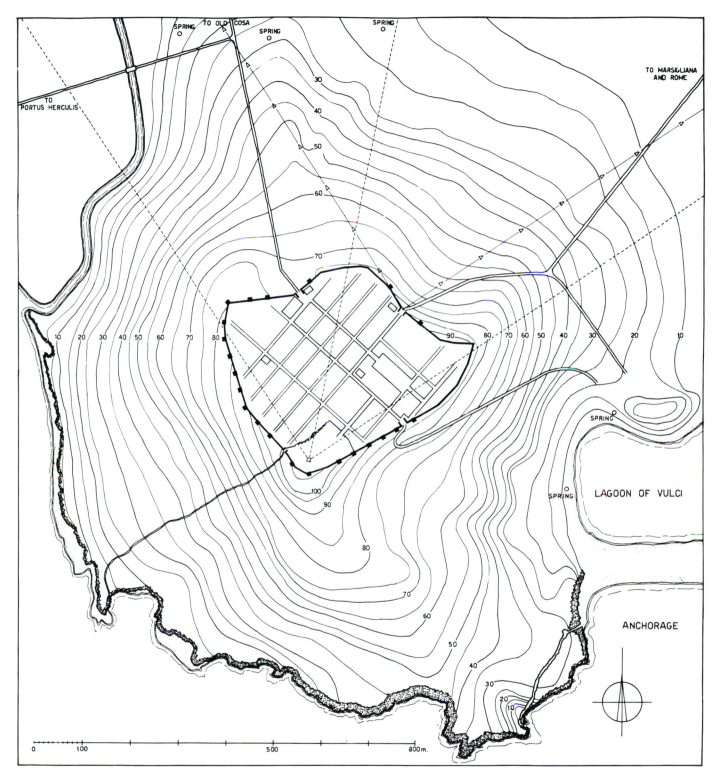

SPRING ○ TO OLD COSA SPRING

SPRING

TO PORTUS HERCULIS

TO MARSIGLIANA AND ROME

30

40

50

60

70

80

90 80 70 60 50 40 30 20 10

10 20 30 40 50 60 70 80 90

SPRING ○

LAGOON OF VULCI

SPRING ○

100

90

80

70

60

50

40

30

20

10

ANCHORAGE

0   100   500   800 m.

Fig. 2.   Hill and town as planned

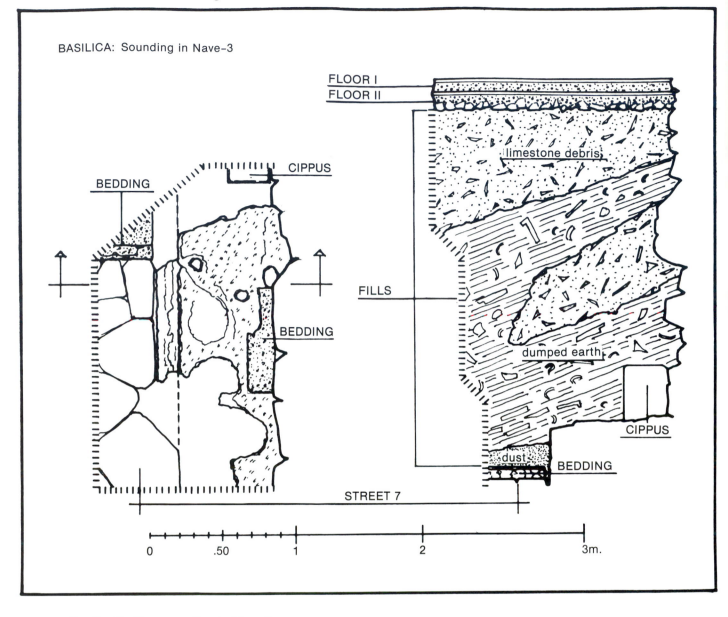

BASILICA: Sounding in Nave-3

FLOOR I
FLOOR II

CIPPUS

BEDDING

limestone debris

BEDDING

FILLS

dumped earth

CIPPUS

dust
BEDDING

STREET 7

0   .50   1   2   3m.

FIG. 3. Basilica, sounding in Nave-3

cippus, and 0.70 m NE along the sidewalk, a similar bedding, perhaps for an inscription. Thus bounded, the area, 514 p.R. (152.14 m) long and 300 p.R. (88.80 m) wide, covered 154,200 square p.R. (13,510 square meters) or about $5\frac{1}{3}$ iugera. It included the lowest slopes of the twin summits of the town-site on the SW and E and gentle declivities toward the N and S. Its SE end was traversed by Street Q, part of which was later incorporated into one of the porticoes of the Forum Square. The area included one of the four large reservoirs that impounded rainwater for the needs of the first settlers,[2] which was essential to the functioning of the Forum and as a central public reserve. Occupying approximately one-tenth of the town-site, the Forum shows the planners' conception of a civic center that would serve not only the citizens residing in the town, probably about twelve percent of the whole, but also the others who dwelt in their colonial territory.

The open Square of the Forum was laid out on the flattest stretch of ground available naturally. This was the low saddle between the S and E heights, which sloped gently northward, originally with a gradient of roughly 17 percent. The rectangular plot, ideally 300 p.R. (88.80 m) by 120 p.R. (35.50 m) or 1 *actus*, provided a surface of 36,000 sq. p.R. or $1\frac{1}{4}$ iugera, running SE–NW, perpendicular to the long blocks of the street plan. It was situated, however, not centrally in the whole zone of the Forum, but with reference to the major streets outside. Its long axis was centered on Street 6, leading to the NW gate of the town, its short axis on Street P, ascending to the Arx, while its SE end was bounded by Street Q. The Square thus both occupied the most suitable terrain and was fitted functionally and visually into the network of streets. From the beginning, however, its eccentric position was poorly related to the frame of its area for expansion.

The laying out of the Square was less precise than might have been desired. Its SW side was accurately perpendicular to Street 5, but the short axis was not, by $1\frac{1}{2}$ degrees. This defective vertical, on which the width of the Square was measured, was also used to calculate the right angle that established its NE side. As a result the Square was slightly trapezoidal, having the long sides convergent toward SE and differing in width from end to end by $6\frac{1}{4}$ p.R. (1.85 m), $\frac{1}{48}$ of the length.

2. Brown 1951, 84–87; Brown 1980, 11, 21.

II. 273–241 B.C.

(Plans II, III; Figs. 4–10; Pls. 1–15)

The first signs of activity in the Forum are of digging and hewing open cisterns and pits. These were dug in the native subsoil and bedrock for the impounding of rainwater and the planting of trees around and along the edges of the Square. All these were closely related to the first building adjacent to the Square, already projected but not, it seems, begun. Its site was the middle of the NE side of the Square, across its short axis and facing the broad street opposite that led to the Arx.

Of the four cisterns that were cut out of the rock at this time, two flanked the building site on the NE side. Approximately parallel with the Square and equidistant from the building, they were roughly equal in size, some $50\frac{3}{4}$ p.R. (15.00 m) long, $11\frac{1}{2}$ to $12\frac{1}{2}$ p.R. (3.40–3.70 m) broad, and, in the NW cistern, 15 p.R. (4.40–4.45 m) deep. The southeastern of the two (Pl. 1) received at its SE end the runoff from the surface. Both of these cisterns were lined with walls 0.65–0.70 m thick of limestone rubblework heavily mortared and finished with a coat of signinum 0.08 m thick.

The other two cisterns, perpendicular to the SW side of the Square and aligned with the NW and SE sides of the building space (Southwest Annex) opposite, were rough rock-cut trenches about 98 and $94\frac{1}{2}$ p.R. (29.00 and 28.00 m) long, 3.40–4.20 m wide, and 11–$10\frac{1}{2}$ p.R. (3.26–3.10 m) deep. Both presumably im-

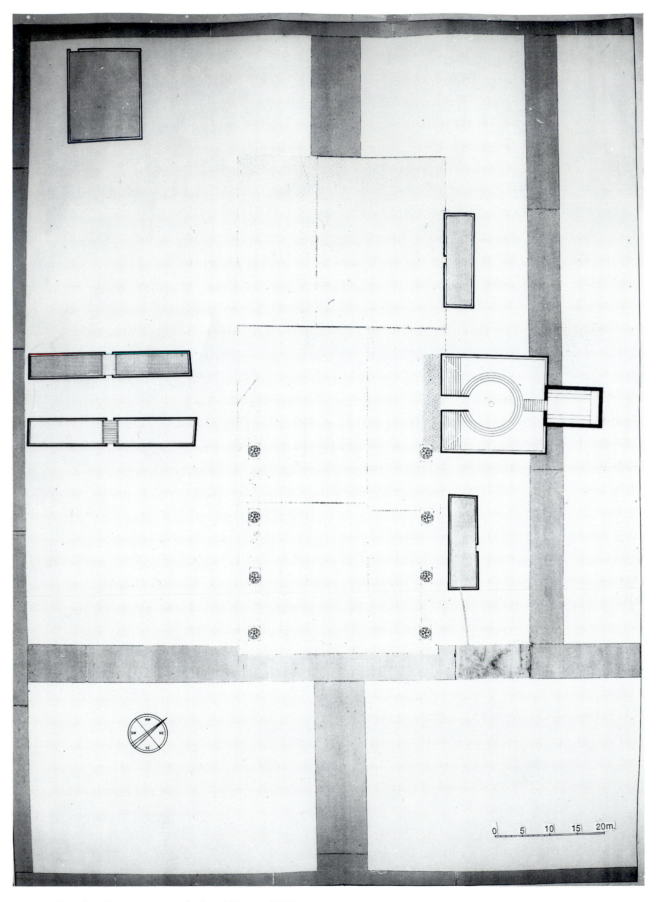

FIG. 4.   Forum, restored plan (A), as of 241 B.C.

pounded the water running down Street P from the Arx. Midway along the length of the NW cistern, pairs of slots were cut into the upper margin of either side, $1\frac{1}{2}$ p.R. (0.45 m) square and 1 p.R. (0.30 m) deep, spaced $8\frac{1}{2}$ p.R. (2.52 m) apart. They appear to have been seating for joists supporting a bridge across the long tank (Pl. 2).[1]

At a rough estimate, the capacity of these four cisterns added about 988,000 liters to the 750,000 that the Reservoir at the western corner of the Forum, dating from before the arrival of the colony, held. The latter no doubt became more a public reserve to use in case of drought or siege. The new cisterns presumably responded to the demands of the Forum not only as a daily and nundinal (market-day) marketplace but also as the common gathering place of the citizens, both engaged in the politics of the city-state and congregating at its festivals. It is to these functions of the Square that the planting of trees may also be attributed (Plan II; Pl. 3).

The pits totaled eight, four each in matching rows along either edge of the SE end of the Square. They were sunk in the sloping and fissured rock, and where it was missing the pit was lined with roughly squared blocks of mortared limestone. Each pit measured approximately 6 p.R. (1.776 m) and 3 p.R. (0.888 m) in breadth and depth from a level offset bedding, $1\frac{13}{16}$ to $1\frac{7}{8}$ p.R. (0.537–0.555 m) wide. This in turn supported a frame of curbstones raised above the adjoining rock or pavement.

The only remaining curbstones found in place, reused for a pit of abridged compass in the SW row, were of local travertine, 0.45–0.52 m wide and 0.30 m high, fastened together with dovetail clamps (Pl. 6; see page 119).

The pits in their original state were considerably larger than the numerous pits that bordered the Roman Forum during the first half of the first century B.C., but of about the same capacity as the largest of the pits that surrounded the temple of Gabii, in much the manner of the Hephaisteion in Athens. All these, despite their various shapes and sizes, were undoubtedly pits for small to medium-sized trees. In the bottom of one of the reduced pits of the SW row at Cosa was found a compact layer of dark sandy loam that, under the microscope, revealed transitory traces of carbonized rootlets. These were identifiable as belonging to trees, but the species could not be determined.[2]

The pits were aligned with the boundaries of the Square, 9 p.R. (2.664 m) in from the SW boundary and 6 p.R. (1.776 m) in from the NE, except for the NW pit, which was 7 p.R. (2.072 m) in. Each of the pits at the SE end was placed 10 p.R. (2.96 m) from the SE boundary, and each NW pit was centered on a line

1. Brown 1951, 81–82; Brown 1980, 22.

2. Roman Forum: *NSc* (1900), 315–17; *RömMitt* 17 (1902), Taf. 1.20; *RömMitt* 20 (1905), Abb. 21; E. De Ruggiero, *Il Foro Romano* (1913), 42–45; *AA* 72 (1957), 165–66; *RömMitt* 83 (1976), 45–48. Gabii: *AA* 83 (1968), 626–31. Hephaisteion: *Hesperia* 6 (1937) 396– 425. Similar tree-pits containing humus are better preserved in Egyptian temple gardens; cf. U. Hölscher, "The Mortuary Temple of Ramses III, Part II" (*The Excavation of Medinet Habu* 4, University of Chicago, Oriental Institute Publications 55 [1951]), 19–21.

two-fifths of the length of the Square from the SW end. The intervals between them were not equal, but increased progressively from SE to NW. The intervals of the NE row, $27\frac{1}{2}$ p.R. (8.14 m), $29\frac{1}{2}$ p.R. (8.73 m), and 32 p.R. (9.47 m), approximate a proportional progression (a:b;;b:c). The same proportion was not maintained in the SW row, where the first two intervals corresponded, but the third was 1 p.R. longer. This anomalous dimension may have resulted from the irregularity in the design of the Square.

Although the purpose of this progressive augment of intervals is not immediately apparent, it is manifest that the two rows of trees defined a special portion of the Square. It was an area of equal sides, 120 by 120 p.R., enclosing $\frac{1}{2}$ iugerum. The trees not only bordered two of its opposite sides, affording welcome shade, but also marked the ends of three broad divisions across it.

The building that occasioned all these works was the first freestanding structure of the Forum, a squarish, open place of assembly with, behind and above this, a covered hall.[3] The town fathers, or the architect, considering the advantages of the sunny SW exposure, placed it on the NE side. Although the design was as compact as possible, the space of only 52 p.R. (15.40 m) between the Square and Street 7 was far too little for the building. Part of the assembly place and the whole hall had to lie on the street outside the boundary. This street, laid out on the sloping rock but not yet leveled or paved, was thus blocked, but probably usable to either side. This was not the last time that this boundary would be disregarded.

The assembly place was enclosed by a rectangular circuit wall 2 p.R. (0.58–0.60 m) thick, built in two faces of brick-like stone slabs with a carefully mortared core of smaller stone and fragments of tile. The stone is the hard calcareous sandstone that was quarried in the plain SE of Cosa; it seems to assume more or less naturally the thin brick-like shapes in which it generally appears in Cosan construction. In the body of the wall the ordinary slabs range from 0.22 m to 0.44 m in length and from 0.035 m to 0.065 m in thickness. Exceptional slabs are as much as 0.51 m in length and 0.095 m in thickness. The stone is gray, sometimes brownish gray in color, deeply pitted and furrowed, and includes many bits of shell and often whole shells. The mortar is coarse and sandy and in most places is exceptionally hard. The beds tend to be relatively heavy, 0.025–0.03 m thick. The slabs are irregularly coursed and staggered. A single leveling course, slightly projecting on the interior, was found in the N corner, 1.11 m below the presumed top of the fill. At the corners is quoining in larger slabs and occasional blocks of the same stone. This general type of construction is widespread locally and is found in a number of Cosan buildings, notably in the walls of the Capitolium on the Arx, where the quoining is more elaborate,[4] and in a number of tombs.[5]

3. L. Richardson, jr, "Cosa and Rome: Comitium and Curia," *Archaeology* 10 (1957), 49–51.

4. Brown 1951, 59; Brown 1960, 31; Brown 1980, 39.

5. Brown 1951, 99, 102.

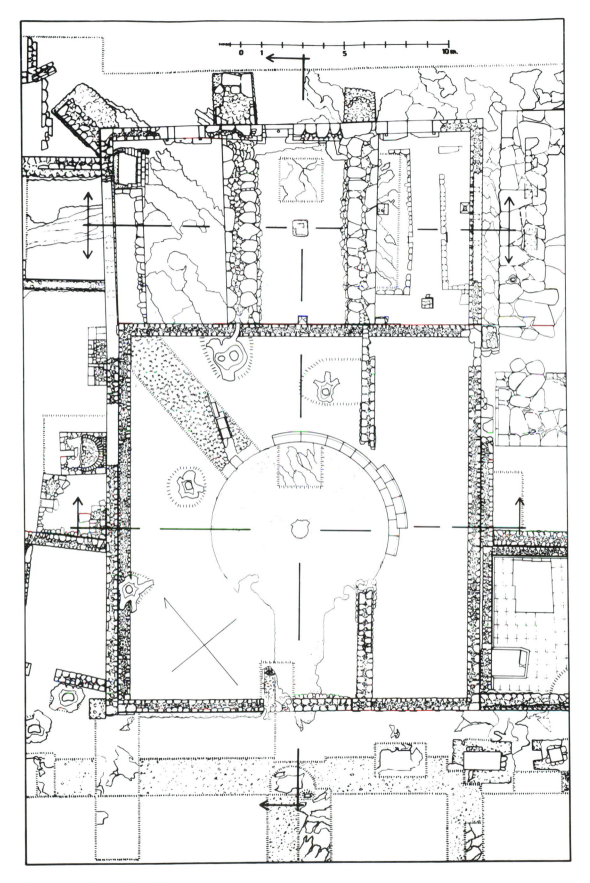

PLAN III. Plan of Comitium

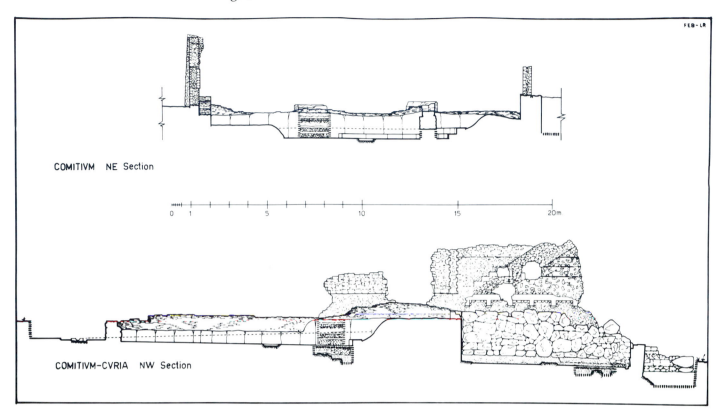

FEB-LR

COMITIVM   NE Section

0   1   5   10   15   20m

COMITIVM-CVRIA   NW Section

Fɪɢ. 5.   Comitium/Curia, NE and NW sections

Where the base of the wall was examined on the NE near the N corner, it was found to consist of a course of small limestone boulders, unmortared, laid on bedrock. The level of this footing had afterward been covered with rammed earth. On the SW (Pl. 8) was found a footing of mortared rubble masonry projecting 0.22–0.27 m beyond the outer face of the wall, descending 0.355 m to hardpan and crests of bedrock. The footing level here, too, was covered with rammed earth.

Inside and out the wall was faced with fine, hard, lime plaster, patches of which survive in varying condition on all four exterior faces and on the NW and SE interior faces. The best preserved remains were found on the exterior at the middle of the NE side (Pl. 7) and along the SW side toward the W corner (Pl. 8), in both of which sectors the wall coat had been covered and preserved by earth fills laid down in antiquity. This plaster bears no trace of color, the undercoat is relatively thin (0.014–0.02 m thick) with an aggregate of coarse sand, and the finishing coat (0.0045–0.009 m thick) is very hard, almost entirely lime with a light aggregate of finely crushed terracotta.

The area enclosed by the wall is a rectangle, perhaps ideally 55 p.R. by 59 p.R. (16.20–16.25 m wide, 17.50–17.55 m long). The SW wall was broken at the middle by an entrance, later blocked, from the Forum. At the time it was

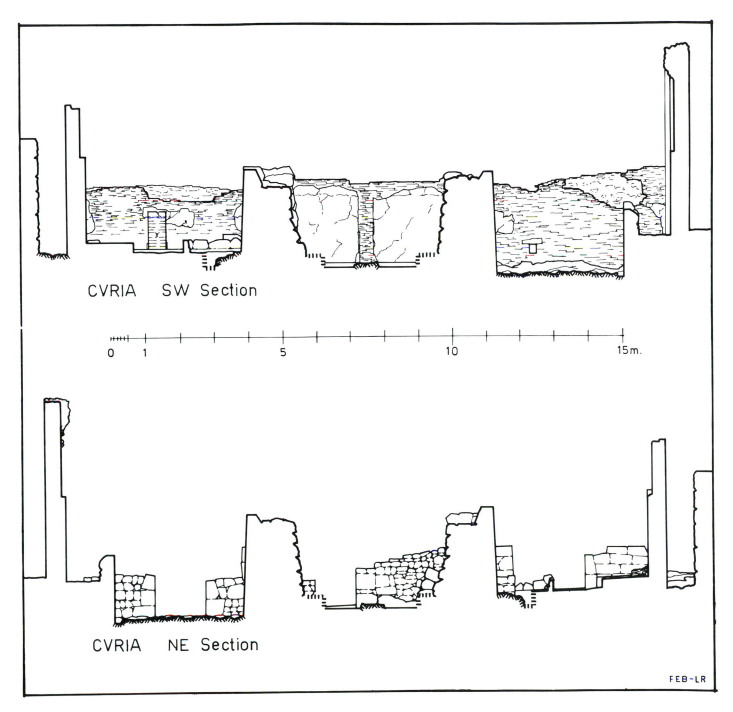

CVRIA   SW Section

0   1   5   10   15m.

CVRIA   NE Section

FEB-LR

Fig. 6.   Curia, SW and NE sections

blocked, if not earlier, this entrance was damaged by the removal of the jambs, which were probably squared or carved stone members. The existing break is 4.47 m wide. On the evidence of the existing pavement of the passage, the original width of the doorway was approximately 2.45 m.

The existing pavement requires explanation. On the one hand, from the evidence of the system of drainage and the section of the fill in the N corner, it would appear that the pavement is original. On the other hand, the material of the pavement, a relatively soft signinum, is unlike that surviving from the base story of the adjoining building, which clearly belongs to the period of the construction of the circuit wall (page 22), and inferior in quality, where one would expect it to be, if at all different, superior, for this enclave opening on the Forum by a wide door must have been used by large crowds, while the basement behind could have been intended for use by only a very few. There is, however, evidence of extensive modification of the building in an immediately subsequent period (pages 46–48), and it may well be that the original pavement had been damaged and broken during that work and was then replaced. In this case, because changing the system of drainage would have entailed complicated and difficult engineering, the original level was maintained and the original pavement completely removed rather than buried under the *rudus* of the new pavement. At all events, the evidence of the fill in the N corner of the enclosure indicates that the central part of the existing arrangement is either original or a careful copy of the original arrangement without significant change.

The existing pavement consists of an entrance passage from the Forum and a circular floor. The pavement of the passage extended out into the open area of the Forum for an unknown distance. In excavation it could be followed in patches for a distance of 2.40 m from the line of the façade wall, beyond which it disappeared. As it was of relatively soft signinum, there is nothing surprising in its disappearance, for it would have broken up under the constant wear and tear of traffic in the Forum. The patches that remain seem to have been protected and preserved thanks to the overlying blocks of a gutter and steps installed along this side of the Forum at the time of the construction of the Basilica early in the third quarter of the second century B.C. (pages 234–36).

Toward its SE end the pavement overlay an unfinished planting pit (Pl. 6), 11 p.R. (3.26 m) from the S corner of the façade, $6\frac{1}{2}$ p.R. (1.92 m) from the wall, and intended to be 5 p.R. (1.48 m) by 3 p.R. (0.89 m). This probably represents an early abandoned scheme, superseded by the pits to the SE. Perhaps a symmetrical twin was intended to the NW for a pair of trees framing the entrance.

In the entrance to the assembly place the rock was worked level to receive a sill, now missing. Inside the opening the passage ran straight for a distance of 4.05 m and emerged in a circular floor surrounded by stone steps. The floor measures 29 p.R. (8.60 m) in diameter and is paved with the same signinum as the passage. The floor is slightly pitched, with the highest points along its S edge, the lowest at its N point, from which a drain leads NNE. The maximum difference is 0.16 m. The floor of the passage is also slightly pitched, so that water falling on it would run down to the circular floor and out through the same drain; the difference in level between the farthest patch of pavement recovered outside the entrance and the floor at the drain mouth is 0.29 m.

The drain is of simple construction. Its floor is a line of tegulae, overlapped as they would be on a roof; the roof is a simple gable of long, untrimmed calcareous sandstone slabs braced against the flanges of the tiles on the E and against a packing of earth between the tile flange and the base of the slab on the W. The triangular section of the drain has a base of c. 0.20 m and a height of c. 0.19 m. At the inner end a single irregular limestone block, c. 0.40 m by 0.50 m, is used for the floor instead of a tegula, and probably the mouth was differently engineered from the rest, but of this nothing more remains. The drain led NNE to a mouth 3.98 m from the N corner of the building. Here the mouth is a box drain cut through the enclosing wall, 0.20 m wide and 0.25 m high (Pl. 5). By calculation from the difference in levels between the floors of the two mouths, which is 0.50 m, the drop of the drain was c. 0.07 m per meter. Beyond the mouth in the NE perimeter wall of the building the water seems not to have been channeled, but simply allowed to spread over the ground and sink in.

In the center of the circular floor is an irregular break in the pavement, c. 0.80 m in diameter and a few centimeters deep, but exposing bedrock, evidently left by the removal of some unidentifiable fixture.

Around the circular floor rose a series of steps built of the light purplish tufa of Vulci. Of these, parts of only the two lowest steps now remain, eleven blocks of the base step, comprising the eastern third, and four of the second, but it is quite clear from the section of the fill and the nature of the construction that several more steps have been completely demolished. The blocks are uniformly 0.52 m wide and 0.33 m high, but vary in length from c. 0.70 m to c. 1.40 m. They are plain and without moldings, but crisply and carefully cut with anathyrosis at the joints and a carefully traced setting line for each successive step. They are laid dry, but bedded and packed behind with fine reddish-brown earth. The steps, except for the lowest, which was sunk somewhat below the level of the pavement (0.06–0.11 m in the parts preserved, depending on the slope of the pavement) were 0.33 m high and 0.40 m wide.

The original number and character of the steps as a structure depends on two sets of *indicia*, the depth of that part of the fill behind the steps that can be regarded as original and the height of the enclosing wall and probable height of the adjacent building on the NE, which was approached by way of the steps.

The fill behind the steps was sectioned in a trench 2 m broad, driven on the diagonal axis from the paved circle to the N corner of the building (Fig. 7; Pls. 9 and 12). Since bedrock falls away from S to N throughout the area of the building, the fill here is presumably deeper than anywhere else, but the upper strata present here were also encountered elsewhere, so the section may be taken as typical. The lowest stratum consisted of broken local limestone in medium-sized

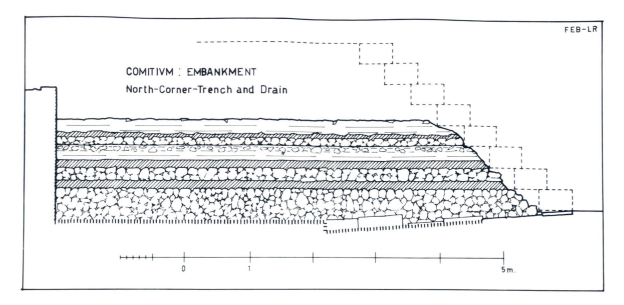

FEB-LR

COMITIVM : EMBANKMENT
North-Corner-Trench and Drain

0   1   5 m.

Fig. 7.   Comitium, sounding in N corner

chunks thrown in without earth packing. It was not explored to bottom, but far enough to indicate that it continued to bedrock. This stratum rose to a height of 0.30 m above the level of the pavement and covered the drain. Above it was a packed stratum of bright yellow clay, c. 0.10 m thick. There succeeded then another stratum of broken limestone, c. 0.20 m thick, and another stratum of yellow clay, c. 0.10 m thick. Then came a stratum of brown earth, c. 0.15 m thick; a stratum of mixed earth and stone, c. 0.15 m thick; and another layer of broken limestone, c. 0.15 m thick. Above this level there was yellowish brown earth with a little broken limestone; this is now preserved for a depth of c. 0.25 m, above which there was only humus.

There is a clear division in this fill between the four lower strata, alternately of broken limestone and yellow clay, and the four upper, where no such order exists. Moreover, the order of the lower strata suggests that the top layer of yellow clay is a finishing, or paving, stratum cushioned on a *rudus* of broken stone, below which lies the *statumen*, a mass of broken stone that provided drainage and protection against the damp from below, covered by a thin leveling stratum of yellow clay.[6] In removing these strata in the sampling trench, it was found that each of the yellow clay strata had a relatively hard surface, produced by ramming with beetles or human feet, the upper harder than the lower.

Hence it appears that the two or three lowest steps must have been part of the original construction, for the character of the drain and evidence of the level of the wall footing on the SW exterior preclude the possibility that the interior floor

6. Vitruvius 7.1 gives rules for the laying of foundations for pavements.

was originally higher and the center lowered by excavation in a remodeling. Moreover, the presence of remains of a plaster facing on the interior of the NW and SE walls like that on the exterior shows that these were at least in part exposed in the original building. These remains are poor, consisting of small patches not more than twenty centimeters in length and breadth. Unfortunately, none of them preserves remains of a lip, such as one would expect to find along the base of such a facing, but the lowest point preserved is c. 1.05 m above the level of the floor and c. 0.35 m above the top surface of the yellow clay pavement, which is in agreement with the other evidence.

The fill, to the top of the yellow clay pavement, rises c. 0.70 m above the circular floor. If there were two steps, these would reach only 0.55 m above the floor; if there were three, they would reach 0.88 m above the floor. Three, therefore, seems the number indicated, on the assumption that behind the steps the floor had sunk a little.

To turn now to the other set of *indicia*, the enclosing wall is still preserved to a height of 96.34 m above sea level (m.a.s.l) at a point near the middle of the SE wall, and the floor of the adjoining building in its third phase stood between 96.68 m.a.s.l. and 96.72 m.a.s.l. The former is binding evidence for the original height of this wall, for the wall shows no sign of addition or alteration and no variation in masonry. The leveling course in the N corner at 95.55 m.a.s.l. is evidently simply that, for although above it the wall projects slightly and the base course of the upper part is of somewhat larger slabs than the rest, there is no material difference in stone or mortar between the two parts. Moreover, the pavement in the lower story of the adjoining building in its first phase stands at 93.14 m.a.s.l., and there is ample evidence that this space was used as a room (pages 22–24). It is difficult to imagine that this room was less than 2.00 m high, as it would have been were the base of the leveling course the original top of the enclosing wall. It seems therefore best to work on the hypothesis that the height of the floor of the adjoining building in its third phase represents the height of this floor throughout the history of the building, which would give the very satisfactory height of 2.50–2.65 m for the base story of the building in its first phase.

In its later periods the adjoining building was approached through the enclosure, and since the connection between the two in their first phase was very close and it is clear that they were of a single build (pages 22–23), one must presume that in the first period this was also the case. Between the three stone steps around the paved circle and the circuit wall must have been wooden steps that gave access to the building behind. Whether these were in concentric circles, as they were later, or whether they were rectilinear banks backed against the enclosing wall is not clear, but since curved steps repeating the height and width of the stone steps would leave a gap of 1.95 m, requiring a bridge between the top step and the threshold of the building behind, rectilinear banks seem more probable. Moreover, whether these banks were built on all four sides, on the three continuous sides, or perhaps only on one, the NE, where they are essential as an approach, remains problematical. Since the plan of the building seems to have been laid out with the idea of completing the steps partly in stone and partly in wood in the original campaign and then continuing the stone stepping at some later time (a measure not infrequently adopted by the Romans in amphitheaters and theaters elsewhere)[7] and because there seems to have been the possibility of making a communication outside to the SE by a stair leading down from the top of the circuit wall (pages 36–37), it seems wisest to assume that steps were installed on at least the three continuous sides.

An adjoining building stood on the major axis of the assembly place, just behind it to the NE. All that is preserved of it today is the pavement of the basement and the footings of two pillars on which the upper story was supported (Fig. 4; Pls. 7 and 13). The pavement is of the same extremely hard signinum as the facing of the enclosure wall, but thicker (0.06–0.065 m thick) and with a heavier aggregate of terracotta. It runs to the facing of the enclosure wall on the SW and rises to the wall so that the joint is masked. The wall here is given a socle, 0.60–0.64 m high, by the application of an extra coat of signinum, which is feathered along its upper edge so that the joint is almost imperceptible. The SE and NW edges of the pavement are hidden under the heavy polygonal walls of a later building, and since the inner faces of these walls are based on earth and threatened to collapse if the excavation were extended, it was impossible to explore under them to any extent. In the E corner of the room, where the polygonal wall is more firmly founded, a trial trench was driven as far as possible. It was found that the pavement continued to a point 1.05 m from the outer face of the SE wall. Beyond the outer faces of the polygonal walls no trace of pavement was encountered at any point, and here excavation was continued to bedrock. Along its NE edge the pavement is broken irregularly on a line, 0.07 m at the SE end and 0.65 m at the NW end, inside the present NE wall. At a point near the E corner of the present room a small fragment of the flange that masked the joint between floor and wall is preserved, and one can be certain that in this dimension the room measured $29\frac{1}{2}$ p.R. (8.73 m). The wall for which this flange is evidence has completely disappeared. It appears either that the walls of the original building were of crude brick or wood, or that they were completely demolished at the time it was rebuilt. Against the notion that they were of stone, it should be observed that there is no trace of bonding or repair in the enclosure wall in the areas where they must have abutted it. In favor of the proposition that they were of light construction is the evidence of the pillars to support the upper story, which would hardly have been necessary in a building of this size (interior: 8.83 m by c. 6.00 m) had there been strong bearing walls along the sides.

7. Cf., e.g., the amphitheater of Pompeii, where the stone seating was installed in sections by magistrates *pro ludis* and was never completed (Overbeck-Mau 185–86).

There were two pillars, one engaged against the SW wall, one freestanding in the middle of the room. The pillar against the SW wall seems to have been given a coat of the signinum with which the wall is faced; the breaks in the wall coat where it was torn out at the time of rebuilding were found very fresh and crisp. Around the base the pavement is finished with a signinum flange. This and the break in the wall coat show that this pillar was c. 0.40 m square. For the base of the pillar in the middle of the room the builders used a crest of bedrock, which they trimmed, somewhat irregularly, and whose edges they covered with the signinum pavement. The cuttings of the crest for the setting of the pillar indicate that this was rectangular, c. 0.40 m by 0.55 m.

In the lowest meter of the earth fill of the building that replaced this one were found numerous small fragments of painted wall plaster, c. 0.01–0.02 m thick (Pl. 14). Their concentration was especially heavy toward the SW wall, but they were not associated with other building material. It seems likely that they are the debris of the decoration of the upper hall of the original building, thrown in here during building operations. They are all fragments of a single decoration in a variant of the Masonry or Pompeian First Style. Here the blocks and string courses were not worked in relief, but simply marked out by pressing a fine twisted cord (0.0015–0.0025 m in diameter) into the wall surface while it was still soft. The colors are red, white, and black. The following elements can be made out: a white surface bordered by a red string course, 0.023–0.029 m wide, with next to it a second red string course, 0.022–0.023 m wide, above which is a white string course, or more likely margin, 0.015–0.018 m wide, and then a black area. The decoration seems to have been one in which there were relatively long, narrow blocks of red and black, each block given a white margin, in courses separated by narrow red string courses. The most probable position for such courses is in a frieze between the main and upper zones.[8] Good comparanda for this decoration, but no exact parallel, have been discovered in the houses excavated on Delos.[9] Nothing similar seems ever to have been discovered at Pompeii. With the plaster were found elements of the floor: 468 mosaic tesserae of dark gray slate, measuring 0.005–0.02 m on a side, and 34 of white limestone, 0.003–0.015 m on a side.

The architectural refinements of the large enclosure, despite its incompleteness and minor discrepancies in measurements, indicate that it was not only an important building but an extremely durable one. The care with which the masonry of the circuit wall was laid, the hardness and polish of its facing, the beauty of the cutting of the tufa blocks of the steps, and the care with which the fill behind them was laid and tamped are all proof that the plan was carefully conceived and meticulously executed. The interior space is squarish, the major axis 1.25–1.30 m longer than the minor. The paved circle is carefully centered on the major axis and the square of the façade wall, leaving the whole difference in

8. See A. Laidlaw, *The First Style in Pompeii: Painting and Architecture* (Rome, 1985), 25–37 and passim.

9. *MonPiot* 14 (1908), 91–98 (M. Brulard); P. Bourneau and J. Ducat, *Guide de Délos*[3] (Paris, 1983), 83–84.

depth to the NE between the circle and the building behind, apparently so that in a later period, when the stone steps had been completed, a narrow terrace would run in front of this building at the top of the stairs. In the earlier period that interval seems to have occurred between the third stone step and a NE bank constructed in wood.

This was the core of the building, and the parts were made to suit it. At the beginning the circuit wall must have been built to the full height it was ultimately to have and must have been finished with a coping and parapet or fence, probably eventually of metal, perhaps at this time of wood; but of these elements nothing identifiable was recovered. The opening to the Forum must have been finished at least with jambs, and evidently with a gate, perhaps with some more elaborate entrance, since there is evidence of considerable damage to the wall in the tearing out of these members at a later time. And in the center of the circular floor must already have stood that small central fixture, the focus of the whole, whose disappearance is so tantalizing (page 19).

From the evidence preserved it is not possible to reconstruct the little building that originally stood behind the enclosure in more than its general lines, but since much of the original building was incorporated in a subsequent rebuilding, and since where changes were made they seem to have been largely rebuildings in stone masonry along the lines of a preceding temporary structure, we are perhaps justified in an attempt at reconstruction employing elements of the second building where other evidence is lacking.

The measurement of the length of the room in the basement story, $29\frac{1}{2}$ p.R. (8.73 m), indicates that the room in the main story was to be 30 p.R. Since the circuit wall of the enclosure is 2 p.R. thick, it is presumed that this thickness was maintained in the basement walls of the building, and a setback of $\frac{1}{2}$ p.R. (0.148 m) at the level of the floor of the main story reduced the thickness of the walls above to $1\frac{1}{2}$ p.R. The façade wall must have been carried on the circuit wall, as it was in later times. The presumed width of the pavement of the basement story, greater than 4.20 m, and the overall width of the building that replaced this, 7.10–7.40 m, suggest that the proportions of the interior of the upper story were 3:2:2, 30 by 20 by 20 p.R., the width two-thirds of the length and the height equal to the width, and it has been so reconstructed in the drawings. The roofing has been reconstructed with timbers of measurements derived from those of temples of comparable size at Cosa, and in the absence of any evidence of terracotta revetment of either this building or subsequent rebuildings, this has been omitted.

Examination of the fill under the pavement of the circular floor in a sounding 2.00 m square made in the NE sector and carried to bedrock showed this to be almost completely sterile. It produced working chips from the blocks of Vulcentine tufa used for the steps, a fragmentary lamp, and a few sherds of black-glaze pottery. The fill consisted of a layer of dark earth, c. 0.20 m thick, over red clay covering and filling the irregularities of the bedrock. Bedrock was encountered at a minimum depth of 0.40 m and a maximum of 0.91 m.

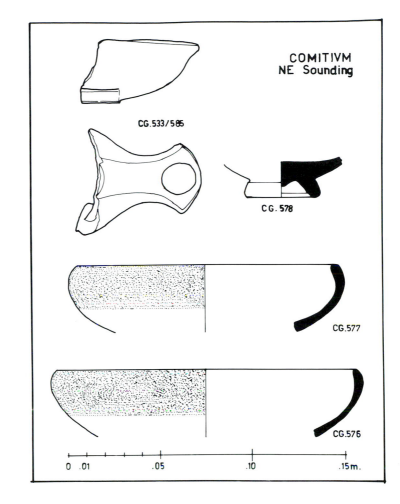

COMITIVM
NE Sounding

CG.533/585

CG.578

CG.577

CG.576

0   .01   .05   .10   .15 m.

FIG. 8. Comitium, NE sounding, potsherds

CG 537 and 585 (Fig. 8). Six joining fragments forming the nozzle and front part of a "truncated cone" lamp, wheel-made of very fine, orange-buff potter's clay and coated with a dense, lusterless black glaze, somewhat mottled at the base. The nozzle flares to its rounded extremity. The base is finished with a bead and the filling-hole ringed by a depressed discus. The type of lamp of which this was a particularly well-made example was in use at Cosa from the outset.[10]

CG 578. This is the base of a small black-glaze bowl or cup, standing on a splayed ring foot, 0.039 m in diameter, which is lightly grooved at the juncture with the base on the outside and rounded on the bottom. The base has a high turning point; the floor is flat and slightly cambered. The clay is a fine buff, orange at the core, the glaze nonlustrous red mottled with black. The fabric and glaze indicate local manufacture.[11]

CG 576 and 577. The rims and upper walls of two bowls of unknown

10. See C. R. Fitch and N. W. Goldman, *Cosa: The Lamps* (forthcoming).

11. Lamboglia 1952, 173.

manufacture, 0.14 m in diameter.[12] They are like L27a-b, but their profile differs from this in the marked thickening of the rim. They are lightly faceted on the exterior. The clay of one is fine grained, very light brown, the other pinkish gray. The glaze is dark gray and nonlustrous, covering the interior but limited to a band terminating c. 0.025 m below the rim on the exterior. The elegance of the profile seems directly derived from the late fourth-century Attic bowls of this shape, appropriate to the second quarter of the third century in Italy.

Examination of the fill under the pavement of the basement of the building behind the enclosure in a sounding 2.00 m square in the NE half of the room and carried to bedrock showed this to be completely sterile, simply the tough red clay of the hill of Cosa dumped over the rough bedrock to make a level floor. Crests of the bedrock appeared almost immediately below the pavement, and its maximum depth was c. 0.40 m.

The date of the complex, therefore, depends almost entirely on its relationship to others in the vicinity. It is clearly older than a small enclosure to the SE that in part abuts the circuit wall near its S corner, for here the plaster facing of the exterior has been preserved by having been protected by the bulwark of this later wall. The smaller enclosure is proved by other evidence to have gone out of use by c. 220 B.C. (pages 37–38), when it was terraced over. The larger enclosure must therefore be dated in the first half-century of the life of the colony, and in view of the unfinished state of its arrangements when it was first put into service, taken together with its important location, the relative refinement of its scheme, and the evident intention of the colonists to keep, complete, and elaborate it, a date before the First Punic War is likely.

The purpose of the enclosure was clearly principally for assembly. The amphitheatral arrangement of the ring of steps and their height of 0.33 m, too steep for comfortable ascent, shows that they are not simply a grandiose approach to the little building lying beyond on the major axis. If the capacity is calculated allowing $1\frac{1}{2}$ p.R. (0.444 m) per place (modern architects allow 0.45 m per place in designing theaters and stadia), the eight steps as reconstructed could have accommodated more than six hundred persons, and others could have stood on the platform between the three stone steps at the base and the wooden banks above. The height of the steps is too little to permit comfortable seating, so it must be presumed that these assemblies stood. The area of the circular floor is too small to imagine that it served as a gladiatorial arena, and those on the lowest step would be surely too dangerously exposed to accident. The amphitheatral arrangement would make this a poor place in which to hold dramatic or musical performances, and there is no dressing room or other accommodation provided for the artists. And so permanent and prominent a theater is unimaginable in a Latin town of this epoch. It can only be the comitium of the colony, the place of public assembly for government

---

12. Lamboglia 1952, 176–77; Morel 1969, 60–66.

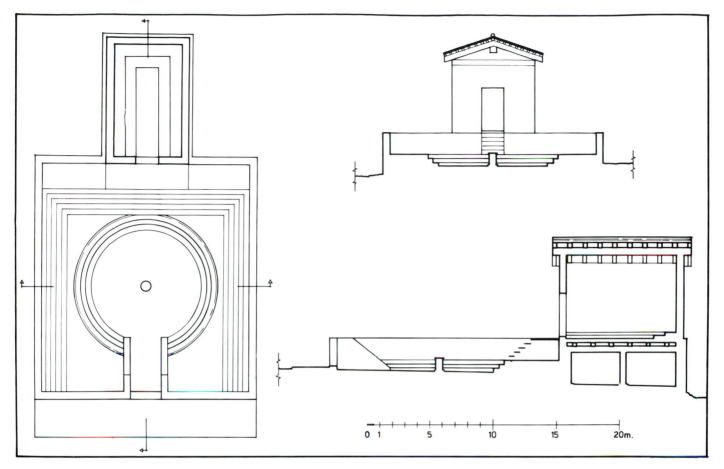

FIG. 9.   Comitium/Curia, restored plan and sections

and political purposes. Only this interpretation accords with the importance shown by its being among the first of the public edifices of the new foundation to be built and by its place on the short axis of the Forum in the middle of the NE side.

Too little is known of the Comitium of Rome[13] to permit detailed comparison of its arrangements with those of Cosa, and the Comitium of Pompeii, if it has been properly identified, is of an entirely different conception.[14] At Cosa, so far as can be seen, there was no rostrum provided, and the speakers may have addressed the citizenry from the central floor. But at Rome the curved front of the "Sullan" rostra suggests that it was originally a segment of a similar amphitheater or so derived, and it may be that a corner of the Comitium of Cosa was also specially

13. E. Gjerstad, "Il Comizio Romano dell'età re-pubblicana," *OpusArch* 2 (Lund, 1941), 97–158; E. Sjöqvist, "Pnyx and Comitium," *Studies Presented to D. M. Robinson* 1 (St. Louis, Mo., 1951), 400–411; J. A. Hanson, *Roman Theater-Temples* (Princeton, 1955), 37–39; L. R. Taylor, *Roman Voting Assemblies* (Ann Arbor, Mich., 1966), 21–23; C. Krause, "Zur bau-lichen Gestalt des republikanischen Comitiums," *RömMitt* 83 (1976), 31–37, 49–54. Cf. F. Coarelli, *Guida archeologica di Roma* (Verona, 1974), 62–67; idem, *PdP* 32 (1977), 166–214; idem, *Il foro romano* 1 (Rome, 1983), 119–60, 2 (Rome, 1985), 11–123.

14. See Overbeck-Mau 136–38; A. Mau, *Pompeji im Leben und Kunst* ²2 (Leipzig, 1908), 87–123.

appointed as a speakers' platform. At Rome the Comitium was a *locus saeptus*,[15] an area enclosed but unroofed like the enclosure at Cosa, and a *templum inauguratum*,[16] a solemn sanctuary containing dedications.[17] No one speaks of any altar in it, but there is no obstacle to its having had an altar, and the break in the center of the pavement at Cosa suggests the fixture removed from it was something small and round, like an altar.

A single-chambered hall standing behind the Comitium on its main axis, dominating it and approached through it, must have had more than ordinary importance. It cannot have been simply a record office. At Rome we know that the Curia Hostilia, situated on the N side of the Comitium, was in similarly close conjunction with the Comitium. Livy (45.24.12) says *in comitio, in uestibulo curiae*, as though the two were architecturally inseparable, and from other passages (Livy 1.36.5; 1.48) we gather that the steps of the Comitium served as the approach to the Curia, much as the cavea of the Theater of Pompey served as the approach to the Temple of Venus Victrix.[18] All the evidence for the Roman Curia and Comitium has been admirably sifted by Sjöqvist,[19] and the main lines of his reconstruction must be accepted. He places the Curia on the axis of the Comitium at the top of the cavea of steps of the Comitium. Since at Cosa this building stands in the same relationship to the Comitium as did the Curia to the Comitium in Rome, the building can only be the Curia of the colony, the hall where the *decuriones* met.

The Curia at Rome should have been inaugurated as a *templum* (Varro, *ap. Gell.* 14.7.7), but since the inauguration had been allowed to lapse, at least since the time of the Sullan rebuilding, we cannot suppose that it had other appurtenances of a religious building. Nor does it appear that there was more than a single chamber in the Curia Hostilia, so it is impossible to determine what purpose the lower story of the Cosan building may have served. The fact that the plaster facing its walls was undecorated suggests that it had no very august purpose. If a stair connected it with the upper story, it may have been a record office, the tabularium of the colony, although in the single remaining wall there is no sign of shelving. If there was no such stair and it opened to the NE, one might suppose that it was let as a shop.

The excavator was also able to clean, photograph, survey, and sound the "Teatro Circolare" of Paestum, Cosa's colonial twin. His results showed that this controversial structure was unquestionably Paestum's comitium and curia, erected somewhat later than Cosa's.[20] Its much larger amphitheater also rose to a platform with the curia behind it, the curia being flanked by two detached halls. More recently, at one end of the forum of Alba Fucens, an analogous building

---

15. Cicero, *Rep.* 2.31.

16. The Ovile in the Campus Martius also was a *templum* (Cicero, *pro Rab.* 11), and the Saepta Iulia that replaced it must have been.

17. See especially F. Coarelli, *Il foro romano* 2 (Rome, 1985), 87–123.

18. Tertullian, *De Spect.* 10; Aulus Gellius 10.1.7; Pliny, *NH* 8.20.

19. Sjöqvist (note 13 above).

20. See Appendix 1 (page 253).

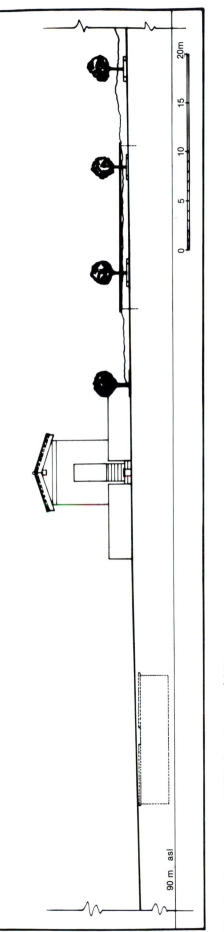

Fig. 10. Forum, restored NE elevation, as of 241 B.C.

has been discovered by trenching.[20] It reveals another circular comitium with a circular foundation at its center. Here the enclosed comitium is flanked by narrow rooms, one longer than the other. It is dated by the excavator to the end of the third century or the first half of the second. The curia was not reached. These three colonial comitia/curiae seem to show a chronological progression of design from the simple to the complex, from the closest to the farthest from the unchanging Roman prototype.

20. H. Mertens, *Alba Fucens* 1 (Brussels, 1969), 98–101; C. Krause (note 14 above), 54–56.

III. 241–209 B.C.

(Plan IV; Figs. 11–16; Pls. 16–26)

After two consecutive decades of war the colonists of Cosa could at last begin to regain their lost momentum, and public works could gradually be resumed in the Forum. They were briefly interrupted, no doubt, in 225 B.C. by the last concerted Gallic raid on Roman territory and by the extraordinary mobilization of Roman manpower that it provoked.[1] The marauding Gauls, who had reached the vicinity of Cosa, were annihilated between two armies in the fields of Telamon only 16 km (10 miles) away. The invasion may not have threatened the defenses of Cosa, but it gave the colonists a foretaste of what Italy was to suffer when Hannibal crossed the Alps seven years later. In that second long war with Carthage all the commonwealth's resources were at stake. After it little was left of men or money to advance the colony.

Immediately SE of the Comitium, a space of only 0.10 m intervening, are the remains of a quadrilateral platform floored with tegulae. This was mutilated, especially along the SW, in the rebuilding of the area in the early second century B.C. (pages 51–56), and certain of the original dimensions are not preserved. In the interior, the NE side, which is the only one wholly preserved, is 6.12 m long; the preserved stretch of the NW side measures 6.38 m; and the preserved stretch

---

1. Polybius 2.25–31; P. Somella, "Antichi campi di battaglia in Italia," *Quaderni dell'Istituto di Topografia* *della Università di Roma* 3 (1967), 9–34.

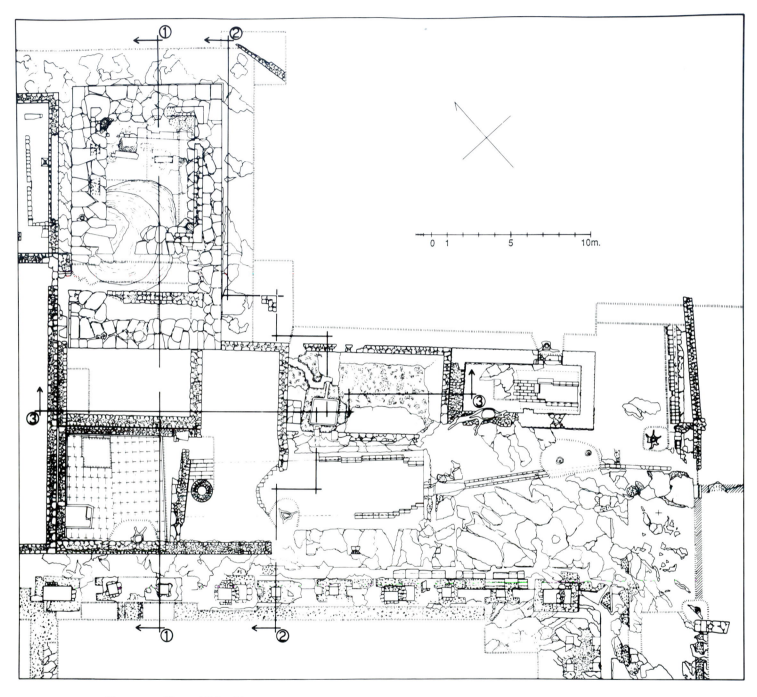

PLAN IV. Plan of E buildings

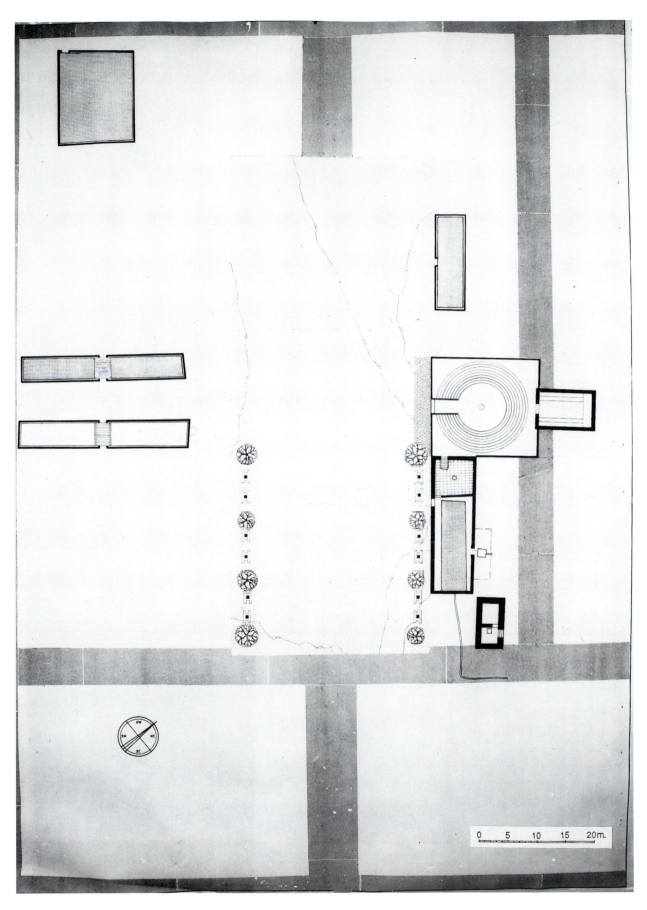

Fig. 11.   Forum, restored plan (B) as of 209 B.C.

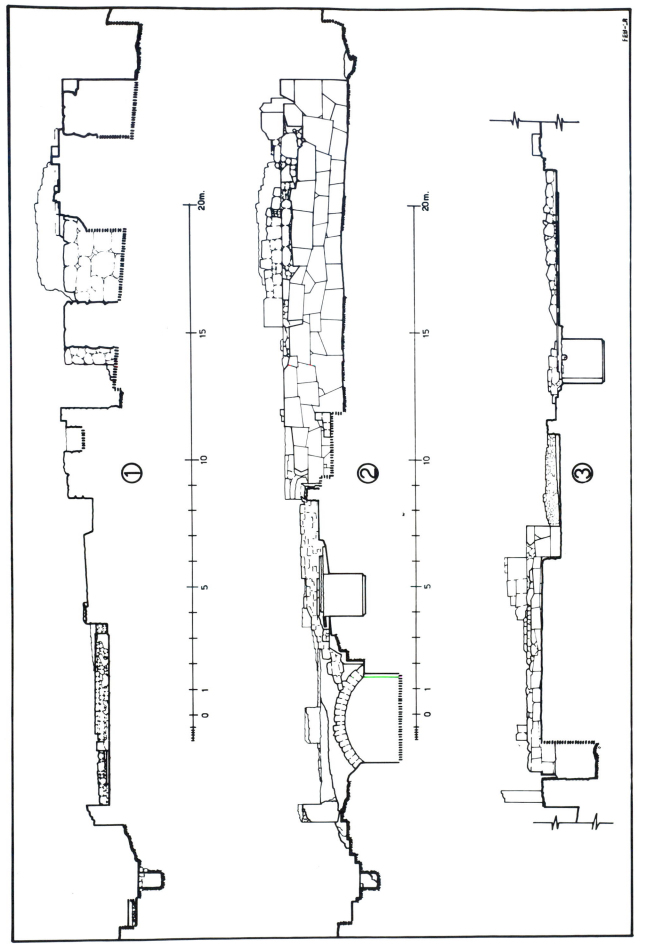

Fig. 12.   Sections of Plan IV

of the SE side, which deviates toward the south, measures 6.25 m. The SW side is not preserved, but since the boundary of the open area of the Forum seems to have been fixed at the time of the foundation of the colony and then never moved, we must suppose that the wall here stood on the line of the later SW wall of the forecourt of Temple B. A line of limestone boulders, unmortared, based on hardpan and crests of bedrock continuing the line of the façade of the Comitium must be the remains of the footing of this wall, for not only is it unlike the upper parts of the existing wall in construction and like the wall foot of the NE side of this enclosure and the wall foot of the Comitium (page 16), but it extends only far enough to have enclosed the tile-paved area (Pl. 27). If the floor ran to the wall and this was of the same dimensions as the others, the NW side would have been c. 7.00 m long, the SE side c. 6.95 m long, and the SW side c. 6.62 m long.

The floor is of ordinary tegulae, 0.48 m by 0.65 m, laid flange down in regular rows and heavily mortared at the joints. A quarter-round flange of mortar, 0.10 m thick, covers the joint of floor and wall. The floor is very slightly inclined toward the W corner, and the maximum difference in level between the E and W corners is 0.11 m.

On the NE side and NW side are remains of an enclosing wall, $1\frac{1}{2}$ p.R. (0.444 m) thick. It is built in two faces of small, roughly squared blocks of the local limestone, cemented with the red clay of the hill, with a core of smaller broken limestone and clay. The faces are irregularly coursed, and there is evidence that there were leveling courses at intervals. There is a single case of through bonding at a point where it appears a jamb was required. Just below the level of the floor is a narrow setback in the enclosing wall. On the interior the wall, where exposed, was faced with a single, thin coat of lime plaster.

This wall is continuous from the jamb mentioned above, 10 p.R. (2.96 m) inside the outer face of the SW wall of the forecourt of Temple B, to a point halfway along the NE side of the floor, where it has been broken, probably deliberately. Although its top is slightly irregular at the SW end of the NW side, for most of the distance the preserved top is a leveling course and maintains a constant height of 93.70–93.73 m.a.s.l. That the wall was originally higher was proved in excavation by the discovery of fragments of the plaster facing at the N corner at a level above this (Pl. 18). This suggests that the wall above this base was of sun-dried brick and simply disintegrated.

Beyond the point where the wall breaks today it continues at a lower level and was found in a trial pit at the N corner of the SE cistern, just to the SE of the floor. From this it appears that the wall did not turn at the E corner of the floor, but continued straight along the NE side of the cistern. Traces of its continuation on the same line, in part as the unmortared boulders of the footing course, in part as mortared repairs to it where it had been broken by later construction, have appeared in the area between the forecourt of Temple B and the SE end of the cistern. And another short fragment was found still abutting the square pier at the W corner of Building L ("Market Building [?]"). Thus its original length appears to have been 48.70 m, and despite its impermanent nature, it appears to have been a boundary, perhaps of the public domain around the Forum. Trace of at least one opening in it, in the form of a jamb block, appears in the remaining bits of the NE stretch between cistern and settling tank.

Against the NW wall of the floor paved with tegulae, at the SW end of this wall, are remains of a flight of steps, 1.25 m wide, built of what was originally sun-dried brick reduced by time to a mass of red clay. The parts that remain were given a facing of lime plaster like that of the wall, and around the base runs a cover-joint of mortar, 0.10 m wide, like that around the edge of the floor. There are two bases for calculating the original appearance of the stair, the depth of the tread of the single remaining step and the height of the riser, and the difference in level between the height of the top of the Comitium wall, to which this led, and the level of the tile floor. By the first calculation there would have been seven steps, each 0.17 m high and 0.30–0.33 m deep; together these would reach a height of 96.34 m.a.s.l., 0.26 m below the presumed height of the Comitium wall (96.60 m.a.s.l.). As the circuit wall of the Comitium is 0.59 m thick, an extra step might have been cut in it (Pl. 25).

The conclusion as suggested by the rounded flange of mortar that edges the floor that this little platform paved with tegulae served as a rain catchment is obvious and inescapable. Yet the water collected here would have had to be impounded in the long cistern that opens to the SE, while the floor slopes perceptibly in the opposite direction, from E to W. This is probably not due to inept engineering, but to the working of a limestone sink near its N corner. There is no trace of any connecting pipe or gutter to carry the flow from the NW side of the floor to the Reservoir; instead there is a narrow trapezoidal space intervening between the SE side and the NW end of the cistern that seems to have been left deliberately to permit insertion there of a collecting gutter, probably of metal. No wall closes the floor on the SE side, and examination of the NW wall shows that no wall bonded in its lower parts was later removed, and indeed such a wall bonded only in its upper parts could hardly have been removed without damage to the flanged floor edge, which instead was here found beautifully fresh and whole, except at the S corner, where it was damaged by the rebuilding of the SW wall. One must therefore conclude that this side of the floor was left open. The floor—a maximum of 44.79 square meters—at Cosa, where today the annual rainfall is c. 0.70 m, would have impounded only about 31.35 cubic meters in a year's time.

The construction of this little catchment shows evidence of haste and consequent flimsiness hardly commensurate with the rock-hewn and polygonal-walled tanks and the thick, polished signinum facings of such works elsewhere in the city. The walls are of small stone cemented with clay with a superstructure of crude brick not because of custom or ignorance, as the Comitium circuit wall demonstrates, but because they were easy to build and were not expected to have to provide long service; and they were faced with a single coat of thin lime plaster that would hardly have protected them for many years, except under cover. In fact, they owe their survival at all to the fact that they were soon deliberately buried under a terrace. And the floor paved with tegulae cannot have been laid for either its durability or its hydraulic properties when signinum would have served far better. It too must be explained as the consequence of economy and haste. Last, one may ask about the stair that mounted the Comitium wall. The stone that quoins the wall just beyond this stair looks like the remains of a deliberate strengthening, as though the original intention of the builders had been to pierce a door through the Comitium wall beyond, but they had later changed their plans and built the stair instead. Such a change in plan might be quite well explained as the adoption of the quickest and easiest solution, rather than as restraint from tampering with an inaugurated templum. Indeed, everything about this little structure suggests the greatest speed and the greatest economy. The thing that is odd about it is that subsequently it became somehow religiously important to the people and was then made first a sacellum and finally a temple.

So in its reconstruction we are forced back on simplicity itself: a small catchment platform, enclosed on three sides with walls, probably of the height of the Comitium wall, of crude brick on a stone base, and on the fourth side probably with a broad metal gutter. It communicated with the Comitium by a relatively narrow stair that must have led over the intervening walls like a stile.

The date of this construction is established by its relation to the Comitium, which it in part abuts, by the meager finds of sherds of cooking wares, together with an odd couple of sherds of black-glaze ware in the fill under the floor in a sounding to bedrock approximately 1.90 m square made after lifting twelve of the tegulae of the pavement, and by the material, especially a dozen coins, found in the mud caked on the floor in a hard stratum that must represent the period of use of the catchment.

The enclosing wall of this building must follow the circuit wall of the Comitium in date, since the latter is faced with plaster on the exterior and the space between the two walls is only c. 0.10 m wide. The comparison of the material found under the pavement with that found under the pavement of the Comitium is inconclusive.

In the sounding in the N corner were extracted a large fragmentary cooking pot (Dyson 1976, Class 10, CF 38–42), probably of mid-third century date, and rim fragments of two black-glaze bowls, L27b, closely akin in biscuit and glaze to the products of the "Atelier des Petites Estampilles."[2] Of the twelve coins,[3] one is illegible; one is from Marseilles, dated after 250 B.C. (CF 2234); one is from Syracuse, dated 304–289 B.C. (CF 2227); three are from Sardinia, dated 241–236 B.C. (CF 2228, CF 2229,

2. Dyson 1976, 28; Morel 1969, 60–66.
3. Coins CF 2224, 2227–31, 2233–37; Buttrey 1980, 16, 21–22, 45 (nos. 2, 5, 9, 15, 17–19, 25–28).

CF 2237); one is from Naples, dated 340–220 B.C. (CF 2236); one is a litra (CF 2230) and one a half-litra (CF 2224), dated by Sydenham to 269–242 B.C.; one is an uncial aes grave, dated by Sydenham to 241–222 B.C. (CF 2231); and one a bit of aes signatum dated by Sydenham to after 299 B.C. (CF 2235). These indicate that the catchment was out of use and terraced over before the beginning of the Second Punic War. The strong suggestion is that it was constructed in a great hurry between the First and Second Punic Wars and was used for only a very short time, perhaps for no more than a single decade.

At the other end of the SE cistern, during the twenty-three years between the wars, the continuation of the NE wall behind the catchment to enclose the cistern it supplied determined the alignment of another building, which was under construction at the W corner of Streets 7 and Q, originally identified as an "Aerarium (?)."[4] Only approximately squared to the plan of the other buildings of the Forum, it is turned broadside to the open Square and is accessible only from the NE (see Plan I; Fig. 13; Pls. 16, 19). The nature of its immediate approach is not clear, but almost certainly this led from the roadway passing between it and Building L ("Market Building [?]") on the SE.

The building measures 9.13–9.14 m by 4.80 m overall, probably ideally 31 p.R. by 16 p.R. (9.18 m by 4.74 m). In its interior it is divided into two rooms by a pair of stubby walls that may be the remains of a buttress arch under the vaulted roof, but if so, it was not centered. The outer of these rooms measures 2.95 m by 3.00 m, evidently 10 p.R. square; the inner measures 3.80 m by 3.00 m, probably 13 p.R. by 10 p.R. The interior wall, 2 p.R. (0.59 m) thick, is bonded into the long walls (Pl. 21); the NE section, which has a finished end, is $1\frac{1}{2}$ p.R. (0.444 m) long. The doorway in this wall, were it symmetrically placed, would have been 7 p.R. broad, which is perhaps excessive. No trace of a sill was found.

The exterior walls are 3 p.R. (0.89 m) thick, thicker than those of any building of comparable size at Cosa, where freestanding walls are apt to be $1\frac{1}{2}$ p.R. (Curia) or 2 p.R. (Temple B) thick. They are built of random rubblework, chunks of limestone either unshaped or with a single spalled face, laid in moderately heavy beds of mortar. The outer face is generally of larger chunks than the inner. There is quoining in large rusticated blocks at the corners (Pl. 20). The bedrock does not seem to have been trimmed to take the foot of the wall, which rests on crests of rock and the hardpan between. In places the footing course projects a few centimeters inside and out, but not regularly. There is a leveling line roughly 5 p.R. (1.50–1.55 m) above the floor, the impost of a vault oriented NW and SE, preserved in the S corner. The radius of the vault would have been 1.48 m, giving the room a maximum height of 3.10 m.

The door to the exterior, pierced in the NE wall 2.10 m from the E corner, was 5 p.R. (1.48 m) wide (Pl. 22). It is now much ruined, and the jambs are missing.

4. Brown 1951, 81.

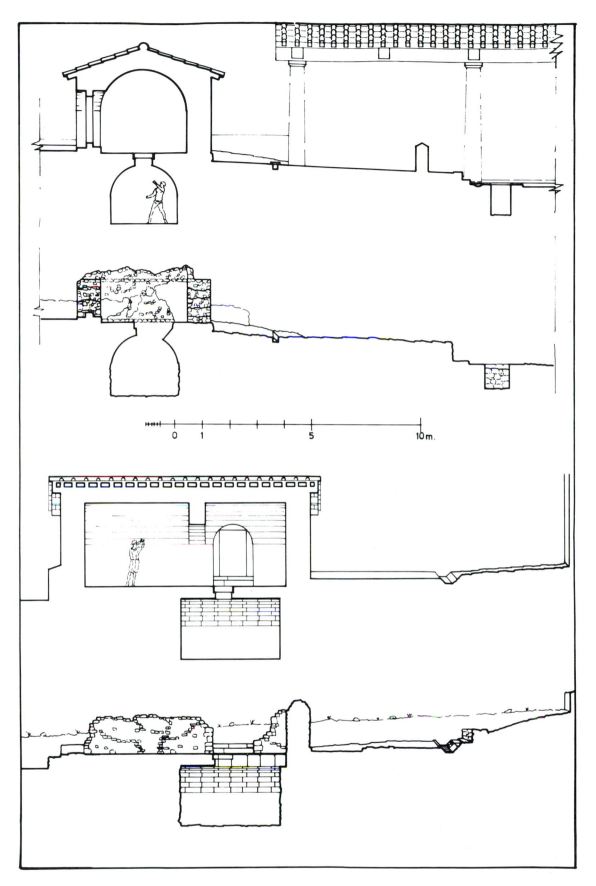

Fig. 13.   Carcer, sections, actual state and restored

The threshold is composed of three blocks, an outer sill, 2 p.R. (0.59 m) wide, and a lower inner sill, 1 p.R. (0.30 m) wide, made in two blocks, the larger of which preserves a rectangular cutting c. 0.08 m long for a pessulus at the center of the doorway tight against the outer sill, while the other has a small round cutting near its center. As there is no trace of cuttings for cardines, we must presume the doors were hung on hinges set in the jambs.

In the interior the walls were faced with relatively coarse signinum, evidently an undercoat for a wall finish that does not survive. Patches of this remain on all walls and nearly to the top of the wall preserved in the S corner. No trace of pavement survives today; the presumption is that it was of wood or earth.

Under the SE half of the building, within the line of its outer walls but so situated as to lie in part under both its rooms, is a small cellar, 3.62 m long and 2.42 m wide. It is evidently in part created out of a small natural fissure, the NW and SE ends being rock-cut, the long sides built of masonry. It is roofed with a segmental vault, nearly a barrel vault, built of well-dressed voussoirs of limestone laid dry. From floor to spring of vault this cellar is 1.21 m high; from floor to keystone it measures 2.23 m. In the crown of the vault, 1.87 m from the SE end of the building, in the line of the door to the exterior, lay the opening to this cellar, a square manhole, 0.70 m on a side and rabbeted 0.07 m for a heavy lid, which is now missing.

This little building seems never to have been part of any other complex. It stood off, solid and somewhat squat. Its only door turned away from the Forum; there is no evidence that it had any window. The spring of its vault is preserved in the S corner, and on the evidence of the vaulting of its cellar we can with some confidence restore a barrel vault, or near barrel vault, to cover it. A simple gable roof of tegulae and imbrices must have finished this. Its floor was either of wood or of beaten earth; its walls were perhaps faced only with tough, practical signinum on the interior. It seems to have existed mainly to cover its cellar, and that cellar was not a cistern, for it is without any hydraulic finish and without conduits.

The collapse of the vault of the building brought down almost the whole of the NW end and thrust the other walls out of plumb, lifting them bodily from their precarious seating on the rock. The growth of olive roots about the ruin compounded the damage. From the earth beneath its walls were extracted sherds of red burnished and ribbed wares that belong to the last period of Cosa's life as a town, but the relation of this building to the town plan and to Temple B shows plainly that it must be a great deal older. A wall running from the S corner of Temple B to the N corner of this building lies off square with the town plan; in part, near Temple B, it is as old as the Augustan restoration of this temple (pages 148–54); in its remainder it seems likely to have been built considerably earlier and to have been broken by the Augustan rebuilding. It probably belongs to the time of the construction of Temple B and was the wall that bounded its forecourt. In that case this cellared building must antedate Temple B, for had it not existed earlier, there would be no explanation for the wall's irregularity. On the other hand, its relation to the SE cistern and the wall bounding this on the NE is uninformative, and the evidence of its construction with great spalled quoins and heavy walls of relatively small limestone rubblework must be used with caution. It is rather strikingly different from the walls of Curia III and Temple B, which are of relatively well dressed small blocks, coursed and with well-dressed quoins. It has therefore been assigned to the period between the First and Second Punic Wars.

The characteristics of so compact a public edifice, within the limits of the Forum but detached from its Square, built massively for strength and impenetrability, might suit either a treasury or a jail, aerarium or carcer. Were it the former, however, one would expect to find it in close conjunction with a temple or facing the Square, whereas it lies along the very limit of the Forum, turned away from the Square. As a treasury its upper chambers would have been taken up with accounts and records, its cellar a strongroom. Yet access to the latter ought to have been under the inner room and have had a better arrangement for moving ingots and coin in and out than a two-foot manhole in its roof. As a jail its relation to the Square is much more like that of its counterpart in Rome, just as its vaulted chambers and underground oubliette make it seem a direct descendant of Rome's Carcer and Tullianum. Livy implies that every city-state had a jail, and Vitruvius prescribes one for every forum.[5] Oddly enough, Cosa's Carcer, if that is what it was, seems to be the only one so far identified outside of Rome.

Another reason for the enclosure of the SE cistern was the addition of installations along either side of the SE part of the Square, which appear to be related to arrangements for voting and mustering (pages 13–14 and 119–20) and to have been made during these years of peace. These were pairs of much smaller pits cut into the rock in the intervals between the trees (Plan IV; Pl. 23). The three pairs on the NE side have been fully exposed. Of those on the SW side only the pair at the SE end and the last pit at the NW end have been uncovered, which has been sufficient, nevertheless, to establish their conformity. The new pits were square, 2 p.R. (0.58–0.60 m) on a side and $2\frac{3}{8}$ p.R. (0.703 m) deep on the average, with a margin of 0.12 m either way. They were somewhat raggedly aligned with the outer sides of the larger pits, and like these their rock walls were pieced out, where necessary, with small blocks of limestone and mortar. The pairs were not centered in the unequal intervals between the tree pits but obeyed a symmetry of their own. The central pair, 10 p.R. (2.96 m) apart, straddled the center point between the two terminal older pits, from which the other two pairs, each $9\frac{1}{2}$ p.R. (2.81 m) apart, were 8 p.R. (2.37 m) distant, leaving intervals between pairs of $22\frac{1}{2}$ p.R. (6.66 m).

Inserted in this manner between the trees, the new pits were in balanced sequence with a slight emphasis on the center, while they were neither less than

5. T. Frank, *Roman Buildings of the Republic* (*PAAR* 3 [1924]), 39–47; G. Lugli, "Il carcere mamertino," *Capitolium* 8 (1932), 232–44; Livy 32.26.17–18 and cf. 26.15.7–8; Vitruvius 5.2.1.

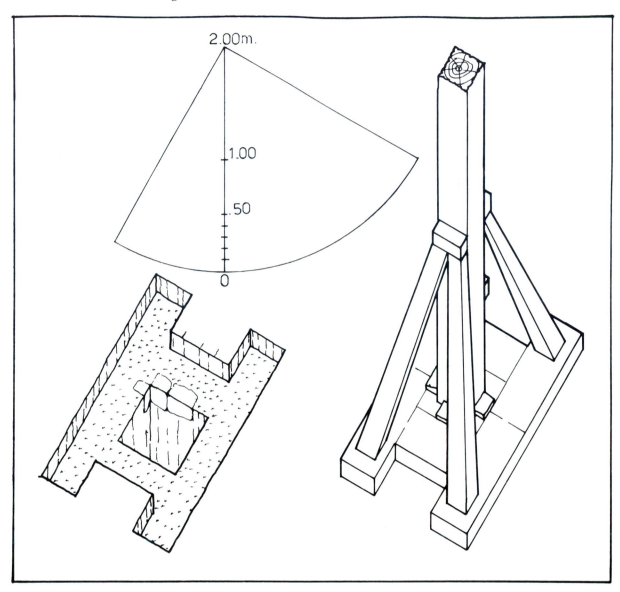

FIG. 14. Hypothetical bracing of posts, axonometric

$5\frac{1}{2}$ p.R. (1.55 m) from a tree-pit, nor more than $10\frac{3}{4}$ p.R. (3.18 m). These new pits, too, were surrounded by offset beddings for the setting of curbstones, distinguished in this case by having lateral extensions, NW and SE from each corner, about $1\frac{1}{4}$ p.R. (0.37 m) long (Pl. 24). Too small for trees, the pits might have held shrubs, such as myrtle, but the peculiar shape of the beddings implies a different purpose. Their projections suggest the function of supporting something fixed in the pits. Pits of these dimensions would have been almost as small as could be made by a workman wielding chisel and hammer. Given the positions of the pairs of pits, facing each other across the aisles of the Square marked by the

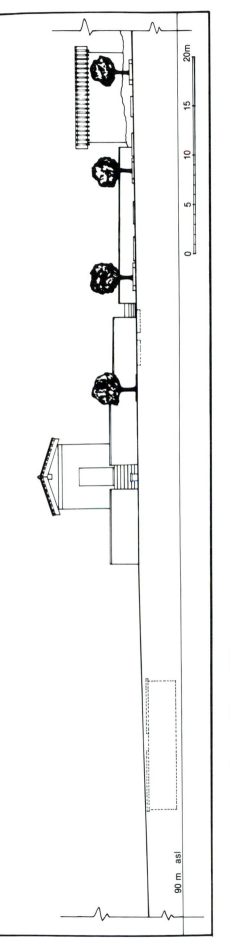

90 m asl

0   5   10   15   20m

Fig. 15.   Forum, restored NE elevation (B), as of 209 B.C.

trees, it is likely that they held posts chocked in the pits and steadied by braces footed in the projections (Fig. 14). This reconstruction proposes that the posts carried awnings to protect the assembled citizenry from the sun on the long comitial days.

Either as a supplement to the NW water catchment or, more likely, as a replacement for it when it was destroyed in the next period (pages 38–48), a second catchment was built along the NE side of the great cistern enclosure, just outside it. Here off the NE side, just SE of center, is a large settling tank with the stub of a feed channel leading toward the cistern. This received water from a narrow channel, 0.13–0.14 m wide, that can be followed for 1.05 m to the NE, where there is a small, basin-like widening in it, beyond which all trace disappears. Consequently, it must remain uncertain whether the channel continued, deviating toward the E, and conveyed water collected somewhere on the Eastern Height, or whether it terminated here and simply channeled into the settling tank water collected on the surrounding catchment. The second theory is perhaps the more logical. There is ample space here for such a catchment, and there is no other obvious source of supply anywhere on this slope of the Eastern Height. The water filtered here cannot have been of very good quality, as the character of the settling tank shows, as does the fact that it was subsequently abandoned and paved over. There is no way of estimating the extent of such a catchment; it could have extended to the SE for the whole length of the cistern; and if supported on terraces of no great height, it could also have extended to the NE.

The settling tank was discovered in excellent condition. In plan it is an irregular quadrilateral approaching a square, 1.70 m on a side and 1.62 m deep. Whether it is fitted into a natural fissure or whether it is an entirely artificial excavation is not clear. The walls are 0.40–0.55 m thick, built of limestone and mortar masonry very like that of the cistern it served. It is entirely lined with a heavy coat of very hard signinum, 0.03–0.039 m thick, that remains sound and watertight today. A flange 0.10–0.12 m wide approaching a quarter-round in profile masks the joint between floor and walls. It is not clear how the walls were finished at the top, nor whether there was a wooden lid, since the top was to some extent mutilated at the time the new pavement was laid. Out of the SW side, off axis toward the NW, leads the signinum-lined channel, 0.24–0.305 m wide, that connected settling tank and cistern. Its mouth in the tank wall was covered with a heavy lead filter plate nailed into position at the four corners with heavy iron spikes and then mortared into the fabric so that only the center was exposed; the surface of the lead was lightly scored so that the signinum would adhere. The plate was found still in position, although its center had been broken, and was cleared and removed. It is 0.408–0.412 m wide, c. 0.39 m high, and c. 0.004 m thick. At the center of the base a strip 0.23 m long and 0.11 m high was bent up and fitted into the mouth of the channel. The center left exposed was roughly circular and pushed out into a shallow bowl. It was pierced with five concentric rings of small holes around a small cluster of holes in the center;

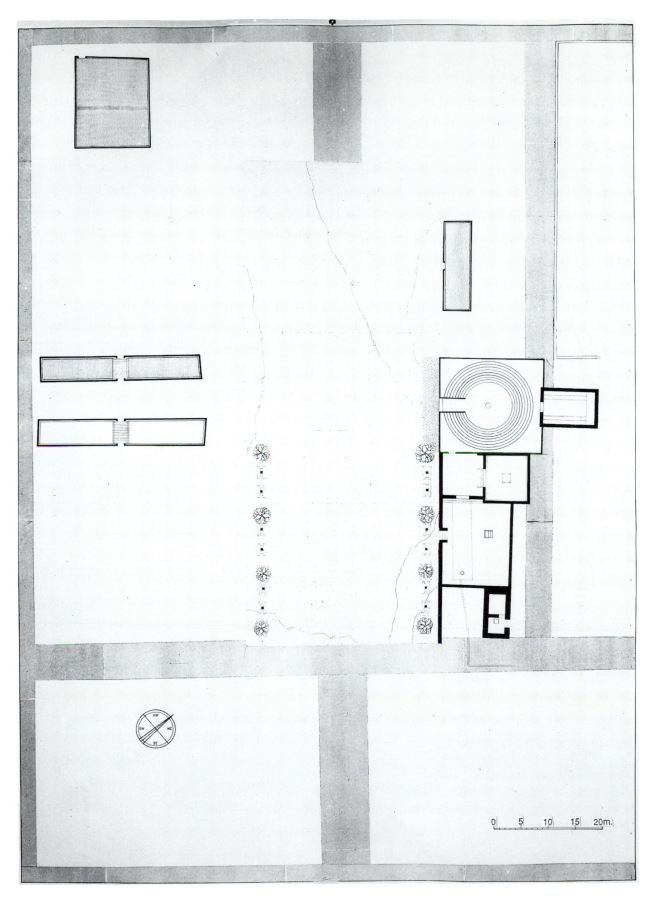

Fig. 16.   Forum, restored plan (C), as of 197 B.C.

these are both square and round and very irregular; the smallest is c. 0.007 m across, the largest c. 0.011 m; the diameter of the largest ring is c. 0.23 m. The channel to which it led is a box drain built of small limestone blocks and mortar and lined with signinum. It is broken 0.80 m from the tank, and beyond this point there is no further trace of it, but since it is only 1.45 m from the cistern at this point, there can be no question as to where it led (Pl. 17).

At the middle of the SE end of the cistern a second channel enters. The way the mouth was cut down in a series of rough steps in a later period so it would enter under the crown of the new vault suggests that this was also part of the original system. But the fact that it represents a different and possibly more sophisticated system of water collection than the catchment suggested above in connection with the settling tank and that it is without a settling tank suggests that it may be a slightly later installation. In the arm emptying into the cistern, the channel is a box drain, $\frac{3}{4}$ p.R. (0.22 m) wide, partly cut in the bedrock, partly built of small stone and mortar, and originally roofed with mortared slabs. It runs somewhat erratically to the SE, in part following a shallow natural fault, to a point opposite the passage between the Carcer and the Market Building,[6] where it turns a near right angle and runs NE, roughly parallel to the NW wall of the Market Building. At a point opposite the W corner of the Market Building it changes from a box drain to an open drain, 0.54 m wide at its top, with a narrow floor, 0.14–0.175 m wide, and sloping sides partly cut in the bedrock, partly built of medium-sized blocks of limestone, c. 0.40 m square, set dry. At present the open drain has been followed in excavation only 5.80 m, but presumably it continues the depth of this large building and caught the drip from the eaves of a portico that ran along the NW side on the exterior. The base of one of the pillars that supported the roof of this portico has been uncovered, as has a stretch of the terrace wall that held the fill under its floor.

At an uncertain date in the third quarter of the third century B.C. a series of alterations was made in the Comitium complex. The stepping of the Comitium itself was completed in stone; the water catchment SE of the Comitium was covered over, reterraced, and raised; and the cistern SE of the catchment was vaulted and terraced over. These changes had the effect of making permanent and monumental what had previously been utilitarian and makeshift. It is therefore logical to connect them with one another as parts of a single project.

The Comitium now took on the aspect it was to keep almost unchanged for nearly five hundred years. As far as sure evidence goes, the circuit wall remained unaltered, but perhaps there were changes in the upper parts that have disappeared. If, for example, the wall was originally crowned by a wooden fence, or parapet, we might expect that at this time there would have been a replacement in bronze or stone. The entrance from the Forum may also have been given a more monumental character than it previously had, for the break in

6. Brown 1951, 82.

the circuit wall measures 4.47 m, while the width of the pavement of the passage through it is only c. 2.45 m. The extra meter at either side would have been ample for the footing of an imposing portal.

The most important change here, however, was the completion of the stepping of the amphitheater in stone. Unfortunately, nothing of the new steps now remains. In a late period, when the Comitium appears to have been converted to use as a threshing floor (page 250), the blocks were prized up and either carted away to be used elsewhere or smashed into small chunks and thrown into a fill of building material, rubbish, and earth that raised the center of the amphitheater. The lower part of the fill behind these steps remains; the upper part was dug out to level the area. In the sampling trench in the N corner of the Comitium the fill consisted of four strata laid on top of the fill for Comitium I (page 19): a stratum of brown earth c. 0.15 m thick, a stratum of earth and stone c. 0.15 m thick, a stratum of broken limestone c. 0.15 m thick, and a stratum of yellowish brown earth including some stone c. 0.25 m thick as preserved. According to our calculations, c. 1.13 m of the fill has been lost.

That the new steps were of the same purplish tufa as the others is proved by the presence of spalls of this tufa in the fill behind them. This tufa, while of an agreeable color and texture and easily worked, is very friable. In the Capitolium of Cosa, built c. 150 B.C., it was used for the stairs, for the slabs that roofed the cistern, and for the altar, but the columns were of nenfro.[7] By the time of the construction of the Basilica, c. 140 B.C., both tufas had been abandoned, except for elements of elaborate carving, in favor of a yellowish travertine, probably quarried at Tarquinia or Saturnia (pages 214–16 and cf. 66n.3).

By calculation from the space available and the known height of the floor of Curia III and IV, 96.60 m.a.s.l., which cannot have varied more than a few centimeters from the height of the floor of Curia II and is known precisely from joist holes and setbacks in the NW and SE walls, one can derive that if the steps were uniform, there must have been eight, each 0.40 m wide, with the base step on which the pavement encroached 0.22–0.27 m high and the others each 0.33 m high. Since such a height and width is not suited to comfortable seating, we must presume that the Cosans stood in their assemblies, as the Romans may also have done. Since a riser of 0.33 m is difficult to negotiate, one might guess that smaller steps, like the radiating stairways in theaters, were cut in the large ones to provide passageways and afford easy access to the Curia, but there is no sign of any such in the blocks remaining, and the base step is preserved in the arc nearest the Curia; that it is also lower than the others must, however, be taken into consideration. If there were no passageways and the capacity is calculated allowing $1\frac{1}{2}$ p.R. (0.444 m) per place, the steps would accommodate about six hundred persons, and there is room behind the steps for a good many more.

Because the existing pavement is different from, and inferior to, the pavement

7. See Brown 1960, 60–69, 73–75, 81–84.

of the basement of Curia I, it seems certain that it belongs to a later period. Because it underlay the blocks of a gutter and steps installed at the time of the construction of the Basilica, c. 140 B.C., it must precede this in date. The time of the completion of the stepping in stone seems the most likely date for it, but the possibility that it was installed at the time of the construction of Curia III cannot be excluded. The pavement is of relatively soft signinum, 0.055 m thick, with a heavy aggregate of coarse gravel and terracotta in small chunks.

Finally, we must consider the small limestone sink at the E corner of the Comitium. Whether this had opened at the time of the foundation of the colony in 273 B.C. is uncertain; it had certainly opened by the beginning of the second century B.C. At some time between these dates it provoked the collapse of a stretch of the base of the SE wall of the Comitium toward the E corner. To repair this damage the Cosans seem not to have patched the wall itself, but to have filled the sink and backed the stretch of wall from the catchment paved with tegulae to the E corner with a buttress wall of dry masonry. The exposed face of this wall is built of roughly rectangular limestone blocks with spalled faces, irregularly but skillfully coursed, occasionally snecked with fragments of tile. At the base are large blocks, the largest of which measures 0.75 m by 0.88 m, snecked with small ones; in the upper parts the face of the wall is of smaller blocks, the core of unshaped chunks of limestone. There is a single leveling course in the parts preserved c. 1.21 m, perhaps ideally 4 p.R., above the foot of the wall (Pl. 28).

From the evidence of the coins found in the mud caked over the floor of tegulae, it appears that the catchment to the SE was rehandled about the same time that the Comitium was completed in permanent and monumental form. The evidence shows only that the area was filled with earth and converted into a high terrace, but it seems likely that this terrace continued to have some very important function, probably now as a sacred precinct. At a slightly later date (pages 51–56) the whole area was again rehandled, and very clearly at that time it had the character of a templum, a high altar platform preceded by a forecourt; it seems logical to suppose that it already had this character earlier, and that it is simply the state of the remains that obscures this.

In the rebuilding of the area as a templum an unfluted limestone drum, slightly tapering but without moldings, 0.60 m in height and 0.60 m in largest diameter, was used as building material in the masonry that supported the stair. Since limestone was never, so far as is known, used for columns at Cosa, this might be the core of an altar, and in that case might have stood on this terrace rather than in the middle of the Comitium, the other possibility (Pl. 26).

The raising of the terrace over the old catchment entailed substantial change only in the SW and SE perimeter walls. The crude brick walls on the NW and NE appear to have continued in use, despite the increased pressure of the fill. The SW wall, along the Forum, was now extended to a length of 13.85 m and made uniform in appearance with the façade wall of the Comitium. The old wall was torn out to the top of the footing course, and the new wall built of chunks of limestone in heavy beds of mortar with a facing on the Forum side of small brick-like slabs of calcareous sandstone (page 14). At its foot it is c. 1.00 m thick. It is based on the footing course of the old wall as far as that extends, but beyond that simply on earth and an occasional outcrop of bedrock. The foot in its extension is still kept fairly regular at the height of the top of the old footing course, 95.01–95.04 m.a.s.l (Pl. 27).

To define the area of this precinct and separate it from the general terrace at the same level that now covered the SE cistern, a SE wall was built at a somewhat higher level than that on the SW. This was later largely destroyed, its SE face torn out and the rest knocked down or buried, so that only a butchered stump remains, but the line of its NW face is still clear. It deviates very slightly toward the E, so that the enclosed area was not quite a perfect square 23 p.R. (6.71 m) on a side, the NE side being some 0.09 m longer, but the intention of the builders is clear. It is built of limestone and mortar masonry, the remaining face only rudely dressed, since it was not exposed, but was hidden in the fill of the terrace. It abuts the SW wall with only a slight attempt at bond and is in part footed on the NW wall of the SE cistern. A gap of 2.39 m near its NE end is probably the work of masons in the construction of Templum Beta a generation later (pages 51–55). The finish of the upper parts and the location of the door that must have pierced it remain uncertain.

The level of the new terrace, 95.70 m.a.s.l., stood 0.90 m below the calculated top of the Comitium wall, so it must be presumed that the top steps of the old crude brick stair continued in use or that a new stair was now built. There is no evidence one way or the other, and none as to how the new terrace was floored.

Since the rehandling of the catchment entailed installation of a wall footed on its NW end and an approach arranged across it, the great SE cistern must now have been vaulted and terraced over. It is easier to presume that the vaulting of the cistern and the rehandling of the catchment are parts of a single scheme in conjunction with the completion of the Comitium in permanent form rather than to think of them as individual events in close sequence yet unrelated to one another (Pls. 1, 32, 33).

To accommodate the vault of the cistern the long walls of the tank were cut down c. 1.15 m to provide imposts, and the vault was then constructed of spalled voussoirs fitted tight by driving in small wedge-like slabs at the joints of the larger blocks where necessary. This has since in large part collapsed, but it survives for c. 5.00 m at the NW end and in the E and S corners. The line of the vault is scored on the SE wall of the tank, but the wall is not gouged to bed the blocks of the vault against it. On its undersurface the vault was faced with signinum, except for a strip 0.39–0.42 m wide along the midline; presumably this strip was left to permit the circulation of air and the escape of mephitic gasses that might collect. In shape the vault is a low, flattened, segmental arch, slightly pointed at the crown; its maximum interior height is c. 0.75 m. It was evidently packed and covered with small stones to the height of the original tank, then covered with a stratum of earth 0.58–0.60 m thick. To reach the top of this terrace a flight of steps must have led up from the open area of the Forum, just SE of the end of the new SW wall along the old catchment where the rock shows evidence of having been worked. The passage here was $7\frac{1}{2}$ p.R. (2.20 m) wide; a rock-cut step along the edge of the Forum must be the bed for a step block. This stands at 94.63 m.a.s.l. and 1.07 m below the top of the new terrace; a flight of six steps with risers of 0.18 m would have been required.

To bring the mouth of the SE channel under the crown of the new vault of the cistern, the SE wall of the cistern and bedrock behind it were cut down in a series of three rough steps, each c. 0.44 m high and 0.29 m wide; these are entirely unfinished and very crudely executed. How the mouth was finished and roofed is not clear. To bring water from the NE catchment a pipe must have been arranged from the settling tank; since there is no sign of working of the side of the cistern along here, presumably this ran over the vault and entered along the midline.

Water could be drawn from the cistern through a drawshaft near the NW end, and another drawshaft in symmetrical position near the SE end may have been destroyed in the collapse of the vault. That surviving, probably not original in its superstructure, is cylindrical, 1.40 m in diameter, with walls 0.42 m thick, built of limestone rubble and mortar masonry plastered over with mortar outside and in. It rises on the crown of the vault only 0.20 m from the NW wall of the cistern; the mouth below it through the vault is rectangular, 0.47 m long and 0.60 m wide. The original drawshaft must have been lower and presumably would have risen only to the new ground level established as a terrace over the cistern vault at 95.70 m.a.s.l. This would have stood 0.58 m above the highest preserved point of the original tank and must have been in continuation of the level of the floor of the catchment to the NE.

All these activities fit into one another and seem to have been parts of a single scheme. There may be slight differences in date among them, but a date for the whole is provided by the coins found in the mud caked on the tiles of the floor of the old rain catchment. The latest of these are dated in the period 241–220 B.C., the period between the First and Second Punic Wars (pages 37–38). Such a date for this monumentalizing of the Comitium complex suits admirably everything else we know and can surmise about Cosan and Roman history.

IV. 209–197 B.C.

(Plan IV; Figs. 17–18; Pls. 27–36)

The crucial year 209 B.C. was the turning point of the war. By 207 central Italy was no longer in danger. Despite the continuous demand on its manpower, Cosa, during the later years of the war, was able to embellish the NE side of the Square modestly with the first purely religious building in the Forum. It was probably motivated by events in the Comitium but involved the whole area from the Comitium to the Carcer and from the Square to Street 7.

NE of the catchment and abutting it and on the Comitium was built a high, solid platform, 9.20–9.30 m wide and 8.65 m front to back. It consists of three new walls, SE, SW, and NE; on the NW side the dry buttress wall built to repair the Comitium was incorporated as a wall, the others being simply made to abut it without bond. It appears that on the ground the builders laid out a square, ideally $29\frac{1}{2}$ p.R. (8.73 m) on a side, in the angle formed by the Comitium buttress and the NE wall of the little precinct. The incorporation of the buttress as one boundary seems to have been part of the original project and also inclusion of the NE wall of the precinct, which affects the overall SE dimension of the finished platform and brings it up to 9.15 m. Ideally, then, the platform was to be 31 p.R. square on the outside.

The new walls are $2\frac{1}{2}$ p.R. (0.74 m) thick; in the NE and SE walls the outer face,

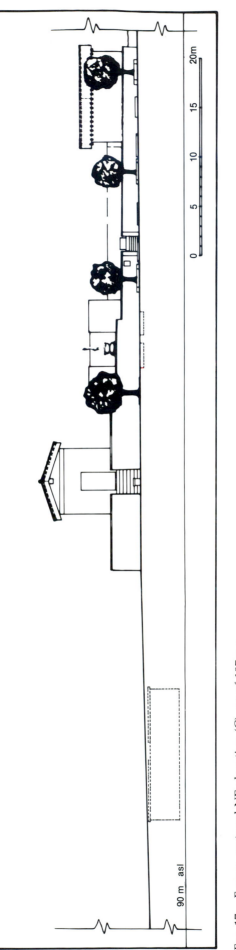

90 m asl

0   5   10   15   20m

Fig. 17.   Forum, restored NE elevation (C), as of 197 B.C.

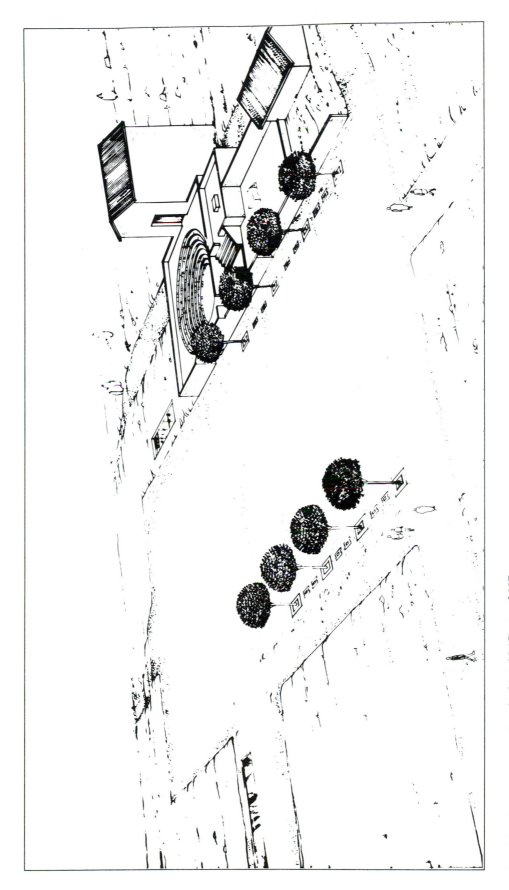

FIG. 18. Forum, perspective, looking N (C), as of 197 B.C.

which was exposed, is dressed, the inner not; in the SW wall, which was backed against the older wall of the precinct and intended to be covered by the stair of approach, neither face is dressed, except at the S corner, where a revetment wall uniform with the dressed faces of the NE and SE walls was added to finish the short stretch between the substructure of the stair and the S corner, 0.80 m long. This was footed on the old catchment wall torn out to the level of the setback under the floor of tegulae to receive it.

The walls are built of the local limestone laid in peppery lime mortar.[1] For the exposed faces the blocks were cut to rectangular or nearly rectangular shapes of widely varying dimensions and laid in broken and irregular courses. In the NE wall (Pl. 29), the only one excavated to bedrock, are two leveling courses, one 0.95–0.98 m above the foot of the wall and one at the level of the floor of the platform, 1.99 m above the foot. The blocks at the base of the wall and immediately above the first leveling course tend to be larger than the rest, but the largest block in the wall is of moderate dimensions, 0.62 m by 0.44 m. In the exposed faces the joints are narrow, with a minimum of mortar, and the wall face was dressed with a point. The interior of the wall consists of broken limestone in fair-sized chunks laid at random in heavy beds of mortar (Pl. 30). The footing of the NE wall was exposed in the excavation and found to consist of a course of unshaped limestone boulders laid on hardpan and bedrock. It is 0.35–0.40 m deep and projects 0.06–0.09 m from the body of the wall.

This small, high, and extremely solid platform was filled with a stratified mass of stone and earth. A sampling trench, 1.50 m wide and 2.75 m long, was excavated to hardpan along the NW wall at the W corner. At the bottom were red clay hardpan and crests of bedrock. Over this were two strata of loose brown earth and broken stone, both rich in potsherds, especially black-glaze wares, with some other material, the lower harder packed than the upper. Together their maximum depth, toward the SW, is 1.45 m; their minimum depth, toward the NE, is 1.10 m. Above these was a layer of rammed clay, bright yellow in color, mixed with limestone gravel, which thickens toward the NE; at the NE end of the trench it is 0.70 m thick, at the SW end 0.45 m. Above this was a thin stratum of brown earth, 0.25 m thick at the NE end of the trench, virtually disappearing at the SW end. It appears that this was laid in at the time of the construction of Temple B to replace a part of the yellow clay stratum that had been dug out at that time and thrown over the area to the SE.

Remains of the superstructure survive only on the NE side, as a stretch of parapet wall 2.77 m long broken at both ends. It was preserved because it was incorporated into the body of the podium of Temple B. On the exterior it is flush with the exterior face of the platform; on the interior it is set back 1 p.R. (0.30 m). In masonry it is identical with the dressed masonry of the exposed faces of the platform walls: small, roughly squared limestone blocks in broken and irregular

1. Brown 1951, 59–60.

courses. Parts of only two courses survive. The wall is c. $1\frac{1}{2}$ p.R. (0.444 m) thick, built in two faces that interlock in many places but are without through bonding in the parts that survive. On the interior a few small fragments of a plaster facing were found close to the base of the wall (Pl. 30). This facing is 0.031 m thick, composed of two coats, each about 0.015 m thick, the undercoat coarse, the finish coat smooth and polished. As found it was without color.

Against the SW wall, near the S corner of the platform, was discovered a mass of mortared masonry 3 p.R. (1.04 m) thick and 0.75 m long as preserved. The chief member of this mass is a slightly tapering, unfluted drum of limestone (page 48). For the installation of this mass the NE wall of the catchment was dismantled to the level of the floor of tegulae and used as footing. It appears that this mass is a support of the stair that led from the terrace in front to the top of the platform. By calculation of the difference between the known height of the catchment terrace, which served as forecourt, 95.70–95.73 m.a.s.l., and the known height of the floor of the platform, 96.86 m.a.s.l., we find that there could have been five steps each 0.23 m high, six steps each 0.19 m high, or seven steps each 0.16 m high. Since in Roman buildings the stairs are almost always rather steeper than in modern buildings, it seems probable that six is the correct number. On the Arx of Cosa the stair of the Capitolium had risers of 0.22 m,[2] but in the rebuilding of the stair of Temple D in the first quarter of the first century B.C. the risers were only 0.185 m high.[3] The treads of the stairs of the Capitolium were 0.351 m wide, those of the rebuilding of Temple D 0.37 m wide; some width not very different from these must be assumed for the treads here.

The datable ceramic material present in the lowest strata of the filling of the platform consists of black-glaze tableware and kitchen ware.

Of the sixty-four black-glaze sherds, five were in Campana A and seven in other non-local fabrics; the rest were of local manufacture.[4] The forms include one bowl of Lamboglia 36, one of 27b, six of 31, one of 63, one saucer with a furrowed rim, and two kylices. The identifiable sherds of kitchen ware were 37:[5] one round-bottomed pan with almond rim and a lid-ledge with reddish brown slip except on the bottom; one flat-bottomed pan, Dyson Class 2 (CF 7); one flat-bottomed pan, Dyson Class 5 (CF 13); one raised pan, Dyson Class 1 (FG 16, 16 IV 12–13); three pots, Dyson Class 2 (CF 19–21, FG 21–27, 16 IV 24–33); one pot, Dyson Class 3 (CF 22–28, FG 28–33, 16 IV 34–37); seven pots, Dyson Class 4 (CF 29–32, FG 34, 35); four pots, Dyson Class 10 (CF 38–41, 16 IV 38); two pots, Dyson Class 15 (FG 37, 16 IV 39–44); and seven bottoms and eight lids. All the forms are current in the third and early second centuries at Cosa. A more precise date for the fill is furnished by a freshly minted triens on the newly issued

2. Brown 1960, 73–75.
3. Brown 1960, 114–15.
4. Lamboglia 1952, 163–66, 170–71, 176–77, 180–

81, 183, 200; Taylor 1957, 177–78.
5. Dyson 1976, 21–22, 23–26, 28, 41–44, 53, 55–57.

sextantal standard, struck around 210 B.C.[6] It can be taken for granted that the platform was built during the last decade of the third century.

The new building seems most probably to have been an independent altar raised on a high platform with a low parapet wall, preceded by a terraced forecourt where the worshipers could assemble.[7] The disproportion in size between forecourt and altar platform is not especially remarkable, since the very existence of the forecourt is due to the previous existence of the rain catchment and the SE cistern and is not a new construction at all. Ordinarily, with an altar of this sort the mass of people would not have entered the sacred precinct but would have simply followed the sacrifice from a distance.

The form of the altar remains a mystery. In the excavation no block that could be assigned to it came to light, and no foundations to support it were encountered. The latter fact makes it probable that it was a small altar like that of the Deus Ignotus on the Palatine in Rome,[8] a notion that is also supported by the possibility that it continued to serve as the altar of Temple B, at which time the size of the altar platform was much reduced. On the other hand most of the independent altars known at Rome are large U-shaped altars,[9] and an altar of this form also stood in the forecourt of the Capitolium of Cosa.[10] So perhaps we should imagine such an altar here, in which case we must presume that it was completely destroyed at the time of the construction of Temple B.

The comparanda for Templum Beta are widely scattered in time and geography, but none comes from a site neighboring Cosa and none is a particularly close or illuminating parallel to the building under discussion. Those in central Italy are square or rectangular platforms in the widest variety of masonry, generally finished with moldings at base and crown. At one side is a stair of approach. In no case does the altar that surmounted the platform survive, but there are good comparanda for the architecture in the many surviving tombs of altar form.

The divinity, or divinities, worshiped at this altar will presumably have been the same as those honored in Temple B, which replaced it. No sacred or votive material especially associated with Templum Beta's separate existence came to light, so the question is best deferred to the discussion of Temple B (pages 197–204).

6. Buttrey 1980, 16, 45 (no. 35 = CF 2232); Crawford 1974, no. 59/2.

7. The author has been unable to locate any comprehensive study of the independent altar as an architectural form.

8. See G. Lugli, *Roma antica, il centro monumentale* (Rome, 1946), 451 and 401, fig. 120.

9. Cf., e.g., the base of such an altar found under the Lapis Niger in the Forum Romanum (Lugli [note 8 above], 121–23; F. Castagnoli et al., *Lavinium II, le tredici are* (Rome, 1975), 89–174.

10. Brown 1960, 80–84.

V. 197–180 B.C.

(Plans V–IX; Figs. 19–39; Pls. 37–75)

Once the long war had ended in 201, those Latin colonies that had felt their losses most severely petitioned the Roman senate for fresh drafts of colonists. Cosa was third in order after Venusia and Narnia in 199.[1] In that year the senate evidently had more urgent priorities and limited recruits. Cosa's first petition was not met. Two years later a second embassy was given license to enroll a thousand householders, provided none had sided with the invader.[2] They were authorized, in effect, to draw volunteers from anywhere in the war-worn alliance, and the senate's confidence in the discretion of the Cosans was no doubt a mark of trust. In any case the arrival of the new draft of colonists set off a burst of activity throughout the colony that would last to the end of the century and regenerate the Forum.

Up to this time no evidence has been found of any permanent building on the public land, except the various structures that had stretched southeastward from the Comitium and Curia. These had sprung up piecemeal, one by one, as they were needed. Now, however, shortly after the reinforcement of the colony, a master plan for the enclosure of the other three sides was undertaken. It comprised eight very similar and unitary buildings filling the space between the

---

1. Livy 31.49.6, 32.2.6–7. Cf. Salmon 1969, 67–68, 101, and n. 172. 2. Livy 33.24.8–9.

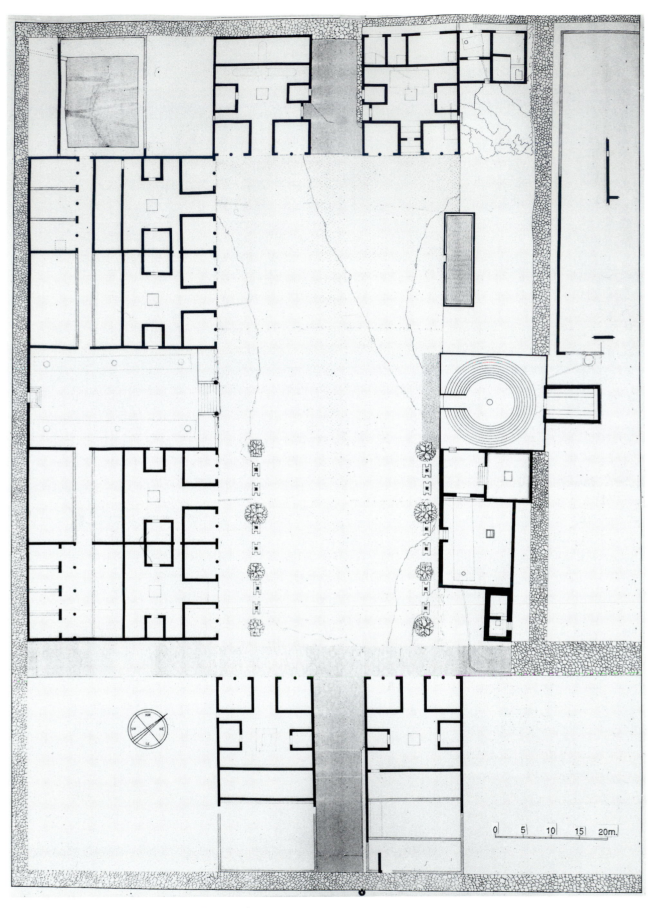

Fig. 19. Forum, restored plan (D), as of 180 B.C.

Square and the bounding streets. Four, in two pairs, along the SW side were separated by an open space opposite the Comitium, while two at either end flanked broad entranceways leading to the Square. Because of the eccentricity of the Square within the surrounding Forum tract (page 9), these buildings varied in length on the three sides, but the portion of each of the buildings that gave to the Square was practically identical with all the others. Each presented a tripartite façade composed of the high, central opening or *fauces* admitting to the interior between the wide doorways of two sizable shops or *tabernae*. The interior behind took the form of an atrium with lateral wings (*alae*) at the back and a room (*cubiculum*) on either side. Beyond these units the rest of each building plot extending to the street behind was treated individually.

Up to this time the surface of the Square, wherever it has been exposed (Pl. 37), was a roughly flat expanse of native rock and hardpan sloping toward the N. Its jagged ridges, fissures, and potholes had, in the course of time and use, been partly worn down and partly filled in, but it was little adapted to the disposal or collection of the rainwater that fell upon it or was discharged from the new roofs around it. Thus the master plan also called for a uniform surface, inclined in a regular plane from south to north, and for porticoes on all three sides before the façades of the new structures.

Unlike the larger and more solid public buildings along the NE side of the Square, whose shells survived one way or another, these buildings were destroyed after about a century when Cosa was sacked. Thereafter some were left in ruins, others in different ways rebuilt for divers uses, only to be abandoned eventually, and all were at last plowed under the meager fields of medieval peasants. We have been able to unearth only a sample of the $1\frac{1}{4}$ acres ($\frac{1}{2}$ hectare) they once covered. One of the buildings has been fully excavated, as have the porticoes around the Square, the façades behind them, the NW entranceway, the upper end of its SE counterpart, and either end of the central open space on the SW. Another building has been explored by numerous soundings, while the major surviving walls along the streets and within the buildings have been uncovered and tested by soundings for floors and the stratified deposits between and beneath them. Allowing for irregularities in construction and differences due to the lie of the land, the outlines of all eight buildings are at least legible.

Atrium Building I

Atrium Building (AB) I was erected on the slope between the N corner of the Square and Street O, bounded on the SW by the NW entranceway from Street 6. The approximate outside dimensions of its somewhat skewed rectangle measured $76\frac{3}{4}$ p.R. (22.72 m) in length and $58\frac{1}{2}$ p.R. (17.32 m) in width. Its SE side

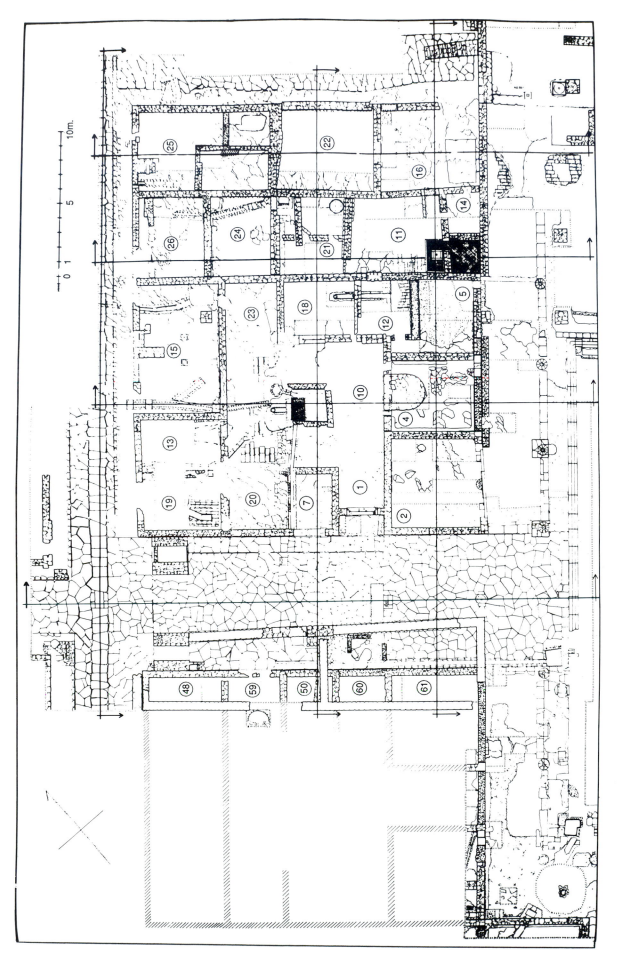

PLAN V. Atrium Buildings I/II

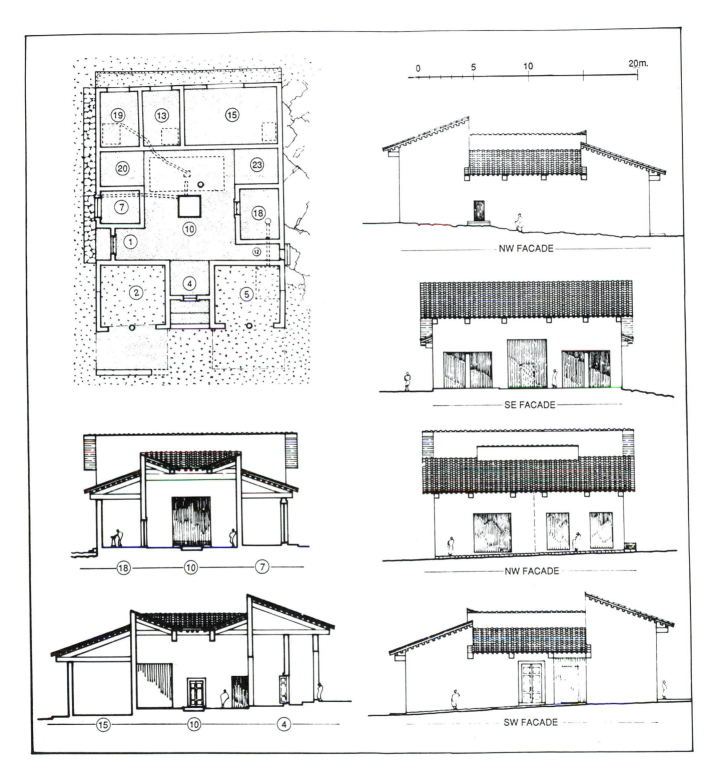

FIG. 20.   AB I, plan, sections, and elevations, restored, first phase

extended some $11\frac{1}{2}$ p.R. (3.40 m) beyond the NE side of the Square. Within this perimeter the building was divided into thirteen spaces, laid out on three transverse levels. The broader middle level included a central atrium (10) with its impluvium, two alae (20, 23), entrance passages on either side (1, 12), a cubiculum off the atrium (18), and another giving on the NW Forum entranceway (7). The upper level, facing the Square, was partitioned into two symmetrical tabernae (2, 5) on either side of the principal entrance (4), the lower into three tabernae (19, 13, 15) of unequal width opening on Street O.

Walls, except in the E quadrant where they had been protected by fills, were found reduced to their lowest courses, especially in the W quadrant. Floors of signinum survived in Rooms 18, 2, and 7, in patches around the impluvium, and in Taberna 15, with traces along the walls in Taberna 13 and Room 20. The bases of the walls were of one build, founded on bedrock or hardpan without footings or worked beds. Along the step between the middle and lower levels, the SE walls of Tabernae 19, 13, and 15 were in part rock-cut. Otherwise all were of coursed rubblework of limestone, roughly squared and closely fitted on the faces, unshaped behind. They were laid in clay in roughly horizontal courses, normally in two interlocking faces. They supported the upper walls, presumably of sun-dried brick. Blocks of the lowest two or three courses were usually larger than the rest, averaging 0.24 m by 0.36 m, as against 0.16 m by 0.24 m above. Exterior corners and reveals were quoined with larger blocks, sometimes of the full thickness of the wall. It is evident that the eight atrium buildings continued the tradition of coursed and clay-bonded rubble masonry surmounted by sun-dried brick seen in the early enclosure SE of the Comitium (pages 35 and 48).

The normal thickness of the walls was $1\frac{1}{2}$ p.R. (0.44–0.45 m), but the SW wall of Cubiculum 18 and the NE of Cubiculum 7, which supported the beams spanning the atrium, were four digits thicker, $1\frac{3}{4}$ p.R. (0.52 m). The NE, NW, and SW walls of Taberna 5 and the NW wall of Taberna 2 had the same width, presumably because of the greater height of these spaces. Construction, to judge from imprecision in the execution of the plan, was hasty. That it was carried out simultaneously by two or more gangs of workmen is attested by vertical seams in the NE and SW exterior walls 3.48 m and 3.80 m from the E and W corners, where the stints of two gangs met.

The walls bounding Atrium 10 enclosed a space measuring 8.28–8.31 m by 10.06–10.21 m, which may be read as planned dimensions of 28 p.R. by $34\frac{1}{2}$ p.R. (8.29 m by 10.21 m). It was floored with signinum without bedding or statumen, except above the haunches of the vault of a cistern. The construction floor that was encountered throughout the SE end was bedrock or virgin soil into which spalls of limestone and clots of clay had been trampled and on which, here and there, a fire-blackened circle gave evidence of the season of the year. The rudus and nucleus of the floor above was 0.12–0.13 m thick, but the finished surface was nowhere preserved.

The impluvium (Pl. 40) was set approximately in the center of the external

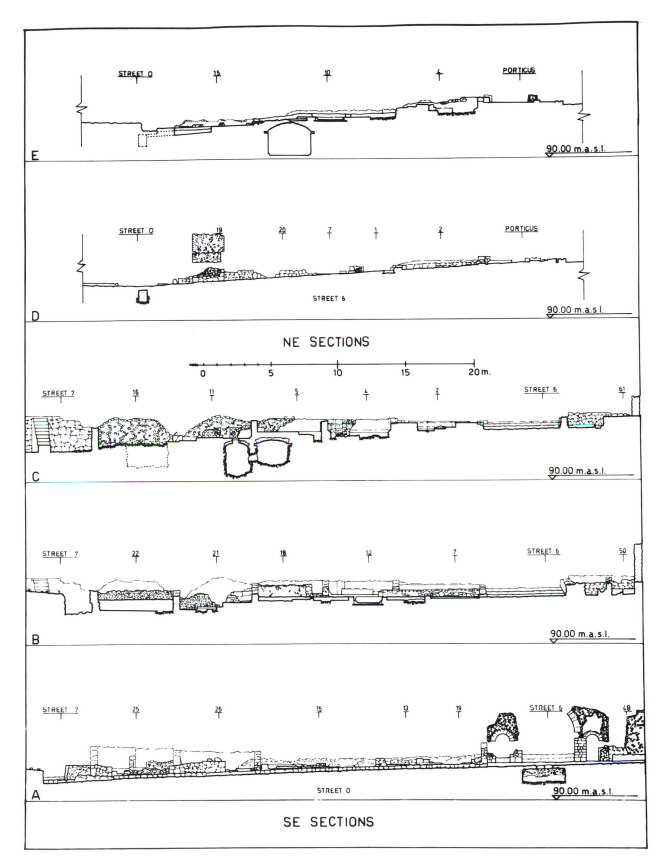

Fig. 21. AB I, sections A–E

rectangle of the structure, at the intersection of the long axis of the atrium and the axis of Cubiculum 7. Its original shape was square, 7 p.R. (2.07 m) on a side: a sunken square, $6\frac{1}{2}$ p.R. (1.924 m) across, with a raised border $\frac{1}{4}$ p.R. (0.074 m) wide. Its floor, 0.20–0.25 m below floor level, was paved in herringbone pattern with small rectangular terracotta bricks, laid edgewise on a carefully worked rock bed and tightly joined with hard, white lime mortar. The frame, which has been fitted into a rabbet cut into the herringbone tiling, had been removed in a later remodeling of the basin. Its floor pitched to a short box drain, 0.26 m wide and 0.15 m deep, walled and floored with fine rubblework, about 0.15 m thick, rendered with signinum and roofed with sections of imbrices. It issued from the NW side of the basin and discharged by a vertical terracotta pipe, 0.22 m in bore and 0.30 m in length, through the vault of the underlying cistern.

This, centered beneath the NW end of the atrium, was accurately hewn in the rock, $23\frac{1}{2}$ p.R. (6.96 m) long, 11 p.R. (3.26 m) wide, and 9 p.R. (2.65–2.70 m) deep, and covered with a low segmental vault. The walls and floor were lined with signinum, 0.05–0.06 m thick, with quarter-round cover-joints of 0.11–0.12 m radius. At the springing line, $6\frac{1}{4}$ p.R. (1.85 m) above the floor, the sides were cut back $\frac{3}{4}$ p.R. (0.22 m) for the impost of the vault. Its arc of thirteen voussoirs, averaging 0.266 m wide on the intrados and 1 p.R. (0.30 m) high, rose only 2 p.R. (0.60 m). The voussoirs were laid without mortar on centering, the sockets for which were cut along the springing, $\frac{1}{2}$ p.R. (0.15 m) square, six on a side, about 1.12 m apart on centers. The spaces above the haunches were leveled up to the crown of the extrados with a filling of broken limestone. The haunch of the vault was also pierced by a roughly hexagonal drawshaft 2 p.R. (0.60 m) across (Pl. 41). Its center lay on the line of the NE side of the impluvium and 2 p.R. (0.60 m) from the SE side of the cistern. The shaft was carried up to floor level by three courses of rough limestone slabs laid dry, which would have supported a puteal. From a point above the center of the vault a drain of imbrices combined to make a pipe and sleeved together ran westward to pass under the NW wall of the atrium and discharge into the soak-away pit of Taberna 19 (cf. Pls. 39, 40, and 50).

A few complete and numerous fragmentary triangular tegulae from the re-entrant angles of the slopes of the atrium were found underlying a later earthen floor (page 249), as they had fallen on the original floor about the impluvium. All appeared to be of one make, of bright pinkish terracotta with a grog of coarse sand and pozzolana and a cream-colored slip, replacements probably, but surely of the original shapes. Each had the configuration of a right-angle triangle, of which the acute angles were chamfered (Fig. 22). Base and hypotenuse were flanged for sleeving together, and the tiles were designed to join along the valleys in lengths of 3 p.R. (0.89 m), including their overlap. They were in two slightly different formats to fit the angles of intersection of an oblong roof converging on a square opening. In one the upper acute angle was of 47°, the lower of 43°. In the other these angles were reversed. None of the long imbrices that

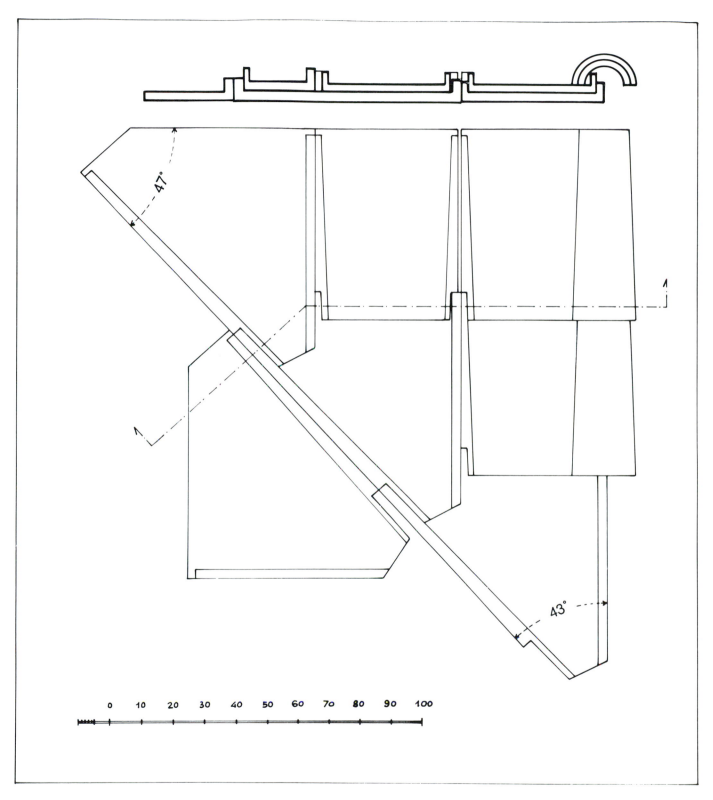

0 10 20 30 40 50 60 70 80 90 100

Fig. 22. AB I, Compluvium tiles

covered their joints along the valleys was found complete. The normal tegulae of the same make, some of which were found with simas (colliciares), measured $1\frac{1}{2}$ p.R. (0.45 m) by $2\frac{1}{8}$ p.R. (0.63 m) and overlapped $\frac{5}{16}$ p.R. (0.093 m). The matching imbrices were of the same length and $\frac{9}{16}-\frac{11}{16}$ p.R. (0.167–0.205 m) in outside diameter. The dimensions of the triangular tiles required that the adjacent tegulae be wider than normal, $1\frac{9}{16}$ p.R. (0.465 m) on the long sides of the opening and $1\frac{3}{4}$ p.R. (0.52 m) on the short. Two tiles of the former width, but none of the latter, were identified. The spaces of the middle level of the building on either side of the atrium correspond in their overall widths of 15 p.R. (4.44 m) but were differently subdivided on the two sides, except for the alae, which opened symmetrically at the NW end of the atrium (Fig. 20, Pl. 39). Each was $13\frac{1}{2}$ p.R. (3.98–3.99 m) deep and 11 p.R. (3.25–3.26 m) wide. Their signinum floors, as the traces along the SW wall of Ala 20 show, stood $\frac{1}{4}$ p.R. (0.07–0.08 m) higher than the floor of the atrium.

A single room (18) having interior dimensions of 12 p.R. (3.55–3.56 m) by $15\frac{5}{8}$ p.R. (4.63 m) opened from the NE side of the atrium. Its floor of signinum, at the same level as the floors of the alae, consisted, like that of the atrium, of a solid rudus, 0.12–0.15 m thick, laid directly on bedrock or the construction floor of earth. None of its finished surface has survived. The doorway was not centered in the SW wall but on the axis of the impluvium. Its doorsill (Pl. 42) of two blocks of local travertine, which is worn, cracked, and buried under the wall at either end, appears to have been prepared for a wider doorway.[3] Traces on sill and threshold indicate that it was adapted for a narrower opening, 3 p.R. (0.89 m) between jambs and 4 p.R. (1.184 m) between reveals. Set level with the pavement inside and flush with the inner face of the wall, it projected $\frac{1}{4}$ p.R. (0.074 m) on the outside with its sill about 0.135 m above the floor of the atrium. The SE doorpost socket was a massive bronze collar fixed in a cutting 0.061 m square, whereas the NW socket was cut directly in the block. A bolt socket, only 0.006 m back of the sill, indicates that the bolt ran in the thickness of the door.

In the E quadrant of the room an irregular strip of floor perpendicular to the SE wall, about 2.00 m long and 0.90–1.20 m wide, was found missing. Beneath it the remains of a box drain ran southeastward under the wall of Cubiculum 18 and Passage 12 to discharge into a soak-away pit under Taberna 5. About 0.24 m wide, it was partly cut in the rock and, like the drain of the impluvium (page 64), was floored and walled with fine rubblework, lined with signinum, and originally roofed with tegulae. The upper end of the drain appears later to have been blocked up at floor level, as though to support something above, while below was placed a decapitated amphora neck angling under the wall. Here, against the wall a vertical section of lead pipe, 0.07 m in diameter, fed into the drain from

3. The local travertine used at Cosa seems to have been brought from at least two quarries, one from the zone of Saturnia-Montemerano, inland 30–35 km to the NW, the other from the coastal region around Tarquinia, 45–55 km to the SE. The former is harder and of grayish tinge, the latter yellowish and friable. Both are generally used for sills, jambs, steps, bases, capitals, and eventually for columns.

above. At floor level it had been mortared into the amphora neck. It is obvious that the flooring was torn up, the drain unroofed, and its upper end partly destroyed at a later stage in the building's history. The drain was found filled with the debris of the floor and the stump of pipe was bent over below floor level.

These hydraulic arrangements seem to indicate that Cubiculum 18 was originally furnished with two basins and ample drainage. One of the basins may well be represented by a fragment of a small bowl of purplish tufa (CE 1182) found on the bottom of the cesspool nearby (Fig. 23). When whole, 0.38 m in diameter at the lip and $\frac{1}{2}$ p.R. (0.15 m) high, it was socketed for a pedestal of $\frac{5}{8}$ p.R. (0.18 m) in upper diameter. On the outside, fasciae at top and bottom were carved framing a series of three cyma moldings, and inside the lip of the shallow bowl was carved a double cyma.

The SW side of the atrium was bounded by the back wall of Room 7, which opened from the NW Forum entranceway. Its NW wall, aligned with that of Room 18, was also of the same length, 12 p.R. (3.55 m), while its width was 10 p.R. (2.96 m). It was floored with signinum, $\frac{1}{2}$ p.R. (0.14–0.15 m) above the floor of the atrium, with which it had no direct communication. This floor too was made up of a rudus 0.08–0.12 m thick laid directly on the trampled construction floor. The finished surface, together with a strip of the plaster at the base of the walls, was found preserved under a second floor. It consisted of a polished coat of hard white plaster over which the finish coat of the walls flared. The scratch and brown coats, 0.014 m and 0.008 m thick, had been applied before the floor was laid.

Of the doorway only a single travertine block at the SE end of the threshold has survived (Fig. 24), together with a bedding for the rest. The block, 2 p.R. (0.592 m) wide and $\frac{3}{4}$ p.R. (0.222 m) thick, projected $\frac{1}{4}$ p.R. (0.074 m) beyond the face of the wall on either side. It was worn but had been crisply worked with a sill, $\frac{7}{8}$ p.R. (0.259 m) wide and $\frac{1}{8}$ p.R. (0.037 m) deep, and the seatings for the jamb and reveal. Joint and tread surfaces were finished with a toothed chisel; the front

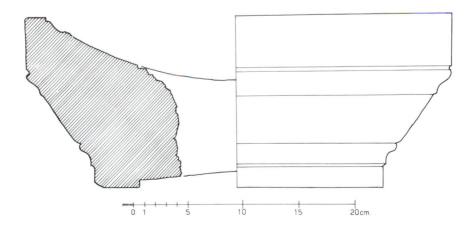

Fig. 23.   AB I, Room 18, basin

0 1   5   10   15   20 cm.

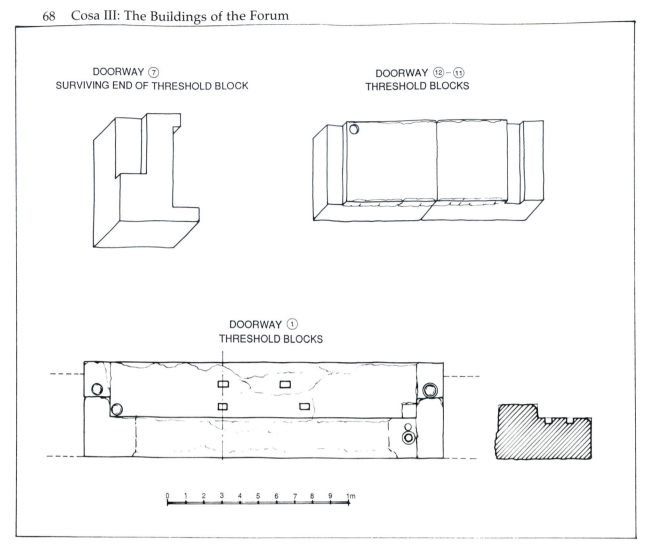

FIG. 24.   AB I, doorsills of Rooms 7, 1, and 12

and wall end were left roughly tooled. The doorway, on the evidence of the block, was framed by jambs 1 p.R. (0.296 m) wide on the outside and $\frac{5}{8}$ p.R. (0.185 m) on the inside, while the bedding for the missing blocks shows that it was centered on the room and of imposing size for so small an apartment, 5 p.R. (1.48 m) wide between the jambs. Alongside the NW wall of the room and across the atrium, beneath the floors and the NE wall of Room 7, ran a shallow box drain $\frac{3}{4}$ p.R. (0.22 m) wide, of the same construction as the drains of the impluvium and Taberna 13, pitching toward the impluvium. It began beside the NW reveal of the doorway, where it must have received the runoff from the roof above through a pipe embedded in the wall.[4]

4. The doorsill block, as found, was not in its original position but raised c. 0.08 m higher on an added bedding of tegula fragments and hard white mortar. The mouth of the pipe had evidently been plugged when the threshold was raised.

The SE end of the atrium opened in three directions to the exterior by three entryways of different sorts. The principal entrance opened on axis from the higher level of the Square. Of the other two the larger (1) was that from the NW entranceway. It, like Room 7, was 10 p.R. (2.96 m) wide and comprised vestibulum, doorway, and fauces. The vestibule, $4\frac{1}{2}$ p.R. (1.33 m) deep, was floored with signinum, whose surface lay 0.18–0.19 m above that of the fauces and atrium. Its rudus, like that of the other floors in this part of the building, was spread directly upon bedrock and the construction floor. As in Room 7, it was finished with a thin, polished coat of white plaster, partially preserved beneath a second flooring.

The doorway, $6\frac{1}{4}$ p.R. (1.70 m) wide between jambs, was not precisely centered. Its massive threshold of travertine, set flush with the face of the wall on the outside and projecting $\frac{1}{4}$ p.R. (0.074 m) on the inside, was found chipped and abraded by long use. The exterior face had been worked to be visible for half its height; the interior made a step of $\frac{3}{4}$ p.R. (0.222 m) down to the floor of the fauces. It consisted of two elements, a large block, $6\frac{1}{4}$ p.R. (1.85 m) wide, and a small one supporting the SE reveal, $1\frac{3}{4}$ p.R. (0.518 m) wide and 1 p.R. (0.296 m) thick. Their visible surfaces had been trimmed for the sill and the beddings for reveals and jambs. As in the doorway 10/18, the right-hand leaf was expected to be the master leaf. Its hinge socket was a shallow cutting, 0.075 m square, for the insertion of a metal shoe. The other was a worn circular hollow c. 0.07 m in top diameter. There were bolt sockets for both leaves, 2 p.R. (0.592 m) from either reveal and 0.045 m from the sill. The doorsill was found, like that of Room 7, not in its original bed but raised 0.05–0.06 m to accord with the later floor of the vestibulum.

Opposite Entryway 1 a corridor (12), 5 p.R. (1.48 m) wide, led in from a narrow doorway on the NE side of the building. Only 3 p.R. (0.89 m) in width, it had a pivot shoe 0.05 m in diameter for a single swinging door. The threshold of two slabs of travertine, each 2 p.R. (0.592 m) long and $\frac{1}{2}$ p.R. (0.148 m) thick, was inserted in the opening of the outer wall and rabbeted for wooden reveal panels. The rabbets were cut $\frac{5}{16}$ p.R. (0.093 m) and 0.028 m deep, one in the end of the SE block, the other $\frac{3}{8}$ p.R. (0.11 m) from the end of the NW block, which was immured to this point. The doorsill stood 0.03–0.04 m above the floor of the passage and 0.40–0.45 m above the ground outside. The NW end of a lower step of limestone was wedged in position on the bedrock, some 0.30 m below the bottom of the threshold. Its outer half, beyond a well-defined line, had been deeply abraded, while the inner half was freshly worked for a joint. Since the face of the doorsill was tooled and unweathered below a line 0.05–0.06 m beneath the edge, there was probably a pair of narrow steps with treads of c. $\frac{3}{4}$ p.R. (0.22 m) and risers of c. 0.15 m and 0.25 m.

The upper level, facing the Square, shows a symmetrical plan of large, squarish rooms on either side of the principal entrance. The elements of the project are easily read, despite changes made for structural reasons and slipshod execution (page 74). The overall outside dimensions are 17.25–17.35 m by 6.32 × 6.71 m, but they betray the projected rectangle $58\frac{1}{2}$ p.R. by $21\frac{3}{8}$ p.R. (17.32 m by 6.33 m) to be divided to produce widths of 20 p.R., $12\frac{1}{4}$ p.R., and 20 p.R. The added thickness of their walls reduced the widths of the rooms on either side of the entrance to $19\frac{3}{4}$ p.R. (5.846 m) and their depth to $18\frac{1}{4}$ p.R. (5.40 m) without reckoning the distortions of the execution.

Since the level of the Square at this time lay about 0.97 m above the pavement of the atrium, Entryway 4 was an inclined passage connecting the two. Radical rebuilding has left little more than the outline of its original form. The demolition of its NE wall (page 238) left only the stump of its foundation at the SE end, a level bedding on the rock, a stretch of its footing of broken stone, and the foundation and first block of its reveal. The lowering of the initial flooring left only short stretches of rough footings and rock beddings of a cross wall nearly in the middle. These remains are the traces of a vestibulum open to the Square and fauces open to the atrium, with a wall and doorway between.

The missing threshold of the outer opening rested on a retaining foundation of rough chunks of limestone. There is nothing to show whether the floors of the vestibulum and fauces were sloped or stepped. The print of the doorway in the cross wall is not preserved, but it is likely that its doorsill and sections of the reveals were reused in the sill of the wide opening of one of the adjacent tabernae (2) and in the walling up of the inner opening of the fauces to the atrium itself in a later renovation (page 249). The doorsill (Fig. 25; Pl. 47) was of travertine, 6 p.R. (1.776 m) long, $1\frac{7}{8}$ p.R. (0.555 m) wide, and $\frac{15}{16}$ p.R. (0.278 m) thick, made for a doorway $4\frac{3}{16}$ p.R. (1.24 m) wide between reveals. The door casing was an L-shaped slab of travertine, cut to revet the reveal and make a frame projecting $\frac{3}{8}$ p.R. (0.11 m).

Save for the cutting down of its back edge to the thickness of the new sill and scuffing of the surface of the sill before the left leaf of the door, the threshold was remarkably unworn. It was designed to be set with the upper 0.17 m of its outer face visible. Joint and exposed surfaces were finished with a toothed chisel of 0.0045 m interval. The bottom and a strip at the base of the face were left rough-broached. The pair of hinge plates, still in their sockets and showing little use, were cast in bronze with convex surfaces within a circular collar to reduce friction.

The room at the S corner of the building, Taberna 2, was first floored 0.32–0.35 m above the natural surface of the Forum with rammed red-ochre clay some 0.16–0.19 m thick above a packing of limestone spalls and detritus, which made up the construction floor. At the center of the NW half of the room this floor, found as usual spattered with clay and broken tile, bore traces of an improvised forge, a horseshoe of baked and reddened soil surrounded by a margin of broken stone with, at one end, a heap of ashes, coals, and tiny lumps of iron. The remains were found of a second makeshift forge sunk below the finished floor against the NW wall, where the wall was shielded by tegulae. Layers of ash signify long use by a smith.

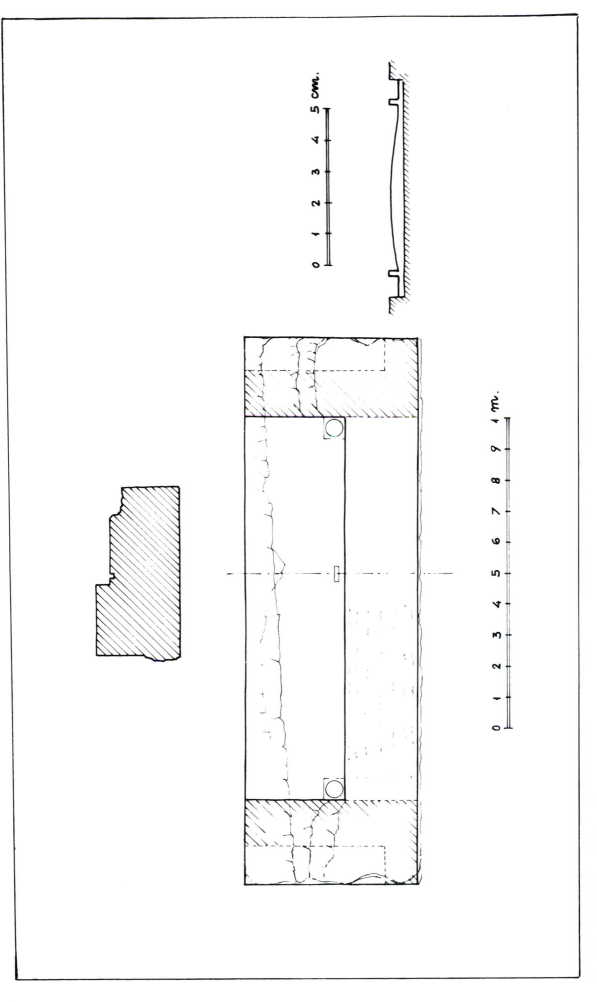

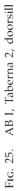

Fig. 25.   AB I, Taberna 2, doorsill

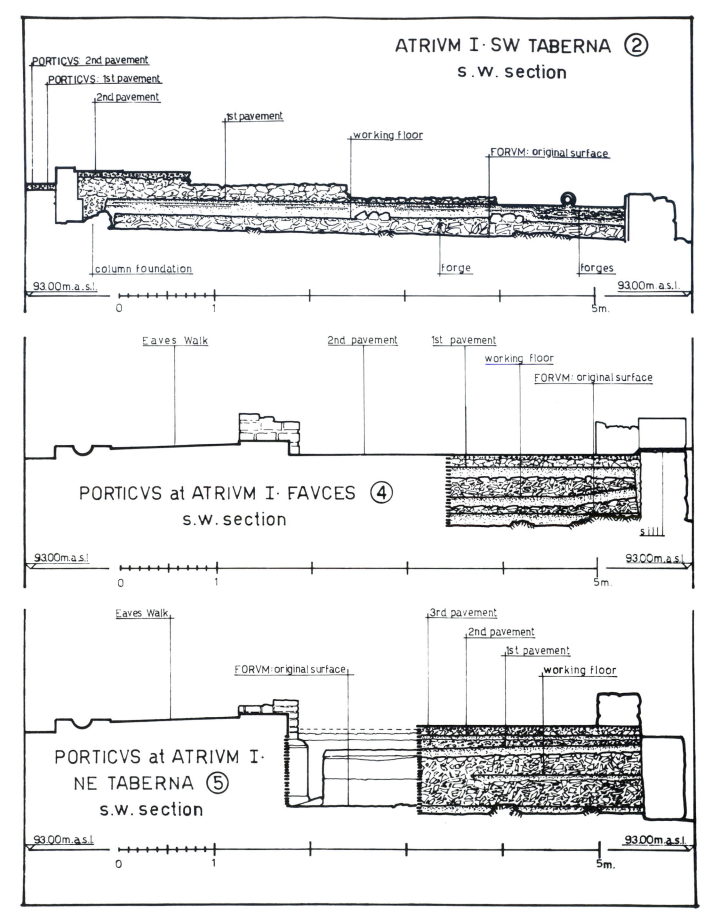

ATRIVM I · SW TABERNA ②
s.w. section

PORTICVS: 2nd pavement
PORTICVS: 1st pavement
2nd pavement
1st pavement
working floor
FORVM: original surface
column foundation
forge
forges
93.00 m.a.s.l.
93.00 m.a.s.l.
0   1   5m.

Eaves Walk
2nd pavement
1st pavement
working floor
FORVM: original surface

PORTICVS at ATRIVM I · FAVCES ④
s.w. section
sill
93.00 m.a.s.l.
93.00 m.a.s.l.
0   1   5m.

Eaves Walk
3rd pavement
2nd pavement
1st pavement
working floor
FORVM: original surface

PORTICVS at ATRIVM I ·
NE TABERNA ⑤
s.w. section
93.00 m.a.s.l.
93.00 m.a.s.l.
0   1   5m.

FIG. 26. AB I, Taberna 2, Fauces 4, and Taberna 5, sections

The opening on the Square, 14½ p.R. (4.30 m) wide between the surviving quoins of its reveals, was divided by a column. Its truncated foundation of fine rubblework, roughly circular and 0.70–0.75 m in diameter, was found beneath the later sill on the axis of and midway between the reveals, standing some 0.18 m above bedrock. On the evidence of two wedge-shaped blocks and a number of fragments of similar blocks all found in the upper pavement, the column itself was built up of sandstone wedges. The surviving pieces have an average thickness of c. 0.07 m. Their chords indicate that there were five or six to a course, while their arcs give overall diameters of 0.40 m and 0.48 m.

What was very probably the capital of this column, or of that in the opening of Taberna 5, was found reused in the later walling of the fauces of Entryway 4 along with three sections of the same jamb casing of which a section was reused in the later sill of Taberna 2. It was a "Tuscan" capital (Fig. 27) of travertine, carved together with a length of shaft of 0.372 m upper diameter and broken off 0.054 m below the necking. The plain abacus, 0.52 m square, accounted for approximately half the height; the low, gently swelling echinus and a shallow cavetto made up the other half. The abacus was dressed with a toothed chisel of the same gauge as that used on the presumed threshold of Entryway 4. The curved surfaces were smooth and faintly striated, as though from turning.

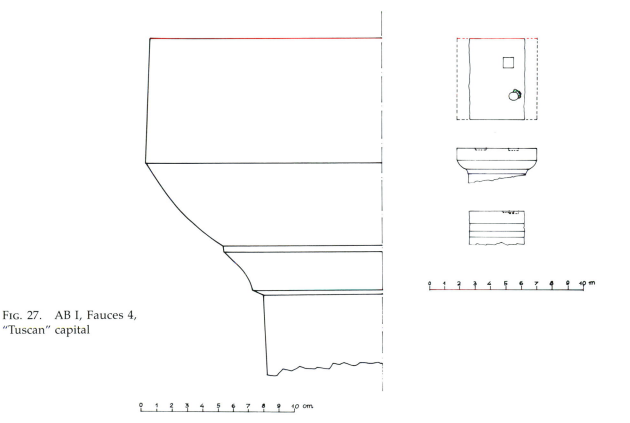

FIG. 27.   AB I, Fauces 4, "Tuscan" capital

Taberna 5, the counterpart of Taberna 2 in the E corner of the building, was radically altered in the course of subsequent rebuilding (page 238), but its original plan is manifest. Enough remains to establish the line of its party wall with Entryway 4 on the SW. The two ends of the bottom course of its NW wall survived the razing of the rest, and the massive foundation blocks of the reveals of its original opening on the Square were found in place. Its original floor, destroyed as was the floor of Entryway 4 in order to lower the level of the room, can be assumed from the level of the Forum outside to have been about 0.20 m below that of Taberna 2. In Taberna 5 it lay on the average 0.70 m or more above bedrock. The lowest 0.55 m or so of this depth was found solidly filled with freshly broken chunks of limestone, packed with chips and earth, preserved under the later floor. The same packing supported the threshold of the opening on the Square, 15 p.R. (4.44 m) across and, presumably, like the opening of Taberna 2 divided by a column.

Beneath the missing floor in the N quadrant of the taberna lay the soak-away pit that received the drain from Room 18 (page 66). A natural fault in the rock had been hewn to a roughly rectangular form, about 3.05 m by 2.30 m and 1.63 m deep, covered by an almost flat segmental vault of thirteen voussoirs with a rise of only 0.25 m. These, 0.30–0.40 m in length, were laid without mortar on centering, the sockets for which were cut along the line of springing, three on a side. While their widths on the intrados approximated 0.20 m, they decreased progressively in height toward the center, from 0.40 m at the springing to 0.20 m at the crown. This was pierced 2 p.R. (0.59 m) from the SE end by the rectangular intake from the floor of the taberna above. It had been securely stoppered with a fitted slab of limestone. The top of the intake, some 0.82 m above, remains buried under the later floor.

The lower level of the building, facing NW on Street O, was some 0.60 m below the middle level and without access to the atrium or alae. Its overall planned dimensions of $58\frac{1}{2}$ p.R. by 21 p.R. (17.32 m by 6.22 m) became, when built, 17.16–17.25 m by 6.06–6.18 m. The plan, unlike that of the upper level, was evidently conceived as a single rectangular space that could be divided into the requisite number of shops. As constructed, they were three built in two stages, at first Taberna 19 and Taberna 13 together, then Taberna 15, as the unbonded corner of 13 indicates. Tabernae 19 and 13 occupied less than half the available space, but they were approximately equal in width, $11\frac{1}{2}$ p.R. (3.40 m). Patches in the E and W corners of the rudus and nucleus in 13 indicated that its signinum floor pitched to its doorway. This relatively wide opening, $6\frac{3}{4}$ p.R. (2.00 m) between its reveals, was centered, and the mortared bedding of the threshold was preserved when the opening was later blocked up. Only the SW reveal of 19 was indicated by a stretch of similar bedding, but its doorway was presumably of the same width as that of 13.

Beneath the floor levels of both tabernae were small rock-cut soak-away pits in their opposite back corners, E and S. That of 19 (Pls. 39, 50), into which the drain from the impluvium of the atrium discharged (page 64), measured about 1.90 m by 1.65 m. Its vault, nine voussoirs across and five to seven long, was found flattened in collapse but intact. Its intake from above was apparently in the S corner, but had been obliterated by the later rehandling of the drainage of the room. In the opposite N corner a drain from the impluvium and a vertical intake pipe were found, joined by a sheet of lead flashing. The soak-away pit of 13, slightly smaller and roughly square, 1.10 m by 0.90 m, had been uncovered and filled in.

The remainder of the space, $28\frac{3}{4}$ p.R. (8.51 m) long, was occupied by a single taberna (Pl. 51) with a correspondingly wide doorway, whose threshold bedding measured 3.45 m long. It was not centered, but shifted SW off axis about 1.00 m. Remains of a signinum floor in the S corner, along the NE wall, and beside the doorway sloped gently from back to front. Patches of roughcast along the base of the NE wall gave evidence for the original plastering. A soak-away pit, as in the other two tabernae, was hewn in the E corner, roughly 1.60 m by 1.20 m on sides and about 1.00 m deep.

Although the two streets that bounded Atrium Building I on the NW and SW had not as yet been paved with stone, raised sidewalks skirted the two façades under the eaves of the building. Along Street O the *crepido* (foundation) ran parallel with the axis of the street, following its inclination and the descending beddings for the doorways of Tabernae 19, 13, and 15. It consisted of a curb of squared limestone blocks resting on the roadbed and close-jointed on the face that retained a fill of firmly rammed earth, broken stone, and detritus. Parallel with the front of Taberna 15 and $4\frac{1}{2}$ p.R. (1.33 m) in width, it gradually widened before 13 and 19 as the alignment of their façades diverged. The other sidewalk, $3\frac{1}{2}$ p.R. (1.035 m) wide and paved with polygonal and trapezoidal stones, ran down the NW entranceway from the SE side of Entryway 1 toward Street O. Its lower end, sheared off by later construction and paving (page 123), would probably have joined the crepido on Street O. NE of the building the natural rock sloped northward to the line of Street 7, where a roadbed had been irregularly cut back along its SW side.

The gradient of the Square in its original state dipped rather steeply along its NW end and particularly toward its N corner. Here, as the SE façade of the Atrium Building was under construction, it was necessary to fill against its rising foundations up to the openings of Vestibulum 4 and Tabernae 2 and 5 (Figs. 26, 2 and 3), which had been designed for a new, gentler gradient. These fills, sectioned by soundings opposite 4 and 5, were stratified in alternating layers of red-ochre soil and broken limestone and capped by temporary floors (cf. page 70). The floors in front of 4 and 5 were tamped and trodden earth, that of 2 was a thin coat of signinum. This last extended at least to the NE reveal of its doorway and was bordered on the Square by a low curb of travertine blocks bedded on the fill parallel to the line of the façade and $12\frac{3}{4}$ p.R. (3.77 m) from it on the projected outer line of the portico. These provisional and differing floors falling gradually toward the Square and stepped gently northeastward indicate that the building was opened for occupancy before the portico and the final pavement were added (Fig. 20).

An overall symmetry pervades the plan of this particular atrium building and is reflected in the openings on the principal façades, toward the Square and the NW entranceway. It must also have been reflected in the main masses of its elevations. The three main parts of the building were probably sharply defined by their levels and by the pitch of their roofs—the middle section clearly articulated by the mass of the central compluviate block of the atrium and the contrasting outward slopes of the lateral spaces. Although the nature of these forms can be inferred from the plan, the state of the remains permits only approximation of their vertical dimensions and appearance. Maximum and minimum limits of height can be applied to some openings, whose proportions were governed by established convention, whereas the height of contiguous structures later added to the building can be estimated with fair probability.

The SE façade of the building was designed to be masked by a portico. The height of its columns, inferred from their lower diameters and capitals, must be understood as supporting a roof continuous with the roof of the upper range of the building (see Fig. 49). At the lower NW end of the building the NW entranceway was at a later time spanned by a monumental archway that abutted the buildings on either side (see Fig. 50). Its total height, deduced from the known heights of its openings and from its general proportions, is most readily conceived as reaching the adjacent roof line of the two buildings.

The height by rule of the doorway of Room 7 on the entranceway establishes the lowest possible line for the eaves of the roof over the spaces on that side of the building and hence of the symmetrical spaces on the other side. Similarly the openings of Tabernae 2 and 5 were regulated by their columns. The capital assigned to these columns having an upper diameter of 0.372 m corresponded to the diameters of the sandstone wedges found in Taberna 2, of which the larger was 0.48 m (page 73). The degree of taper and the height of the shaft prevalent at Cosa calls for a lower diameter of 0.48–0.50 m and a height of 3.12–3.50 m. Again, the proportional relations of the atrium suggest that a rule of thumb, like the Vitruvian precept (6.3.4) that the height of an atrium should equal three-fourths of its width, may be applied. This height of 21 p.R. (6.22 m) is in full accord with the heights that can be conjectured on other grounds.

If, then, the pitch of the roofs be assumed to have been about 20° or six digits per foot, which seems to be about average in the houses of Pompeii and Herculaneum, the combination of these various elements of probability produces a reconstruction that is structurally coherent and consistent with what else we know of architectural practice at Cosa. This serves as our tentative model for the other atrium buildings that have been less thoroughly explored.

The earlier sequence of building SE of the Comitium and Curia in the Forum had been completed in the final years of the third century, and it has been assumed that the extensive design of which Atrium Building I was a part was related to the arrival of new colonists and begun soon after 197 B.C. (page 57). The excavation of AB I revealed no earlier structure on its site. The rough bedrock and hardpan of its middle and lower levels, as well as the stratified fills above the rock of its upper level, were immediately overlaid by the construction floors of earth and limestone chips (page 62). Into these a scattering of more or less minute potsherds had been trodden, unsuitable for precise classification, but definitely types of local manufacture, like those found in the fill of the Sacellum (page 55), for example. The construction floors, however, also yielded five coins, two toward the back of Taberna 13, one in Corridor 12, and two in the sounding outside Taberna 5. Four had been struck in Rome and one in Sardinia, ranging in date from just after 211 to about 200 B.C., and all five were slightly worn.[5] These briefly circulated pieces of the issues of the last half of the war suggest money brought in by the new colonists.

Atrium Building II

The other atrium building that faced the NW end of the Square on the other side of the NW entranceway was seated on the same rocky terrain as its counterpart, sloping down from the Square to Street O and from SW to NE. The functional divisions of the building were doubtless laid out in the same order of three descending levels. Only the SE and NE façades have been exposed and trenched on the inside to verify the positions of openings and bonded walls within. These prove that one building was conceived as the looking glass image of the other, alike in plan and build, with insignificant variations of dimensions. Taberna 61 of AB II across the entranceway corresponded to Taberna 2 of AB I, 60 to 1, 50 to 7, 59 to 20, and 48 to 19. The entryways and tabernae facing the Square were identical, just as the walls of each were of the same thicknesses and their coursed rubble construction indistinguishable.

The openings of Entryway 60 and Room 50 (Pl. 52) were presently blocked up with identical rubblework, because of a change in the system of conduits from the Square that required an open channel along the SW side of the NW entranceway (page 115). Both were evidently then turned into rooms that opened off the atrium. The partition and doorway of 60, which had separated vestibulum and fauces, was removed, leaving its indented points of bond in evidence on either side, while the joints of the outer blocking of both left their traces in the rebuilding. A sounding in the space of 60 found its original construc-

---

5. CD 913 (Buttrey 1980, 55; Crawford 1974, 56/1). CD 916 (Buttrey 1980, 54; Crawford 1974, 56). CE 522 (Buttrey 1980, 48; Crawford 1974, 113/2). CE 572 (Buttrey 1980, 42; Crawford 1974, 56/2). CE 859 (Buttrey 1980, 36; Crawford 1974, 64/6a).

tion floor resting on hardpan and partly overlaid by a bonding bed of clay (cf. page 62). It lay about 0.44 m above the unpaved entranceway, and 0.48 m above it the remains of the signinum floor of the fauces were still in place. It is plain that the higher level of the rock formation under the atrium would have made necessary three or four steps in the vestibulum between the entranceway and the doorway, which would have stood almost a meter above the doorway opposite. Similarly, a sounding in Room 50 exposed the rudus of its floor some 0.50 m above the entranceway and the construction floor 0.20 m below it. Again, two or three steps must have been needed to reach its level. A box drain beside them, matching the drain running under Room 7 to the impluvium of AB I, here pitched in the same direction but was not a collector and flowed from the atrium to the entranceway.

The cistern of AB II, placed in approximately the same position as its counterpart across the way (Fig. 28), was of a different plan and dimensions but of about the same capacity. It is now visible and accessible from the surface at one end. The plan is essentially a T, having legs only $4\frac{1}{2}$ p.R. (1.33 m) wide and semicircular ends. The crossbar beneath the NW end of the atrium and the two alae is $38\frac{1}{4}$ p.R. (11.32 m) long and the vertical $17\frac{1}{2}$ p.R. (5.18 m), the SW side of which coincided with the axis of the atrium. Its short prolongation southeastward, which probably permitted introducing a drawshaft beside the impluvium, was found choked with fallen masonry. The NE leg of the crossbar, covered by a segmental vault of unmortared limestone voussoirs, was at some time walled off to the height of the springing to serve as a separate tank. The other two legs, perhaps at the same time, were revaulted with mortared sandstone slabs, and an arch of the same construction was inserted to support the vault at its juncture with the crossbar.

The three openings facing the Square were blocked up at various times (page 240), but the remaining plastered quoins of their reveals were left in place (Fig. 29; Pl. 53). In front of them stratified fills similar to those of AB I (page 75) provided an apron for access to the tabernae and entryway before the portico was built. From the E corner of the building to the SW taberna the apron of rammed earth before the NE taberna (61) and the entryway was curbed, like that of Taberna 2 of the twin building, with travertine slabs. They were dressed on the entranceway and on the projected outer line of the portico to come but were left rough behind. Some 0.70 m beyond the curb and 16 p.R. (4.74 m) from the façade of Taberna 61 two rectangular pits were sunk, $14\frac{1}{2}$ p.R. (4.29 m) apart on centers, one centered on the SW reveal, the other's outer side aligned with the NE reveal.

The pits, roughly $1\frac{1}{4}$ p.R. by $1\frac{5}{8}$ p.R. (0.37 m by 0.48 m), were cut through the fill into the rock, one 0.75 m deep and the other 0.96 m. They were revetted above the rock with finely mortared rubblework, which was offset with lid-stops of stone on two opposite sides, 0.16–0.18 m below the mouth. These pits, slightly less than one-half the size of the post holes along the sides of the Square (pages 41–44), were certainly to serve for the stepping of posts and, when these were

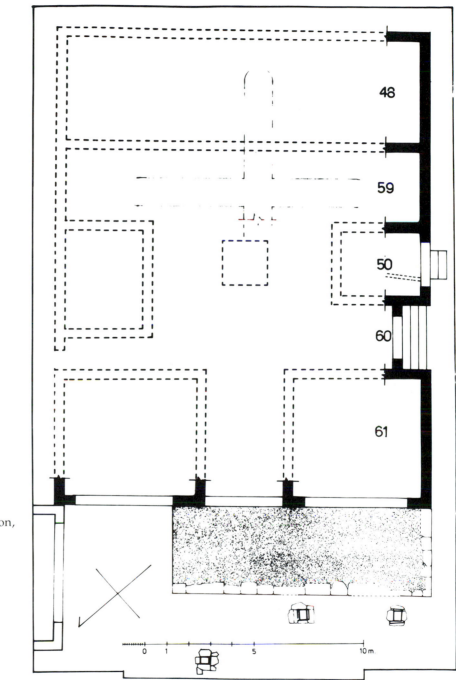

FIG. 28.   AB II, plan,
schematic reconstruction,
first phase

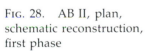

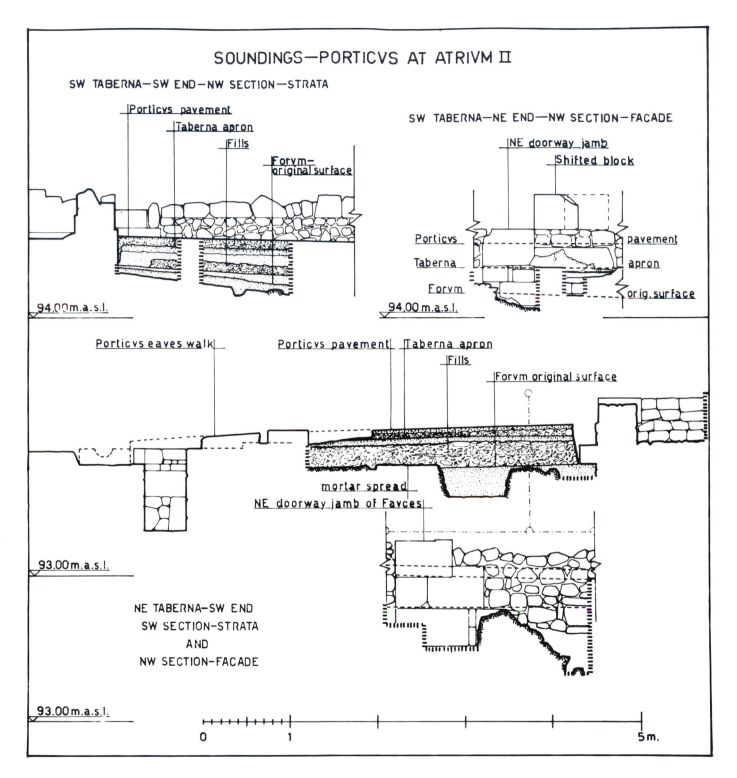

SOUNDINGS—PORTICVS AT ATRIVM II

SW TABERNA—SW END—NW SECTION—STRATA

Porticvs pavement

Taberna apron

Fills

Forvm—
original surface

SW TABERNA—NE END—NW SECTION—FACADE

NE doorway jamb

Shifted block

Porticvs   pavement

Taberna   apron

Forvm   orig. surface

94.00 m.a.s.l.

94.00 m.a.s.l.

Porticvs eaves walk

Porticvs pavement

Taberna apron

Fills

Forvm original surface

mortar spread

NE doorway jamb of Favces

93.00 m.a.s.l.

NE TABERNA—SW END

SW SECTION—STRATA

AND

NW SECTION—FACADE

93.00 m.a.s.l.

0   1   5 m.

Fig. 29.   AB II, SE façade, soundings

unstepped, to be covered so as to create no hazard. Their positions with respect to the taberna suggest that the posts would have supported an awning above and in front of the doorway of the shop. This in turn implies that the leaseholder had the right, not only to his taberna, but also to the space in front of it, down to the edge of the Square, which was later defined by a gutter (page 114).

Atrium Building II was shorter than AB I by about 0.50 m, the width perhaps of a wall, and not accurately aligned with either end of AB I. It appears that when the irregularity was noticed the outer walls of Tabernae 2 and 13/19 were angled in an attempt to bring the corners of the two buildings opposite. If this was the case, it is an indication that they were constructed at the same time. Moreover, whereas the construction floors of AB I produced a number of coins (page 77) but no datable potsherds, the deep fills of Entryway 60 and Room 50 of AB II yielded one plate and three black-glaze bowls of local manufacture from the end of the third or beginning of the second century.[6]

Atrium Buildings VII and VIII

The pair of atrium buildings at the short SE end of the Square faced Street Q with the SE entranceway between them. The frontage of buildings and entranceway corresponded to those at the opposite end of the Square to within 0.06 m, the individual buildings somewhat less exactly. The length of these buildings from Street Q to Street R was approximately 120 p.R. (35.50 m), an *actus,* nearly one and one-third times the length of the NW buildings. The virgin terrain upon which they were erected was rocky and rough, falling SSW from the Eastern Height and S and SE from Street Q. It required vertical cutting of the rock on the NE and filling within retaining walls on the SW in order to achieve relatively horizontal flooring in either building.

Atrium Building VII has been explored by means of trenches from 1.40 m to 5.30 m in width from Street Q along the NE side to a depth of 19.00 m and along the SW side to a depth of 6.50 m, along the entire NW façade, along the main axis of the building southeastward to a depth of some 18.50 m, and by three detached soundings. This exploration revealed the remains of most of the units around the atrium (4, 6, 8, and 12), the exterior walls of the two tabernae (1 and

6. CE 1016 (Lamboglia 1952, 5/21; Taylor 1957, A7). CE 353 (Lamboglia 1952, 27b; Taylor 1957, A21a). CE 418 (Lamboglia 1952, 31; Taylor 1957, A18). CE 1036 (bowl with overhanging convex rim; Taylor 1957, A31a/b); Mercando 1963, tav. 1.6, 2.7, 4.3, and 9–11 (end of the third century B.C.); see M. Torelli, "Il donario di M. Fulvio Flacco nell'area di S. Omobono" (*Studi di topografia romana,* Quaderni dell'Istituto di Topografia Antica dell'Università di Roma 5 [1968], 71–75); Morel 1965, nos. 147, 455, 461; form derived from Attic bowls of the fifth century (cf. The Athenian Agora 12, *Black and Plain Pottery,* nos. 777, 953, 958–83, 817–22) and copied in fourth-century bucchero (cf. *PBSR* 38 [1970], 72–73, fig. nos. 14–18).

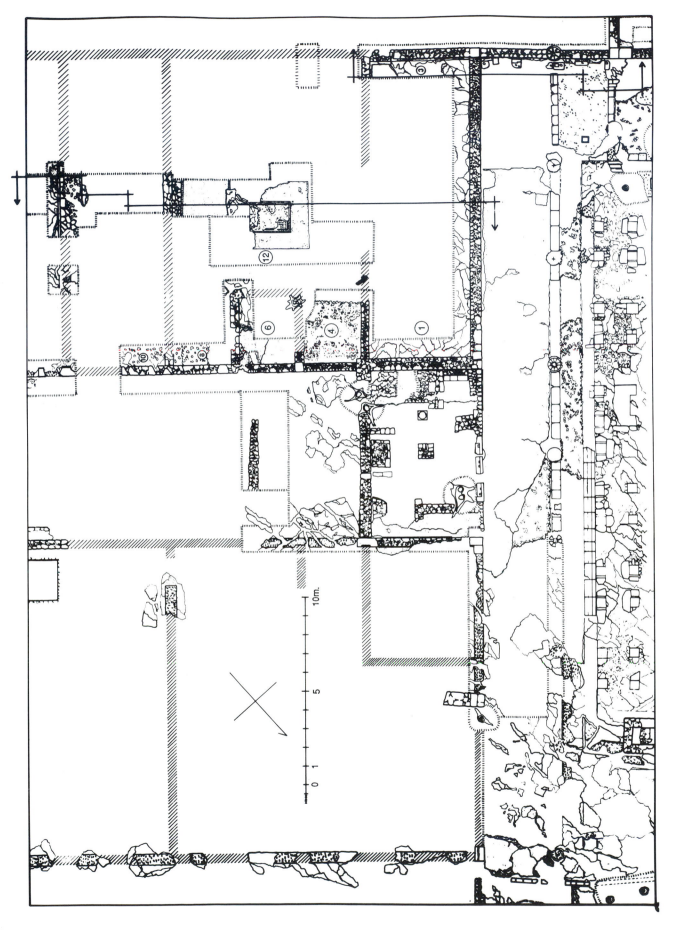

PLAN VI. Atrium Buildings VII/VIII

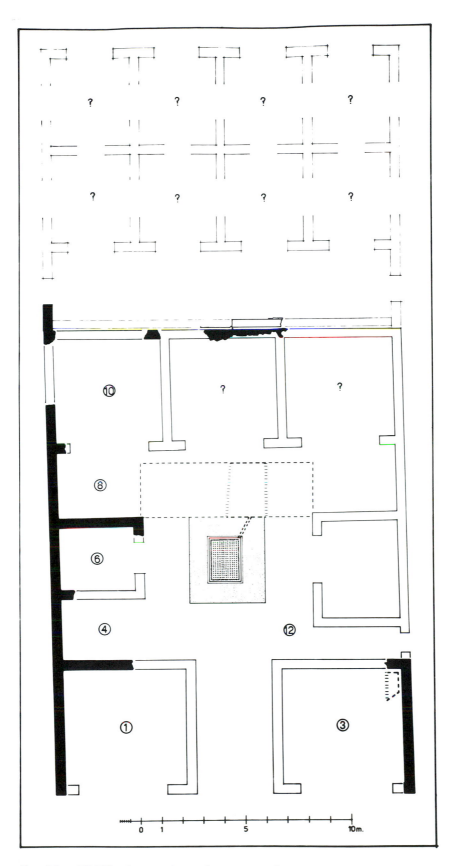

Fig. 30. AB VII, plan, conjectural reconstruction

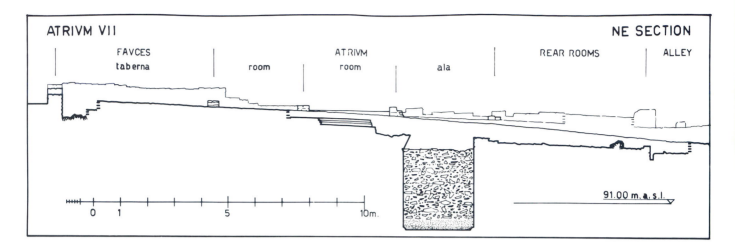

Fig. 31.   AB VII, section, center, looking NE

3), a band across the building behind the atrium on the same level as Unit 10 and presumably made up of rooms parallel to it, and a fourth unit at a lower level separated from the rest by a passage and extending to Street R. In every trench and sounding the walls were found razed, robbed, and in part rebuilt from the spoil. What is left are foundations and worked beddings in the rock. The foundations, found chiefly in the trench along the SE entranceway, are of the same construction as those of Atrium Buildings I and II (cf. page 62), normally $1\frac{1}{2}$ p.R. (0.44 m) in thickness, except for the stump of the SE wall of Unit 8, which is $1\frac{5}{8}$ p.R. (0.48 m) thick (Pl. 54).

The lower courses of the outer face of the NE wall of Taberna 1 remained in place along with the lower courses of the NW half of its back wall. Of Taberna 3 the lowest quoin blocks of its W corner, the remains of the foundation of its SW wall, and the lowest blocks of the return of its SE wall were still in place (Pl. 55). While these elements are enough to show that the depth of the two tabernae and the entryway to the atrium was 21–$21\frac{1}{4}$ p.R. (6.21–6.29 m) and that the length of the NW façade was $57\frac{3}{4}$ p.R. (17.10 m), neither the wall with its openings nor the floors within were found. The trench along the SW side, however, sectioned the lowest meter or so of the deep fill of red-ochre earth laid in under the floor of Unit 3 and encountered in its E corner part of a cesspool or soak-away pit. Hewn in the rock, this contained under its later filling a thick layer of sediment left from use (page 87).

The surface of the rock under Taberna 1 and the earth fill under Taberna 3 indicate that their missing floors stood considerably higher than the floor of the atrium. There the central trench exposed the impluvium (Pl. 56), a rectangular basin, 5 by 7 p.R. (1.48 by 2.07 m), sunk $\frac{3}{4}$ p.R. (0.22 m) below a frame of signinum, 3–$3\frac{1}{2}$ p.R. (0.89–1.035 m) in width, pitching to the basin. The edges of

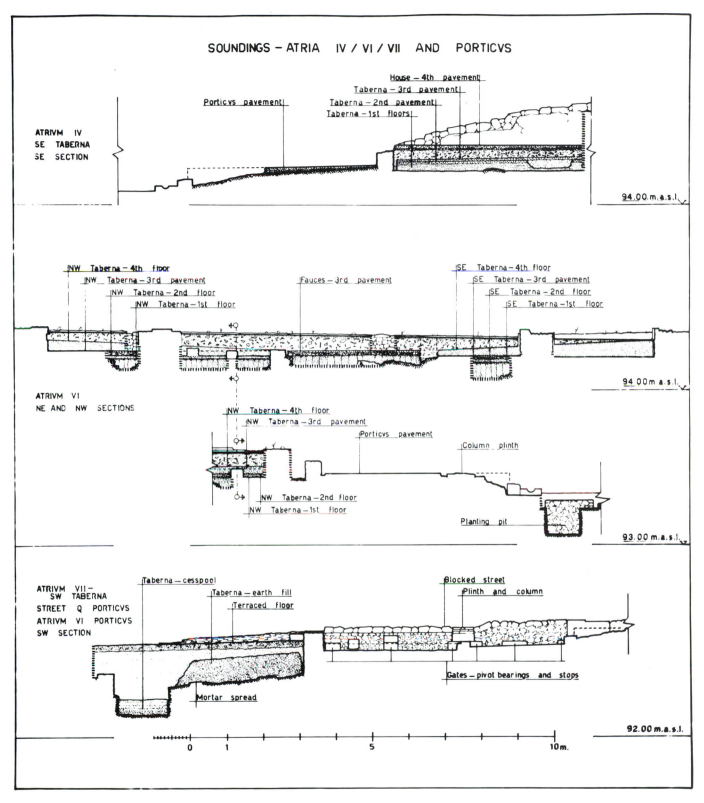

SOUNDINGS – ATRIA IV / VI / VII AND PORTICVS

House – 4th pavement
Taberna – 3rd pavement
Porticvs pavement
Taberna – 2nd pavement
Taberna – 1st floors

ATRIVM IV
SE TABERNA
SE SECTION

94.00.m.a.s.l.

NW Taberna – 4th floor
NW Taberna – 3rd pavement   Fauces – 3rd pavement   SE Taberna – 4th floor
NW Taberna – 2nd floor   SE Taberna – 3rd pavement
NW Taberna – 1st floor   SE Taberna – 2nd floor
                                                                SE Taberna – 1st floor

ATRIVM VI
NE AND NW SECTIONS

94.00 m.a.s.l.

NW Taberna – 4th floor
NW Taberna – 3rd pavement
Porticvs pavement
Column plinth

NW Taberna – 2nd floor
NW Taberna – 1st floor

Planting pit

93.00 m.a.s.l.

ATRIVM VII –
SW TABERNA
STREET Q PORTICVS
ATRIVM VI PORTICVS
SW SECTION

Taberna – cesspool
Taberna – earth fill   Blocked street
Terraced floor   Plinth and column

Mortar spread   Gates – pivot bearings and stops

92.00 m.a.s.l.

0 1   5   10 m.

FIG. 32.   AB VII, section, Taberna 3, looking SW; AB VI, NE and NW sections; AB IV, SE Taberna, SE section this apron were smoothly plastered to a depth of $\frac{3}{16}$ p.R. (0.055 m), at which level the floor of the atrium appeared, on the SW, NW, and NE sides, to have been hard-rammed earth mixed with crushed terracotta and gravel. The rim of the impluvium was also of signinum in two steps; the floor was decorated with large, white limestone tesserae, $\frac{1}{16}$ p.R. (0.018 m) on a side, in a pattern of squares within a border.

From its S corner a box drain of fine rubblework sloped toward the cistern. It was $\frac{3}{8}$ p.R. (0.11 m) in width and height, resembling the original drains of AB I, but here provided with a slotted sluice gate at the impluvium end in the form of a tile cut in pentagonal shape. The cistern, sectioned by a 2.00-m-wide trench (Pl. 57), proved to be $8\frac{3}{4}$ p.R. (2.59 m) wide above the quarter-round cover-joints at the bottom, and its higher NW side was found to stand 3.50 m high. This would have been only some 0.40 m below the floor, as reconstructed above. The signinum facing was uninterrupted to the top of this canted wall, and on neither side was there trace of a ledge or sockets for centering. Presumably the cistern had a flat wooden roof instead of a vault.

The NE trench brought to light the remains of the truncated walls and floors of the spaces that flanked that side of the atrium. These answered to the same spaces that bordered, on the SW side, the atrium of AB I. Thus Room 4 of AB VII corresponds to Entryway 1 of AB I, Room 6 to Room 7, and Ala 8 to Ala 20. None of these, however, had access from the SE entranceway, and Rooms 4 and 6 must have opened on the atrium. The nucleus of the signinum floor of Room 6 was found virtually intact across its NE end, lying about $1\frac{1}{8}$ p.R. (0.33 m) above the earth floor of the atrium. The floors of Room 4 and Ala 8, to judge by the rudus of one and the statumen of the other, would have come to the same elevated floor level. On the other side of the atrium a sounding across the line of the outer SW wall failed to discover either wall or floor, but it is assumed that a room and corridor, like 18 and 12 of AB I, were once there.

The stump of the lowest course of the rear wall of the atrium emerged in the NE trench (Pl. 54), and in the central trench a section of its foundation. The height of the statumen of the floor behind the first and of the fill of earth and rock behind the second demonstrates that Unit 10 and a band of its width extending across the building lay at approximately the same level as the atrium. Its SE retaining wall was discovered in the E sounding, the center trench, and a sounding between. A large quoin block of the NE wall had been carefully dressed to make a bond with the SE wall, and in the trench a 4.00-m stretch of its lowest courses, founded on the leveled rock and backed with irregularly fitted blocks, was uncovered. The middle of the retaining wall would have to have risen to 1.37 m to meet the floor level of Unit 10, which, given the unbroken NE wall, presumably had entry from the atrium. No cross wall is visible within Unit 10, but this, of course, does not prove that there was none, nor that traces are not to be found in the unexcavated area. Without cross walls the inner dimensions of the area, $55\frac{3}{4}$ p.R. (16.50 m) by 17 p.R. (5.03 m), call to mind a long warehouse or barn, neither of which seems suitable. More likely the space was divided into at least three rooms.

The main portion of AB VII, which opened on the Square and corresponded to the atria of AB I and II, occupied only three-fifths of the length of the building plot. The remainder, situated on a lower level and detached from the upper complex, was presumably served by the SE entranceway and/or by Street R. It has not been investigated, except in the E sounding and the SE end of the central trench. The last block in the sounding was found to be the bottom quoin of the NW reveal of an opening, 4 p.R. (1.185 m) from the SE retaining wall of Unit 10. In the central trench the foot of this wall formed one side of a narrow continuous channel worked in the rock, 0.09–0.10 m wide and sloping southwestward. On its other side ran a step parallel to the wall, $1\frac{1}{4}$ p.R. (0.37 m) wide, of compact rubblework coated with hard signinum, which turned up from the tread evidently to face a second riser (Pl. 58). The opening from the SE entranceway and the gutter-like channel combine to suggest a passageway between walls that was given a gutter on one margin for drainage. This suggests the presence of a separate building on the SE, which may have consisted of rows of tabernae or storerooms back to back off the passageway and Street R (Fig. 30).

Dates are scanty, but the fill under the missing floor of Taberna 3, sectioned by the SW trench (page 84), yielded a denarius only slightly worn but thickly patinated[7] struck in the last decade of the third century and some thirty-seven legible potsherds, all of which were current at the end of the third and the beginning of the second century B.C.

> Black-glaze of Campana A and at least three local fabrics: two Taylor saucers with furrowed rim; two plates of Lamboglia 5; five bowls of 27; one bowl of 31. Kitchen ware: two brimmed pans with bulging walls and offset rim; one pan of Dyson Class 4; four pots of Dyson Class 1; one pot of Dyson Class 2; three pots of Dyson Class 3; four pots of Dyson Class 4; one pot of Dyson Class 10. Storage ware: one amphora of Will Class 1; one amphora of Corinthian form; and one amphora with blunted, wedge-shaped rim.[8]

The area occupied by Atrium Building VIII off the E corner of the Square appears to have been the most devastated of the Forum, and consequently it is now archaeologically the least promising. Trial trenches along either side of its W corner exposed meager remains of walls and rock-cut beddings. Along the NE side the debris of its tumbled wall has piled a wide talus, and elsewhere the eroded mantle of earth reveals the bedrock and a scatter of building blocks. Only the outlines of the characteristic layout of the building emerge.

The lowest quoins at either end of the façade on Street Q have survived to establish its width of $58\frac{5}{8}$ p.R. (17.35 m). The basis of the NE outer wall of the

---

7. C70.450 (Buttrey 1980, no. 41; Crawford 1974, 53/2).

8. Mercando 1963 provides for this collection a

striking Roman comparison toward the end of the third century B.C. (see note 6 above, p. 81).

building was the edge of a scarp hewn in the rock, 1.50–2.00 m down to the inner floor level. The chiseled beddings above can be traced some 26.00 m southeastward from the N corner. The SW trench uncovered 11.65 m of the wall and its beddings at the NW end on that side. Beyond a gap of c. 10.20 m a stretch of the wall visible on the surface, c. 8.30 m long, was skirted by a narrow sidewalk, broken 5.00 m from the end of the structure. The SE façade is marked by the single reveal block of a doorway on Street R, 2.75 m from the S corner.

Within this perimeter some of the normal units of the building type can be discerned. The wall of the SW taberna along the SE entranceway ends with a massive quoin rabbeted to bond with its SE wall, $21\frac{5}{8}$ p.R. (6.40 m) from the principal façade. There the width of the taberna is marked by a deeper, right-angled bedding, evidently for the SW reveal of the vestibulum, 23 p.R. (6.81 m) from the W corner of this façade. Assuming that the NE taberna had the same dimensions, the entryway would have been $12\frac{5}{8}$ p.R. (3.73 m) wide, a trifle larger than those of AB I and II. One of the beddings, cut into the crests of rock in prolongation of the SW wall, was also rabbeted for a joint with a cross wall. It was 10 p.R. (2.96 m) from the back wall of the adjacent taberna, in line with the wall of Room 4 of AB VII and in the same position as Entryways 1 and 60 at the other end of the Square (pages 69 and 77). Another isolated crest of rock, about 6.40 m beyond, was found worked with a broad bedding parallel to the principal façade, sunk in the rock in line with the SE wall of the atrium of the building across the way. It came to an end 2.00 m from the inner face of the SW wall, but the bedding continued on the surface of the crest until it fell away.

This kind of cutting presupposes the quoin of the reveal of a doorway from the atrium and the level bedding of a sill, which indicate an arrangement of the spaces beyond the atrium unlike those of AB VII. The latter had a striking difference of levels and an opening presumed to be for a passageway; the former contained an uninterrupted wall, behind which the terrain sloped more or less uniformly. The SW wall along this slope runs beside a cistern, 22 p.R. (6.50 m) long, perhaps bracketed by cross walls. If so, the remaining wall, attached to the reveal block on Street R, may have been part of a series of narrow tabernae, perhaps as many as eight, with storerooms behind, while a row of rooms of indeterminate size opened to the SE from the atrium. Here the crepido along the NE side of the entranceway may have reached only as far as an opening into them, since no sign of its continuation to Street Q was visible in the SW trench.

A second "Tuscan" travertine capital that was later reused in the shrine of Liber Pater between AB VII and AB VIII (page 251) was probably removed from one or another of the four tabernae facing the Square (Pl. 59). It was found remarkably fresh, of slightly smaller diameter than the one suggested for AB I, Taberna 2 (page 73), but similar. At the beginning all the wide openings of the sixteen tabernae on the Square may have had median columns of this order to support the wooden beams above their doors.

Atrium Buildings III and IV

The four atrium buildings aligned along the SW side of the Square were designed in pairs with median party walls and an open space between (page 59). Both pairs extended from the Square to Street 5, 115 p.R. (34.04 m) at the NW end and c. $115\frac{3}{4}$ p.R. (34.27 m) at the SE end, a slight divergence. From Street Q to the corner of AB II the width of the frontage on the Square to either side of the projected width of the Comitium determined the widths of the paired buildings, each more than a foot broader than AB I, II, VII, and VIII. The façade of AB III and IV on the Square measured 118 p.R. (34.93 m). Their site was the foot of the long declivity from the Arx to the Square; within their building plots the sloping rock fell about 2.80 m, a grade of 8 percent.

The excavation of the NE façade of AB III and a narrow trench behind exposed much of the lowest courses of its original tabernae and fauces. Including its party wall with AB IV, the façade measured $59\frac{1}{2}$ p.R. (17.60 m), the two tabernae, $23\frac{1}{2}$ and $23\frac{1}{4}$ p.R. (6.95 m and 6.88 m), and the entryway, $12\frac{3}{4}$ p.R. (3.78 m). The quoin blocks of the NW taberna and its NW and SE walls were of the usual squared limestone rubble set in clay, overlapping the quoining of the SW wall of AB II (Pl. 61; cf. Fig. 29). The imprint at the SE of its robbed reveal quoin was a bedding of tile chips, $4\frac{5}{8}$ p.R. (1.37 m) from the corner. The NW and party walls on either side of the SE taberna with their quoins were also preserved, as was the SE reveal quoin (Pl. 62). Here the remnants of a hard earth floor amid outcrops of rock appear to have been the construction floor, and under its surface lay a sextantal as, only somewhat circulated, minted in central Italy between 211 and 208 B.C.[9]

The NW wall of this building was spared by the plow, and more than two-thirds of it has been uncovered (Pl. 63). At $56\frac{3}{8}$ p.R. (16.68 m) from the NE façade a short, bonded cross wall and reveal with one end of a threshold show where an interior room opened off the atrium. The signinum floor beside it lay about 0.45 m above the earth floor before the NE entryway. A second, similar partition wall, 16 p.R. (4.73 m) beyond, bounded the space behind the atrium. This area, subdivided or not, resembles the corresponding spaces in AB VII and VIII (pages 86 and 88). Just beyond, the NW wall was interrupted by an opening, $7\frac{1}{8}$ p.R. (2.11 m) wide, that communicated with the paved walkway skirting the open reservoir in the W corner of the Forum area (pages 8 and 119). Its signinum pavement stood about 0.13 m above the bedding of the doorway and had abutted the missing sill. The two bottom reveal blocks were found in place, whereas the sill was removed when the opening was narrowed later to $2\frac{3}{4}$ p.R. (0.81 m) (page 249).

A sounding (Pl. 65) showed that the original SW reveal projected southeastward to make a pier, $1\frac{1}{2}$ p.R. (0.45 m) wide, followed by an opening that was later

9. C69.223 (Buttrey 1980, 34; Crawford 1974, 59/2).

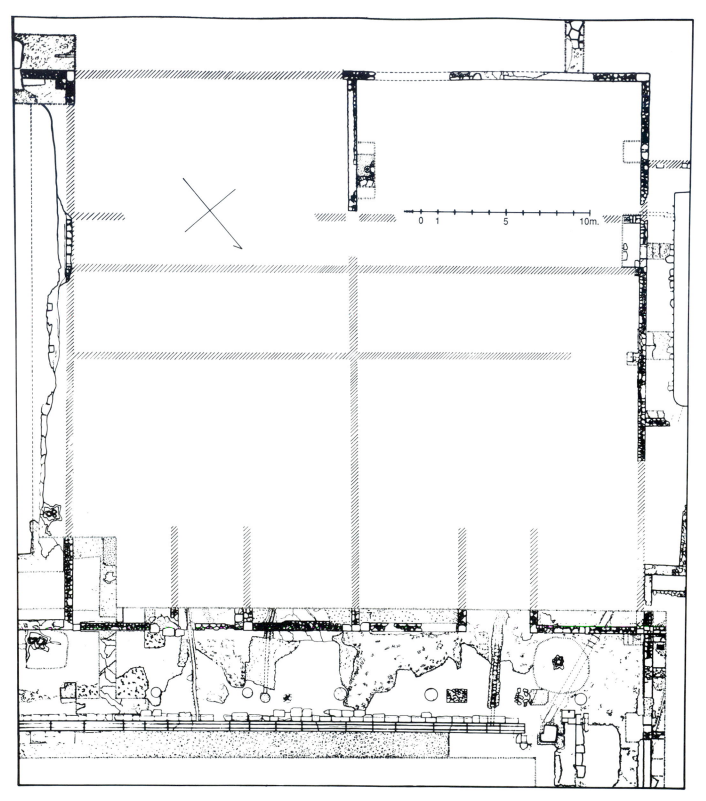

PLAN VII.   Atrium Buildings III/IV

walled up. The space from the pier to the NE wall was 9 p.R. (2.66 m), at which point the end of a limestone step was uncovered along with two battered flagstones set on the trimmed rock and hardpan. In the stratum immediately above were scattered a number of fragments of sandstone slabs from a demolished column that had evidently stood nearby. The narrow space and the flagstones suggest an open passageway through the building, and the pier and column imply a series of openings along its SW side giving access to a row of rooms. These would presumably have been tabernae of the columnar kind found in AB I facing the Square (pages 69–74). Here, however, they must have faced in, since they lay some 1.70 m below the surface of Street 5; and along the inside face of the NW pier of the putative taberna a conduit under the floor fed into the adjacent reservoir.

The terminal quoin of the NW wall at the W corner of AB III was in place, but the wall along the street and the SW end of the party wall shared by the two buildings had been rebuilt in a later period (page 249). A trench along the NW side of the latter revealed the top of the earlier wall beneath, and a sounding was dug to confirm the presence of the earlier wall at the other end (Fig. 33; Pl. 66). The original party wall proved to have been in part built on and in part cut in the rock to a depth of 1.42–1.52 m from its rough surface down to a level bed, which had been covered with a signinum floor about 0.12 m thick, at the same level as the flagstones of the passageway in the NW sounding. Where the cutting encountered a large fissure in the rock, and above the top of the rock, the wall was constructed of limestone masonry bonded with clay and plastered to a height of $5\frac{3}{4}$ p.R. (1.70 m) above the floor. On top of this was laid a band of five courses of tegulae, alternately presenting their flanges and their sections and set in lime mortar, to form a level bed $6\frac{7}{8}$ p.R. (2.04 m) from the floor. At its NE end, however, the sounding met a tumbled pile of blocks and quoins of a fallen pier or piers, while nearby stood the fragment of a column of mortared sandstone wedges, fallen upright in the red-ochre debris of sun-dried bricks that covered the floor. It was 0.35 m in diameter and identical with the pieces found at the other end of the conjectural passageway (*supra*). Just below it, where the floor was broken away, the edge of a circular drawhole was visible, piercing the vault of a cesspool or soak-away pit. It recalls the similar features in the tabernae of AB I and VII and the fragmentary column in the opening of Taberna 2 of AB I. All in all, our soundings confirm the presumption of a number of similar tabernae along the SW end of AB III.

These shops and their open passageway, sunk in the rock and leveled, must have been of the same height. Their wall plates of tiles must also have supported the low ceiling beams that bore the weight of the shops or warehouses above in a second story facing Street 5. The sloping street, when paved, was about 2.09 m above the floor of the SE taberna below and 1.72 m above that of the NW taberna, and to approach the upper shops steps or ramps must have been necessary.

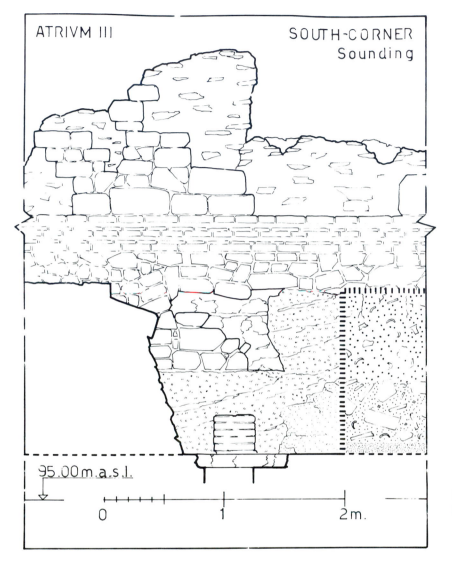

FIG. 33.   AB III, section,
S sounding, looking SE

The same rock formation stepping down from Street 5 to the Square that determined the floor levels of AB III can be observed in the cutting for the old cistern on the SE (page 11; Pl. 2) and must also have underlain Atrium Building IV. This makes it likely that the gentle ascent of the floors of AB III, only about 0.85 m, was maintained in the corresponding sequence of spaces in AB IV. On this assumption no trial trench or sounding was opened in the SE part of the building.

The only indications that the SW passageway of AB III continued across AB IV in the same way to an opening into the Forum Annex (page 101) are six large limestone blocks emerging from the earth in line with the SE wall of AB IV exactly opposite the position of the NW doorway into the passageway. The NE block remains in its original position, mortared against a visible meter of the rubblework of the SE wall, the counterpart of the NE reveal of the opposite doorway. Its upper surface, 0.53 m long, is horizontal and dressed to receive a block above. The other five blocks stand on edge with interstices prepared for a bond of lime mortar. They fill precisely the amount of space between the reveals at the other end of the passageway, blocking what must have been an opening.

As in AB III, excavation brought to light the NE façade of the building, to which a sounding was added in the E corner. On the Square, AB IV was wider than its mate by 0.19 m, which was applied to enlarge the vestibulum to $13\frac{1}{2}$ p.R. (4.00 m), while both tabernae, measuring $23\frac{5}{6}$ p.R. (6.90 m) in width, were practically the same as those of AB III. In spite of rebuilding, devastation, and plowing, the lowest courses of most of the original walls and quoins along the façade and in the sounding have survived, as have the rammed-earth floors of both tabernae. The NW taberna impounded rain collected in a small, hemispherical catch basin hewn in an outcrop of rock 4.10 m in front of its façade, from which it was channeled inward. This was yet another use of the area before the shop (cf. pages 78–81). Outside the opening of the SE taberna, where the rock sloped to the Square, a strip averaging 2 p.R. (0.55–0.65 m) wide was worked level for a walkway under the eaves.

The sounding in the E corner of the SE taberna, 5.20 m by 2.60 m, uncovered a series of superimposed floors. The construction floor was leveled between outcrops of rock with limestone chips and detritus from the rising walls (Fig. 33). A succession of trodden earth surfaces, altogether some 0.24 m thick, testifies to the first activity in the taberna before the erection of the portico in front. The earth of these floors was permeated with carbon, both dust and nodules. In the W corner of the sounding (approximately at the back center of the shop) was part of a shallow rectangular pit, which deepened with each successive floor. It was filled with layers of ash and sand, lumps of charcoal, and quantities of slag, along with globules of copper and lead or tin. The pit was no doubt a forge and the first leaseholder a smith.

Atrium Buildings V and VI

The second pair of SW atrium buildings was built on the same rocky descent as the first, but here it dropped off along its eastern flank toward Street Q. AB V/VI was thus narrower than AB III/IV by $1\frac{3}{4}$ p.R. (0.56 m), a difference distributed between the two vestibula, which were narrowed by just this much. What remains of the original walls and floors of the alternating shops and entryways has been exposed in the excavation of their façades and the open strip before them.

At the N corner of the NW taberna of AB V outcrops of bedrock were chiseled

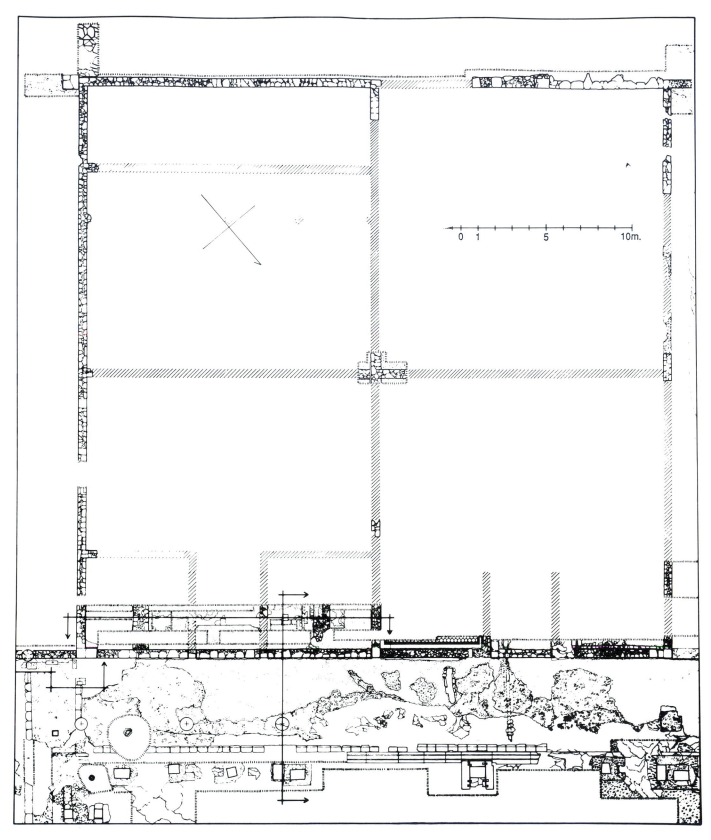

PLAN VIII. Atrium Buildings V/VI

down to grade, fitting the bottom corner quoin and a smaller block beside it (Pl. 67). The reveal quoin adjoined this but was tipped sideways in a later blocking up of the opening (page 240). Beyond the corner quoin the stretch of the base of the NW wall was built in the usual square-faced limestone rubblework bonded with clay. The quoins and masonry of the SE wall of the taberna were later removed, leaving leveled beddings on the rock. A sounding within, along a crack in a later signinum floor, laid bare the construction floor over the rock and two shallow trampled earth floors above it. The later signinum and mosaic floors of the rooms above the original entryway and SE taberna (page 240) respected their limits, and the remains of their common wall and the beddings of the wall end and NW quoin of the taberna were clearly imprinted on the rock.

On the façade of Atrium Building VI all three original openings were at some time blocked up, leaving visible only the three lowest wall-end quoins and the massive angle block at the E corner. Our excavation trench was therefore moved inward (Fig. 32). The lower courses of the NW party wall with AB V were found in place, while only a few foundation blocks of the SE wall of the taberna emerged from the cut. The first floor was of beaten earth and char above hardpan sprinkled with limestone chips. Toward the SE wall a roughly squared limestone block was embedded in the floor, about 0.35 m high, with various cuts or sockets for attachments on the top (Pl. 68). It stood above a second earthen floor, some 0.10 m thick, with grayish ash trodden into the surface, under which lay bits of iron and slag, a broken stylus of bone, and fragments of black-glaze bowls and a cooking pot.[10] The context suggests metalworking of some sort and perhaps the keeping of accounts (cf. pages 70 and 93).

The common wall of the fauces and SE taberna had, at least within the trench, been totally demolished, its position and width marked only by the edges of later floors on either side. What remained of the lowest earthen floor, topping a sterile fill above the rock, sloped upward toward the level of the atrium. The original SE wall of the taberna, back of the angle-quoin, stood approximately 0.95 m above the rock, retaining the fill under the two floors of beaten earth, one on top of the other, as in the NW taberna, both laid before the addition of the portico.

Back of these excavations the perimeter and party walls of both atrium buildings were here and there visible on the surface. Elsewhere their tops were exposed in shallow trenches, while the central conjunction of the two buildings was examined in a sounding to their floors. The original walls were recognizable from their level beddings on the rock, from their rough footings below the grade of the roadbed of Street 5, and from the masonry characteristic of all the atrium buildings (Pl. 69). Some of these walls, especially at the E and S corners and in the central sounding (Fig. 34), were used as foundations for later walls at higher levels.

---

10. The black glaze forms (Lamboglia 1952, 27, 28) are of local manufacture, as is the pot (Dyson 1976, Class 2).

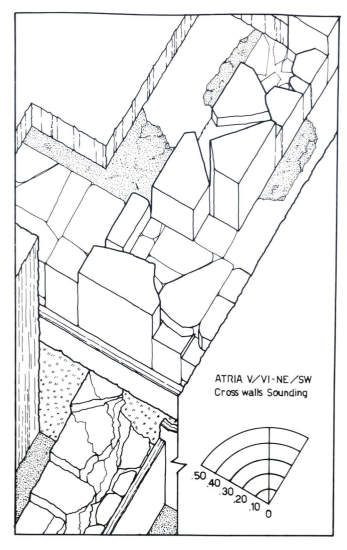

ATRIA V/VI-NE/SW
Cross walls Sounding

.50 .40 .30 .20 .10 0

Fig. 34.   AB V/VI, axonometric, cross walls, facing W

The SE wall of AB VI showed no access from Street Q, standing some 0.65 m to 0.35 m above the original interior floors. Along its inner face, however, there remained, projecting at right angles, the ends of three cross walls and an engaged column. The first of these, SW of the NE façade, marked the back walls of the two tabernae. The second was in line with the cross wall that divided the atrium from the SW half of the complex and was also disclosed in the central sounding. There the cross wall had been hewn out of the rock down to 0.62 m, and the resulting floors on either side were at the same level. Since the original floor of the NW taberna of AB VI in line with the floors in the sounding was within 0.01 m of their level, it appears that a single floor level was maintained the length of the building. Southwestward, 29 p.R. (8.59 m) beyond the cross wall, the engaged column, which was $1\frac{11}{16}$ p.R. (0.50 m) in diameter and constructed of wedge-shaped slabs of sandstone (pages 73, 88, and 91), was found bonded into the wall (Pl. 70). The third wall end, $8\frac{1}{2}$ p.R. (2.51 m) beyond, was $15\frac{5}{8}$ p.R. (4.63 m) from the SW wall. The top of the latter, descending southeastward 2.25–0.41 m above the projected floors, showed no sign of any opening.

These *disiecta membra* seem to suggest, but not to copy, the arrangements found in the SW parts of AB III/IV. Here the half-column, which is nearly in line with the NE walls and columns of the tabernae of AB III/IV, implies an inner portico across the width of AB VI and likely of AB V. The wall behind it, because of its limited width, would probably have enclosed a number of spaces. That these were tabernae is strongly suggested by the other atrium buildings. In this position tabernae and portico together would have supported the second story of tabernae or horrea opening on Street 5 (page 91). The portico might have faced a broad open space, or more probably another nearer wall, answering to the NE wall of the passageway of AB III/IV. That wall did not come to light in the shallow SW trench but could probably be found at a lower level, in which case the band to the NE, like the analogous space in AB III/IV and AB VII/VIII, would also have been accessible from the atria.

In general, then, it may be concluded that Atrium Buildings I, II, VII, and VIII, which stepped down from either short end of the Square, were designed to have only tabernae opening on the bounding streets, whereas the four on the SW slope (AB III, IV, V, VI), which stepped gradually up or maintained an artificial level, were planned to have basement tabernae facing a mews and tabernae or horrea above these opening onto a street.

Southwest Annex

The master plan of the buildings along the SW side of the Forum also incorporated the empty tract between Atrium Buildings IV and V. The shelving rock originally sloped about 10 p.R. (2.96 m) to the Square between the open tanks that were aligned from the beginning with the sides of the Comitium (page 11). It was now bounded on either side by the walls of AB IV and V and was centered exactly on the axis of the Comitium. It has been partially excavated across either end, on the Square and on Street 5. Its width on the street was $60\frac{3}{4}$ p.R. (17.98 m), while on the Square it was $61\frac{1}{2}$ p.R. (18.20 m), which is $2\frac{1}{2}$ p.R. (0.74 m) wider than the Comitium.

The new design preserved the view up Street P to the Arx and made of the open space a special sort of annex to the Forum, accessible from the Square and from Street 5. It was to some degree leveled by lowering the upper half of the rocky slope about 0.90 m and raising the lower half by spreading the waste rock from above over its surface. The result was a gentle inclination of the signinum surface of 2.2 percent toward the Square and of about the same amount toward

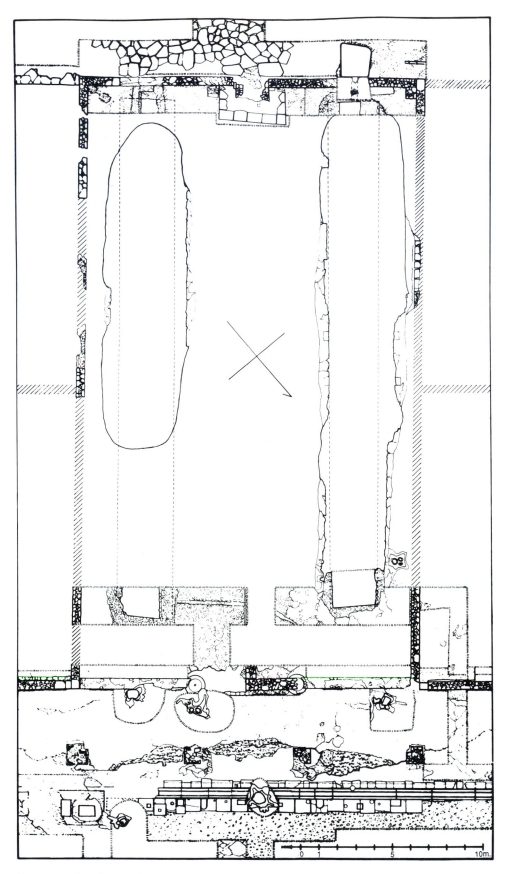

PLAN IX. Southwest Annex

the SE from wall to wall. Concurrently, the tops of the tanks were brought level to the grade and their irregular sides were lined and regularized with mortared rubble masonry to support vaults. These were nearly barrel vaults and were faced with signinum along with the walls, cover-joints, and floors. In this manner the cisterns were reduced in width but enlarged in depth: the NW cistern, 95 p.R. (28.12 m) long, 11 p.R. (3.26 m) deep, and 9 p.R. (2.66 m) wide; the SE cistern, $97\frac{3}{4}$ p.R. (28.94 m) long, $10\frac{1}{2}$ p.R. (3.11 m) deep, and 10 p.R. (2.96 m) wide.

The NW cistern was fed by the runoff from Street P by means of a diagonal curbing across the pavement of Street 5 that channeled the flow into a settling tank at the SW end of the cistern, while the SE cistern was apparently filled by collecting the rainfall on the pavement of the Annex. The capacity of the two cisterns would have been about 500 cubic meters. Water was drawn through puteals (well-curbs), perhaps six in number, of which three fragments were found on the bottom of the NE end of the SE cistern. One of these was a piece of the base, another of the wall, and a third a splinter from the inside (Fig. 39). Carved from a block of grayish violet tufa from Vulci, its exposed surfaces were polished smooth and the resting surface roughly tooled. The bore was vertical, 0.40 m in diameter, and the outer wall tapered upward from 0.82 m to 0.725 m. The top was missing, but the taper shows that it stood higher than 0.60 m.

Entrance from the Square to the Annex led through a monumental bicolumnar gateway and up a flight of stairs. Of the gateway only the two column bases, also of the tufa of Vulci, remain, flanking the axis of the opening, 15 p.R. (4.44 m) apart and $19\frac{1}{2}$ p.R. (5.77 m) from either wall. Each base, 0.355 m high, was composed of a cylindrical plinth, $3\frac{3}{4}$ p.R. (1.11 m) in diameter, or one-fourth of the interval, and a bulging quarter-round torus, supporting a column whose radius was the height of the base (Fig. 35; Pl. 71). The missing columns were bedded on rings of anathyrosis some 0.12 m wide, and at the center of each a square, tapered mortise had been cut, $\frac{3}{8}$ p.R. (0.11 m) on a side at the top, $\frac{1}{4}$ p.R. (0.074 m) at the bottom, and the same in depth. This kind of tapered mortise suits the insertion of the mandrel of a lathe, and the numerous shallow grooves in the soft stone of the bases suggest turning. Short of displacing them to inspect the undersides, it cannot be proved. This type of "Tuscan" profile was current in the late fourth, third, and early second centuries throughout Etruria and Latium;[11] these were probably the first of the type at Cosa and perhaps the last.[12]

The columns themselves stood 4.84 m apart. Their lower diameters of 0.71 m would by the Vitruvian rule have been tapered to upper diameters of three-fourths of the lower, 0.532 m.[13] At Cosa the heights of attested columns range from $6\frac{1}{2}$ to 7 lower diameters, and the columns in question, freestanding or lightly loaded, were presumably in the higher range, $6\frac{3}{4}$ to 7, here 4.80–4.97 m, framing

11. E.g., *MAAR* 28 (1965), 118, no. 34.5 (Vulci); 119, no. 34.18 (Caere); 119, no. 35.11 (Lavinium); 118, no. 38.5 (Minturnae).

12. Cf. *MAAR* 26 (1960), 65–66, 114.

13. Vitruvius 3.4.4.

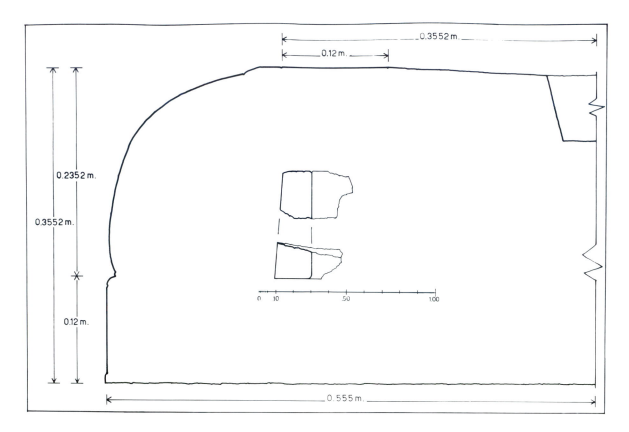

FIG. 35.   Forum Annex, sections, bicolumnar monument, well-curb

an approximate square. An architrave or entablature, if there was one, spanning some 5.00 m, must necessarily have been of wood.[14] The bearing surface for the bases was dressed on the bedrock in a roughly rectangular bay some 1.55 m below the calculated height of the NE end of the pavement of the Annex. Tangential to the plinths and between them, the signinum pavement of the portico, when laid, abutted what could only have been the bottom step of a flight ascending to the Annex. No block of these steps appeared in the trenches behind the bases, but a rising embankment of limestone aggregate laid in clay must be remains of their bedding. The height to be reached, however, would require just seven risers of $\frac{3}{4}$ p.R. (0.222 m), following another Vitruvian rule that also limited treads to between $1\frac{1}{2}$ p.R. (0.444 m) and 2 p.R. (0.592 m).[15] As treads, the radius of the plinths, $1\frac{7}{8}$ p.R. (0.555 m), would have been appropriately related to the columns and have brought the top of the stair to the top of the NE walls of the cisterns. These in turn would have formed the ends of two open exedrae, one on either side of the stair. The stairs, of course, must have been flanked by retaining

14. Not only are stone architraves unknown at Cosa, but wooden architraves with entablatures constructed of rubble masonry finished with stucco are the rule elsewhere for such buildings.

15. Vitruvius 3.4.4.

walls and railings on either side. Of these nothing remains except the imprint of one on the SE column base. Centered on its SW side, a strip 0.45–0.50 m wide was protected from the wear and weathering that the rest of the base showed (Pl. 71).

The excavation along the other end of the Annex disclosed a complementary design of a central stair between two exedrae. In this case the stair offered access, descending from Street 5 to the center with a return to the entrance wall to either side. What was left of it (Pl. 72) was essentially the travertine bedding blocks for the bottom step, measuring 12 p.R. (3.55 m) on the front and $6\frac{5}{8}$ p.R. (1.96 m) on the sides, within which stood the lower half of the foundation of the upper platform. This was 6 p.R. (1.776 m) by $3\frac{3}{4}$ p.R. (1.10 m), walled with rough-hewn limestone and broken tile and filled and tamped with clay. Three treads of c. 1 p.R. (0.296 m) and presumably four risers of $\frac{3}{4}$ p.R. (0.222 m) would have reached the top of the platform, where a threshold between the reveals of the wide opening in the SW wall led in from Street 5. The shallow exedrae above the ends of the cisterns, approximately twice as wide as the stairs, were clearly a studied design of fifths. Moreover, through the SE wall of the Annex there was probably access to the open passageway that served the SW tabernae of AB V/VI. Like the later blocked gateway at the other end (pages 89–91), this presumed gateway lies in a gap with an outcrop of rock in the right place dressed as though to receive a sill.

These eight similar buildings that symmetrically enclosed three sides of the Forum Square were not only economically built but strictly functional. The spaces of each that open on the Square, on Streets O and R, and on the public passageways through the four SW buildings were evidently all shops, commercial or industrial: sixteen on the Square, six on Street O, sixteen or so on Street R, and fourteen on the passageways, for a probable total of fifty-two. On Street 5, the busiest thoroughfare in the town, the tabernae and/or horrea above the walls of the shops below could not be numbered, since they had all been totally destroyed. These shops no doubt provided the goods necessary for townspeople and farmers alike, releasing the Square for the daily market in foodstuffs, as well as the larger nundinal markets, public assemblies, and festivals. At the same time these shops and warehouses would have been a source of public revenue, if only from their rents.

Behind each of the pairs of tabernae facing the Square, the vestibulum, and fauces, the atrium with its alae takes the forms of the core of a contemporary Roman house, yet they were obviously not designed as dwellings. Their most striking feature is the absence of regular living quarters. The entrances from the NW entranceway of AB I and II made them unusually accessible. Room 18 of AB I had the position of a cubiculum but was simply a nondescript room with doors, except for its arrangements for drainage (pages 66–67), whatever its function. In short, what we have exposed or conjectured about the eight atria may best be defined as an adaptation of the central component of a typical atrium house for public or commercial purposes.

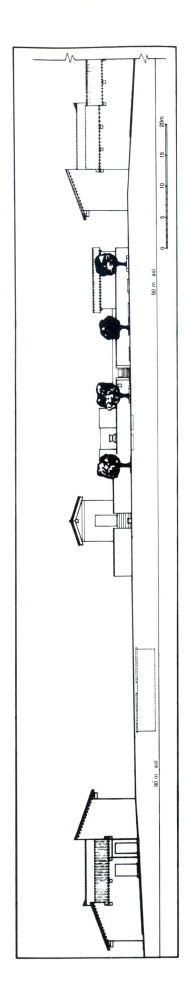

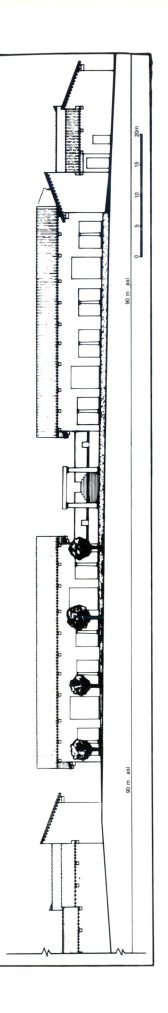

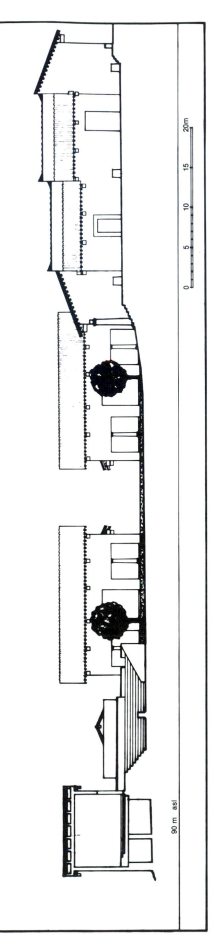

Fig. 36.   Forum, as of 180 B.C., elevations and sections, NE, SW, and SE

They can, however, be related to certain buildings in republican Rome known by the term *atrium* specifically mentioned by ancient writers:[16] Atrium Publicum, the public record office on the Capitoline, predecessor of the Tabularium;[17] Atrium Libertatis, the office and archive of the censors;[18] Atrium Sutorium, guildhall of the shoemakers, also used each year on March 23 for the rite of the Tubilustrium;[19] Atria Licinia, an auction hall;[20] and Atria Maenium et Titium (with their four tabernae), which were replaced by the Basilica Porcia.[21] Their common designation appears to record a stage in Roman architecture when the central space of the house—ample, uncluttered by supports, covered except for its source of light—was adapted to a wide range of public uses. In the Rome of the third century these atria seem to have been both various and scattered. In the colonial early second century of Cosa the atria had been brought together in the master plan for its forum, or so it seems. In any case, where none of the Roman atria have survived, the atria of Cosa can provide their pattern, and conversely the atria of Rome can suggest some of the functions that those at Cosa may have acquired.

The SW Annex (pages 97–101) probably had its specific and important place in the master plan. Whatever it was, it should have been somehow connected with the abundant supply of water provided by its two lateral cisterns. The stairs and gateway on Street 5, while they served the public, were also at the end of the shortest road between the Annex and the lagoon and anchorage below the city, via the SE Gate in the walls (page 3 and Fig. 2). The lagoon and the sea were the town's sources of fresh fish, crustaceans, and mollusks, and the numerous oyster and clam shells that have turned up in the Square are a sign that the citizens had a place nearby to obtain them.[22] The Annex, a paved area with fresh water at hand, fills the requirements of an outdoor fishmarket, which Cosa would not have been without. The Roman Forum in the third century was flanked by its Forum Piscarium on one side,[23] and the architect at Cosa may well have been prompted to fit his Forum Piscarium into an equivalent place in his design. One might even propose that the bicolumnar monument that set off the Annex from the Square honored a public-spirited citizen who had donated it from the profits of his fishery.

These eight structures, the central open space, and three avenues covering the

16. *TLL* 2.1102. 59–1103.29 *"atria sacro vel publico usui destinata."* The material has been discussed by E. Wistrand, "Ante Atria" (*AIRRS* 4°, 2 [1932]), 55–63, and E. Welin, *Studien zur Topographie des Forum Romanum* (*AIRRS* 8°, 6 [1953]), 179–219.

17. Livy 24.10.9 (214 B.C.); cf. Polybius 3.26.1. Remains: *BullCom* 67 (1939), 201; A. M. Colini, *Il tempio di Veiove*, 13, fig. 6; *BullCom* 70 (1942), 6, fig. 2.

18. Livy 25.7.11 (212 B.C.); 34.44.5; 43.16.13; 45.15.5; Festus 277L; Granius Licinianus p. 10 (Flemisch).

19. Varro, *Ling.* 6.14; Festus 480L; Fasti Praen., *CIL* 1².234.

20. Cicero, *Quinct.* 3.13, 6.25; Servius *ad Aen.* 1.726; cf. *atrium auctionarium*, Cicero, *Leg. Agr.* 1.3.7; *CIL* 9.3307.

21. Livy 39.44.7.

22. On Cosan bronze coinage a dolphin symbol identified Cosa as a port and fishery (Buttrey 1980, 22 and pl. 2).

23. Livy 26.27.3; 40.51.5; Plautus, *Curc.* 474.

areas from the Square to the bounding Streets 5 and 7, O and R (pages 3–9) did not occupy the total surface of the Forum rectangle. At the corners of the delimited boundary there remained rectangular plots of various sizes, because of the eccentric location of the open Square. In the W corner the Reservoir and its surroundings left a space of $42\frac{1}{2}$ p.R. (12.50 m) beside AB II and 75 p.R. (22.20 m) from AB III to Street O, while between AB I and Street 7 the N corner of empty space was 77 p.R. (22.80 m) by 40 p.R. (11.84 m). Between AB VIII and Street 7 in the E corner was a longer expanse, 120 p.R. (35.52 m) by $37\frac{1}{2}$ p.R. (11.10 m), and in the S corner between Streets 5 and Q and AB VII, largest of all, was a space 121 p.R. (35.80 m) by $113\frac{1}{2}$ p.R. (33.60 m). Once the eight atrium buildings had been erected, it appears that these four plots were free to be sold or leased.

Only one of these plots has been fully excavated and initially probably only part of it was developed, because of its suitable location in the N corner on

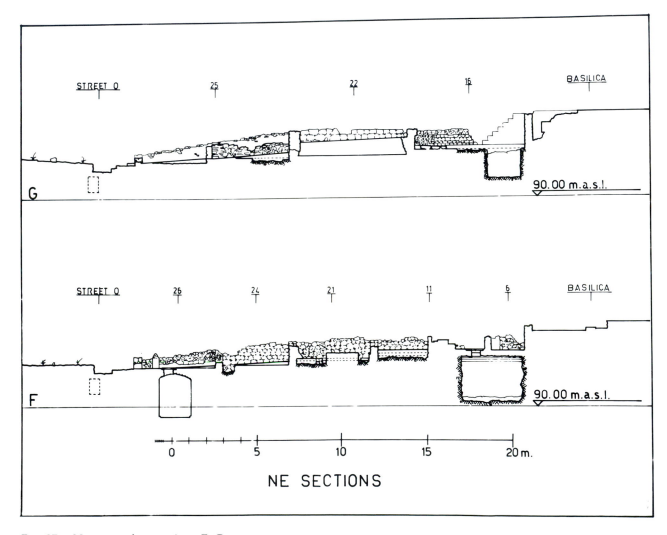

FIG. 37.   N corner plot, sections F, G

Streets O and 7 in line with Tabernae 15, 13, and 19 of AB I. The rest of the plot behind was walled and partly roofed within twenty years (pages 135–138). The first two buildings were Tabernae 25 and 24/26, each consisting of two spaces of different sorts. Taberna 25 had a wide doorway on Street O and within was doubly partitioned. One of these partitions crossed in the middle from the SW side to delimit about three-fifths of the space, while the other, from the NE wall about two-thirds of the way back from the front, walled off the remaining two-fifths. The larger space, on the right, was paved with lozenge-shaped bricks of terracotta. The smaller contained a shallow pit or basin cut in the rock, 0.70 m deep, and was unpaved. Between the ends of the two partitions a step finished the higher signinum pavement of the forepart of the taberna. This special arrangement suggests a butchershop. The partitioned areas were virtually out of sight. One was roofed and paved for the slaughtering, dressing, and flushing, the other, open above for catching rainwater, would hold the slops. Out in front the butcher would be selling his meats. The neighboring Taberna 24/26 was of the same size as the other but divided across by a central wall. Under the outer room a capacious cistern, holding 16.34 cubic meters, was filled with water collected in the open space behind the building and from the NE roof of AB I. A drain of fine rubblework, $\frac{1}{2}$ p.R. (0.148 m) wide and high, passed from the E

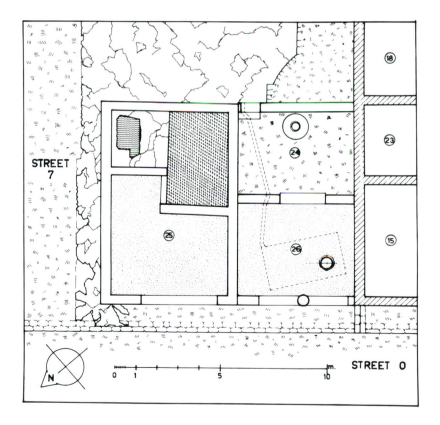

FIG. 38. N corner plot, Tabernae 25 and 24/26, I

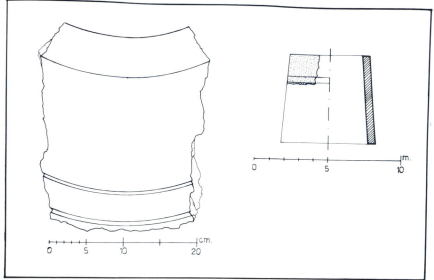

Fig. 39.   Street O,
sidewalk before Taberna
25, rim of puteal,
presumably from Taberna
26

exterior corner under the E doorway in the back wall and under the signinum floors of the two rooms to discharge into the E corner of the cistern. Its drawshaft was rabbeted at the top for a well-curb centered on the SW half of the wide door from the street. A fragment of the puteal was rammed into the fill of the walk before the adjacent Taberna 25 (Fig. 39). It had been broken from a slightly tapering cylinder of Vulci tufa, $1\frac{7}{8}$ p.R. (0.55 m) in outer diameter at the top, $\frac{3}{16}$ p.R. (0.055 m) thick, and profiled with a pair of grooves. If the taper was constant, it would have reached the diameter of the setting ring in the floor, with a height of c. 2 p.R. (0.60 m). The entrance, like those of the tabernae on the Square, was divided by a column. Later on that too was done away with (page 240), but it left twenty-five fragments of its travertine capital under a new pavement. When recomposed it proved to be the same size and shape (Pl. 75) as the others (Fig. 27, Pl. 59). The doorway to the inner room revealed only the flattened remains of a large *dolium* (storage jar) in the depression that had once steadied it. Perhaps one might think not of a taberna, but of a *popina*, or cook-shop. A single coin found in the undisturbed fill along the conduit under the floor of Taberna 24 was a small bronze of Massilia dated in the second half of the third century B.C.[24]

24. CF 588 (Buttrey 1980, 3; McClean 1.6.45–46).

VI. 180–175 B.C.

(Plans I–X; Figs. 40–55; Pls. 76–100)

It was noted in the previous chapter (pages 70, 75–77, and 95) that the Atrium Buildings, as soon as erected one by one, were put to temporary use until the grading and resurfacing of the Square could be completed. This entailed also the laying of gutters that served as curbs around all four sides, as well as settling basins and conduits to convey rainwater from the adjacent roofs to the Reservoir in the W corner of the Forum (pages 8 and 114–19). This program, it appears, then allowed the builders to be shifted to another point on the Square, namely the Curia (pages 22–23), which had not yet been given its permanent form.

The provisional Curia had weathered some eighty years, and the time had come for a completely new building, both solid and imposing. The podium of the new Curia was of dry polygonal masonry of the gray pitted limestone of the hill of Cosa. It was apparently never a perfect rectangle; because of subsequent damage the walls no longer stand true, but the evidence is that the back wall was always some 0.40 m longer than the façade, both side walls somewhat splayed, and the SE wall some 0.22 m longer than the NW. In the superstructure, the façade wall of which must have been based on the Comitium circuit wall, the S and N corners would have been right angles, the E corner slightly acute, c. 87°, and the W corner slightly obtuse, c. 93°. At present the SW (façade) end mea-

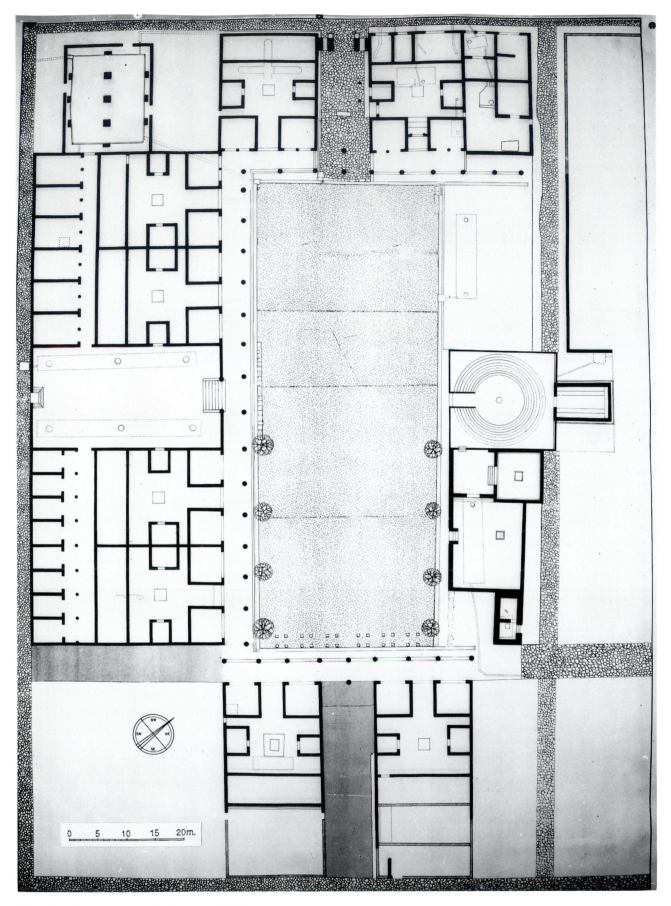

Fɪɢ. 40.   Forum, restored plan, as of 180 ʙ.ᴄ.

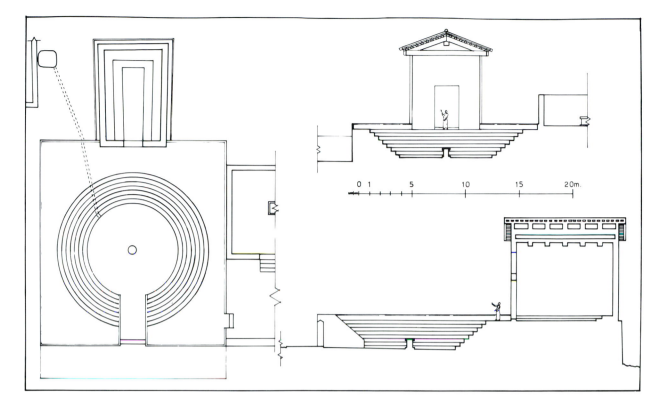

FIG. 41.   Comitium/Curia, phase 2, restored plan and sections

sures 7.18 m, the NE 7.55 m; the SE side measures 9.80 m, the NW 9.53 m.
Ideally, the podium should have been 24 p.R. by 32 p.R. and 7.504 m by 9.472 m.

Like the walls of the fortifications of the city, the three walls of the podium (on
the SW there is no wall, the podium simply abutting the circuit wall of the
Comitium) were built in two faces, the outer face neatly fitted and dressed
smooth, the inner face built of rough boulders left as they came from the quarry,
snecked with smaller stones. The space between the two faces is packed with
smaller stones and spalls. The outer face is based on crests of bedrock, trimmed a
little to make beds for the blocks, but the bed is not continuous, and between
crests are gaps of as much as 1.75 m where the wall rests on earth. The footing
was covered by the ancient ground level to a depth of c. 0.30 m. The blocks tend
to be quadrilateral or pentagonal in shape and are laid in courses. The NW wall,
the better preserved of the long walls, now stands five courses high; apparently
a single course is missing at the top. The blocks are laid dry and without
anathyrosis; the joint beds are from 0.25 m to 0.35 m deep. There are occasional
joggles in horizontal and oblique joints, but most difficulties in fitting were met
by snecking with small triangular blocks. Such snecking is much commoner in
the masonry here than in that of the city walls[1] or that of Temple B, built c. 175

1. Brown 1951, 33–35; Brown 1980, 19.

B.C. (pages 143–45). The blocks are large, larger than a building of this size warrants, but none is colossal; the largest is 1.42 m long and 0.64 m high. The outer face of the podium is battered; the degree of batter is regularly c. 4 percent.

The engineering of the podium is clarified by the evidence of the inner face of the wall and of the fill at the SW end, which was found undisturbed. The fill was of the native red clay of the hill, laid in strata that followed the coursing of the inner face of the wall. The base of this inner face, however, does not rest on the pavement surviving from Curia I, but on a hard layer of fill, c. 0.60–0.70 m deep. It appears that this fill was bedded in and rammed, probably with beetles, as a first operation. Then the first course of the rough inner face of the wall was laid; then a second layer of fill was bedded in after the wall course was completed. The construction continued in this fashion, courses of the wall and layers of the fill alternating. There were slight differences in the consistency and color of the earth in the various strata of fill (the lowest stratum was rammed; the middle strata were loose), but the significant differences among them were in the content of building material and in the floors that divided one from another. In the SW end of the first working floor and the stratum just above were numerous small fragments of wall plaster, remains of a decoration in a variant of the Masonry, or Pompeian First Style (page 23). These have been assigned to the upper hall of Curia I. The floor that overlay this stratum was thickly strewn with pearls of lime mortar and tiny fragments of wall plaster. The wall plaster seems to be simply more fragments of what was found in larger pieces below, ground underfoot by the workers as they laid the next course of the wall, but the mortar should be evidence of building activity, perhaps of the pavement or parapet of the Comitium. These lumps of mortar continued through the next stratum above, which consisted of relatively loose earth. Here were also encountered many chips and small fragments of purplish Vulci tufa, evidently spalls from the working of the upper steps of the Comitium. The floor finishing this stratum again contained many small lumps of mortar. The fourth stratum of fill was full of dark, blackish red lumps of mortar. Above this there was only humus.

Thus we can follow for a little while the progress of work in the new Curia. The first step must have been laying of the stratum of rammed red clay. This was probably done while the old Curia was still standing. On this was bedded the first course of the inner face of the podium wall. Then the old Curia building was dismantled. This accounts for the presence of bits of its decoration in the fill behind this course. Whether the whole building was wrecked at this time or only the superstructure remains unknown, but the polygonal blocks of the outer face of the podium are noticeably thinner than those of the inner face and almost never exceed the two-foot thickness of the walls of Curia I. Moreover, the blocks of the outer face are not, for the most part, interlocking with those of the inner; where they are, the fitting together of the faces seems to have required some maneuvering. And the packing between the two faces is of chunks of limestone rather large for such work in Cosa. The evidence, then, suggests that the inner face was constructed before the outer and that the outer was accommodated to the inner as dressing. One may wonder to what extent this was simply the consequence of the greater labor of dressing polygonal masonry, since the upper layers of the fill show evidence of other construction activity, in particular chips from the dressing of Vulci tufa for the Comitium, an indication that the fill was probably not laid and completed as a single job, but proceeded at intervals as the walls rose.

Mingled with the earth throughout the fills were a few coins and potsherds, some of which joined across the layers. Three of the coins were legible. One was a fragment of aes signatum, another a sextantal as of the mint of Rome from shortly after 211 b.c., and the third a sextantal semis struck in Luceria between 211 and 208 b.c. The latter two had been rubbed in circulation, but their major features were clear (cf. page 77).[2] The sherds of black-glaze tableware were the most abundant and the most useful in dating the fill, together with a Rhodian amphora stamp.

Local wares comprised about 90 percent of the 108 pieces in the fill, and of the 80 identifiable plates and bowls 55 percent were the shapes that were favored during the late third and early second centuries b.c. These were Lamboglia Forms 27 and 31 and Taylor's saucer with furrowed rim. Other forms of the period were fewer, with five examples of Taylor's plate with upturned rim, one of Lamboglia Form 51 and one of Lamboglia Form 36. Of the few imported pieces there was one rim of gray-matt ware (page 26), Lamboglia Form 27, and four bowls of Lamboglia Form 31 and one of Form 33b in Campana A; in Campana B there was one Lamboglia Form 6 and one fragment of a plate of unidentifiable form. The stamp of the amphora handle seems to be conclusive. It reads ΕΠΙ ΑΡΙ / ΤΟΔΑΜΟΥ / ΠΑΝΑΜΟΥ, and it dates c. 180 b.c., not earlier than 183.[3]

Of the building that stood on this podium nothing remains; it was apparently demolished at the time of the construction of Curia III. It was probably a single-chambered hall, since there is no evidence of foundations for interior walls in the podium. It was probably built of small, spalled limestone blocks and mortar in broken and irregular courses, as were the superstructure of the towers of the city walls[4] and Temples D[5] and B (page 145), since this appears to have been the usual style of construction for important buildings in this period. Toward the top, where it is well preserved, the podium wall is c. 1.50 m thick, evidently ideally 5 p.R. (1.48 m). If, as seems probable since there is no change in the Comitium wall, which continued to serve as footing for the façade wall, the walls of the new Curia ran on the outer face of the podium walls and were $1\frac{1}{2}$ p.R. thick, then following the pattern of the walls of the earlier Curia, they were probably

2. Aes signatum (Buttrey 1980, 25); sextantal as (Buttrey 1980, 32; Crawford 1974, 56/2); sextantal semis (Buttrey 1980, 37; Crawford 1974, 97).

3. V. R. Grace and M. Savatianou-Petropoulakos, *Délos*, fasc. 27 (1970), 277–382, "Les timbres amphoriques grecs," 291, 304 (EII).

4. Brown 1951, 38–41.

5. Brown 1960, 28–32.

set back $\frac{1}{2}$ p.R. (0.148 m) from the face of the podium. We may assume that the setback was finished with a molding of purple tufa, although no fragment that could be assigned to it was found in the excavation.

The interior of the Curia must have measured approximately 6.00–6.40 m by 9.00–9.22 m, probably ideally 20 p.R. by 30 p.R. (5.92 m by 8.88 m). The height of the ceiling has been set at 20 p.R., so the proportions of the interior volume become 3:2:2, the height equal to the width, the width two-thirds of the length. These seem to have been the proportions suitable for such a building at Cosa (but see also Vitruvius 5.2).

Because of the paucity of positive evidence, most of the building can be reconstructed only hypothetically. In view of the extremely broad walls of the podium, steps or platforms have been restored like those of the Curia Iulia in Rome and the curia of Sabratha, two along each side and one at the back, on which the *decuriones* could sit. These would have been 3 p.R. (0.888 m) wide. The roofing has been reconstructed with timbers of measurements derived from those of temples of comparable size at Cosa, and in the absence of any evidence of terracotta revetment, this has been omitted. No fragment of an acroterion was found in the excavation, and the building is too modest to have admitted the introduction of a bank of windows in the façade. The podium suggests a deep-eaved superstructure similar to a Tuscan temple; if this is correct, then the door must have been imposing and would have made a frame of suitable dignity for the magistrate who addressed an assembly in the Comitium from it. But if it was not sufficient to light the interior (and it must have stood open during meetings of the ordo, as that of the Curia Hostilia always did) a single window above and proportioned to it seems all that would have been required. There is only a great axial door in the rather larger Curia of Pompeii.[6]

The finished Comitium and the new Curia now extended $95\frac{1}{2}$ p.R. (28.27 m) back from the Square, and it appears that the entire rectangle, 59 p.R. (17.46) in width, including the open areas on either side of the Curia, had been delimited for future use. Just inside the assumed NW and NE lines of demarcation, at the lowest point on the bedrock, a squarish basin 7 p.R. (2.07 m) on a side was hewn out of the rock to a depth of 1.50 m (Plan III, Pl. 77). It was lined with random rubble of limestone in fine white mortar and rendered with roughcast. The cutting was reduced by the lining to a tank with rounded corners about 1.58 m by 1.75 m having a floor of signinum with a quarter-round cover-joint. This would have collected the rainwater from the NE roof of the Curia and from the Comitium. The drain from the latter (page 18), if prolonged on the same axis, would have entered the S corner of the tank. The tank itself could have held only

---

6. H. A. Grueber, *Coins of the Roman Republic in the British Museum* (London, 1910), 2.46 (a temple), 3, fig. 60.3–4; C. C. E. Huelsen, *Recenti scavi del Foro Romano* (1910), 18, fig. 14; A. Bartoli, *Curia senatus* (Monumenti Romani 3 [1963]), 4–5 and tav. 95. For further references to curia buildings, see *TAPA* 100 (1969), 529 (L. R. Taylor and R. T. Scott).

about 4.50 cubic meters, whereas the catchment area would have yielded about 60 cubic meters per year. It was therefore a dry well or soak-away pit.

The location of the tank indicates that the NW line of demarcation had been made parallel to that side of the Curia, and probably at the same time that the tank was building, a wall was erected along the NW side of that limit. The evidence is a short truncated angle at the end of a much longer wall running along the NE side of Street 7. This wall and its angle, 0.45 m above the sloping rock, are remarkably like the lining of the tank; built of smallish limestone rubble laid in hard white mortar and rendered with roughcast. The exposed segments of the long wall (page 207) showed evidence neither of openings from the street nor of walls at right angles; but the remains of contemporary walls, 6.00–8.00 m

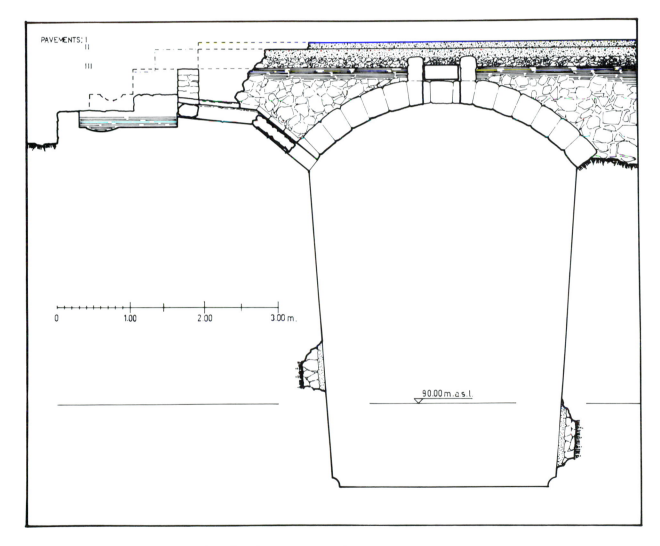

FIG. 42.   NW cistern and settling basin, cross section

northeastward, suggest houses. The S angle alongside the Curia was found bedded in a later wall (page 230) on the same line.

It is probable, if not certain, that during the work on the Curia the old open tank NW of the Comitium had been vaulted and the area leveled by means of a retaining wall along the SW side of Street 7 (page 11 and Fig. 3). The rubblework sides of the tank with their signinum facing, like that of its twin SE of the Comitium (pages 11, 46, and 49–50), show a splay from 3.10 m at bottom to 3.70 m, and the vault was segmental with a rise of only 0.70 m on a radius of 2.85 m. On the intrados the fifteen voussoirs were each about 0.30 m wide and roughly 0.42 m high, the keystone reaching 5.55 m above the floor, with a drawhole at either end (Fig. 42). At the NW end of the area a strip of the surface of its hard, tamped earthen floor was uncovered, standing some 0.10 m above the crown of the vault, while on its NE edge the retaining wall rises 0.12 m higher.

The grading of the Square was a matter of eliminating outcrops of the bedrock, of filling crevices, and of spreading a metaling of crushed rock and spalls over the uneven surface. Some of this had been done haphazardly from time to time, but now an even bed required a proper gradient, sloping from SE to NW (cf. page 9 and Pls. 37 and 78). The surface layer has been exposed all around the Square in trenches from 1.00 m to 2.50 m wide, with two trenches each 3.00 m wide crossing the Square in the middle. Something like a clay court, 0.10 m to 0.25 m deep, it was composed of clayey, red-ochre earth mixed with broken limestone of about fist size on the average and thoroughly tamped. Its gradient is marked by gutters along the margins, but in the course of constant use it settled in places, was trampled, pitted, and irregularly patched and renewed.

The gutters that bordered the Square were positioned to catch the rainwater from the eaves of the three porticoes that were yet to be built and to collect the runoff from the older installations along the NE side. Of the gutter blocks on all four sides approximately 40 percent have survived. These fifty-one blocks of local travertine arrived quarry-faced, 0.60–0.70 m in breadth and 0.15–0.30 m in thickness, and of very different lengths from 0.83 m to 3.81 m, with an average length of about 1.50 m. Except where sides of blocks were to be fitted to other members, as along the SE side of the Square, only the tops of the blocks were dressed, reduced to a uniform width of 2 p.R. (0.592 m) and finished down to a depth of 0.03 m along the edge that faced the Square, marking its periphery, while the gutter channels conveyed the rainwater from the surrounding buildings and spaces into the three separate settling basins.

The largest of these (Fig. 42) was across the gutter on the NE edge of the Square at the SE end of the newly vaulted cistern (*supra* and Plan X). The floor of its gutter from the E corner of the Square, dropping $2\frac{1}{2}$ p.R. (0.74 m) over the length of 60.40 m, gave the flow of water greater velocity than elsewhere. It carried the runoff from the open spaces of the area beside the Carcer (pages 44–46), the forecourt of the Sacellum (pages 51–56), and part of the area NW of the Comitium. The basin, 1.35 m by 1.22 m, was shallow but had a circular silting trap just below the intake. Behind the seatings for the gutters on either side the walls of the basin rose to the height of the floor that covered the vault of the cistern and the conduit from the basin.

The other two settling basins received the rainwater from the roofing of all the porticoes and atria that pitched toward the Square and discharged it into the Reservoir in the W corner of the Forum. The basin in the W corner of the Square (Pl. 80) received the drip from Atrium Building VIII, the SE entranceway, AB VII, AB VI, AB V, the Southwest Annex, AB IV, AB III, and AB II. The gutters that conveyed it measured approximately 130.00 m long, descending at a gradient of 5 percent. The rectangular basin, about 1.00 m square and 0.41 m deep below the water level, had a capacity of 40 liters or 15 gallons.

Its counterpart was the settling tank at the top of the NW entranceway (Fig. 43) that served the entranceway, AB I, and some time later an addition to the portico in front of AB I northeastward. It also gathered in the runoff from most of the area NW of the Comitium. Together this system of channels amounted to some 56.00 m in length.

The conduits that led from the two settling basins to the Reservoir were dissimilar. The one from the W corner of the Square ran almost straight to the E corner of the Reservoir. It was a box drain, with floor and sides $1\frac{3}{8}$ p.R. (0.403 m) wide and high constructed of fine rubblework, floored with tegulae, and coated with watertight signinum. As far as the façade of AB III it was vaulted, but under the wall and beyond, as far as visible, it was roofed with tegulae. Its discharge into the Reservoir was by a circular opening, $1\frac{1}{2}$ p.R. (0.45 m) in diameter, framed with rubblework (Pl. 81). Its length must have been about 21.50 m and its drop 0.22 m.

The second conduit, leaving the top of the NW entranceway, was an open channel (Fig. 43, Pl. 52) of semicircular section with a radius of 0.20 m. Skirting the NE face of AB II, it was first 0.35 m below the surface, then rose gradually until, as it turned to hug the NW face of the building, its floor stood 0.57 m above the sloping pavement of Street O. At some point along the way toward the N corner of the Reservoir it went under the street, turning again to reach its goal through a pipe 0.14 m in diameter, framed in a square limestone collar of 0.38 m on a side (Pl. 82). Its tortuous journey, descending 0.56 m, was approximately 58.40 m long. The installation of this at first depressed and then elevated conduit along the SW side of the NW entranceway was evidently the reason for the blocking up of the openings on this side of AB II (page 77). This indicates that at one point a single settling basin and conduit in the W corner of the Square was deemed sufficient to dispatch the requisite volume of water, but that ultimately it was found necessary to double it.

The Reservoir itself (Figs. 44 and 45, Pl. 83), one of the four receptacles built in anticipation of the first colonists (page 8), needed only the conduits from the Square and a structural canopy to prevent the invasion of vegetation and evaporation. The original floor of the Reservoir, where it was sounded, was 0.30–0.39 m

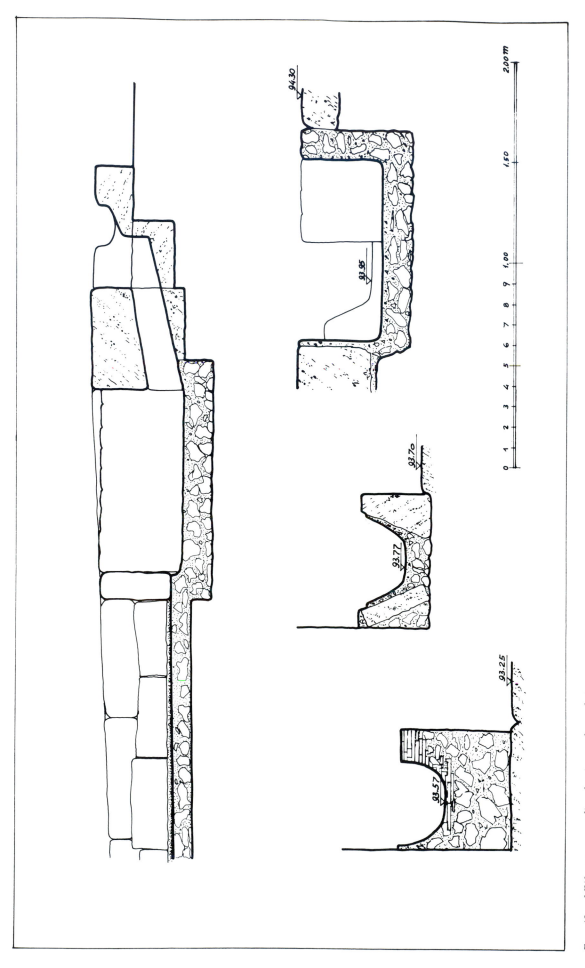

Fig. 43. NW gutter, settling basin, and conduit, cross sections

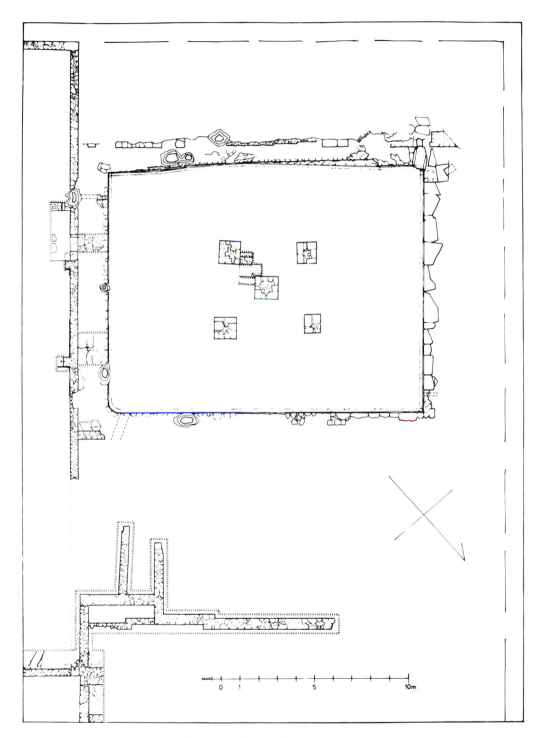

Fig. 44.   Forum Reservoir and surroundings, plan, actual state

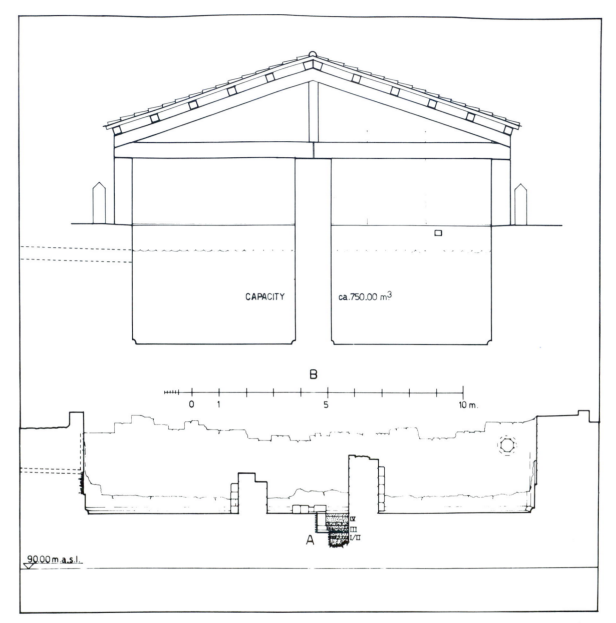

CAPACITY   ca.750.00 m³

B

0   1   5   10 m.

A

90.00 m.a.s.l.

FIG. 45.   (A) Forum Reservoir, section, actual state, looking NE; (B) Forum Reservoir, section, restored, looking SE

above the uneven bedrock. Leveled up 0.14–0.21 m with limestone chunks and spalls and rammed, it was spread with a layer of limestone chips in dark mortar and then surfaced with chips of tile in hard white signinum. The new conduits, entering from E and N, were not on a level but 10 p.R. (2.95 m) and 7 p.R. (2.08 m) above this floor. The discrepancy means that while in normal conditions both conduits performed, at exceptional times the lower of the two would be submerged and would have to be stoppered, leaving only one to function.

The sounding, approximately in the center of the floor, exposed a square pier, $4\frac{1}{2}$ p.R. (1.335 m) on a side, resting on the original floor and standing about 0.31 m above the later of the two successive floors. Below these the pier preserves its thick coat of hard signinum and its quarter-round cover-joint at the base. It was built of dry ashlar masonry, quoined at the corners, in three courses of roughly 0.32 m each around a core of spalls and pulverized rock. So sturdy a support in this position demands a purpose, which in this case must have been the roofing of the Reservoir, most likely a gable roof running NW–SE. Two more corresponding piers in line on the long axis would have sufficed. They and their three tie-beams were probably lifted above the narrow walkways atop the walls of the Reservoir enough to allow water to be drawn from it.

The gutters, as raised margins around the Square, entailed a slight reduction of its former rectangle (page 8), and the various pits on the NE and SW sides along its SE half were either buried or reduced in size. All twelve sockets for holding posts (pages 41–44) were now filled and tamped with earth and chips of stone beneath the new pavement of the Square. The eight larger planting pits for trees (pages 13–14) were diminished to about one-third of their original size, still adequate for small trees. These new pits, now 3 by $2\frac{1}{4}$ p.R. (0.89 m by 0.67 m), were walled up with good rubblework $1\frac{1}{2}$ p.R. (0.44 m) thick in the W and N corners of the old pits to support travertine curbs level with the gutters (Pls. 3, 67). The single curbing that has survived shows that the old blocks were used for it. The NW end block was simply lifted to a higher position. The SE end block was moved northwestward to its new support, while one of the long SW or NE side blocks was cut to the new length and fastened with a dovetail clamp identical to the original clamps.

Probably at the same time a more complex sequence of post holes was being hewn in the rock bordering most of the gutter across the SE end of the Square. These were two rows of sockets, grouped in fours (Pl. 84), placed at the corners of six squares with sides of $7\frac{1}{2}$ p.R. (2.22 m) and separated by five intervals. Four of the intervals, to the left and right of the center, were the same as the squares, while the one in the middle was wider, $10\frac{1}{2}$ p.R. (3.11 m) wide. In this interval a single extra socket beside the gutter was placed off-center at the S corner. These twenty-five quadrangular sockets were $1\frac{3}{4}$ p.R. (0.518) on a side and $3\frac{3}{4}$ p.R. (1.11 m) deep on the average. Each had ledges inside its mouth on opposite sides for a lid, of which three were found still in place, about $\frac{1}{2}$ p.R. (0.148 m) thick. Two still had their iron lifting rings (Pl. 85). Thus the sockets were opened at certain times and otherwise closed; when they were opened, a post must have been inserted in each shaft, while the intervals between became passageways.

A comparable system of similar square pits was discovered in 1950–52 in the forum of the Latin colony of Alba Fucens, founded in 303 B.C. The excavators have dated the sockets to the second half of the second century B.C. The arrangement was at the SE end of the forum, as at Cosa, and at first consisted of a row of eleven paired pits, broadside to the square. Each pair was separated from the next by an equal interval. Each square socket was revetted with slabs of stone on sides and bottom and was about $1\frac{1}{2}$ p.R. (0.45 m) across and 2 p.R. (0.60 m) deep. Each was fitted with a stone lid, as the one found in place indicated. At this stage, it seems, the posts supported lintels over the intervals.[7]

The abandoned sockets along the sides of the Square at Cosa evidently held posts to define three aisles through which the first citizens queued for voting or military enlistment. If this was also the function of the more numerous sockets along the SE end of the Square, then the new aisles and posts were required because more lanes were needed for the new colonists. At the assemblies the posts in the corners of the six squares would have been used to support continuous cover for the officials who supervised as the citizens passed through their five corridors, three for the old Cosans and two for the newly added colonists.

The erratic twenty-fifth socket in the wider middle opening (Pl. 86) may have been simply a faulty beginning in plan, since the pit in line with this in the second row was never cut. Or it may have been placed just off center for a post of a special kind. Perhaps, for example, it was for the *vexillum* of the colony, a banner on a crosspiece, planted there to signal the day of the annual selection of the new cohort of the colony.[8] Moreover, that wide central interval, certainly not necessary just for queueing, suggests that the sockets were designed for other uses as well. One of these might have been the erection of temporary stages and scenery with central portals. The sockets for the temporary *scaenae* in the contemporary theaters of Pergamon and Syracuse offer close parallels, while vases from Greece and Magna Graecia picture the wooden structures that were used. Rome's theaters at this time were busy, but none has survived; Cosa's arrangement may possibly reflect them.[9]

The streets that bounded the Forum and led from the Square were at this time being paved and provided with conduits and curbings for carrying off sewage and rainwater. Some of the streets were bordered with sidewalks and others not, but excepting the unpaved streets, all were surfaced with thick-set flags of limestone. These were trapezoidal or polygonal, having lengths from 2.00 m to 0.50 m and thicknesses from 0.30 m to 0.18 m, laid on flattened bedrock or on fills of ballast and tamped with sand. After the sidewalk beside AB I (page 75) came the paving of the NW entranceway, which left two spaces in the center of the pavement at the top of the entranceway for two column bases of the portico to come. At the same time the conduit along the NE side of AB II (page 115) was built. Along the upper half of the conduit the paving stones of the street were set back in place overlapping the outer edge of the channel below, which, after it rose above street level, was carried on the paving stones beneath. At the bottom of

7. F. De Visscher and J. Mertens, *BullCom* 74 (1951–52), appendix 17, 3–14; J. Mertens, *Alba Fucens I* (Brussels, 1969), 92–96; C. Krause, *RömMitt* 83 (1976), 45–47.

8. Cicero, *De Leg. Agr.* 2.86; *Phil.* 2.112; Plutarch, *C. Gracch.* 11.

9. *Altertümer von Pergamon* 4 (1896), 12–14 and Taf. 4, 5; *Palladio* 17 (1967), 115–46; M. Bieber, *The History of the Greek and Roman Theater* 2d ed. (Princeton, 1961), 62–63, 129–46, 167–68.

the entranceway the paving ended on a straight line, above which the Fornices (pages 123–28) were to be placed.

Street O met Street 6, and beyond their meeting they spread to the SE in an apron to abut their flagstones against those of the NW entranceway (Pl. 87). Under Street O ran one of the mains of the sewer system, running out the NE Gate at the bottom. The section was roughly 2 p.R. (0.59 m) wide and 3 p.R. (0.89 m) high, covered, as part of the paving, with large, trapezoidal blocks, some 1 p.R. (0.295 m) thick and 4 p.R. (1.185 m) in length (Fig. 46). The rain falling on the surface of the street was diverted into the Reservoir beside the gate.[10] Similarly Street 5 meshed with Street P at their meeting, where, at the summit of Street 5, Street P's runoff was channeled into the NW cistern of the SW Annex (page 99). Street 5 on its way downward to the NW housed another main, which, turning under Street K, debouched from the NW Gate. This conduit, like that of Street O, was 2 p.R. (0.59 m) wide; but being deeper below the surface, it was covered by a stone gable of slabs set against keystones (Pl. 88). Again, the surface rainfall was diverted to the settling tank and NW Reservoir beside the gate.

Finally, Street 7 met Street O with a step and a seam across its sidewalk, indicating that it was paved somewhat later. This would have been after the delimitation of the area around the Curia (page 112) but before Temple B raised its podium over the flagstones of the street (page 143), sometime between 170 and 150 B.C. Street Q and the SE entranceway were never paved within the Forum. The courses of both had been trimmed down and cavities filled by spreading a thick rudus upon them, but no more.

Across the SE entranceway, some 6.40 m from the Square, a sounding was opened, 3.70 m wide, down to the rock and hardpan beneath the rudus (Pl. 89). Amid the ballast were found 334 sherds, of which 246 were black-glaze tableware, similar to those found under the floor of the Curia (page 111), of the kind prevailing at Cosa from the late third century B.C. to the early second. The local potteries provided some 90 percent of the lot, while the imported pieces consisted of eleven fragments of Campana A, five of Campana B, and three of Calene ware of the second half of the third century B.C. Saucers with furrowed rim and bowls of Lamboglia Forms 27a–b, 31, 36, and 51 made up three-quarters of the local ware. Three coins were found as well: C68.212, 213, and 214. These were contemporary with the ceramics. Of these C68.213 was a semi-uncia of 215–213 B.C.[11]

Next in order in the master plan (pages 57–59) came the porticoes skirting the Atrium Buildings, crossing the SW Annex and the entranceway at either end, as the surface dropped from SE to NW, $2\frac{3}{4}$ p.R. (0.815 m). The Porticus at the SE end swallowed up part of Street Q, its columns bordered by a curb from end to end

---

10. Brown 1951, 85; Brown 1980, 11.   11. Buttrey 1980, 40, no. 30; Crawford 1974, 38/7.

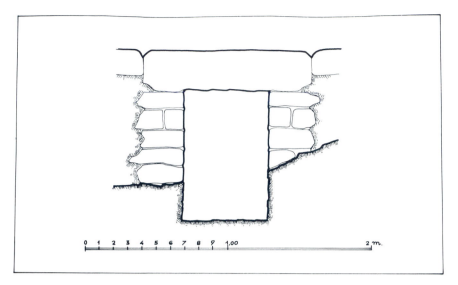

0 1 2 3 4 5 6 7 8 9 1.00   2 m.

FIG. 46. Main sewer under Street O, section at Street 6

across the SE entranceway, while the curbs between columns before AB I and II stopped at either side of the paved NW entranceway (Pl. 90). The aisle of the SW Porticus was raised above the gutter by two steps, risers and treads measuring $\frac{3}{4}$ p.R. (0.22 m) and 1 p.R. (0.30 m) (Pl. 79). The total number of columns was thirty-four, of which two were later eliminated when piers were placed across the SW Annex. Of the rest there remain stumps of nine columns and twenty-three settings. Twelve settings were circular plinths of travertine, from 0.60 m to 0.90 m in diameter and of various heights, depending on the depth of the underlying rock (Pl. 91).[12] Eleven beds were worked level on the rock surface. The nine fragments of shafts, of which the longest is only about 0.50 m, were $2\frac{1}{8}$ p.R. (0.63 m) in diameter, and like the columns of the tabernae (pages 73, 76, 91, and 96) were built up with wedge-shaped slabs of sandstone usually about 0.08 m thick, eight to ten making a round. The taper of the columns, following Vitruvius's "Tuscanic" order (4.7.2), as in the temples of the Arx,[13] would make them about 0.472 m at the top. Pieces of four travertine capitals from the SW Porticus fit the columns. They were of the "Tuscanic" kind (Pl. 92), roughly dressed and, like the shaft, to be plastered and finished in detail, adding about 0.04–0.05 m to their diameter and thus something to the calculated height of $15\frac{1}{16}$ p.R. (4.46 m) of the columns. The columns had no visible bases, although some of the wider plinths were inturned to the bottoms of the columns below the signinum flooring.

The tangents of the columns were placed 14 p.R. (4.14 m) from the walls behind and 18 p.R. (5.32 m) from the SE gutter, $18\frac{1}{2}$ p.R. (5.47 m) from the NW gutter, $18\frac{3}{4}$ p.R. (5.54 m) from the SW gutter. The centering of the columns was

12. R. Delbrück, *Hellenistische Bauten in Latium*, vol. 2 (Strasbourg, 1912), 30, Taf. 16; P. B. Vittucci, *Forma Italia, Regio I*, vol. 5 (Rome, 1968), 78, 96, figs. 141, 142, 150.

13. Brown 1960, 37, 91–92, 111–13.

not uniform, nor were they aligned regularly with the inner, perpendicular walls of the tabernae and vestibula. Generally, however, the columns of the SE and SW porticoes and those in front of AB I framed these openings, without being centered on them, as though each Atrium Building were to be seen from a vantage point along the middle of the Square. The spaces between columns were from $18\frac{3}{16}$ p.R. (5.38 m) to $13\frac{3}{16}$ p.R. (3.90 m), but they tended to hover around $16\frac{3}{8}$ p.R. (4.84 m), wider than the height of the columns by one or two Roman feet. The W corner of the colonnade, where the SW and NW Atrium Buildings II and III met, evidently presented difficulties in column placement. Only two columns stood in front of AB II, with intercolumniations of $20\frac{5}{16}$ p.R. (6.01 m) and $21\frac{1}{2}$ p.R. (6.37 m) on centers. The latter had been moved out from the SW wall $\frac{3}{4}$ p.R. (0.22 m) to $14\frac{3}{4}$ p.R. (4.36 m), presumably to support an architrave less than $22\frac{1}{4}$ p.R. (6.59 m) long. This, of course, lengthened the regular tangents of the first two of the columns of the SW Porticus. The next column was necessarily very close, at a distance of only $9\frac{1}{4}$ p.R. (2.74 m), the narrowest intercolumniation of the lot, and was drawn back some 0.09 m, so as to adjust to the third column and the normal tangents of the Porticus.

Two antefixes (Pl. 93) to cover the ends of the imbrices of the roofs, one on the SE portico and another on the SW, were found. Both rose from a plain fascia with a strut behind. They show a female head, frontal, 0.09 m high, with a classical oval face, heavy chin and cheeks, lidded eyes, and moderate forehead. The hair waves symmetrically over the forehead and ears, descending in crimped tresses to the shoulders. Above a roll across the crown of the head rises a palmette of central sword-blade leaf, c. 0.095 m high, with incurling leaves on each side (sword and pruning hook). To either side of the head is an eight-petaled rosette. Here and there were traces of buff slip and paint. The general effect is archaistic, the head being an unidentified divinity.

The generally broad spaces of the porticoes required, in the Roman way, heavy timber architraves as well as projecting principal rafters, extending from the lean-to roofs of the tabernae and vestibula (page 76) and across the two entranceways and the entrance to the SW Annex. The porticoes behind the columns, floored with signinum, were for strolling well protected from the elements, and the overhang outside made an additional continuous, though narrow, walk around three sides of the Square. The SW Porticus, well designed with its two steps and its back to the sun, was the best of all from which to watch assemblies, shows, and the lively activity of the forum (Fig. 49).

The unpaved rectangles left toward the lower end of the NW entranceway (page 121) were intended to accommodate a triple archway, or Fornices, a wide central opening and narrow lateral passageways, built before or just after the Porticus. Facing the juncture of Streets 6 and O as they climbed from the NW and NE Gates, the Fornices marked the real and symbolic passage between the rest of the town and the public world of the Forum. Its ruin, split in two halves canted off their supports, is still one of the most conspicuous features of Ansedonia (Pl. 94).

FIG. 47.   Fornices, SW half, standing in A.D. 1793

It was described and illustrated in 1793 by the first known modern visitor, when one half was still standing (Fig. 47), and it was marked on the first published map of the site, showing it fallen in 1810.[14] The unexcavated remains were examined in 1948, and an attempt was made to classify and date them.[15] Excavation has given a more accurate notion of the monument itself and its spatial and temporal context. The four piers of the archways, standing 0.45 m to 1.05 m above the pavement, were set from the NW façades of AB I and II on Street O about 1.00 m to 0.84 m (pages 127–28; Pl. 94) for a frame. The major fallen element includes the whole SW lateral vault and a little less than the lower quarter of the central vault. The other fallen mass includes only the NE lateral vault above the springing. The length of each pier was 8 p.R. (2.37 m). Their widths and intervals were, from NE to SW: 2 p.R. (0.59 m), $3\frac{3}{8}$ p.R. (1.00 m), $2\frac{15}{16}$

14. G. Santi, *Viaggio secondo per le due provincie senesi* (Pisa, 1798), 140–41, tav. 4; G. Micali, *Antichi monumenti per servire all'opera intitolata l'Italia avanti il dominio dei Romani* (Florence, 1810), tav. 4.

15. Brown 1951, 73–75, 111.

p.R. (0.87 m), 13 p.R. (3.85 m), $2\frac{15}{16}$ p.R. (0.87 m), $3\frac{1}{8}$ p.R. (0.925 m), $2\frac{3}{8}$ p.R. (0.70 m), altogether $29\frac{3}{4}$ p.R. (8.81 m). These dimensions, some coherent and others not, must have been the result of a schematic project for a triple gateway to cross a 30-foot space between buildings. It evidently called for a central span of 13 feet, flanked by wings of equal widths and pierced by lateral openings of one-fourth the width of the central span, where the relative dimensions would have been: $2–3\frac{1}{2}–3–13–3\frac{1}{2}–2$ (Fig. 48). This symmetrical scheme, however, was impossible to realize under the circumstances. The space was not 30 feet but $29\frac{3}{4}$. The SW pier

Fig. 48.   Fornices, NW face, assembled and restored

had to carry the conduit along the NW entranceway (page 115) through a terracotta pipe with a diameter of 1 p.R. (0.296 m).

Hence the pier was enlarged and the other piers and intervals reduced, except the central span and the NE pier. Originally the NE face of the SW pier was almost completely masked to a height of about 3 p.R. (0.89 m) by a mass of rubblework masonry, $2\frac{1}{4}$ p.R. (0.67 m) thick, footed on the pavement of Street O, which here had no sidewalk. This supported and enclosed the continuation of the pipe that traversed the pier to carry it around the N corner of AB II. About 0.80 m past the angle of the building the pipe became an open conduit again, running SW toward the reservoir. The right angle of pipe had been broken from its jacket, of which the stumps alone remained, while the conduit was preserved to the limit of the excavation.

Each pair of piers on either side of the central opening was erected on a level footing of rubblework laid against the existing edge of the apron of Street 6 (page 121) and in accord with its downward slope northeastward, yet raising the heads of their arches to the same horizontal plane (Pls. 94, 95). The piers were of solid limestone rubblework, roughly coursed on all four faces, with larger stones, more regular and closely jointed, on the principal faces. Above the narrow leveling course, 0.09–0.10 m high, that marked the impost line, the three vaults were framed at either end with rings of limestone voussoirs. Around and above the faces of the archways the random rubblework was more or less uniformly broken limestone, with stones measuring 0.20 m by 0.25 m on the average. The vaults were of similar random rubblework, laid on centering in a bed of mortar that bears the imprint of its planking on widths of $\frac{1}{2}$ p.R. (0.15 m).

The SW vault sprang from a height of 5 p.R. (1.48 m) above the footing. Its NW end was framed with an arch of nine almost uniform voussoirs, 0.155–0.165 m wide on the intrados, squared off on the extrados, about $1\frac{1}{4}$ p.R. (0.37 m) high and 0.20–0.30 m deep. The arch at the SE end was of eleven voussoirs, regularly 0.13–0.135 m wide on the intrados and 0.29–0.30 m high, with a right springer 0.39 m high and keystone of 0.33 m. The NE vault, if on the same proportions, would have sprung about 1.60 m above the footing. From the size and position of the two remaining voussoirs on the NW face and the imprint of the others left in the rubblework, that arch was of eleven voussoirs of 0.14–0.145 m on the intrados, 1 p.R. (0.29–0.30 m) high, and 0.20–0.40 m deep. The other face was too damaged to provide information. The central vault sprang at a height of $7\frac{1}{4}$ p.R. (2.146 m) above the SW footing. The five remaining voussoirs of its NW face, uniformly 0.47 m high and cut roughly to the curve of the extrados, were unequal in width and depth. The springer, 0.31 m by 0.31 m, was followed by blocks 0.425 m by 0.29 m, 0.19 m by 0.62 m, 0.29 m by 0.27 m, and 0.17 m by 0.53 m, which give the appearance of a header-and-stretcher bond of alternately wide and narrow voussoirs, originally at least twenty-one in number. On the SE face the surviving springer and next voussoir were 0.42 m and 0.44 m high, not cut to a curve. Their other dimensions, 0.33 m by 0.22 m and 0.29 m by 0.30 m, do not suffice to indicate a similar alternation of wide and narrow, although the imprint above the latter suggests a narrow header.

These facings were not meant to be visible, as is shown by a large patch of the original stucco on the NW face above the SW arch. The finish coat has scaled off. The scratch coat is the hard structural mortar, spread thin to even the rough surface of the rubblework. The brown coat is heavy and sandy, some 0.02 m thick. Enough remains to show that the scratch coat covered the voussoirs of the arches. The brown coat ends above the SW arch with a well-defined double edge on a curve concentric with the intrados and about 1 p.R. (0.30 m) above it, implying an attached stucco molding defining the archivolt.

Before each of the middle piers on the NW side of the arch the paving framed a shallow rectangular space, 3 p.R. (0.89 m) wide, $3\frac{3}{4}$ p.R. (1.11 m) long, and $\frac{3}{8}$ p.R. (0.18–0.19 m) deep, floored with a level bed of fine rubblework. The outer angle of the NE space next to the central passage was protected by a roughly tapered fender block, some 0.32 m by 0.45 m at the base and $1\frac{1}{4}$ p.R. (0.37 m) high. The socket of a similar fender was found beside the corresponding angle of the other space. Both spaces were presumably fitted with rectangular plinths of stone, which have left no clue to their original height, except that they must have concealed the face of the footing of the piers behind them. Protection against damage from traffic implies that the plinths carried valuable members. The fact that no similar spaces appear on the other side of the central opening would seem to preclude that these were columns. It is possible that statues could have been placed in this position, but considering the shape of the spaces, the plinths may also have supported rectangular stone basins, *labra*.[16]

The crown of the vault of the central passage, as it has been reconstructed on paper (Fig. 48), would have reached approximately 14 p.R. (4.14 m) at its NW end, one foot higher than its diameter. It is natural to assume that the archivolt of the main arch was outlined with a stucco molding similar to, but larger than, the moldings of the lateral archivolts. This broad, low, central arch seems to echo the appearance of the gates in Cosa's walls. They are 12 to $10\frac{1}{2}$ p.R. (3.55 m to 3.11 m) in width and $14\frac{1}{2}$ to $12\frac{5}{6}$ p.R. (4.29 m to 3.75 m) in height, while one of them, the SE Gate, was also set back from the curtains on either side. If the Fornices at the Forum imitated the gates and curtains of the town wall, they would have been about as high as the Atrium Buildings on either side. It so happens that a wing on either side of the central opening, as projected, would have been exactly the right height to meet the top of the Atrium Buildings (page 76), and the triple archway would have had the overall proportions of 4:3. Fornix and fornices were early types of architecture, like arcus, but they functioned as iani,[17] transitions

---

16. The first mentioned *fornices* at Rome were those of L. Stertinius and P. Cornelius Scipio Africanus (196 and 190 B.C.), both of whom placed *signa* on their triumphal arches, presumably on top, while Scipio set *marmorea duo labra ante fornicem* (Livy 33.27.3–5, 37.3.7). Cf. H. Kähler, *RE*, zweite Reihe 13 (1939), 377–78; G. A. Mansuelli, *ArchEspArq* 27 (1954), 93–178; M. Pallottino, *EAA* 1 (1958), 588–99.

17. Cicero, *Nat.Deor.* 2.67: "*transitiones perviae iani . . . nominantur.*"

from one place to another and important change. At the same time that Cosa's Fornices were rising, one of the censors of 174 b.c. seems to have provided the colonies of Pisaurum and Potentia and the municipium Fundi with iani.[18] These, too, dignified their fora.

The newly achieved master plan of the Forum now appears to have added certain necessary refinements that enhanced the efficiency of the Square and the NW entranceway. These secondary furnishings were probably completed in a very few years.

One of these was an apron of a single line of slabs of travertine abutting the outer side of the gutter along the SW Annex. It ran from the NW end of the Annex probably originally to the SE end but now stops short at the first tree-pit there, $59\frac{5}{16}$ p.R. (17.56 m) long. There are sixteen remaining original slabs. Two others were later replaced by three. The last slab on the NW was smooth; in each of the others are one or two sockets, twenty in all, and two more appear beyond the gutter, sunk in the step behind. Ten of the sockets are rectangular, measuring from 0.58 m by 0.46 m to 0.10 m by 0.05 m, nine circular, having diameters of 0.27 m to 0.05 m. Two of the rectangular sockets have a semicircular end, 0.65 m by 0.34 m and 0.50 m by 0.30 m. The depths of the sockets range from 0.15 m to 0.30 m.

These must all have been mortises to receive tenons supporting pillars or cylindrical shafts larger than the mortises. The broader pillars, presumably of stone, would have been inscribed, while others footed in the smaller mortises were presumably of wood, square or round, and would have had tablets attached. The large rectangular sockets seem to have separated the apron into three spaces. The two rectangular sockets with semicircular ends are perpendicular to the portico behind and centered, one on either side of the middle. The largest rectangular socket is parallel to the portico and beside the unsocketed NW slab, and it is not unlikely that the missing slabs at the SE end showed the same or a similar arrangement. If so, these four were probably the first erected and inscribed. All the others are smaller and haphazardly spaced, evidently erected over many years. All may have faced the Annex, proclaiming the regulations, measures, and prices of the fish market (page 103).

At the same time as the laying of the apron, or possibly before, the exedrae on either side of the stairs up to the Annex floor (pages 100–101) were closed with 2-foot walls of random rubblework run between the bicolumnar gateway (pages 99–100) and the NW and SE walls on either side. Behind the rubblework walls the exedrae were filled with fresh rock and clay, a fill extending to the retaining walls supporting the ends of the two cisterns. The new walls now stand only to 1.23 m, but the sloping fill reaches the height of the floor of the Annex, 1.55 m. Atop the walls there must have been parapets of a certain height. At the base of the outer face the pavements of the portico overlapped the thick undercoats and

18. Livy 41.27.13.

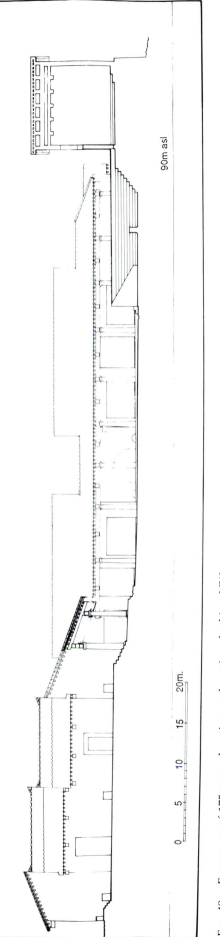

90m asl

0 5 10 15 20m.

Fig. 49. Forum, as of 175 B.C., elevation and section, looking NW

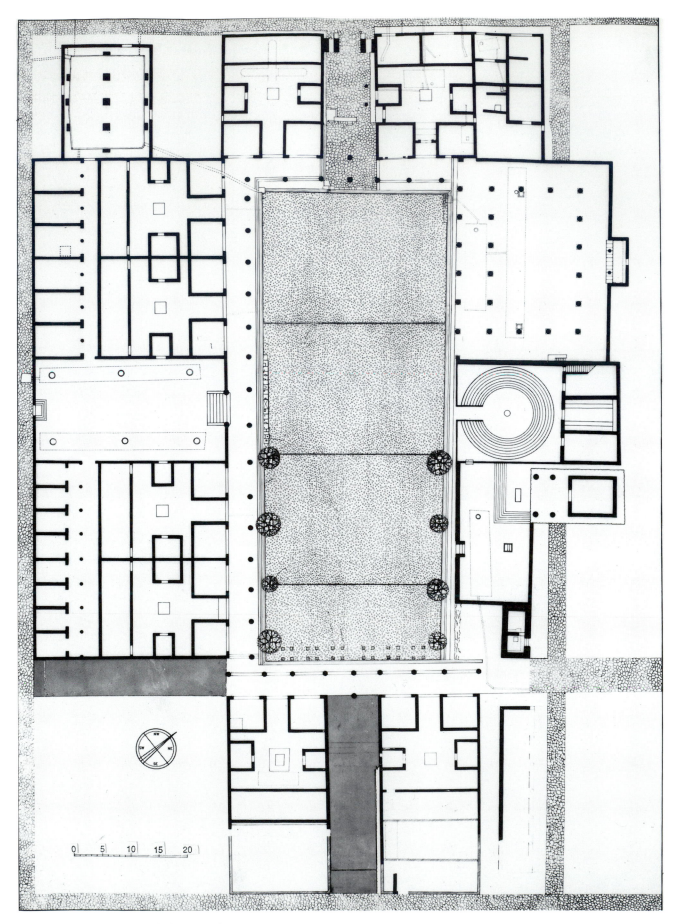

Fig. 50. Forum, restored plan, as of 140 B.C.

some of the topcoats of the finish of the walls. Since the blocking up of the exedrae is best explained as an alteration to provide walls facing the apron and stelae on which to display something, another possibility may be considered, the *forma* or cadaster of the colony of Cosa.[19]

This would have mapped the land, sea and streams, the roads, farmlands, woodlands and pasture, and above all the grid that designated the plots of the colonists.[20] The surveyor's document would have been engraved on bronze in two copies, one plate for the colony and another for Rome; but for the citizens of a particular area there was often a larger and clearer *forma* provided. The remains of two such *formae* carved on marble are well known, one at Rome itself and the other at the colony of Orange/Arausio on the Rhone.[21] Both were displayed in public places. The Square of Cosa's Forum was its assembly place, SE of its short axis from the Comitium to the Annex. The latter, its exedrae blocked by the new wall, would have been suitable for the display of the *forma* of Cosa's territory, not in marble but in paint on plaster (Fig. 51).[22] In the Square the colonists could see on the map their farmsteads and the roads and waters near them, as well as the colony's woodland and pasturage. The row of stelae in front might have advertised the regulations, old and new, governing daily times and places for selling, buying, and bartering, or perhaps for the transfer of lands.

The NW entranceway, by the Fornices below and the Porticus above, had become a smaller enclosed court, 63 p.R. (18.85 m) long and 30 p.R. (8.88 m) wide. On its long axis, 40 p.R. (11.84 m) back of the iani, were the legible traces of the central feature of the court. A number of flagstones had been prized up across the axis, others chopped or deeply chiseled along the edges of a rectangle, 8 p.R. (2.37 m) by $2\frac{3}{4}$ p.R. (0.815 m). The rock bed of the cavity was found covered with remains of a mortared bed of broken limestone some 0.12 m below the flagstones around it. Against the SE edge of the rectangle and centered on it, a single course of four limestone blocks formed a plinth 3 p.R. (0.89 m) long, 2 p.R. (0.59 m) wide, and $\frac{3}{4}$ p.R. (0.22 m) high, of which the rear half was worn smooth and the edge rounded, the front encrusted with mortar. These remains reveal the presence in the center of the court of a rectangular platform of stone or rubblework approached from behind by a pair of steps. The riser at the bottom indicates that the height of the platform above the pavement would have been $2\frac{1}{4}$ p.R. (0.67 m), equivalent to $2\frac{1}{2}$ p.R. (0.74 m) on the front, and this estimate is confirmed by the later enlargement of the platform.

The platform set on axis in the midst of this public place, at a fixed distance from the archway, accessible by steps from behind, could hardly be other than a

19. F. Castagnoli, "Le 'forme' delle colonie romane e le miniature dei codici dei gromatici, *MemLinc* 7.4 (1944), 83–118; Brown 1980, 41–42.

20. F. Blume et al., *Die Schriften der römische Feldmesser* (Berlin, 1848–52): Frontinus 1.58, fig. 167; Hyginus 108–34, 167–208, figs. 127–205; O. A. W.

Dilke, *The Roman Land Surveyors* (Newton Abbot, Devon., 1971), 66–125.

21. G. Carettoni et al., *La pianta marmorea di Roma antica* (Rome, 1960); A. Piganiol, *Les Documents cadestraux de la colonie romaine d'Orange* (*Gallia*, supp. 16).

22. F. Castagnoli (above, note 19), 98–118.

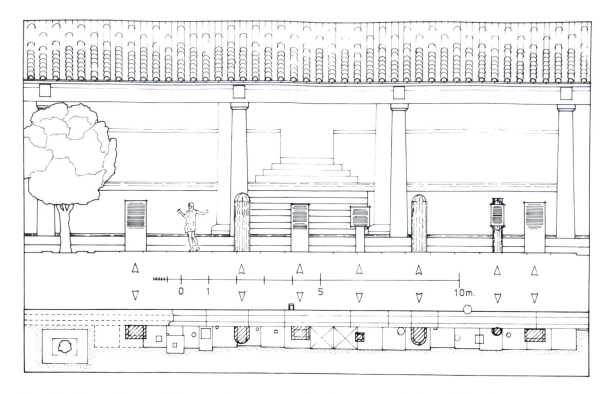

Fig. 51.   Forum Square, SW center along apron and sockets, restored plan and elevation

judicial *suggestus* or *tribunal,* the platform on which the appropriate magistrate or *iudex* placed his curule chair or his *bisellium* to hold court or accept petitions. Its presence would have converted the normal enclosed space into a courtroom and the slope of pavement below accommodated the *corona*, the watchers of the proceedings.[23]

Furthermore, part of Atrium Building I might well have been used for judiciary preliminaries to trial, official jurisdiction, or private arbitration with advocates. Vestibulum 1 (page 69; Pl. 44) was beside the *tribunal,* and benches had been inserted on either side of it, built of roof tiles overlaid with plaster. Just beside it was Room 7 (pages 67–68; Pl. 43) with its impressive doorway on the entranceway, which now included a bicolumnar porch. The SE plinth of the pair of columns was found in place, a cube of limestone $1\frac{7}{8}$ p.R. (0.55 m) on a side, projecting 0.13 m above the pavement. Its counterpart, which must have stood 0.29–0.30 m above the pavement, had been removed, leaving a socket 0.42 m wide filled with a mortar bedding and a bed chiseled on the adjacent flagstones 0.135 m wide. The plinths were set on the axes of the side walls of the room, $11\frac{1}{2}$ p.R. (3.40 m) apart and $5\frac{1}{2}$ p.R. (1.63 m) from the façade. Of the

23. *DarSag,* s.v. "Tribunal" (V. Chapot); H. D.   s.v. "Tribunal" (E. Weiss, 1937).
Johnson, *The Roman Tribunal* (Baltimore, 1927); *RE,*

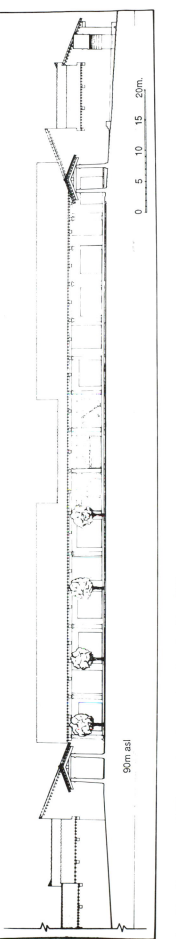

Fig. 52. Forum, as of 175 B.C., elevation and section, looking SW

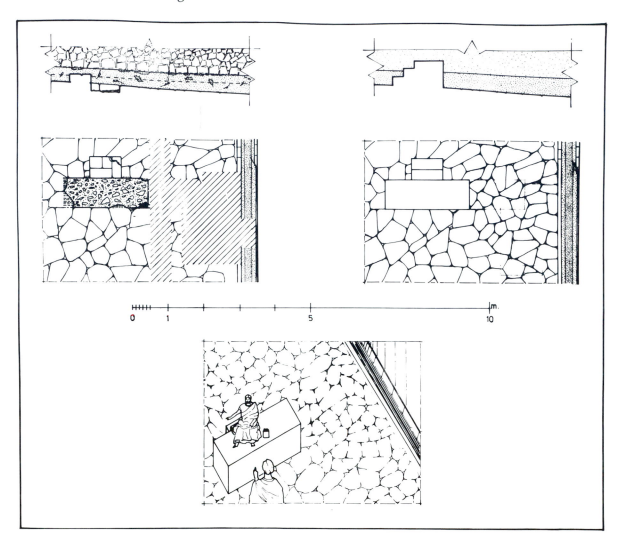

FIG. 53.   NW entranceway, *suggestus*, plans, sections, and axonometric

shafts of the columns no vestige was found, probably because they were constructed of the sandstone slabs commonly employed about the Forum (pages
73, 76, 91, 96, and 122).

The capitals, however, were of travertine and of uncommon type. Two fragments of these were found, mutilated, within a radius of 15 m from the plinths.
The first, about a third of the whole, top to bottom, was discovered in the filling
of the conduit opposite (page 115), and a sizable fragment of echinus and necking appeared in an upper level of the fauces of AB I (Room 1). The second, also
about a third of the whole, was built into the wall that blocked up the opening of
the NE taberna of AB II (page 240). These are Tuscan capitals, $\frac{7}{16}$ p.R. (0.13 m)
high, worked together with sections of shafts of an upper diameter of 0.32 m.
The abacus, $1\frac{5}{8}$ p.R. (0.48 m) square, capped a quarter-round echinus and deep

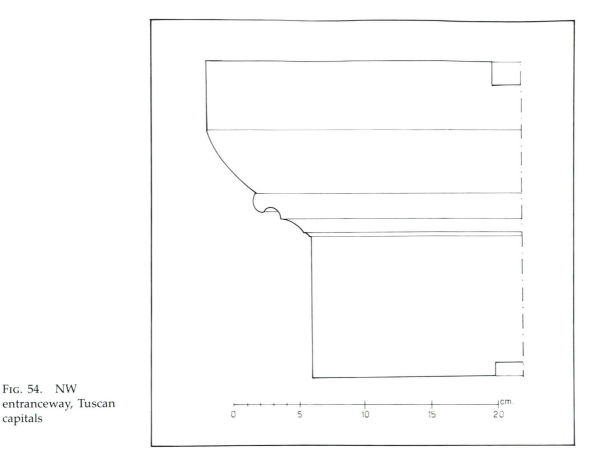

FIG. 54. NW
entranceway, Tuscan
capitals

necking, made up of a shallow double cavetto crowned with a hawksbeak.[24]
Given the measurement of the abacus and the proportions prevailing at Cosa,
the columns would have been $11\frac{3}{8}$ p.R. (3.37 m) high, suitable for carrying a shed
roof over the doorway and framing the door with a porch of square façade.

The remaining unbuilt area adjacent to the AB I plot, SE of Tabernae 25 and
24/26 (pages 104–5), was soon built up. The steps in the process are plain, and
although they cannot be dated precisely, no more than a score or so of years
could have elapsed before the NW Porticus was extended to cover the lengthened façade on the Forum.

The first step was the erection of a shop or storehouse (Room 22) behind
Taberna 25 and accessible from the open area to the SE. The SE wall of Taberna
25 made a party wall, against the ends of which the NE and SW walls of the new
structure were abutted without bond. The new walls, enclosing a somewhat
irregular rectangle 6.50–6.65 m by 6.90–7.00 m, were found standing, four to
nine courses, 0.70–1.60 m, high, largely out of plumb beneath a later rebuilding

24. *MAAR* 28 (1965), 42 (Cosa CE 300; C67.447);
40.1–7.

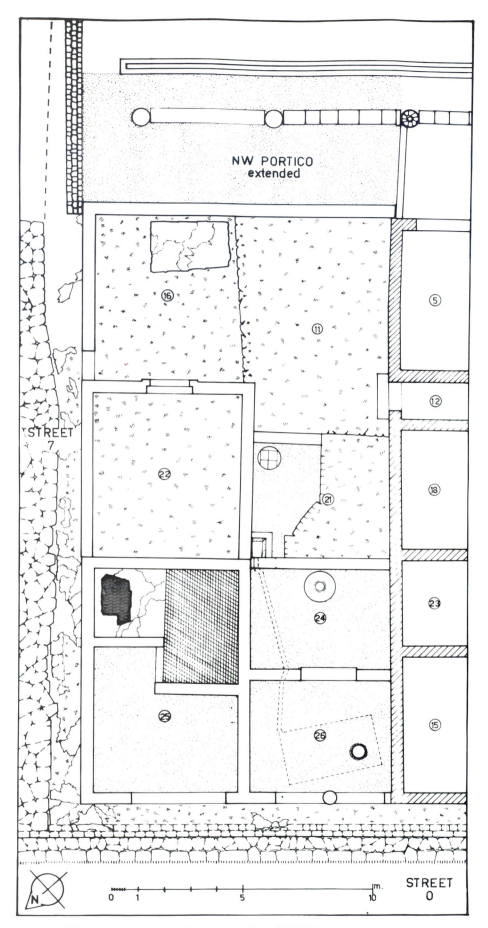

Fig. 55.   N corner plot, Areas 11, 16, 21, 22 and NW Porticus Annex

(page 240). The new walls, $1\frac{5}{8}$ p.R. (0.48 m) thick, were similar in build to the earlier walls nearby. The room was floored with rammed earth, laid directly on the construction floor over bedrock. The jambs and plinths of the doorway have been torn out, but their imprint shows that the opening was 6 p.R. (1.77 m) wide. The shape of the room implies that the gable ran NW/SE, perpendicular to the gables of Tabernae 25 and 24/26. Quantities of shattered roofing found in the room and an absence of ceiling material point to an open timber roof with eaves overhanging the crepido of Street 7 on one side by about 4 p.R. (1.184 m) and the same on the other side.

Next the remaining L-shaped open area of the plot was enclosed with a wall along its two open sides. The longer leg faced the flank of the Comitium across open terrain, and still stands 2.00 m to 3.00 m high. It was laid out with its inner face on the line of the façade of AB I, overlapping it for half its thickness to about the NE curb of the Porticus. The shorter leg, on Street 7, standing up to 1.20 m high, was erected so as to leave a doorway of $3\frac{3}{4}$ p.R. (1.11 m) at its juncture with the E angle of Room 22. Walled up, apparently at the same time as the SE doorway of Room 22, this showed no sign of its frame. The new walls were of coursed rubblework, $1\frac{3}{4}$ p.R. (0.52 m) thick, closely resembling the walls of Room 22 (Pl. 100). Like Room 22 also, the area of the ell was roughly leveled by knocking off outcrops and filling crevices, making steps 0.29 m and 0.42 m high up from Rooms 21 and 16 to the S corner (Area 11). These yards, Areas 11 and 16, had pavements of trampled earth, and opposite the doorway from 22 to 16 a refuse pit, close beside the SE wall, was hewn in the rock, roughly rectangular, 3.00 m by 1.88 m and about 1.68 m deep. It shows no trace of roofing or of the entry of a drain. Area 21 was now cut off from 24 by walling up the rear doorway of 24 with solid rubblework, yet still served as the catchment to supply the cistern of Taberna 26. In the corner behind the blocked doorway was sunk a rectangular basin, $1\frac{1}{4}$ p.R. (0.37 m) deep with a quarter-round cover-joint at the base, lined with signinum. It was evidently designed to receive via a downspout the runoff from the SW slope of the roof of Room 22, as well as from the roofs of 24 and 18 in AB I. At the opposite end of Area 21 and presumably well under the protection of the eaves of 22, a circular charcoal oven, *focus* or *fornax*, was let 0.06–0.08 m into a signinum pavement. The circle of its floor, against which the paving stopped, was paved with sawn and fitted segments of tile, reddened and smutted by fire.

Whatever the original use of Room 22, the enclosure of the area apparently was connected with AB I, with which it communicated through Corridor 12. The disposal of refuse in the pit in one end of the ell and the installation for cooking at the other find their likeliest explanation if Room 18 was used as a public hospice (page 101).

The angle of the enclosure abutted the end of the rough retaining wall back of the NW cistern on the Square that ran along the SW side of Street 7 (page 114; Pl. 100) as far as the NW side of the Comitium. The wall of the SE enclosure was now masked by an extension of the NW Porticus, of which the first 4.50 m of the floor and its curbing were found preserved intact beneath a later floor (page 216). The full extension, however, is readily restored with two columns, spaced approximately like those at the other end, 5.12 m apart on centers.[25] The extension was floored with signinum on a rising grade along AB I and similarly bordered by a curb of travertine, set with its outer face tangent to the foot of the columns. The curbing blocks varied in length from $1\frac{3}{4}$ p.R. (0.52 m) to 3 p.R. (0.89 m), but all were $1\frac{7}{8}$ p.R. (0.55 m) wide and stood $\frac{3}{8}$ p.R. (0.11 m) above the flooring. Against the end column of AB I was a slab $\frac{5}{8}$ p.R. (0.185 m) higher than the curbs, and more slabs evidently ran across the Porticus set in a trough in the flooring to differentiate the two porches. This new expansion of the NW Porticus was without tabernae but faced a bay from the Square, stretching to the Comitium. The area was unpaved but was supplied with water from the NW cistern (page 11); perhaps it served as the Forum Boarium of Cosa.

25. The later floor was that of the Basilica. It is reasonably certain that a circular drum of travertine supporting a stump of three slabs of sandstone, 0.83 m high and 0.815 m wide, placed under the S corner of the Basilica is the remains of one of the two columns (see page 232).

VII. 175–150 B.C.

(Plans III, IV; Figs. 56–58; Pls. 101–8)

While minor but noteworthy changes were taking place in the course of implementing the master plan for the Forum, the older NE side of the Square was undergoing major remodeling. The second Curia served for only fifteen or twenty years before new spaces were required, and the areas demarcated by the Comitium on either side of the Curia podium were used.

The remains of the original structure of Curia III are relatively meager, because some of its walls collapsed and were rebuilt in antiquity and others were torn out and modified. What survives amounts to the SE wall and the SE stretch of the base of the NE wall, but from these the plan of the new building can be deduced.

To build Curia III the superstructure of Curia II seems to have been demolished to the level of the podium, and the Curia now became a building of three parallel halls facing on, and filling the width of, the NE side of the Comitium. The central hall, a reconstruction of Curia II, was flanked by slightly smaller halls on the SE and NW.

The angle of the new building at its E corner is not a perfect right angle. The only right angle in the SE hall is its S corner, where it abuts the Comitium; the others are adjusted to fit the slightly irregular podium of Curia II. In the NW hall it was probably the N corner that was a right angle, for that would make the back line of the building continuous. The maximum depth of the SE hall (along its SE wall) was c. 9.50 m, while the maximum depth of the NW hall (along its SE wall) would have been only c. 9.15 m. The minimum depth of the NW hall (along its NW wall) would have been c. 9.00 m. This striking irregularity in the construction can be blamed partly on the fact that the builders were incorporating the central part of the NE wall of the podium of Curia II in the fabric of the new NE wall of Curia III and on the fact that the podium wall had not been built absolutely true in the beginning. But also, and this cannot be escaped, there is a haphazardness in the plan and lines of the building that suggests haste and indifference to precision of design.

The SE wall of the new Curia abuts the E corner of the Comitium without any attempt at bond. Presumably the NW wall was similarly abutted and unbonded. The new exterior walls, 2 p.R. (0.59–0.60 m) thick at the base, were built of spalled limestone blocks, roughly squared and of various sizes, but none very large, laid in irregular courses snecked with limestone chips. In the part preserved the courses show some tendency to diminish in height as they rise; then above a leveling course higher courses appear again. The mortar is peppery and not very strong; when it was uncovered, the face of the wall was found to be badly in need of pointing. The wall is built in two faces, without through bond except at the corners, doorways, and wall junctures, where there is quoining in larger, carefully squared blocks. To provide a better bond, the E corner of the podium of Curia II was torn out and rebuilt, so the wall ran continuous here, although it changed from limestone block and mortar to dry polygonal masonry in its middle stretch. Probably the N corner of the podium was similarly torn out and rebuilt, but this was destroyed subsequently, so certainty is impossible. The wall, where preserved, is footed on bedrock, but without a footing course, and the bedrock was not trimmed to receive it. In the base of the SE wall three leveling courses can be seen.

At 96.31–96.35 m.a.s.l. is a setback of 0.14–0.15 m, probably ideally $\frac{1}{2}$ p.R., on the inner face of the SE wall. This was clearly for a floor; just below it are sockets for joists to support a floor. These are c. $\frac{3}{4}$ p.R. (0.222 m) square at intervals of 1.25–1.30 m. Originally there must have been six such joists; traces of three remain. Remains of construction of this period above the setback show only a windowless wall a maximum of 5.47 m long and 1.05 m high. This shows no trace of either wall finish or pavement.

In the NE wall of the SE hall's lower story is a doorway 2.14 m wide. Its jambs are quoined, but untrimmed; its threshold is composed of two blocks of limestone, 0.96 m and 1.18 m long. The sill is 0.59 m wide, the thickness of the wall, cut down behind 0.03 m to mask the lower edge of the door that closed against it. Just behind the jamb on either side is a shallow square cutting, 0.10–0.11 m on a side, for the metal shoe of a *cardo*. The central portion, where there might have been slots for *pessuli* that secured the leaves, has been broken away. A generally similar doorway in the NE wall of the NW hall is so much narrower (1.46 m) that it is probably of later date. Inside the lower story of the SE hall there is no evidence of pavement or new plaster; the floor seems to have been simply beaten earth.

From the remains it is not possible to reconstruct the building in all its details, but the erratic nature of the plan and the expedient of incorporating the podium of Curia II into the fabric of the new building suggest that the simpler the reconstruction, the better. In our reconstruction the walls of the new Curia chamber, the central hall, have been run on the lines of those of Curia II, and the NE walls of the new side chambers have been made to agree with it in having a setback along the rear façade at the height of the top of the podium, although there was none along the sides. The doors to the new side chambers have been made somewhat smaller than that of the Curia, since they were clearly less important, and have been moved from the axes of these chambers toward the Curia for aesthetic reasons.

The problem of roofing the new building cannot be resolved on the basis of the evidence, since the wall is not preserved high enough to show joist holes. There are five possibilities: The roof of Curia II was almost certainly a gable running NE/SW; the roof of Curia III may have been an extension of this gable, ugly as that would be. Or it may have been a gable running NW/SE. The third possibility is that it was a series of three gables oriented NE/SW, one over each hall, but in this case it is not clear how the roof was drained, which is a serious problem. The fourth possibility, that there was a clerestory arrangement with the roof of the Curia rising above those to either side and simple lean-to roofs over the lateral halls, assumes a knowledge of clerestory architecture rather too early for Cosa. Finally, there may have been a gable running NE/SW over the Curia chamber and gables running NW/SE over the side chambers, a roof like that of the temple of Concordia in Rome. This seems aesthetically the best solution and so has been adopted. The height of the ceiling has been kept the same as that of Curia II and the roof reconstructed with timbers of the same measurements.

It is not certain which preceded, Templum Beta or Curia III. The lack of rewarding fills under the floors and around the foundations of Curia III means that its dating must depend on its relationship to other buildings, and Templum Beta is at no point tangent to it. But since Templum Beta was a modest structure and soon replaced by Temple B, and since Curia III was rather grandiose, at least in concept, it seems likely that Templum Beta is the earlier. It has been dated with some confidence at 209–197 B.C. (pages 51–56), which is the terminus post quem for Curia III, if the interpretation of the circumstances leading to its construction is correct; and if 180–175 B.C. is accepted as the date of Curia II, Curia III must follow that.

The NW face of the podium of Temple B was left unfinished in rough boulders clearly because the proximity of the SE wall of Curia III made working the stone into polygonal blocks an extremely difficult task, while on the other hand it effectively concealed this side of the temple podium from view. There can be no doubt that Curia III preceded Temple B. The date of Temple B is fixed by both the style of its terracotta revetments and the material found in the fill of the podium, 175–150 B.C. (pages 154–55); this is the terminus ante quem for Curia III. In the period of twenty-odd years in which the date of Curia III can fluctuate, the first half must be preferred.

The basement story of the SE hall of Curia III is well preserved, but so little survives of the three halls that faced on the Comitium that we can do no more than conjecture about their original appearance and use. The central hall must have continued to be the Curia proper and has been reconstructed with the broad steps along the sides presumed for Curia II (page 112). Indeed no change in its interior arrangements is envisaged. Those to either side must have served related functions, so closely are they tied to the Comitium/Curia complex. In the late Curia of Rome there was a tripartite division into Curia proper, Atrium Minervae, and court between. The architecture and function of the Atrium Minervae and court still remain, however, too obscure for them to be used as comparanda.[1] On the S side of the Forum of Pompeii are three large parallel halls, separate buildings, but all parts of a single architectural complex and concept, that offer an interesting parallel to the triad of Cosa. Here again, unfortunately, the identification of the individual members of the group has been questioned, although they are generally regarded as the Curia and other municipal offices of the city.[2] A third parallel is the series of three parallel halls opening on the Comitium of Paestum, where, too, the individual members cannot be identified (pages 259–63). Probably one or both of the side chambers was a tabularium, or archives, since the proceedings of the senate of the colony must have been recorded and filed, and in nearly a hundred years from the foundation of the colony these would have amounted to a considerable mass.

The rooms created in the basement stories of the new NW and SE halls evidently opened only to the NE, away from the Comitium and Forum, and were without connection with the chambers above. In view of the lack of windows and rustic finish of the SE room, it is perhaps best to presume that these had no public function, perhaps were even let out as shops.

Only some thirty to forty years after its construction, Templum Beta, the sacellum built by the SE side of the Comitium, was seriously damaged by the collapse of part of the NE wall of the altar platform, its collapse evidently provoked by an enlargement of the limestone sink noted earlier in this area (page 48). Instead of repairing the templum, the Cosans took this opportunity to replace it with a proper temple building. The planning of this temple is highly

1. See A. Bartoli, *Curia Senatus* (Monumenti romani 3, Istituto di Studi Romani [Rome, 1963]); N. Lamboglia, "Uno scavo didattico dietro la curia senatus e la topografia del foro di Cesare," *RendPontAcc* 37 (1966), 105; E. Nash, "Secretarium Senatus," in *In Memoriam Otto J. Brendel, Essays in Archaeology and*

the Humanities (Mainz, 1976), 191–204.

2. For the buildings at the S end of the Forum of Pompeii, see R. Bartocini, "La curia di Sabratha," *OAL* 1 (1950), 30, with bibliography; G. Fuchs in *RömMitt* 64 (1957), 154; L. Richardson, jr, *Pompeii, An Architectural History* (Baltimore, 1988), 269–73.

intricate, clearly designed to preserve as much as possible of the older sacred structure while rebuilding the sanctuary in an entirely new form. Similarly intricate planning has been discovered at a number of temple sites in central Italy and seems always to have been prompted by religious scruples.[3]

The new temple, Temple B, is raised on a massive podium with walls of polygonal masonry. Today the dimensions of the podium taken near the top measure 16.32–16.52 m by 9.59–9.80 m, probably ideally 55 p.R. by 33 p.R. (16.28 m by 9.77 m); the discrepancy is due to irregularities in the plan and damage worked by the roots of trees. The podium is placed overlapping the altar platform of Templum Beta so as to cover it for a depth of 3.55–3.60 m on the NE and to leave the remainder, 5.13 m in depth, as an apron, slightly off axis, in front of the temple. To build the temple podium the SE wall of Beta's platform was torn out for a length of c. 3.30 m, 0.88 m from its E corner, and the platform fill was sectioned by a trench c. 2.70 m wide running NW/SE.

The masonry of the NE, SE, and SW walls of the podium of Temple B strongly resembles that of the city walls of Cosa, except that the blocks in the podium are somewhat smaller, probably reflecting the difference in the sizes of the works, rather than their difference in date.[4] The stone is the gray pitted limestone of the hill of Cosa. The outer face of the wall is footed on bedrock, apparently trimmed to beds to receive the individual blocks as they were shaped. The wall is built in two faces, without through bonding, the outer highly finished where it was to be exposed, the inner left in unworked boulders. The irregular space between the two faces is packed with the spalls from the working of the blocks of the outer face. The outer face is of polygonal blocks with a tendency to quadrangular and pentagonal shapes. On both NE and SE it is built in four courses, except at the corners, which suggests that like the podium of Curia II (pages 107–11) it was constructed a course at a time. At the corners are larger masses with level, or nearly level, joint beds, which give a slight effect of quoining. The joints are tightly fitted, without anathyrosis, the joint beds usually 0.50–0.85 m deep, but sometimes as little as 0.33 m. Joggles occur in horizontal and oblique joints, and there is occasional snecking with small triangular blocks. There is no effect of arching and no appreciable batter. A count of blocks in the SE face gives an average surface area of 0.60 square meters.

The exterior face of the NE and SE walls is highly dressed. That of the SW wall, the principal façade, is highly dressed only at the S corner, where it was exposed. Where it was covered by the altar apron in front of the temple the joints are not so tightly fitted, and the face of the wall is more summarily chiseled. The NW wall, parallel to the SE wall of Curia III, presents a curious mixture of finishes. At the N corner, where the wall was exposed, the high finish of the NE

3. See, e.g., L. Crema, *L'architettura romana* (Enciclopedia classica, sez. 3, vol. 12.1 [Turin, 1959]), 45–58; A. Boethius and J. B. Ward-Perkins, *Etruscan and* *Roman Architecture* (Pelican History of Art [Harmondsworth, 1970]), 132–48.

4. Brown 1951, 28–58.

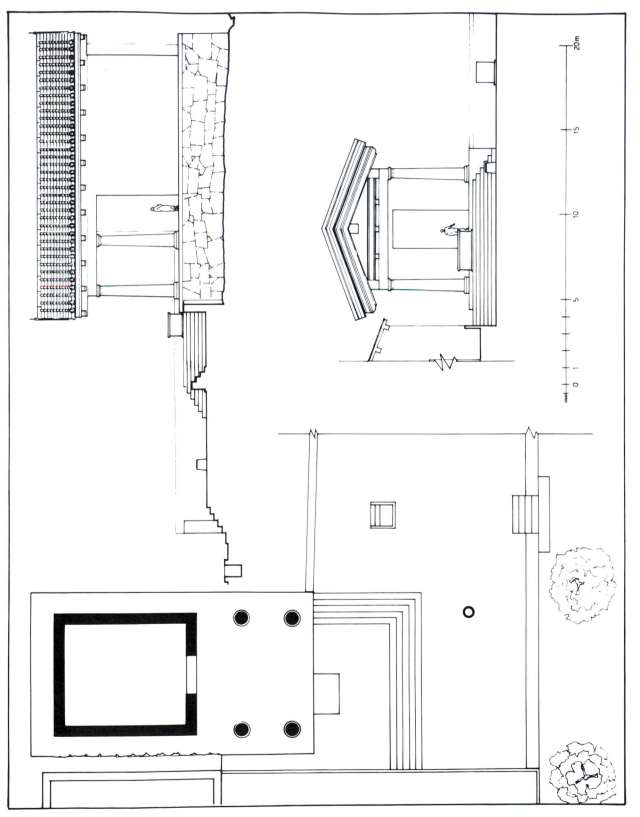

Fig. 56. Temple B, plan and SW and SE elevations

wall continues for a distance of 1.30 m. At the W corner, as far as the NE wall of Templum Beta, on which it abuts, the rougher finish of the SW front is maintained. The remainder of the wall is simply of unworked boulders piled up and snecked with smaller stone, the same construction that is used for the inner face of such podium walls. It is evident that this exterior face was left unfinished because the proximity of the Curia made working the blocks extremely difficult and also effectively hid this side of the podium from public view. An error of 0.10–0.11 m in the alignment of the lower courses of the stretch from the W corner to the NE wall of Templum Beta, evidently due to the interference of Beta's wall in the sight-line, is corrected in the top course.

The walls of this podium, although all clearly of one build and essentially of one masonry, are of varying thickness. The NW, NE, and SE walls are $7\frac{1}{2}$ p.R. (2.20–2.25 m) thick. The SW principal façade wall, however, is only 6 p.R. (1.75–1.85 m) thick.

In the interior of this podium were found ruins of a foundation wall built in two faces of unworked boulders of limestone bonded with the lateral walls. This carried the façade wall of the cella. Its axis lay 7.10 m behind the front of the podium; its width was only $5\frac{1}{2}$ p.R. (c. 1.60 m). The two compartments of the podium were both filled with a mass of red clay and other material in which no clear stratification could be detected.

Of the superstructure of the temple very little remains, only the base of most of the SE wall and short stretches of the bases of the SW, NW, and NE walls. Fortunately, the E and S corners and the SE jamb of the doorway to the cella are preserved, and these permit a reasonably certain reconstruction of the plan of the whole. On the exterior the cella measured 8.45 m by 7.23 m, presumably originally 28 p.R. by 24 p.R. (8.29 m by 7.10 m); on the axis of the walls it would have measured 7.69 m by 6.51 m.

The cella walls are 2 p.R. (0.59 m) thick, built of roughly squared blocks of the local limestone of medium size in two faces, which interlock but are without through bonding except at corners and at the doorway, where there is quoining in larger blocks of the same stone. The masonry is mortared, the mortar whitish and not especially strong. The blocks have spalled faces and are laid in irregular courses snecked with spalls; parts of only the two lowest courses survive. The walls run on the inner face of the podium wall, not on its axis, and are set back 4 p.R. (1.18 m) from the outer face of the podium along the sides, $4\frac{1}{2}$ p.R. (1.33 m) along the back. A tufa or sandstone molding similar to those found on the Arx of Cosa[5] must have run as toichobate to hide the unsightly joint between wall and podium, but no fragment that could be assigned to this came to light in the excavation.

The interior of the cella of the temple, 24 p.R. by 20 p.R. (ideally 7.10 m by 5.92 m), was found considerably modified by rebuildings and alterations of the medi-

5. See Brown 1960, 69–72.

eval period, as well as tragically damaged by the vandalism of clandestine diggers. No plaster at all was found on the remaining stretches of wall, but except in the W quadrant where the diggers had torn their pit, there were remains of two successive pavements. The upper one proved medieval and was lifted, the lower exposed and followed over the area SW of a medieval step built along the NE end of the cella. It was found to be everywhere badly broken and extensively and untidily patched with herringbone and lozenge bricks but appears to be the original pavement. It is of pale gray mortar, very friable, over a rudus c. 0.11 m thick, without statumen.

In the pavement and in the excavation of the fill in the center of the podium no trace of foundations for the base of the cult statue was encountered. These might have been removed in the course of modifications, but it is at least probable that the original cult image, or images, were of terracotta, as were the cult statues on the Arx, in which case there would have been no need for foundations.[6]

The width of the doorway is deduced from the single remaining jamb to have been $7\frac{1}{2}$ p.R. (2.22 m) between reveals. No trace of threshold or closure remains in the opening today, nor is there any sign in the jamb of damage caused by its removal. It must have been carefully fitted to the opening, and some of the blocks built into the step of the medieval period in the NE end of the cella may belong to it. Three blocks of travertine very crisply cut and badly worn along one edge but without cuttings for fittings may be blocks of the outer sill that ran across the opening. These are 0.90 m, 0.35 m, and 0.29 m long, uniformly 0.444 m wide and 0.35–0.40 m high. Another block of travertine is 0.89 m long, .048–0.50 m wide, and 0.29 m high and preserves in one end a rectangular cutting 0.16 m long, 0.135 m wide, and 0.02 m deep. This shows all the characteristics of an inner sill block, the cutting designed to hold the metal shoe in which the *cardo* turned. It would have fitted in the opening against the jamb and held the doorpost, evidently of rather large diameter. Yet another travertine block, 1.15 m long and 0.30 m high, may have belonged to this doorway too, but is now too broken to be positively identified.

The area of the pronaos is relatively deep, $22\frac{1}{2}$ p.R. (6.66 m), in contrast to the 4.29–4.37 m of Temple D on the Arx, which is a contemporary building of similar size.[7] Here there is now no trace of column settings. These must have been swept away in the medieval period, when it lost whatever remained of its pavement. This is shown by the remains of the superstructure of Templum Beta embedded in it to have been more than 0.13 m thick and more than 0.15 m above the pavement of the cella. Because the façade wall of the podium is conspicuously lighter than the side and back walls, it appears that it was not designed to hold columns and that what columns there were stood on the broad lateral walls.

In the excavation of Temple B the column elements discovered were far too small ever to have stood in the pronaos. Evidently these were salvaged from

6. See Brown 1960, 28–30, 50–58.   7. See Brown 1960, 25–47.

houses and villas in the neighborhood and used to decorate the little church built in the ruins of the cella in the eleventh century. But deep in the material used at the same time to fill and level the center of the Comitium was a nearly complete capital of travertine that would suit Temple B and no other building in the near neighborhood. Presumably it belonged to the W corner column and in the final collapse of the temple roof was toppled here and simply buried under rubbish. It is of the Hellenistic Tuscan order, the shaft plain and the abacus square. The abacus measures 0.71 m on a side and is 0.095 m deep (Pl. 108). The echinus is a steep, somewhat angular curve, 0.055 m deep, trimmed with a sharply angular necking band, 0.028 m deep, above a length of shaft of 0.073 m. The top edge of the abacus has been chipped away in a rough bevel, c. 0.05 m high and 0.074 m deep, on all four sides so that weight would fall only on the strong central block. The underside of the preserved shaft is gently convex to ensure firm seating on the shaft. In top and base surfaces are cuttings, c. 0.043 m by 0.048 m by 0.023 m, presumably for the lathe on which it was turned. The convex underside of the capital suggests that the column shaft was constructed of masonry of small sandstone slabs, like those of Temple D[8] and the Forum Porticus (pages 121–23). This was apparently usual at Cosa in this period.

Just in front of the temple the part of the platform of Templum Beta that was not engulfed in the podium of Temple B formed a small apron, slightly off axis to the NW. It was 5.13 m deep and 9.25 m wide. Clearly this must have held the altar of the temple, but since no fragment of this or trace of foundations for it was found, it is impossible to say what its form was. The absence of traces of foundations suggests that it was a small altar that would not require foundations, like the altar of the Deus Ignotus on the Palatine at Rome.[9] It seems likely that this was the original altar of Templum Beta and continued in use. If it stood tight against the podium of the temple, it need not have changed its location.

On two sides, SE and SW, the altar platform was approached by stairs. These might have been built in part of the blocks of the original stair of Templum Beta, but since the stair was now greatly enlarged, it is perhaps best to presume that it was completely rebuilt. The SE end of the substructure of the Templum Beta stair was now largely demolished, and the stair was continued around the corner of the apron to the S corner of the podium of Temple B. This is proved by the fact that the breach made in the SE wall of the platform of the templum to build the temple podium was repaired between the remaining part of the platform wall and the new temple podium with a wall of unshaped and unmortared boulders, clear indication that though the wall continued in use in this period, it was hidden from sight. The number of steps is calculated to have been six. The level of the forecourt of the temple was c. 95.70 m.a.s.l., that of the top of the altar platform c. 97.04; the six steps would each have been c. 0.22 m high, and if the

8. Brown 1960, 30–31.

9. See G. Lugli, *Roma antica, il centro monumentale*   (Rome, 1946), 401–3.

treads were 0.25 m wide they would fit neatly in the space at the S corner of the temple. No block that could have been part of the steps came to light in the excavation.

The level of the forecourt provided for the temple seems to have remained that of the forecourt of Templum Beta, of which it was an adaptation. The boundaries on the NW and SW and the approach from the Forum remained where and what they had been (pages 49–56). The NE boundary, however, was moved 5.13 m to the NE, and it seems likely that the SE boundary would have then been demolished and rebuilt in its entirety. The new NE forecourt wall, apparently of rather simple and rude construction, ran from the S corner of the temple podium to the N corner of the Carcer, so that it does not square with either of these buildings. It was clearly in its NW part rebuilt after the fire of the Augustan period, so only the SE stretch has any claim to being original, and even this is suspect because of the rehandling and repairing of the area at a later period (pages 245–50). The only part of the SE wall that survives is the NE stretch backed against the Carcer, which would have been a new creation of this period. Whether that stood on the line of the SE boundary of the terrace over the SE cistern is not clear; presumably it did not, for had it, the relationship of that boundary to the Carcer would be very odd indeed. However, originally were this terrace bounded on the SE, that boundary would still have lain somewhere in this vicinity.

The stretches of the walls that might be original have been destroyed to the top of the footing courses, which are simply set in earth. These are $1\frac{1}{2}$ p.R. (0.44 m) thick, built in two faces of small limestone boulders with a single spalled face. The faces do not interlock, and there is no through bonding, the space between the faces being filled with smaller stone and mortar. Presumably the upper parts of the walls were similar, and the walls were faced with mortar or plaster. Thus the builders created a somewhat irregular yard in front of the temple 12.30 m wide at its widest point and 24.60 m long at its longest, perhaps deliberately in the proportion 1:2.

No pavement was discovered at any point in this yard. Southeast of the temple stair a level beaten earth floor was found and followed over an area c. 5.00 m by 7.00 m. On this were found fragments of the decoration of the temple that fell here when the temple burned. The presumption is that the yard was floored with beaten earth throughout.

The formula for the reconstruction of the temple is deduced from the measurements of the cella and the relation of the measurements of the abacus of the single surviving capital to the width of the cella, which is 1:10. The temple building was the studied architectural part, curiously unrelated to the severe mass of the podium on which it stood. The podium projected beyond the building 4 p.R. along the sides, $4\frac{1}{2}$ p.R. in back, and $2\frac{1}{2}$ p.R. in front. Along the sides the line of the eaves just overhung the podium; in back it fell almost flush with it; in front the roof projected to draw the altar platform into union with it.

In overall dimensions the temple building measured 24 p.R. by 48 p.R. (7.104 m by 14.208 m) in the proportion 1:2. The pronaos would have been 20 p.R. (5.92 m) deep, the cella 28 p.R. (8.288 m) deep, in the proportion 5:7. The proportions of the pronaos, 20 p.R. by 24 p.R. would have been 5:6, the dimensions the reverse of those of the interior of the cella, where the proportion was 6:5. On the exterior the cella was 24 p.R. by 28 p.R., in the proportion 6:7. The lower diameter of the columns, provided by the abacus of the capital, was 0.71 m, the upper diameter 0.56 m. The projection of the bases can be presumed to have been approximately equal to the taper of the shaft, 0.15 m. The height of the columns, calculated as $6\frac{2}{3}$ diameters, would be 16 p.R. (4.736 m), two-thirds the width of the temple. On axis the spacing of the columns would have been 22 p.R. (6.512 m), the façade intercolumniation 5.8016 m, and the flank intercolumniation 5.2096 m, a difference of 2 p.R.

The height of the opening of the doorway is expected to have been twice its width, $7\frac{1}{2}$ p.R. (2.22 m). Its head ought to have come approximately level with the bottom of the capitals in order to leave space around it for a trim. If we presume that the sill of the door was raised only 0.026 m above the pavement of the pronaos, the requirement is met precisely.

The roofing of the temple is reconstructed on analogy with Temple D on the Arx of Cosa.[10] The terracotta revetment plaques of the decoration of the roof do not include architrave plaques, so we must restore the roof's height on probability. Its thickness is given by the upper diameter of the columns and the chipping away of the top edges of the abacus, 0.56 m. On analogy with Temple D, the height of the architrave of which is known ($1\frac{1}{2}$ p.R., 0.444 m), the height here has been restored as $1\frac{3}{4}$ p.R. (0.518 m). The dominant horizontal timbers, the joists or *tigna*, which spanned the whole of pronaos and cella and projected front and back, would have been beams of the weight of the architrave, 0.56 m thick over the lateral walls, where they ran as wall-plates and were loaded with the main rafters (*cantherii*), lighter over the central space, where they are restored as three, each 1 p.R. (0.296 m) thick, at intervals of 1.569 m on centers. A height of $1\frac{1}{2}$ p.R. (0.444 m) has been given them. Their projection front and back, if reconstructed by the formula of Vitruvius (4.7) as one-fourth the height of the columns, would fall $\frac{1}{2}$ p.R. short of covering the podium in back, while in front it would overhang the altar platform by $1\frac{1}{2}$ p.R. Since a heavy roof was part of the aesthetic of the Tuscan temple, it seems possible that the overhang was $\frac{1}{2}$ p.R. greater than normal and contributed to the archaistic quality that is shown by other elements to have been deliberate in this temple, but we have not had the temerity to abandon the Vitruvian formula and so reconstruct it. The failure of the joists as reconstructed to cover the podium in back is hard to understand in view of the parallels but must have had the visual effect of carrying the line of the edge of the sima to the ground.

10. See Brown 1960, 37–42.

Over the *tigna* the triangular wall of the tympanum was constructed to support the rooftree (*columen*). The angle of the gable has been set at 20°, which seems to be the average pitch of ancient roofs and has the aesthetic advantage of bringing the projecting ends of the *cantherii* level with the projecting mutules. The rooftree was probably of the same thickness as the lateral mutules, 0.56 m, since upon these elements were carried the main rafters.

The main rafters overhung the lateral walls of the temple, and their projection is fixed by Vitruvius's formula for determining the *stillicidium,* the total overhang or line of the lip of the eaves tiles: one-third the height of the columns.[11] This would fall 1.58 m beyond the side walls, and some 0.30 m of this would be the projection of the eaves tiles and revetments beyond the timbers of the roof. The projection of the *cantherii* has therefore been calculated as 1.28 m. Since the *cantherii* are the counterparts along the sides of the *tigna* on the front and back of the temple, they have been reconstructed as timbers of the same dimensions, 1 p.R. (0.296 m) thick and $1\frac{1}{2}$ p.R. (0.444 m) high. These are imagined to have been twelve in number, spaced at intervals of 1.184 m.

Above the *cantherii* ran the purlins (*templa*), perpendicular to the *cantherii,* restored as $\frac{3}{4}$ p.R. square; above these came the rafters, or *asseres,* restored as $\frac{1}{2}$ p.R. square, and above these the planking, or *opercula.* The tiling of the roof was carried out in tegulae of the standard $1\frac{1}{2}$ p.R. by 2 p.R. size, and imbrices to match; there would have been thirty-seven files of eleven tegulae, thirty-five of eleven imbrices, on either slope. The files of tiles at either end of the roof were sima tiles, rabbeted to take the raking sima decorated with strigillation. This in turn carried a pierced cresting. The undersurface of the tiles that projected along the eaves must have been painted with some pattern, but of these no fragment was recovered. The imbrices just above the eaves tiles were molded in one piece with the antefixes; these, 1 p.R. (0.296 m) in diameter, stood close together, with only half a diameter intervening.

Below and close against the eaves tiles on the sides and the sima on the front and back to mask the cluster of small timbers (*opercula, asseres,* and *templa*) ran a series of terracotta revetment plaques, $1\frac{1}{2}$ p.R. (0.444 m) high. Since the sum of small timbers is estimated to have been only 0.389–0.407 m high, the lower edge of these would have hung free over the *cantherii.* The regular position of the nailholes for the attachment of these plaques indicates that they were fastened to planking, or *antepagmenta,* that covered the ends of the small timbers.

The triangular space of the pediment may have been floored with a roof of lighter timbers than those of the main roof, but since it was filled with sculpture at one-half life size that was nailed to a wooden background, it seems better to suppose that it was simply floored with planking. Support for this notion can be found in the absence of any second series of revetment plaques for the masking of a roof. The engineering of the pediment's background is unclear from the

11. See Brown 1960, 39n.26.

evidence, but probably it stood flush, or nearly flush, with the façade, fitted around the *columen,* so that the sculptors could take advantage of the undecorated *cantherii* as background for the freestanding heads of the figures.

The effect and aesthetic of the temple as a whole is hard to appreciate. It stood in many ways aloof from the Forum, accessible only indirectly, protected by a high, blank wall. The façade could be appreciated only from a distance or very close at hand. On entering and climbing to the terraced forecourt one's first view was the oblique one, façade and flank together, set off and lofty above another stair. The precinct did not extend around the temple but stopped level with its façade, where a very Roman wall prevented the architectural sightseer from continuing around it. The temple shrank toward the protective bulk of the Curia.

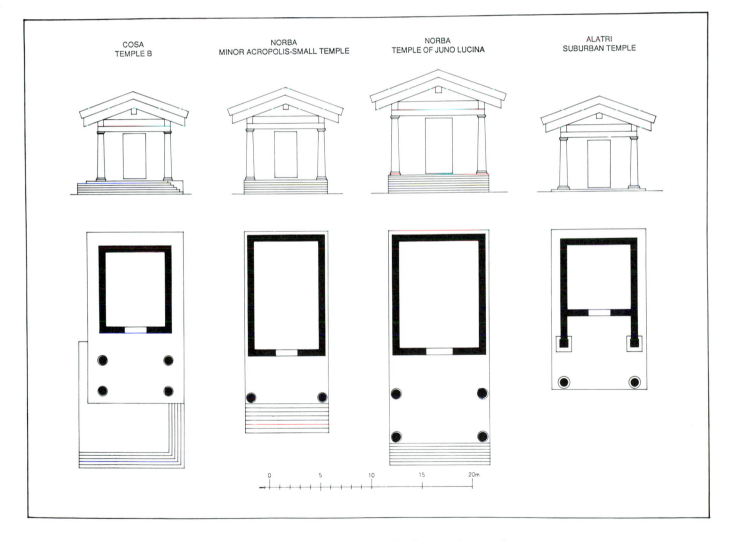

FIG. 57.   Temple B, comparison in plan and elevation with other similar temples

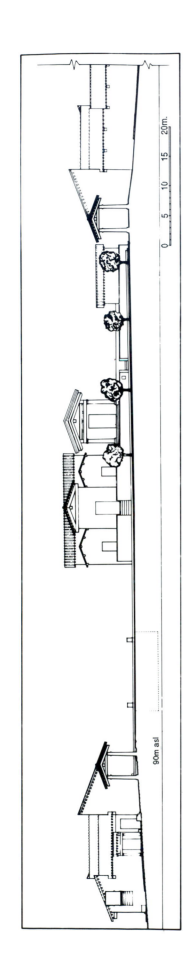

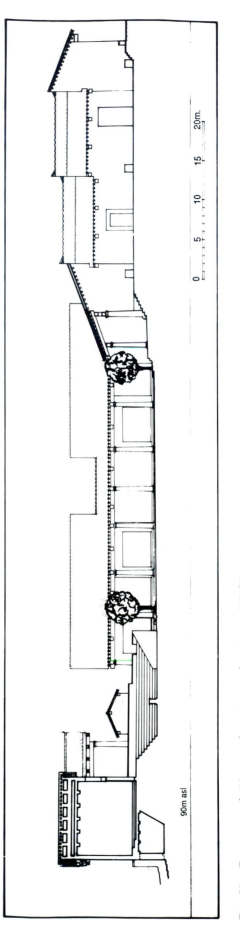

90m asl

90m asl

Fig. 58. Forum, as of 150 B.C., elevations and sections, NE/SE

The full view of the flank could be seen only by one coming from the Eastern Height along the road beyond the Carcer. From there the temple must have seemed dainty, almost precarious, poised lightly somewhat forward on the elegantly finished block of the massive podium that must have seemed big and high for it. From here the cella, withdrawing behind the great open pronaos, will have seemed very little more imposing in volume than the pronaos, if as much. And the absence of terracottas along the architrave and crown of the wall must have made the roof seem to sit very lightly, almost jauntily.

On the façade the temple would have been overshadowed by the Curia and would have seemed the more insubstantial for the steep flight of steps rising to the altar platform, but it would not have had to contend with the beauty of its podium and its seat on it. It would have seemed gracious, if simple, the spread of its eaves just covering the lines of the sides of the podium, the projection of the roof forward welcoming the worshiper into the pronaos and the door to the cella. In the pronaos the columns stood 16 p.R. (4.736 m) high, half the width of the temple podium, and were surmounted by a pediment whose apex, without acroterion, rose some 3.80 m higher. But this would have seemed far less ponderous than other such pediments, for instead of their weight of bands of repetitious terracotta plaques, it carried only a minimum: a single line of nailed plaques under sima and pierced cresting, and instead it was enlivened with sculpture, a dramatic assembly of active figures.

All this takes us back in time to the simple archaic temples about which we know so little, the temples whose revetment was spare and confined to essentials. But in those the aesthetic was refined, the simas and crestings massive things of beauty, the antefixes imposing or flamboyant, and the pediments or figures mounted on the rooftree splendid and sinister, full of secret life. Here the patterns of the revetment are fussy, ill suited to the scale of the building, the antefixes overdecorated bowls, the pedimental sculpture agitated and theatrical. Its ugliness is not provincialism. For some reason not immediately apparent, the Cosans wanted their temple to look much older than in fact it was, but went about achieving this in what seems a misguided manner (Figs. 56, 57).[12]

12. See L. Richardson 1960, 179–82.

Addendum 1
Temple B, Tiles and Terracotta Revetments
(Pls. 109–19)

In the course of excavations very numerous fragments of tiles, revetment plaques, and terracotta sculpture were discovered in areas around Temple B, especially close to the base of the walls of the podium along the sides and back. Determination of their position on the temple from study of the location of the fragments is complicated by the fact that in the clandestine excavation of the temple in the nineteenth century a large mass of building material and debris was disturbed and moved. Consequently, the evidence from all areas to the NW, including the narrow passage between Temple B and the SE wall of Curia III, where the finds were particularly rich, is untrustworthy. On the other hand, along the SE side of the temple the lower strata were discovered undisturbed, and since many of the fragments found here were soot blackened and mingled with ashes and other marks of a conflagration that destroyed the roof of the temple in the first part of the first century after Christ, the evidence here can be regarded as reliable. Such evidence is important in only a single case.

The original set of temple terracottas seems to have been of two manufactures, clearly distinct but each represented in the whole range of plaques used on the temple. In Fabric A, far the rarer fabric and not used for the freehand pedimental sculpture, the clay is buff in color, sometimes tending to pinkish or brownish, with a grog of fine peppery sea sand. The pieces were carefully pressed and retouched and slipped after pressing, and the firing is hard. The plaques were given a white priming coat before being painted, and good traces of the color frequently survive. In Fabric B the clay is red-orange in color in the antefixes and revetment plaques, varying from red-orange through brown and buff in the fragments of pedimental sculpture, with a very heavy grog of red-brown pozzolana ground to the consistency of coarse birdseed and mixed with a little fine gravel and small pearls of lime. The pressing is not always careful; the plaques are frequently pocked with air bubbles, and the piercing of the open cresting, which was done with a knife after pressing, is hasty and careless. There was little other retouching of the plaques after pressing; the slip was brushed on; and the firing is relatively soft, so that most of the fragments are badly weathered, especially along breaks. Like the plaques of Fabric A, those of Fabric B were given a white priming coat before being painted, but perhaps because of the softness of the firing, little of this or of the color survives.

The explanation of the enormous difference between the two fabrics is both important and difficult. The absence of pozzolana in the grog of Fabric A suggests that it is the older fabric; the inexpertness of the manufacture of the plaques of Fabric B suggests that they were an experiment with a new technique. Two explanations seem possible: first, that the pieces of Fabric A were imported from some other city where the use of pozzolana as grog was not yet developed, and these were then imitated at Cosa in Fabric B, or second, that the pieces of Fabric A were old pieces manufactured for the decoration of another Cosan temple and left in storage together with their matrices, which were then brought out and used for the decoration of the new temple. The second explanation seems far more probable. Were the pieces of Fabric A imported, it is hard to see why both matrices and a few finished plaques should have been imported together, and the matrices used for Fabric B must be original because there is no difference in measurements between the fragments of the two sets. Moreover, there is considerable circumstantial evidence to support the second explanation. Fabric A appears identical to the fabric of a set of plaques, some of them almost the same designs as those of Temple B, which were found used as building material in the walls of the cistern of the Capitolium of Cosa.[1] Those plaques are certainly remains of an earlier temple on the Arx, destroyed at the time of the building of the Capitolium, and the Capitolium must be dated within a few years of Temple B.[2] The use of plaques of the same design for the decoration of several temples of a city is well attested at Cerveteri, Orvieto, and Civita Castellana. And the designs of the Temple B plaques are rather third than second century in style. Despite the introduction of pedimental sculpture, an important innovation in the architecture of the Tuscan temple, Temple B is really more representative of the early, more regional architecture of the colony than it is of a new architecture that was beginning to spread through Italy after the Second Punic War.

Roof Tiles

In spite of the usual mass of tile fragments encountered in the excavation of the temple, no whole tiles were recovered and no fragments of ordinary imbrices or tegulae in either Fabric A or Fabric B. A number of fragments of tiles preserving one whole measurement, length or width, were collected, however, and these are evidence enough to be certain that the roof was entirely of ordinary imbrices and tegulae, the tegulae $1\frac{1}{2}$ p.R. by 2 p.R. (ideally 0.444 m by 0.592 m), the imbrices 1 p.R. (0.296 m) wide at the broad end. The tiles were of a great range of fabric, testimony to repairs of the roof at short intervals during the life of the temple, but no single fabric clearly predominated. No fragment that could be identified as belonging to an eaves tile was discovered, so it is

1. See L. Richardson 1960, 151–69, esp. 151–53.   2. Brown 1960, 102–3.

impossible to say whether these were decorated with a painted border on their undersurface.

Lateral Antefixes

TYPE A: SHELL ANTEFIX WITH A HEAD OF SILENUS (Pl. 109).

HEIGHT 0.296 M, WIDTH 0.296 M.

Seventeen fragments representing at least five antefixes were recovered. Two of the fragments are large, five small; all are of Fabric B. Nine of the fragments were found in areas NW of the temple that must be classed as dump areas; five, including the large fragments, were found in areas to the SE.

The antefix shows a benign Silenus head in a circular shell with a border of inscribed palmettes. The head is round with a bald, high-domed skull and leans far forward out of the shell. Around the temples is what appears to be a ribbon with round bosses or flowers at the center of the brow and above the ears. The ears are small and human and are spread against the background. The eyes have heavy lids and are of a kindly expression. The nose is small at the base, broad and flattened at the tip. The mouth is small with plump lips. A fairly heavy beard in thick curling tufts covers the lower cheeks and chin and spreads on the background. The head is without a neck and emerges from a smooth ground, which is separated from the border by a narrow fillet.

The border is decorated with small five-leaved palmettes, each inscribed by a fillet that curls up under the base of the palmette in volutes. The base of the palmette is a small knob; the leaves are sword-and-sickle. Between each pair of palmettes is a small palmette of three leaves as filling ornament. The edge of the shell is smooth, not scalloped, marked with a deep groove.

The base of the antefix is cut into the base of the circular shell without a worked transition. It is decorated with an egg molding between grooves that runs at an angle and gives the antefix a tipped appearance. It is not clear whether or not there were menisci. At the back is a flying strut of oval section.

The only color preserved is red, which is found at several points on the face.

TYPE B: SHELL ANTEFIX WITH THE HEAD OF A MAENAD
(Pls. 110, 111).

HEIGHT 0.296 M, WIDTH 0.296 M.

Eight fragments represent at least four antefixes. Only two of the fragments are of good size; all are of Fabric B. Six of the fragments were found in dump areas; none was found in a place where it might have fallen from the roof.

The head is framed in a shell with a plain edge decorated with a border of palmettes. The face is full, but youthful; like the Silenus it leaned far forward out of the shell. The hair is parted in the middle and drawn smooth over the crown with a loose wavy roll along the brow before a low stephane. The ears lie close to the head, half covered by the hair, without earrings. The features are small and clustered in the center of the face. The eyes are wide, the nose straight, the lips plump with a somewhat pursed look. The cheeks, jaw, and throat are heavy. Around the base of the throat runs a narrow band, like a necklace. The head stands against a plain ground set off from the border by a fillet.

The border is decorated with alternating S-spirals set in a zigzag, the triangular spaces between filled with palmettes of five leaves, sword-and-sickle, alternately standing and hanging. The edge of the shell is plain, marked with a shallow groove.

The base of the antefix is poorly preserved. The ornament appears to be either a row of paterae or flowers, or else a guilloche.

The only trace of color preserved is a trace of bright pink on one cheek.

In addition to the assigned fragments, there are nineteen fragments of these antefixes that cannot be assigned specifically to either the Silenus or the maenad type but belong to one or the other. Two of these are fragments of shells, eleven are fragments of struts, and six are fragments of tiles and terracotta packing from the joint between antefix and shell.

No close parallels for these antefixes are known; the best parallels come from the Arx of Cosa itself.[3]

Pedimental Antefixes

DIAMETER 0.23 M, HEIGHT 0.235 M.
Seven fragments represent at least two antefixes. Two of the fragments are large, three very small. The fabric is neither A nor B, but a brownish pink clay with a grog of a little finely ground pozzolana fired at a low temperature. The fragments all come from a single area, the dump in the passage between Temple B and the SE wall of Curia III.

The antefixes show a youthful satyr's head framed in a shell worked with a vine pattern. The satyr wears a smooth cap, or perhaps a flap of his nebris pulled over his head. Along the forehead are thick short locks of hair, and from the

---

3. L. Richardson 1960, 154–58, 186–88.

temples grow stubby horns. The ears are large and pointed. The ridge of the brow is heavy, the eyes deeply set. The nose is slightly snub, spreading at the tip and with large nostrils. The mouth has thick lips, slightly parted. At the base of the throat is knotted a nebris.

The shell is decorated with a serpentine vine along which grow tendrils, star flowers, and sprays of leaves. The edge of the shell and the base of the antefix are plain. From the preserved fragments it is impossible to tell whether there were menisci, but presumably there were, since the antefixes of this type found on the Arx had menisci. Behind is a flying strut of round section.

There are traces of red on the satyr's flesh, yellow on the nebris, and black on the ground of the border.

A number of fragments of other antefixes of this type and of its counterpart with a female head were discovered on the Arx of Cosa, where they were assigned to Temple D; they seem also to have been used as replacements on the Temple of Jupiter.[4] The fact that the fragments we have might have belonged to only two antefixes and were found out of context suggests that they might be strays or might be replacements for lateral antefixes in a late period when the difference in size was of small concern. Since, however, it seems likely that there was a little roof in the front of the pediment of a Tuscan temple even after pedimental sculpture had been introduced, there is some reason for believing that antefixes might have continued in use here, in which case these could be the antefixes of the pediment of this temple.[5]

Raking Cornice (Pl. 112)

HEIGHT 0.378 M, LENGTH 0.60 M.

Thirty fragments represent at least seven plaques of the type. Of these three are large, ten very small; three are of Fabric A, the others of Fabric B. The fragments were found in areas on all sides of the temple, eleven in areas to the NW that must be classed as dump, twelve in areas to the SE, including five fragments (among them the three large fragments) from the conflagration level. Only two fragments were found on the NE side of the temple and only two in the forecourt. It appears that when the roof fell, it slipped to either side and did not fall forward or back.

The design is in two zones. The upper zone is a series of narrow convex strigils turned out very sharply at a right angle at the top under a low, plain cornice in which there is a slot for setting an open cresting. The strigil tips project slightly

---

4. L. Richardson 1960, 174–75, 186–88.   5. See E. H. Richardson 1960, 303–12.

and are rounded; the strigils terminate at the base in a horizontal fillet of rectangular section and are separated from one another by flat channels, as though they were simply applied to a ground plate. The lower zone is a flat ground decorated with palmettes in low relief of two types alternating. One is a palmette of seven leaves, sword-and-sickle, with a solid semicircular base; the lowest pair of side leaves curl upward, the other two pair down. The other palmette is of five leaves, sword-and-sickle, with an oval bead for a base; both pair of side leaves curl up. Around this palmette runs an inscribing ribbon of bead section that curls up under the base of the palmette in a pair of simple volutes. To fill the interstices between each pair of palmettes circular beads are added in the field, one above and one below, and one is inserted at the base of each inscribed palmette. At the base of this zone to finish it runs a second plain fillet, below which is a deep tenon for insertion in another member.

A few traces of paint survive. On one fragment the coloring of the strigilation is preserved; the strigils are orange, the spaces between them blue, yellow, and red, repeating. In the lower zone the only color preserved is on the base fillet; it is red.

On the backs of these fragments are very numerous traces of hard white mortar mixed with black sand. It is evident that such a cornice, simply inserted in a base member and expected to carry an open cresting, would be extremely fragile, yet there is no sign of strutting of any sort on the pieces preserved. It appears that instead of strutting, a low wall was built on the tiles and the plaques then mortared against this.

Presumably the terminal plaque of this series was finished with some sort of acroterial figure or animal, but no fragment that can be assigned to any of these was recovered. One plaque, however, was cut differently from the others, the cut falling between the third and fourth palmettes instead on the center line of the fifth. Probably this was the plaque just before the terminal plaque on the right-hand slope of the roof. Possibly some of the fragments assigned to columen plaques are actually fragments from these figured plaques, but there is no way of telling what they might be.

Tiles for the Setting of the Raking Cornice (Pl. 113)

HEIGHT 0.07 M, LENGTH PRESUMABLY C. 0.592 M.
Three fragments from three different tiles; one is of Fabric A, two of Fabric B. Two fragments were found SE of the temple, one NW.

The terminal tegulae along the raking edge of the roof were specially designed to hold the raking cornice. Along the outer edge, instead of the usual flange, there was a torus set off above and below by narrow steps, the whole 0.07 m high. Behind the torus is a wide mortise with slightly flaring walls to receive the tenon at the base of the raking cornice. It is 0.034 m wide at the top, 0.026 m wide at the bottom, and 0.026 m deep.

A few traces of red paint survive on one of the fragments, but not enough to show whether the torus was solid red or whether there were stripes or a design in several colors. The step under the torus seems to have been painted solid red.

Open Cresting A (Pl. 114)

HEIGHT 0.318 M, LENGTH UNKNOWN.

Three fragments are all possibly from the same plaque, all of Fabric A. Two were found in the dumps of the clandestine excavation NW of Temple B, one in the late fill in the middle of the Comitium.

The design is closely related to that of open cresting B and is reconstructed from a number of fragments of identical plaques found on the Arx of Cosa, especially in the vicinity of Temple D.[6] At the base of the cresting is a plain tenon for insertion in the raking cornice, above which runs a narrow fillet. The main field is decorated with piercing in four zones. At the base are pierced semicircles with a three-leaved sword-and-sickle palmette between each pair. In the middle are two staggered rows of pierced circles with a ribbon of bead section run in serpentine loops around them. At the top is another row of pierced circles connected to one another by arching ribbons of bead section. Between each pair of these circles is a triangular bead, and above this stands a small palmette of seven leaves, sword-and-sickle. The top edge of the plaques is cut in a rounded zigzag over the tops of the palmettes, and there seem to have been menisci inserted in alternate crests.

The traces of color on the fragments show that the triangular bead in the top zone was light blue and the field under the arching ribbons and the faces of the pierced circles of this zone were red. The faces of the pierced semicircles and their field were also red. The serpentine ribbon was blue.

Fragments of identical crestings have been found at Talamone and Tarquinia. The fact that only three fragments of this cresting were found in the vicinity of Temple B inevitably raises doubts that it was used on that temple, but the facts that it is of Fabric A and a close relation of open cresting B, which was certainly used on the temple, increase this probability.

6. L. Richardson 1960, 189–91.

Open Cresting B (Pl. 115)

HEIGHT 0.275 M, LENGTH 0.537 M.

Sixty-six fragments represent at least five plaques of this type. Most of the fragments are small; only one is of considerable size; all are of Fabric B. The fragments were found in concentration toward the NW of Temple B, some forty in the NW room of Curia III and just outside this room to the NE, especially in the lower levels in these areas. Thirteen more were found in the dumps of the clandestine excavation and six in the Comitium. Only three were found in areas to the SE of the temple and only three in the forecourt, but one of the latter was the single large fragment of the cresting. The explanation of this distribution seems to be that at the time the temple roof burned the cresting had been relegated to the rear façade, having been replaced on the main façade sometime earlier with another cresting.

The design of the cresting is simple and severe. At the base is a tenon to fit in the raking cornice, above which runs a plain fillet of rectangular section. The main field is pierced in four zones. At the base is a row of pierced pointed arches without decoration. In the middle are two staggered rows of pierced circles with a relief ribbon run in serpentine loops around them. At the top is a row of smaller pierced circles from which spring palmettes of five club-shaped leaves standing well apart. The top edge of the plaques is cut in a rounded zigzag along the top of this row of palmettes, and in each crest is a hole for fixing a meniscus or similar element. In one of these holes was discovered a small fragment of iron inserted without a lead setting.

Traces of color show that the fillet at the base was red, and possibly the serpentine ribbon in the middle field was also red, but the colors of the ground and the palmettes are not preserved.

Along the tenon at the base is pierced a row of small holes, usually rectangular in section and tapering from front to back, as though made with a small nail after pressing and before firing. The interval between these holes is not known, but the frequency of their occurrence in the fragments suggests that it was relatively short, perhaps c. 0.15 m. The obvious explanation of these is that they were for wires to lace the cresting to the raking cornice, but corresponding holes do not appear in the raking cornice, and some of the holes do not go through the plate. Possibly they were for short nails that braced the cresting in its mortise and gave the setting of lead or mortar better purchase.

A somewhat larger and much more beautifully executed version of the same cresting is known from a number of fragments found on the Arx of Cosa and associated there with the Temple of Jupiter.[7] In those fragments the fabric is identical with Fabric A, heavy and with a grog of sea sand, and the

---

7. L. Richardson 1960, 159–60.

pressing and piercing are careful and expert. In these the piercing is carelessly done, evidently after pressing, and the plaques were not retouched before firing. Presumably this set of plaques was made from a matrix taken from a plate of the other with the successive shrinking in firing that is a familiar phenomenon.

The other near relation of this cresting is open cresting A and its duplicates from Talamone and Tarquinia.

Revetment Plaques with a Design of Crossed Ribbons (Pl. 116)

HEIGHT 0.45 M, WIDTH 0.517 M.

One hundred thirty-nine fragments were recovered, most of them relatively small, but one consisting of about half a plaque and several equal to one-quarter of a plaque or more. By far the large majority of fragments are of Fabric B, but a small group are of Fabric A. The fragments were found on all sides of the temple in great quantity, especially along the SE side and in the conflagration level on this side, many of them being blackened by the fire.

The design of the plaque is in three zones. At the top is a deep cavetto under a plain cornice; this is decorated with a Lesbian leaf, somewhat schematically drawn, and set off from the main field by a fillet of rectangular section. The main field is decorated with a pattern of diagonally crossed ribbons rolled in volutes at their ends that frame stylized flowers of two sorts. In the square spaces across the middle of the field are star flowers of eight lozenge-shaped petals radiating from a button center; between the ends of these petals appear the tips of leaves or other petals. In the triangular spaces at the top and bottom of the field are flowers seen in profile, a stem from which branch two leaves and a lily-like trumpet springing outward in points under a central group of three small drops. At the bottom of the field is a second fillet. The lower border consists of two elements, a chain of small hanging palmettes alternating with lilies, connected by arching and interlacing stems, and a row of short dentils connected along the top by a fillet.

Despite the great number of fragments, comparatively little of the color is preserved. The Lesbian leaf was painted red, black, and blue and possibly other colors, the flower sometimes black, the leaf sometimes blue and sometimes red. The fillets and crossed ribbons of the main field were red, parts of the flowers at least bright blue. The ground of the chain of palmettes and lilies was black.

These plaques are a variant of a type found in quantity on the Arx of Cosa, many of the fragments built into the walls of the cistern of the Capitolium.[8] The minor differences are principally in workmanship; the cistern group plaques are of great refinement of design and manufacture, while the Temple B plaques show carelessness in the design of the Lesbian leaf and poor pressing and firing. The other notable difference is in the length of the dentils; in the cistern group plaques the dentils are long, 0.086 m, while in the Temple B plaques they measure only 0.025 m. There are small variations in many other measurements, and it appears also from the existence of fragments of Fabric A among the Temple B plaques that there had been separate matrices from the beginning. Moreover, the difference in measurements is not of a type that could be explained as shrinkage in the manufacture of a new matrix from an existing plaque.

The discovery of fragments of these plaques in such large numbers on all sides of the temple and especially all along the SE side can only mean that they were used to revet some part that appeared on all sides. They are therefore thought to have covered the combination of small timbers (*opercula, asseres* and *templa*) that made up the covering of the roof under the tiles, nailed to planking (*antepagmenta*) that masked the ends of these small members. As the height of the plaques (0.45 m) is greater than the calculated sum of the small timbers (0.389–0.407 m), so the lower edge would have hung free over the *cantherii*. The possibility that these plaques were used to revet more than one member has been considered and rejected. The other beams of the roof must have been either painted or left undecorated.

Repair of the Decoration

Sometime in the later part of the second century B.C., or perhaps more likely in the first quarter of the first century, it became necessary to repair the terracotta decoration of Temple B. Probably there were leaks in the roof by then, and one may assume that while the scaffolding to repair it was up, it was decided to touch up the decoration as well. It was not a question of redecoration, but rather of filling in the gaps, and for this a variety of expedients was employed. Some of the pieces that were obtained must have been antiques, entirely out of fashion at this time. Others were designed in the current fashion but poorly made, formulaic designs clumsily pressed and finished. In the case of the open cresting we can see that the original cresting was probably entirely, or almost entirely, removed from the front of the temple and relegated to the back to make way for the new design. In the case of the nailed revetment plaques the new ones seem simply to have been inserted at random.

8. L. Richardson 1960, 163–64.

ANTEFIXES (Pl. 117)

MAXIMUM HEIGHT AND WIDTH 0.36 M.

Two closely related types of antefix are represented, one by a single, almost complete, shell without the head it framed and without its base, the other by eight fragments of shell pressed in a matrix that was a blurred and retouched version of the other. They all come from areas classed as surface.

The almost complete shell is decorated with a deep border of S-spirals alternating in direction from which rise alternate palmettes and lilies. The palmettes are of five club-shaped leaves, except the central one, which has seven, springing from small arches. The lilies have prominent sepals above a drop-shaped base from which rise pointed petals in two zones of three each. Each center petal has a central rib. The outer edge of the shell is scalloped to follow the top of the border, and the head at the center was set off by a narrow fillet. Traces of bright pink are preserved on the ground around the S-spirals in several places, but no other color. There is a trace of a gooseneck strut behind, but none of a meniscus.

The clay is bright reddish brown over a grayish brown core with a heavy grog of very fine black sand. The antefix does not appear to have been slipped. The firing is hard, and neither surface nor break is badly weathered. The antefix was given a heavy white priming coat before being painted.

The fragments of imitations of this show pointed and rounded scalloping in the trimming of the outer edge at the sides and a thickening of the wall to strengthen it at the top, so that there is a scalloped border here in relief within a plain-edged bowl. The ground of the border was black, and there is a trace of pink on one lily. It is not clear whether there was a meniscus. There was a thick flying strut of round section behind.

The clay is creamy to pinkish buff, of even color. The grog is of augite and black sand, used sparingly. The pieces were slipped before firing, and the firing is moderately hard with a slight tendency to weather. The pieces were given a heavy white priming coat before being painted.

An excellent parallel for this design is offered by an antefix from Orvieto dated by Andrén fourth or third century B.C.[9]

OPEN CRESTING (Pl. 118)

HEIGHT 0.37 M, LENGTH 0.505 M.

Thirty-nine fragments were recovered, of which two are large and fourteen small, the minimum number of plaques represented being five. The fragments were widely scattered, but there was a concentration of them at the S corner of

---

9. Andrén 2: pl. 72, fig. 244.

the temple, especially in the lower levels, which suggests that this cresting decorated the main façade of the temple at the time it burned. Several of the fragments show fire blackening. The relative rarity of fragments found NE of the temple indicates it was not used on the rear façade.

The design is the familiar one of pierced triskelia and figure-eights under a row of palmettes. At the base is a tenon for insertion in a raking cornice, above which runs a fillet, concave with rolled edges. The main field is filled with a zone of pierced triskelia inscribed in circles alternating with figure-eights, also pierced, with open arches above and below them. All the ribbons of this design are slightly concave with rolled edges. The triskelia have little discs at their centers and turn clockwise. Under them hang fleurs-de-lis in low relief. At the top of the plaque stands a row of palmettes of seven club-shaped leaves springing from small pierced arches. The upper edge of the plaque is scalloped around the five center leaves of each palmette, and there is a hole for a meniscus in the center leaf of each. In two cases a stump of iron with a lead setting is preserved. In two other cases a rivet of lead was driven through the front of the plate to secure the meniscus. There are numerous traces of red on the fleur-de-lis, the figure-eight and the arches above and below it, the top palmettes, and at least one arm of the triskelion, but of no other color.

The clay is generally light pinkish buff, sometimes brownish. The grog is pozzolana used in moderation and ground fine. The pressing is only fair, and the piercing not everywhere careful. The plates were given a good buff slip and fired hard. The breaks are jagged and have not weathered.

Open crestings of this design are common among later Hellenistic decorations. At least two close parallels to this one were found on the Arx of Cosa and appear to have decorated the Capitolium.[10] Their main difference from these is that the triskelia turn counterclockwise.

REVETMENT PLAQUES OF SERPENTINE DESIGN (Pl. 119)

HEIGHT OVERALL 0.425 M, EFFECTIVE HEIGHT TO COVER BEAMS 0.365 M, WIDTH 0.34 M, MAXIMUM PROJECTION OF CORNICE 0.08 M.

Thirty-four fragments, only one of which is large and seventeen of which are small, represent at least five plaques, but probably more; they were found in widely scattered areas around Temple B, twelve in areas that must be classified as dump, but with a certain concentration along the SE side of the temple in the lower levels, which indicates these were hanging on the temple roof when it burned.

The design is the familiar one of a ribbon run in serpentine loops filled with

10. L. Richardson 1960, 210–11, 240–42.

palmettes under a strigilated top border. The strigils are concave, the passages between them slightly narrower than the strigils; there are eleven strigils to a plaque springing from a roll and crowned with a plain cornice. The main field is covered with a series of palmettes alternately standing and hanging surrounded by a concave ribbon run in serpentine loops. The palmettes are of five well-rounded leaves, each leaf bordered and given a pronounced cushion center, springing from a drop-shaped base. They are connected by reversing S-spirals with volute ends that curl over under each palmette and are bound together by a plain band. These S-spirals zigzag back and forth across the center of the design. As filling ornaments there is a series of triangles containing darts along the top and a series of ribbed lozenges across the middle. The lower edge of the plaque is cut in scallops following the loops of the serpentine ribbon. A series of three nail holes appears in the strigilation, but none in the main field. The only traces of color are red, found at a few points on the ribbons and palmette leaves but without a clear pattern.

The clay is a fine light tan, sometimes with a pinkish core, with a grog of pozzolana used with moderation. The pressing is only moderately careful, and the surface is frequently pitted with small bubbles of air. The firing is hard, and breaks do not weather badly. The plaques were given a white priming coat before being painted.

Good parallels for the design are extremely common in late Hellenistic temple terracottas. The best perhaps is one at a considerably larger scale that comes from the Arx of Cosa, where it was used on the Capitolium in the fourth period of its decoration at the end of the first quarter of the first century B.C.[11] Others not so close have a wider spread in chronology.

11. L. Richardson 1960, 257–58.

Addendum 2

Terracotta Sculpture from Temple B

(Pls. 120–225)

In the excavation of Temple B were found more than two hundred and fifty fragments of terracotta sculpture. Of these, one hundred and thirty are of a coarse fabric, with an exceptionally heavy grog, thick-walled, and porous, with the texture characteristic of architectural terracottas of the original decoration of the temple, both mold-made plaques and antefixes and hand-modeled reliefs. The other fragments, not all of a single manufacture, are of better levigated clay with a fine grog and the dense, smooth texture characteristic of mold-made votive terracottas. These are designated in this report by the terms "architectural" and "votive," although votive figures were sometimes made of "architectural" clay, as for example, the famous portrait bust of a young woman now in the Vatican found in a votive stips at Caere (Cerveteri) in 1826 and a fine portrait of a young man also in the Vatican.[1] Both busts were modeled by hand; apparently the coarser, livelier "architectural" fabric lent itself better to modeling than the fine dense clay used for most ex-votos. On the other hand mold-made ex-votos were occasionally made of "architectural" clay; there are two examples from the Arx at Cosa.[2] And large-scale ex-votos were sometimes modeled by hand in the "votive" fabric (see below II i and ii).

I i. Pedimental Sculpture

Seventy-five fragments assignable to the pediment of Temple B were recovered, of which sixteen are composed of a number of joining fragments. Twenty-five are parts of figures at one-half life size; twelve are parts of background plaques, often with relief; thirty-eight are miscellaneous unidentifiable scraps, a few of which may have belonged to the frieze I ii (pages 182–84). All but eight fragments, a knee (I i 16a) and seven indeterminate scraps, were found either in the

The text of this report was written in 1954. Since then Hellenistic terracotta pedimental sculpture from Etruria and Latium has been studied by a number of scholars. A recent survey of the subjects and forms of the pediments appears in F.-H. Massa-Pairault, *Recherches sur l'art et l'artisanat etrusco-italique à l'époque hellénistique* (École Française de Rome, 1985), 135–85.

The footnotes in this chapter have been revised and supplemented accordingly.

1. Vatican inv. 14107; R. West, *Römische Porträt-Plastik* (Munich, 1933), pl. 23, fig. 92. Vatican inv. 13848; ibid., pl. 7, fig. 20.

2. E. H. Richardson 1960, 378–79, nos. 3 and 4, figs. 93, 94.

excavation along the SE side of the podium of Temple B or in the Comitium/
Curia to the NW.

Fabric. The clay varies in color from red-orange through medium brown to
buff. It is coarse in texture with an exceptionally heavy grog of large angular
grains of dark red pozzolana mixed with a little coarse sand and occasional small
pearls of lime. The exposed surface was originally covered with a fine buff slip
that more or less concealed the grog, but the sculptures were fired at a relatively
low temperature and tend to weather badly. As a result the slip on most fragments has entirely disappeared, and the surface is often deeply pitted. The
breaks are rough and crumbly. No trace of paint or priming coat is preserved.

Most of the pieces are thick walled, although the heads I i 14 and I i 15a and the
torso I i 15b are notable exceptions. The foot I i 13c, leg I i 19, arm I i 22, and hand
I i 16b are solid. The modeling is skillful and lively. That of the heads, particularly
I i 14 and I i 15a, is delicate; the drapery falls in a variety of crisp, sharp-edged
folds with relatively little attempt at distinguishing the texture of different fabrics, although the weights of fabrics are differentiated, at least where one lies
over another (e.g., I i 17; cf. I i 15b with I i 18).

CATALOGUE: BACKGROUND PLAQUES

The fabric of the following twelve fragments, like that of the figures, is coarse
and crumbly, and probably partly for this reason, they are uncommonly thick,
ranging from 0.025 m to 0.055 m. The average thickness varies between 0.028 m
and 0.032 m. The underside was packed against planking, but in wads, so as to
leave gaps and hollows in the back surface. Two fragments show a ridge made
by the edge of one of the boards against which the clay was worked. The
background plaques of the pediments from Civita Alba show the same peculiari-
ties, marks of planking and folds and fissures in the wadded clay of the underside.[3] Zuffa, in his important publication of this pediment, argues that the clay of
these plaques must have been relatively dry when it was worked,[4] but the great
thickness of the walls of the background may better explain this particular in the
Cosan fragments.

The upper surface is rough and irregular, in places scratched and grooved with
a sharp tool, in places swept by broad, shallow parallel grooves, as if by the
knuckles of a closed fist, in places roughened with added strips and crusts of
clay. In two cases folds of drapery are modeled on the surface; in another the tips
of two long flight feathers of a wing have been added in relief. A fourth has a

3. Bologna, Museo Civico: Andrén 1: 298–300, 2:
pls. 98–100; Massa-Pairault, 143–46.

4. M. Zuffa, "I frontoni e il fregio di Civitalba nel
Museo Civico di Bologna," *Studi in onore di Aristide
Calderini e Roberto Paribeni* 3 (Milan, 1956), 272, and
fig. 2 on 276.

surface covered with drapery, which projects at roughly a right angle. A section of a finished edge is preserved on five pieces; this is in no case a straight edge but always slightly curved and beveled so that the separate members locked into one another to make a continuous frieze. The same sort of joining occurs in the pediments of Civita Alba and Talamone.[5] Nail holes, which were pierced before firing for fastening the plaques to a wooden backing, appear along broken edges on three fragments. There is no trace of any supporting wall to carry the statues forward from the background plane, nor is there any broken fragment in this fabric that could have been part of such a wall, as there were in the pediments of the Temple of Jupiter and the Capitolium on the Arx at Cosa.[6] The figures of this pediment evidently did not project so boldly as those of the Arx temples; instead they were attached to the background plaques directly, or by their drapery. In this, again, the pediment of Temple B resembles those of Civita Alba and Talamone;[7] probably it was characteristic of the whole group of mythological pediments of this period.

I i 1 (*Pl. 120*). A large fragment made up of six joining fragments showing the ends of two long feathers appliquéd in relief at the left. Along the left side is a convex finished edge, beveled at the back. The feathers were roughly modeled, a heavy groove drawn down the center of each and short, slanting, oval strokes run in chevrons along these.

L. 0.345 m; w. 0.185 m; th. 0.022–0.032 m.

I i 2 (*Pl. 121*). A large fragment, the surface covered with moving drapery. One deep fold curves to the left from the right upper and lower corners; two shallower folds, forked above, appear to the left. At the right side of the fragment a round shield, convex with an offset rim, projects from the background along its diameter. Along the left of the fragment something has been broken away from the surface, very likely the figure that held this shield. Below the shield on the right is a concave finished edge.

L. 0.25 m; w. 0.175 m; th. 0.022–0.048 m; l. of finished edge 0.12 m.

I i 3. Part of a thick plaque with one slightly convex finished edge. A stiff rectangular appliqué with a rippled surface, probably a corner of drapery, is attached to the face.

L. 0.22 m; w. 0.06 m; th. 0.036–0.055 m.

I i 4. Fragment preserving one slightly concave finished edge and portions of two nail holes along the broken edge.

L. 0.17 m; w. 0.07 m; th. 0.025–0.035 m.

5. Civita Alba: Andrén 1.298; Zuffa, (note 4 above), 274–80. Talamone: Andrén 1: 228; O. W. von Vacano, "Ödipus zwischen den Viergespannen," *RömMitt* 68 (1961) 45.

6. E. H. Richardson 1960, 315, figs. 3 and 4, 335, fig. 24a.

7. Talamone: Andrén 1: 228, 2: pl. 82, fig. 85; O. W. von Vacano, B. von Freytag gen. Loringhoff, *Il frontone di Talamone e il mito dei "Sette a Tebe"* (Catalogo della mostra, Firenze, Museo Archeologico, 14 febbraio–3 ottobre 1982), figs. 1–22, pls. 2–11. Civita Alba: Andrén 1: 298, 2: pls. 98–100.

I i 5. A large piece composed of three joining fragments. Extremely rough surface and heavily wadded back.

L. 0.223 m; w. 0.22 m; th. 0.029–0.032 m.

I i 6. Similar fragment.

L. 0.172 m; w. 0.135 m; th. 0.029–0.032 m.

I i 7. Similar fragment. The back shows the impression of the edge of a plank of the backing against which the artist worked.

L. 0.165 m; w. 0.13 m; th. 0.028–0.033 m.

I i 8. Similar fragment, the surface roughened in broad shallow stripes. A small portion of a nail hole appears at one broken edge, and a small section of finished edge is preserved.

L. 0.183 m; w. 0.155 m; th. 0.032–0.035 m; l. of finished edge 0.045 m.

I i 9. Large fragment with a very rough surface, preserving part of a finished edge and a small portion of a nail hole at one broken edge. Across the back appears the line of a board of the backing.

L. 0.24 m; 0.22 m; th. 0.028–0.05 m; l. of finished edge 0.07 m.

I i 10. Small fragment.

L. 0.10 m; w. 0.06 m; th. 0.025–0.03 m.

I i 11. Small fragment.

L. 0.093 m; w. 0.08 m; th. 0.03 m.

I i 12. A large piece composed of three joining fragments. Two parallel folds of drapery, slightly curved, are modeled on the face. From the inner fold something has been broken away; presumably this was a figure whose drapery made the attachment to the background.

L. 0.20 m; w. 0.33 m; th. 0.02–0.034 m.

CATALOGUE: FIGURES

I i 13. Three fragments of a bearded man wearing a Phrygian cap.

a (Pls. 122–124). The head and part of the neck. The face is a broad oval, the forehead low with a transverse furrow and heavy brow ridges, the nose short and straight, the eyes wide, set in shallow sockets, the mouth half open. The heavy hair falls in thick, shaggy locks only slightly curling over the forehead and temples; the moustache and close, full beard frame the mouth and cover the jaw and chin. The right ear has a long lobe; the left is not indicated. The cap sits high on the thick hair; it has a narrow, slightly flaring brim with a small but distinct peak over the middle of the forehead; on the brim, above the right ear, is an irregular knob, apparently remains of an ornamental volute. The elongated crown of the cap is rolled forward and tucked under; the surface of the cap is pulled in very shallow ridges, transverse across the front of the crown, spiral toward the crown (Pl. 122). The material of the cap seems to be leather, rather than cloth or metal.

The left side of the head behind the jutting tip of the beard (Pl. 124) is only roughly modeled and is unfinished. The head therefore must have been turned three-quarters left in the pediment. The surface is badly weathered and deeply pitted.

Ht. 0.18 m; w. 0.115 m.

b (*Pl. 125*). Part of the left upper arm wearing a tunic with a short, tight sleeve slit partway up the outer seam. The underside of the arm has been broken away from some attachment, probably the body. The fragment is thick walled, but hollow; the surface is badly weathered.

L. 0.098 m; w. 0.055 m; max. th. of wall 0.024 m.

c (*Pl. 126*). Right foot wearing a soldier's, or hunter's, boot of soft leather, which leaves the toes free. The foot is broken off at the ankle; the great toe, the ends of the other toes, and a part of the heel are missing. At the break on the inner side of the ankle is a rough projection, a bit of the folded cuff of the boot. The foot is worked solid, the surface badly weathered.

L. 0.11 m; ht. 0.074 m; w. 0.054 m.

The color and quality of the clay, as well as the factors of scale and weathering, of these pieces make it certain that they belong to a single figure. It is not easy, however, to reconstruct his full costume. The toeless half boot was worn by hunters and soldiers, and also by the gods Bacchus and Diana on occasion. It was intended for strenuous outdoor activity in rough country.[8] The tunic with a short, slit sleeve was worn in Greece only by laborers, but in Rome by both soldiers and civilians.[9] The headless pedimental warrior from the Arx at Cosa wears such a tunic; so does the togatus of the Via San Gregorio pediment at Rome.[10] The cap, to judge from the shallow transverse and spiral ridges of the surface (Pl. 122), should be of some pliant material, but the sharply flaring brim with its stiff peak over the forehead and the ornament above the right ear suggest that it is metal or leather and is a helmet rather than a cap.

A helmet shaped like a Phrygian cap is not uncommon in Hellenistic art, but normally the peak is higher and the rim cut to fit around the ear; it is normally also provided with a neck guard and usually with peltate cheekpieces.[11] Furthermore, it sits lower and fits closer to the head than this. On a few Etruscan urns, however, a warrior does wear such a helmet without cheekpieces, and the helmet worn by Pelops on an urn in Florence showing Myrtilus at the altar attacked by Pelops and Hippodameia is in the shape of a Phrygian cap without cheekpieces or neck guard and is perched high on his head, as

8. G. Lippold, *Die Skulpturen des Vaticanischen Museums* 3.2 (Berlin, 1956), 137 no. 46, pl. 63; 203 no. 68, pl. 96; 233 no. 6, pl. 110; West (note 1 above), pl. 40, figs. 169, 170, 172; Brunn-Körte 2.1: pl. 12, fig. 4.

9. M. Bieber, *Griechische Kleidung* (Berlin/Leipzig, 1928), 16, fig. 19 on p. 14; L. M. Wilson, *The Clothing of the Ancient Romans* (Johns Hopkins University Studies in Archaeology 24 [Baltimore, 1938]), 57, pl. 63, fig. 70.

10. E. H. Richardson 1960, 315, fig. 4, 316–17; Andrén 2: pl. 112, fig. 397.

11. *Pergamum* 2, text 96, 103, pls. 44, fig. 1, helmet on right. *Pergamum* 3.2 pls. 16, 35, fig. 2.

here.[12] The peak of Pelops's helmet there, however, is much higher and more flaring than this. Whether this headpiece is a helmet or a cap, and whether its wearer is a warrior or a hunter, must remain, for the time being, in doubt.

I i 14. Two fragments of the head of a young woman wearing a cap or folded kerchief.

a (*Pl. 127*). The throat, chin, lower right cheek, and mouth of the figure. The face was broad, but the chin is narrow and delicate, softly cleft. The lower lip rolls downward; the upper lip is scarcely indicated. The head was raised and twisted to the left. The mouth is open, and its expression is suggestive of emotion.

Ht. 0.08 m; w. 0.06 m; max. th. 0.016 m.

b (*Pl. 128*). The right ear, part of the cheek and neck, and the side of the skull. The ear is oval with a long, rounded lobe; behind it the hair is brushed in a neat horizontal band under a cap or kerchief of soft material drawn into shallow folds. The hair in front of the ear is indicated by faint, wavy striations; on the neck the striations are deeper and make an irregular chevron pattern.

Ht. 0.077 m; w. 0.057 m; max. th. 0.014 m.

This is one of two thin-walled figures from this pediment. The twist of the neck and the parted lips give this head an emotional character like the anguish of the head of a girl from Arezzo, although less intense.[13] The Arretine head, a mourning or frightened woman from a pedimental group of the second century B.C., wears a soft cap, much less neatly and closely fitted than this one seems to have been. Similar headdresses are often worn by female figures in Greece of the classical and Hellenistic periods and are much affected by maenads and bacchantes on Neo-Attic reliefs from Greece and Italy.[14]

I i 15. Three fragments of a young man wearing a cloak.

a (*Pl. 129*). A triangular fragment from the front of the face, showing the forehead, eyes, and nose. The forehead is high and straight with a slight thickening of the brow ridges and the root of the nose. The nose makes a continuous line with the forehead, thickening slightly at the bridge; the strongly curling wings of the nostrils are outlined by sharp furrows. The wide eyes are shadowed by the heavy brow ridge; the heavy upper lids are sharp-edged, the lower lids thinner and softer. The left eye is larger and less plastic than the right, and the brow shows the beginning of a flare. Two thick, tousled curls and the stumps of three more fall forward over the forehead; their tips curl under and to either side. The surface of each lock is deeply striated.

12. Florence, Museo Archeologico: Brunn-Körte 2.1, pl. 53, fig. 2; Giglioli pl. 399, fig. 4.

13. Florence, Museo Archeologico: Andrén 2: pl. 90, fig. 322; Giglioli pl. 378, fig. 3.

14. E.g., a bronze figure of a bathing girl from Beroea, in Munich, now dated late second or early first century B.C.: M. Maass, *Antikensammlungen München, Griechische und römische Bildwerke* (Munich, 1979), 28–29, no. 11; W. Lamb, *Greek and Roman Bronzes* (London, 1929), 170, pl. 62 b and c; K. A. Neugebauer, *Antike Bronzestatuetten* (Berlin, 1921), 79, fig. 42. Attic grave stelae of the fourth century: M. Bieber, *The Sculpture of the Hellenistic Age* (New York, 1955), figs. 3 and 6. Campana plaques: H. von Rohden and H. Winnefeld, *Die antiken Terrakotten* 4.2 (Berlin/Stuttgart, 1911), pls. 47, 57, 98.

Ht. 0.095 m; w. 0.065 m; max. th. 0.02 m.

The high, smooth forehead, thickened at the root of the nose, and the heavy, springy locks of hair with their deep striations recall the head of Paris from Arezzo, although unlike that head's, the eyes of the Cosan head are blank.[15]

b (*Pl. 130*). Upper torso, nude except for a cloak thrown over the left shoulder. The base of the throat, the left shoulder and breast, the thoracic arch and the beginning of the ribs on the right side are preserved. The modeling is expert, although in very low relief; the broad planes of the chest and ribcage are diversified by delicate indications of muscle and bone; the nipple of the left breast is indicated by an added pellet of clay. The drapery falls from the left shoulder in somewhat irregular parallel folds, folding inward toward the body.

Ht. 0.20 m; w. 0.24 m; max. th. 0.03 m.

c (*Pl. 131*). Pubes.

Ht. 0.065 m; w. 0.05 m; max. th. 0.03 m.

This figure is thin-walled like the head I i 14 and unlike any other figure known from this pediment.

I i 16. Two fragments of a young male figure.

a (*Pl. 132*). Nude right knee. The kneecap, with a shallow transverse groove, and the bulge on the inner side of the knee are preserved. Most of the surface is covered with a hard white slip.

Ht. 0.09 m; w. 0.05 m; max. th. 0.03 m.

b (*Pl. 133*). Right wrist and base of the right hand, the fingers broken away. The hand was open with the palm turned out from the wrist and the fingers spread. The surface is slipped like that of I i 16a. Solid.

L. 0.08 m; w. 0.05 m.

I i 17 (*Pl. 134*). Left breast and shoulder of a female figure wearing a dress with a high girdle and a cloak. The dress is apparently the narrow Hellenistic peplos fashionable both in Greece and in Italy from the third century B.C. It is usually, as here, girt high under the breasts and frequently worn with a heavy cloak.[16] Here the dress is pulled into tight, straight folds over the small, pointed breast and gathered in reeded folds just below it. The heavy cloak falls in irregular folds over the shoulder and upper arm; its inner edge is bunched into a roll. At the back the figure is only roughly finished, and a rough, wadded projection, perhaps the floating end of the cloak, attached it to the background.

Ht. 0.191 m; w. 0.19 m; max. th. 0.075 m.

I i 18 (*Pl. 135*). Draped right leg of a standing figure. Its straightness and the stiff knee indicate that this was the supporting leg of the figure. Heavy drapery falls from a point somewhere above the preserved top of the fragment; it is pulled

---

15. Andrén 2: pl. 89, fig. 318; Giglioli pl. 378, figs 1 and 2.

16. S. Haynes, "The Bronze Priests and Priestesses from Nemi," *RömMitt* 67 (1960), 34–47, pls. 12–14, fig. 1; 15; 17, figs. 5 and 6; 18, figs. 6–9; D. B. Thompson, "Three Centuries of Hellenistic Terracottas," *Hesperia* 28 (1959), 135, 145–46; M. Bieber, *Entwicklungsgeschichte der griechischen Tracht von der vorgriechischen Zeit bis zur römischen Kaiserzeit* (Berlin, 1934), 35, 38, pls. 34, 39–41.

into folds that loop downward across the front of the thigh and break in a fall of crinkled folds across the ankle and instep of the foot, now missing. A heavy cascade of folds, the edge of this garment, falls along the inside of the leg; the hanging edge is turned back on itself to make a laddered fold. Its lower edge spreads to the sides and forward as it breaks on the ground.

Ht. 0.37 m; w. 0.13 m.

The back of this fragment is hollow and the piece has been broken from its background; the leg was intended to be seen in front view, as it is shown in Plate 135. Both sides of this fragment are finished and well preserved, which leaves the pose of the figure's left leg in some doubt.

Drapery like this, pulled rather tight across the supporting leg and with the free edge hanging in folds between the legs, is not common. The edge of the cloak of a seated figure may fall between the legs as, for example, the cloak of the seated goddess from the Via San Gregorio pediment[17] or that of the half nude Andromeda in the Villa Giulia museum in Rome.[18] The edge of the cloak of a figure in motion may also hang like this, as does that of the Apollo from Luni[19] and that of the youngest Niobid in the Vatican.[20] But this figure from Temple B is neither seated nor in motion. The only plausible explanation is that this was a half nude standing figure similar to the nymphs in the background of the group of the discovery of Ariadne from Civita Alba,[21] where the figure's cloak hangs from the left shoulder and is pulled loosely across the back and caught between the legs, covering one completely and leaving the other exposed. The sharp pull of the drapery along the inside of the supporting leg is also best explained by presuming this arrangement. To judge from the slenderness and delicacy of the leg, this was a female figure.

I i 19 (*Pls. 136, 137*). Nude left leg of a female figure. The leg is broken above the knee, which is slightly bent, and at the ankle. At the back a flaring addition attached it to the background (Pl. 137). The leg was meant to be seen from the front, the knee projecting 0.14 m beyond the plane of the background, the ankle only 0.052 m. Solid.

Ht. 0.32 m; w. 0.06 m.

Although this graceful left leg would admirably suit the figure of I i 18, it does not join with that fragment, nor will any arrangement of the two bring them close enough together to permit their association. Evidently the pediment contained two less than fully clad female figures.

I i 20 (*Pl. 138*). Fragment of a forearm wearing a rope-twist bracelet. The modeling is perfunctory. The underside is unfinished and shows marks of attachment. Pierced lengthwise.

L. 0.10 m; max. w. 0.047 m.

17. Andrén 2: pl. 110, fig. 393.
18. Andrén 2: pl. 56, fig. 184.
19. Andrén 2: pl. 93, fig. 337.
20. Lippold (note 8 above), 428 no. 24, pl. 181;

Bieber (note 14 above), fig. 256.
    21. Andrén 2: pl. 98, fig. 355, pl. 100, fig. 359;
Zuffa (note 4 above), 277, fig. 3, 279, fig. 4.

This forearm might belong to the draped female figure I i 17, to one of the half-nude figures I i 18 and I i 19, or less probably, because of its thickness and variation in the fabric, to the head I i 14.

I i 21 (Pl. 139). Right forearm and hand stretched out stiffly. The hand is open, bent back, palm out; the fingers were spread. Fingers and thumb are missing. The modeling is perfunctory; the outside of the arm above the wrist and the hand were attached to the background, or to some object, perhaps, to judge by color and texture, to the altar I i 27. Pierced lengthwise.

L. 0.17 m; w. 0.05 m.

I i 22 (Pls. 140, 141). Left arm wrapped in a cloak, the hand outstretched. The arm is designed to stretch out perpendicular to the background toward the spectator, the open hand reaching forward. Fingers and thumb are now missing. The drapery is twisted around the arm so that one corner falls across the inner plane of the wrist (Pl. 140). After the arm and drapery had been modeled they were pressed, perhaps between boards, into a roughly rectangular block, leaving a hollow underneath and a roughly flattened surface on top, inside and out. At the back, toward the elbow, on top, a twist of clay is the beginning of another fold of drapery above the arm (Pl. 141). The whole piece has been broken from its background. At the outside of the wrist the edge of the drapery is carefully flattened and smoothed to fit against another finished edge. Solid.

L. 0.19 m; ht. at break 0.095 m; w. at break 0.057 m.

I i 23 (Pl. 142). Bent right knee. The figure, apparently male, was kneeling on a flat surface. A fold of drapery is caught under the shin, and two rounded folds cross the thigh somewhat above the knee. The piece is hollow, modeled in high relief like I i 18. The back is flat and has been broken from its background. The surface is badly chipped and deeply pitted.

Ht. 0.145 m; w. 0.10 m; max. th. 0.052 m.

I i 24. Seven fragments of drapery from a single female figure.

a (Pl. 143). Part of a cloak drawn across the waist. The upper edge is wound in a tight roll; a series of crushed V-shaped folds falls below. Above the rolled edge four parallel folds slightly oblique to the vertical are part of the dress worn under the cloak.

L. 0.14 m; w. 0.126 m; max. th. 0.035 m.

b. Front of a thigh, across which drapery is pulled in narrow, slanting, interlocking folds.

Ht. 0.134 m; w. 0.10 m; max. th. 0.02 m.

c (Pl. 144). Lower leg with the knee slightly bent covered by drapery in narrow parallel folds that sweep gently to the right. The heavier folds at the right side of the leg are rectangular in section. At the bottom the drapery flares slightly, as though it brushed the ground.

Ht. 0.265 m; w. 0.11 m; max. th. 0.028 m.

d. Fragment of twisted drapery.

Ht. 0.07 m; w. 0.098 m; max. th. 0.028 m.

e. Parts of two long hanging folds, rectangular in section, like those of I i 24c (Pl. 144).

L. 0.17 m; w. 0.055 m; max. th. 0.03 m.

f. End of a deep, rectangular fold of hanging drapery.

L. 0.095 m; w. 0.045 m; max. th. 0.041 m.

g. Small fragment with two sharp, shallow folds of drapery.

L. 0.07 m; w. 0.035 m; max. th. 0.02 m.

These seven fragments come from the loose peplos and cloak of a female figure. The cloak must have been worn like that of a figure from Celle at Civita Castellana, covering the left shoulder and drawn around the hips, where its upper edge is wound in a heavy roll across the waist, while below it falls in V-shaped folds.[22] The material of the cloak in the Cosan fragment is not, so far as can be determined from fragment a, differentiated from that of the dress, so one cannot tell whether fragments b, c, and g were parts of the cloak or the dress. Fragments e and f must come from the cloak.

I i 25 (*Pl. 145*). Fragment of the upper part of a large right wing. The outer finished edge, to the left of the fragment, is thickened and rolled inward, its surface rendered with small irregular pellets of clay added separately. The flat under surface of the wing is covered with a broad scale pattern, its shallow grooves worked freehand with a blunt tool. Something has broken away from the surface of the fragment on the right. The back is unfinished but stood free of the background except at the right, where it has been broken from its background.

Ht. 0.13 m; w. 0.125 m; max. th. 0.03 m.

This fragment shows the upper part of the wing, two of whose feathers are appliquéd to the surface of the background plaque fragment I i 1 (Pl. 120). The wings of the "genius" in the pediment from Talamone[23] and those of the three central figures, Eros and two Lasas, in the Civita Alba pediment[24] are designed in the same way, the upper part modeled separately, the long feathers carried in relief against the background plaque. The outer edge of these wings is thickened and rolled inward in the same way, and the upper part of the wings of the Talamone figure is covered with scale pattern in low incision. The scales are to be read as short covert feathers or wing linings, each with its central rib.[25]

I i 26 (*Pl. 146*). Small disc with a raised rim and central boss, a button or brooch.

Diam. 0.03–0.034 m.

Large, round buttons of this sort were used to fasten a variety of things: a man's cloak on the right shoulder, a woman's dress on both shoulders, the so-called Girdle of Venus between the breasts. See, e.g., the cloaks of the young

22. Andrén 2: pl. 26, fig. 93; Giglioli pl. 316, fig. 2.

23. Andrén 2: pl. 82, fig. 285; von Vacano (note 5 above), pl. 10, fig. 2; von Vacano–von Freytag (note 7 above), 254–56, figs. 125–27.

24. Andrén 2: pl. 99, fig. 357; Zuffa (note 4 above), 274, fig. 4.

25. von Vacano (note 5 above), pl. 10, fig. 2. Cf. also the wings of certain Victories on Campana plaques: von Rohden-Winnefeld (note 14 above), pl. 21, fig. 2, pl. 37, fig. 1, pl. 38, pl. 105, figs. 1–3.

warrior from Bieda and the paedagogus from Luni,[26] the dress of the Muse Thalia from Tivoli,[27] and the Girdle of Venus worn by death demons on a number of sarcophagi and ash urns.[28]

I i 27 (Pl. 147). Corner of an altar hung with a garland. The altar is designed to be seen obliquely and perhaps below eye level. The garland is a narrow rope set with flattened pellets of clay to represent short stiff leaves; most of these have been either damaged or broken off.

Ht. 0.13 m; w. 0.095 m; max. th. 0.06 m.

An altar shown from an angle, often with a figure seated or kneeling on the top, is a familiar element in scenes on Etruscan urns and in other Etruscan and Roman engravings and reliefs.[29] Such an altar is part of the central composition of the pediment from Via San Gregorio in Rome.[30]

I i 28 (Pl. 148). Five joining fragments showing an enclosure wall or the façade of a building on which are hung a looped garland and a patera. The wall is capped with a projecting cornice of two somewhat irregular stepped fasciae, preserved only to the right. The garland, like that of I i 27, is a narrow rope thickly set with flattened pellets to represent leaves. The patera was worked in very low relief, in its deeper relief actually impressed in the surface of the wall, and has almost entirely disappeared through weathering. Six of the bowl's ribs and six drop-shaped bosses between them are still legible. On the weathered surface above the patera can be seen the line of the missing right half of the loop of the garland and the beginning of the curve of a second loop.

The cornice is cut off sharply at its left end by a plain finished edge 0.057 m. high. On the top surface of the cornice at this corner is a keyhole-shaped socket, 0.045 m long and c. 0.01 m deep, partly filled with mortar. The cutting was made before the piece was fired and must have served as the setting for a clamp to attach some element or object to the top, or to attach the wall itself to something to the left. The second possibility is the likelier, since the left half of the wall lacks a cornice but has a plain finished top edge. And an appliquéd pinch of clay on the upper surface of the cornice to the right and another scrap on its face just above a break in the front surface indicate that some figure or object was attached to, or hung over the top of, this wall.

The wall itself is simply a screen, without depth; it must have been part of the background of the pediment. There is part of a large nail hole, 0.02 m in diameter, at the lower left of the fragment, but the piece was not modeled against wooden planking like the other surviving background plaques; its back is rough and shows the marks of fingerprints, and behind the patera are three deep holes,

---

26. Andrén 2: pl. 80, fig. 280, pl. 95, fig. 339.

27. Bieber (note 16 above), pl. 34; Lippold (note 8 above), 3.1, pl. 4, no. 508.

28. Giglioli pls. 351, 397, fig. 1, 401, fig. 4.

29. Andrén 2: pl. 83, fig. 293; Giglioli pl. 403, fig. 2; von Rohden-Winnefeld (note 14 above), pl. 124, fig. 2; I. Ryberg, *Rites of the State Religion in Roman Art* (MAAR 22 [1955]), pl. 4, fig. 9, pl. 9, fig. 19c, pl. 25, fig. 39a, pl. 29, fig. 45e, pl. 43, fig. 66.

30. Andrén 2: pl. 110, fig. 393; Ryberg (note 29 above), pl. 6, fig. 14.

0.009 m in diameter, presumably the prints of three sticks put in as props while the piece was being modeled.

Ht. 0.335 m; w. 0.445 m; w. of cornice 0.06 m; ht. of cornice 0.055 m; average th. of plaque 0.035 m.

This architectural fragment might be read as the decorated front of a large altar, were it not for the fact that we already have another unmistakable altar (I i 27, Pl. 147) that was a significant element in the pedimental composition and jutted out into it. This, then, must be something else. It must be, I think, part of the wall of the precinct in which the altar stood, and its garlands and patera are then forerunners of the garlands and paterae on the interior face of the screen wall of the Ara Pacis Augustae.[31] Similar precinct walls are shown behind scenes of sacrifice on Augustan and later imperial reliefs,[32] but I know of no republican parallel for this motif. The closest is, perhaps, the garland wound with ribbons at the base of a Praenestine cista of the Hellenistic period, now in Berlin, showing a triumphal procession and sacrifice.[33] This garland runs straight, horizontally below the frieze, and above each downward dip of the ribbon wound in serpentine loops around it is a group of three circular elements. Two of these are simply series of concentric circles, but the larger, central device seems to be a patera with a morning-glory pattern, rather than the usual bead-and-drop. If this reading is correct, then the wall itself, which was cut off at the left and clamped to something beside it, may have fitted against the right lower corner of the *columen* of the temple.

The pediment of Temple B contained the following figures, positively identified among the fragments: a bearded man (I i 13) wearing a Phrygian cap, a tunic and half boots; since his head is turned to the left and its left side is only roughly finished, he must have stood in the left half of the pediment; two young male figures (I i 15 and I i 16), one nude except for a cloak; two draped female figures (I i 17 and I i 24); a young woman wearing a soft cap or kerchief (I i 14); this head might possibly belong with the drapery of I i 24, but the fabric is somewhat different; one half-draped female figure (I i 18) and another half-draped or nude (I i 19); a kneeling male figure (I i 23); two gesticulating figures (I i 21 and I i 22); a winged figure (I i 25), probably the same as I i 18 or I i 19. There was, then, a minimum of ten figures. In addition the composition included an altar (I i 27), the wall of a sanctuary (I i 28), and a shield (I i 2). It remains to be seen what the subject of the pedimental composition might have been.

Like the groups from Civita Alba and Talamone,[34] the figures of this pediment

---

31. E. Nash, *Pictorial Dictionary of Ancient Rome* (London, 1961), 1:65, fig. 62; E. Simon, *Ara Pacis Augustae* (Greenwich, Conn., n.d.), pls. 7–8.

32. Ryberg (note 29 above), pl. 15, fig. 28b, pl. 25, fig. 39a, pl. 29, fig. 45e.

33. Giglioli pl. 293, fig. 2, pl. 294, fig. 1; Ryberg (note 29 above), 20–22, pl. 6, fig. 13 (dated third

century); L. B. Warren (Larissa Bonfante), *AJA* 68 (1964), 35–42 and pls. 13–16, dates this c. 100 B.C.

34. von Vacano (note 5 above), 46–49, gives a number of cogent reasons why the large winged figure in the center of the reconstructed pediment in Florence should be removed from it.

are all of a single scale, in this case one-half life size, and the pediment itself had a continuous background. The scene represented was evidently tense and dramatic, on the evidence of the open mouths of I i 13 and I i 14, the outstretched arms of I i 21 and I i 22, and the kneeling figure I i 23. This cannot have been a pediment of the "assembly type," like the group of Apollo and the Muses and the Capitoline triad from Luni, the Via San Gregorio pediment at Rome, and the pediment of the Capitolium at Cosa,[35] where the figures were not only arranged in a quiet, relatively static composition but were also graded in scale from the center toward the outer angles of the pediment. Like the pediments from Talamone and Civita Alba, this from Temple B at Cosa must have shown a mythological scene.

In his studies of the Talamone pediment von Vacano has demonstrated that not only the subject but the iconography of that pediment has its closest, indeed its only real parallels in a number of reliefs decorating ash urns from Volterra.[36] So it seems legitimate and reasonable to examine the subjects of other ash urns for a possible interpretation of our pediment. In the corpus assembled by Brunn-Körte, a great many reliefs show action that takes place around or before an altar. In several the altar is an essential part of the composition: the Recognition of Paris,[37] Telephus in the Greek Camp,[38] the Sacrifice of Iphigenia,[39] the Murder of Myrtilus.[40] An altar also appears occasionally in scenes of the Death of Troilus,[41] the Sacrifice of Polyxena,[42] the Murder of Agamemnon,[43] the Murder of Clytemnestra,[44] Orestes and Iphigenia among the Taurians,[45] the Punishment of Dirce,[46] and a few other scenes of sacrifice or murder to which names cannot be put.[47] Of these the scene that has the most details in common with our fragmentary pediment is the first, the Recognition of Paris.[48]

The number of figures varies greatly among the several versions of the scene, as it does in any other similar series of representations from Etruria,[49] but the essential composition seems to have included the young Paris, nude except for a swirling cloak and a Phrygian cap, who kneels on one knee on the altar in the center of the scene (Pls. 149–154). In all but two cases he kneels on his right knee; almost always he holds a drawn sword in one hand and a palm branch in the

35. Andrén 2: pls. 93–94, 110–12; E. H. Richardson 1960, 307–8, 364–65.

36. von Vacano (note 5 above), 12–37, 52, 57–63; idem, *RömMitt* 76 (1969), 141–61.

37. Brunn-Körte 1: pls. 1–16, figs. 1–34.

38. Brunn-Körte 1: pls. 26–34, figs. 1–4, 7–8, 11–17.

39. Brunn-Körte 1: pls. 35–47, figs. 1–26.

40. Brunn-Körte 2.1: pls. 53–56, figs. 1–8.

41. Brunn-Körte 1: pl. 61, figs. 27–28, pls. 62–65, figs. 29–36.

42. Brunn-Körte 1: pl. 73, fig. 2.

43. Brunn-Körte 1: pl. 74, fig. 2.

44. Brunn-Körte 1: pl. 80, figs. 10–11.

45. Brunn-Körte 1: pl. 84, fig. 1.

46. Brunn-Körte 2.1: pl. 5, fig. 4.

47. Brunn-Körte 2.2: pl. 77, figs. 5–6, pl. 79, figs. 1–2, pls. 80–81, figs. 1–3, pl. 82, figs. 1–2, pls. 85–86, figs. 8–10, pl. 110, fig. 1.

48. The story is preserved in Hyginus, fab. 91; cf. Brunn-Körte 1: 4–5.

49. F. Messerschmidt, "Probleme der etruskischen Malerei des Hellenismus," *JdI* 45 (1930), 64–74, 75–82; J. D. Beazley, *Etruscan Vase Painting* (Oxford, 1947), 58–59, 87–92.

other and turns his head back toward a young man wearing a long tunic and armed with sword and shield who approaches from the right, while a second young man, nude except for a cloak but also armed with sword and shield, threatens him from the left (Pls. 149, 150). In many cases an elderly bearded man wearing a Phrygian cap and the long sleeved tunic of a king,[50] evidently Priam, stands to the right of the central group (Pls. 149, 151, 154),[51] while a half nude female figure, usually winged, stands protectively between Paris and the nude youth on the left (Pls. 149–151).[52] Sometimes Paris's protectress has a counterpart on the right; the one on the left is winged, the other winged or wingless, but in either case evidently a divinity (Pl. 152).[53] In addition to these, a woman brandishing an axe (Pl. 153)[54] and a man wearing a priest's cap with a tall *apex* may appear to the right (Pls. 153, 154),[55] whereas in two examples a second warrior wearing a corselet stands behind the nude warrior on the left, while a woman wearing a diadem grasps his right arm and tries to restrain him (Pl. 154).[56] In these last two reliefs the left of the scene is closed by a bearded man wearing a Phrygian cap, a short tunic, and half boots and a small boy, nude except for a cloak (Pl. 154).

If we try to fit our fragments into this scene, the altar (I i 27) must have stood in the center and the bent right knee (I i 23) with its folds of drapery must have belonged to Paris, kneeling on it. The wing (I i 25) should belong to the winged protectress of Paris who stands to the left of the altar, and the draped leg (I i 18) should also be hers (see especially Pl. 151). The nude leg (I i 19) may be given to his other divine protectress on the right. The young man (I i 15) may be the warrior to the left of the winged figure or the priest on the right, since in one case this figure, too, is nude (Pl. 154). The bearded man in the Phrygian cap (I i 13) cannot be Priam, who always stands to the right, but might well be the man wearing a short tunic and half boots at the left of the scene (Pl. 154). The draped female figures (I i 17 and I i 24) might be the woman with the axe (Pl. 153) and the woman who clings to the warrior's arm (Pl. 154), although the head (I i 14) seems a better choice for the latter. The male figure (I i 16) might be a priest (Helenus), the nude warrior (Deiphobus), or the young boy at the far left of the scene (Troilus ?).

None of the urn reliefs shows a precinct wall hung with garlands, like fragment I i 28, as background, but a few bits of architectural detail do appear: a door,[57] a column carrying an architrave that frames the scene (Pl. 152), and a column

50. von Vacano (note 5 above), 52 and n. 139.

51. Brunn-Körte 1: pls. 1–14, figs. 2, 3, 7, 8, 11, 17, 20, 26–29.

52. Brunn-Körte 1: pls. 1–14, figs. 1, 3–30.

53. Aphrodite (?): Brunn-Körte 1: 13, pls. 10–11, 13, figs. 22, 24, 28. On pl. 9, fig. 21, a winged Vanth stands between Paris and the warrior on the right, and on pl. 7, figs. 14 and 15, a similar figure closes the composition at the extreme right.

54. Cassandra: Brunn-Körte 1: 14–15, pls. 8, 11–13, figs. 18, 24 (where the lady with the axe is a nude figure wearing hunter's boots and a trailing cloak).

55. Helenus: Brunn-Körte 1: pls. 12, 14, figs. 25, 29.

56. Hector and Hecuba: Brunn-Körte 1: 18, pl. 14, figs. 29–30.

57. Brunn-Körte 1: pl. 2, fig. 5.

crowned with an omphalos.[58] And architectural details in the background of mythological scenes are, in any case, part of the vocabulary of Hellenistic relief, as, for example, in the Telephus frieze from the great altar of Pergamum.[59]

This highly speculative reconstruction has a pleasant neatness in that every surviving fragment of our pediment that can be identified can be fitted somewhere into the iconography of the Recognition of Paris as given by the ash urns, and no other scene will accommodate so many of our fragments. The subject is not known to have been used elsewhere for a pedimental group, but each of the existing mythological pediments from Etruria is unique in subject: the Seven Against Thebes at Talamone,[60] the Discovery of Ariadne at Civita Alba,[61] the Judgment of Paris (?) at Arezzo,[62] the Rescue of Andromeda at Civita Castellana,[63] and the Slaughter of the Niobids at Luni.[64] Therefore there is no reason why the subject of the pediment of Temple B at Cosa could not be the Recognition of Paris. As supporting evidence the reader should remember that this story was the basis of tragedies not only by Sophocles and Euripides, but also by Ennius, toward the end of whose life this temple is to be dated.[65]

The subject of a mythological pediment, unlike a pediment of the "assembly type," provides no clue to the divinity to whom the temple was dedicated. Unfortunately, for none of these Hellenistic mythological pediments can the identity of the divinity of the temple be positively established by other evidence. The great sanctuary at Pyrgi has provided us with a splendid and intricate mythological composition, at first thought to be part of a pedimental group but now recognized as the revetment of the *columen* of Temple A, the Tuscan temple of the first half of the fifth century.[66] According to the archaeological evidence this temple was dedicated to the Etruscan goddess Uni,[67] although Greek writers call the goddess of the sanctuary Eileithyia or Leucothea.[68] The mythological scene has recently been identified as an episode from the Seven Against Thebes.[69] Why

58. Brunn-Körte 1: pls. 6–7, figs. 13, 14, and perhaps pl. 14, fig. 30.

59. *Pergamum* 3.2 Plates, pls. 31–33.

60. Andrén 2: pl. 82, fig. 285; von Vacano (note 5 above), 47, fig. 2, pls. 10–11.

61. Andrén 2: pls. 98–100; Zuffa (note 4 above), 277, fig. 3, 279, fig. 4.

62. Andrén 2: pl. 89, figs. 318–19; Massa-Pairault, 166, 175–76, suggests that these fragments and a group from Vulci may, in fact, be parts of a scene of the Recognition of Paris.

63. Andrén 2: pl. 56, fig. 184.

64. L. Banti, *Luni* (Florence, 1937), 49, pls. 18–22 A–P; Andrén 2: pl. 95, figs. 339–40, pl. 96, figs. 344–45; Massa-Pairault, 148–49, suggests that this pediment represented the Death of Troilus.

65. Brunn-Körte 1: 4–5, 15. Ennius died c. 169 B.C.

66. M. Pallottino, "Scavi nel santuario etrusco di Pyrgi," *ArchClass* 10 (1958), 315–22; idem, *ArchClass* 11 (1959), 251–52, pls. 87–90; G. Colonna, *NSc* 1959, 143–263; idem, *NSc* 1970 supplement 2, 48–71, pls. 1–2.

67. G. Colonna, *NSc* 1959, 225–26, 227, figs. 79–80. The gold plaques found in the sanctuary in 1964, which identify the Etruscan Uni with the Phoenician Astarte, belonged to Temple B. See G. Colonna, *ArchClass* 16 (1964), 56; M. Pallottino, *ArchClass* 16 (1964), 112.

68. Aristotle, *Oec.* 2 p. 1349b, 35–36; Strabo 5.2.8.

69. E. Paribeni, "La perplessità di Athene. Per una corretta lettura del frontone di Pyrgi," *ArchClass* 21 (1969), 53–57, pls. 17–19; G. Colonna, *ArchClass* 21 (1969), 295–96, pl. 107; idem, *NSc* 1970 supplement 2, 48–71, pls. 1–2; I. Krauskopf, *Der thebanische Sagenkreis und andere griechische Sagen in der etruskischen Kunst* (Mainz, 1974), 43–45, 108, See 6, pl. 17.

this scene, whose central figures are Athena, Zeus, Tydeus, and Melanippus, should have been chosen for Uni's temple is impossible to guess; it seems an arbitrary and capricious choice. But such lack of direct allusion to the divinity in the pediment is not uncommon even in Greece. Although the subjects of both pediments of the Parthenon are suitable to its goddess, and that of the east pediment of the temple of Zeus at Olympia is at least suited to the site, the west pediment's Battle of the Lapiths and Centaurs with Apollo as its central figure has no obvious or even apparent connection with the cult of Zeus. Both pediments of the temple of Aphaia on Aegina, showing the two wars between Greeks and Trojans, have Athena as the central figure, but there is no evidence that she and Aphaia were the same goddess.

I ii. Frieze

Seven fragments of a frieze of racing chariots at small scale of the same fabric as the pedimental sculpture and certain other architectural terracottas were found in the excavation of Temple B. Parts of two chariots and of at least three horses are preserved, as is the long skirt of one of the charioteers. The chariots, the lower part of a charioteer's body, and one horse are modeled in very low relief. The head and neck of another horse are in high relief and projected deeply from the background. One foreleg of a horse is modeled in the round. Such a combination of very low and very high relief also appears in a fragment of a small frieze of the Hellenistic period from Cerveteri, now in Florence, which shows two horses galloping in harness.[70] The hind legs of the off-horse and the inner hind leg of the near horse are in low relief; the outer hind leg of the near horse is in high relief, while his forelegs and head were clearly in the round. I know of no other Hellenistic terracotta frieze from Italy that combines these extremes of relief.

The chariot has an early archaic form that appears on terracotta friezes of the mid-sixth century B.C. at Tarquinia, Cerveteri, and Veii.[71] It has a low-slung, heavy platform and a scoop or coal-scuttle shaped body to protect the driver's legs. Loop handrails are attached to the body high at the back to assist the charioteer in mounting. The Caeretan chariots have a five-spoked wheel;[72] the wheel of the example from Tarquinia has seven spokes.[73] On the Cosan fragment

---

70. Florence, Museo Archeologico, inv. no. 84073; Andrén 1: 19 no. I: 3a. Andrén lists this fragment with the archaic terracottas, but the style is unmistakably Hellenistic.

71. H. Nachod, *Der Rennwagen bei den Italiken* (Leipzig, 1921), 60 no. 74a–d; E. D. Van Buren, *Figurative Terra-Cotta Revetments in Etruria and Latium*

in the VI and V Centuries B.C. (London, 1921), 65 (iv) Caere, Veii, Corneto; Andrén 1: 15–17 nos. I: 1a, 1d, 2: pl. 4, figs. 6–7 (Caere); 1: 10 no. 3 (Veii); 1: 67 no. I: 1c, 2: pl. 22, fig. 75 right (Tarquinia).

72. Andrén 2: pl. 4, figs. 6–7.

73. Andrén 2: pl. 22, fig. 75 right.

(Pl. 155) the back of the chariot with its loop handrails is clearly shown, and the wheel has six spokes.

A six-spoked wheel was common in Etruria from the late archaic period down to Roman times,[74] but the chariot with a coal-scuttle body and wide looping handrails seems to have passed out of fashion after the mid-sixth century. The later archaic Etruscan chariot, of which the bronze chariot from Monteleone in New York is an example,[75] is illustrated on terracotta friezes from Tuscania, Rome, and Velletri;[76] and classical Etruscan chariots were derived from this late archaic type,[77] whereas Hellenistic chariots seem to have had a square platform and low parapet walls variously cut and ornamented.[78] The man who designed the Cosan frieze must have seen somewhere an early archaic representation of chariots, perhaps a part of the ancient terracotta frieze at Tarquinia.

The charioteer of the Cosan frieze wears a long dress, like most Greek charioteers and a few Etruscan charioteers of the late archaic period,[79] but unlike theirs, which hang stiffly, tight to the figure, his dress swings loosely behind like the garments of the charioteers of the Mausoleum frieze.[80] The horses are moving left.

CATALOGUE

I ii 1 (*Pl. 155*). Fragment showing the back half of an archaic coal-scuttle chariot with looping handrails and most of its six-spoked wheel. The long skirt of the charioteer can be seen through the loop of the handrail and flying out behind the chariot. The back of the relief is irregular, slightly concave and rough, with fingermarks and added patches of clay.

Ht. 0.198 m; w. 0.15 m; max. th. 0.025 m.

I ii 2 (*Pl. 156*). Fragment of the wheel of a similar chariot, showing parts of two spokes and a segment of the rim.

Ht. 0.06 m; w. 0.08 m; max. th. 0.02 m.

74. E.g., late archaic friezes of chariots drawn by winged horses from Rome and Velletri (Andrén 2: pl. 104, fig. 371, pl. 126, figs. 442–43), an early classical cippus from Chiusi, now in Palermo (Giglioli pl. 148, fig. 2), an ash urn from Volterra (Giglioli pl. 402, fig. 1), and a number of Campana plaques (von Rohden-Winnefeld [note 14 above], pls. 73, 78, 87, fig. 1).

75. New York, Metropolitan Museum of Art. See G. M. A. Richter, *Greek Etruscan and Roman Bronzes in the Metropolitan Museum of Art* (New York, 1915), 17–29 no. 40; Nachod (note 71 above), 43–48; Giglioli pl. 88, fig. 1, pls. 89–90.

76. Andrén 2: pl. 24, fig. 88, pl. 104, fig. 371, pl. 126, figs. 442–43.

77. Giglioli pl. 148, fig. 2; Nachod (note 71 above), 58 no. 67 and pl. 3. Both come from Chiusi.

78. Andrén 2: pl. 50, fig. 160 (Civita Castellana, Lo Scasato), pl. 82, fig. 285 (Talamone), pl. 101, fig. 360 (Civita Alba). Nachod (note 71 above) considers this type of chariot Gaulish.

79. Bronze charioteer in the Delphi Museum (R. Lullies and M. Hirmer, *Greek Sculpture* 2 [New York, 1960], pls. 102–104); Andrén 2: pl. 15, fig. 50 (Caere), pl. 104, fig. 371 (Rome); Giglioli pl. 98, fig. 2 (Velletri), pl. 100, fig. 3 (Rome).

80. London, British Museum; see A. H. Smith, *A Catalogue of Sculpture in the Department of Greek and Roman Antiquities, British Museum* 2 (London, 1900), 120, no. 1037, pl. 18.

I ii 3 (Pl. 157). The end of a horse's muzzle in profile, in low relief, with the nostril distended and mouth half open. A fragment of the bridle, a projecting rounded boss, appears at the break on the right side just beyond the corner of the mouth.

Ht. 0.037 m; w. 0.039 m; max. th. 0.015 m.

I ii 4 (Pl. 158). Fragment of a horse's head in profile, in low relief, showing part of the left cheek and eye. A crescent-shaped appliqué, evidently part of the harness, rests on the horse's nose forward of the eye. Possibly from the same head as I ii 3.

Ht. 0.04 m; w. 0.05 m; max. th. 0.016 m.

I ii 5 (Pl. 159). Part of a horse's chest and left foreleg bent sharply at the shoulder so that the leg was swung stiffly forward. The back is hollow, the piece modeled in relatively high relief with thin walls.

Ht. 0.08 m; w. 0.074 m; max. th. 0.03 m.

I ii 6 (Pl. 160). The neck and a small part of the left cheek of a horse with a hogged mane, modeled in the round but retouched on the left side only. The right side was attached to the background of the frieze by a wedge of clay where the neck joined the shoulder. The angle of this wedge, which survives, shows that the head and neck turned out in three-quarters view. At the base of the neck can be seen the broad collar of the harness, and on the cheek is a flattened disc, also part of the harness. The fragment is hollow, with relatively thin walls.

Ht. 0.09 m; w. 0.09 m; max. th. 0.017 m.

I ii 7 (Pl. 161). A horse's foreleg modeled in the round but carefully retouched only on the left side. The ankle joint is relatively thick, the hoof long and tapering. The leg was lifted in motion, but it is impossible to tell from the fragment whether this was a walk or a gallop.

L. 0.08 m; w. at break 0.015 m.

Although a number of figured friezes of the Hellenistic period have come to light in Etruria,[81] there is no evidence as to their position on the temples, or even whether they were part of the temple decoration. They cannot have been, as the archaic terracotta friezes were, decorations for the architrave or gable of the temple, but they might have decorated the cella wall, either inside or out, or perhaps the altar or the base of the cult statue.

I iii. Fragments of Life-Size Statuary

In addition to the half life-size pedimental figures and the small frieze of racing chariots, sixty-seven fragments of life-size figures and drapery on a scale to suit these, modeled freehand, were found in the excavation of surface levels in and

81. Cerveteri: Andrén 1: 19 no. I: 3. Civita Alba: Andrén 2: pl. 101. Cosa, Temple D: E. H. Richardson 1960, 328, C 1–10, figs. 18–19. Sovana: Andrén 2: pl. 81, figs. 281–82. Vetulonia: Andrén 2: pl. 84, figs. 294–97.

around Temple B. Three more of similar manufacture come from the surface levels of the Basilica, nearby to the NW. The fabric of these fragments strongly resembles that of the pediment and frieze but is not precisely the same, and it varies so from fragment to fragment that it is possible with the help of its evidence to distinguish at least six separate works, divided among statues and half figures. At least four of these were not freestanding, but were attached to terracotta backgrounds.

I iii 1. Eighteen fragments apparently belong to the bust or half figure of a woman attached to a heavy background designed to be nailed to a wall or wooden support.

Fabric. The clay is buff with a clear light red surface covered by a buff skin; the grog is of fine sand mixed with somewhat coarser grains of red pozzolana, used sparingly. The pieces are relatively heavy, the breaks irregular but not crumbly, and of a sandy texture.

Style. The fragment of the head (I iii 1a) is carefully modeled with a nice contrast between the smooth surface of the forehead and the rough texture of the hair. The drapery is boldly worked, smooth and heavy, falling in regular, straight folds.

a (Pl. 162). A fragment of the head of a female figure preserving the right eye, part of the forehead, and three wavy tresses of hair. The eye is wide, with crisp-edged lids, the upper more strongly curved than the lower. It is set deep under the eyebrow, a sharp ridge, softening somewhat toward the outer corner. The forehead is low and smooth, and three thick tresses of hair are brushed back and to the side, making a gently curving frame above. The texture of the hair is rough and lively, retouched carelessly with a point. The curve of the crown of the head above these locks is smooth and appears unfinished; presumably there were other locks, or possibly a diadem, modeled separately, that have broken off.

Ht. 0.11 m; w. 0.12 m; max. th. 0.04 m.

b–j. Nine fragments of drapery. One, b (Pl. 163), shows three folds of thin drapery fanning out from a point a little above the top of the fragment, probably part of a chiton. The others, c–j (Pls. 164–166), are heavy, smooth drapery with close vertical folds. Occasionally a short horizontal nick, evidently deliberate, crosses a part of one fold (see Pl. 164). These fragments must come from a cloak, rather than a skirt, since, as will appear below, the figure of which these are fragments was a half figure or bust.

k. A fragment of the base edge of the bust (cf. the much better preserved example II i 7, Pl. 215). The outer surface is convex and crossed by faint, irregular horizontal folds, probably representing fine drapery. The concave inner surface is rough. The trimming edge is finished smooth, 0.011 m wide, with an inner setting band, offset c. 0.005 m lower, which is summarily smoothed and hatched with crisscross scratching. Along the broken edge of the fragment is what seems to be part of a nail or bolt hole, 0.012 m in diameter, which suggests that the bust was bolted to a base of some sort.

Ht. 0.075 m; w. 0.10 m; max. th. 0.06 m.

l (Pl. 167). A thick fragment, one surface finished with long crude streaks made with the tips of the fingers, the other roughly flattened and marked with very fine grooving, like I iii k. Along the broken edge of the fragment is preserved part of a nail hole, 0.015 m in diameter. This is apparently a fragment of a background plaque.

L. 0.105 m; w. 0.07 m; max. th. 0.038 m.

m (*Pl. 168*). Part of a strut or supporting wall. One edge is roughly finished with a rounded surface; the surface intended to be seen is smoothed and shows the beginning of a fold of drapery.

Ht. 0.09 m; w. 0.10 m; max. th. 0.037 m.

In addition to the above there are five fragments of this group the character of which cannot be determined.

The head, the head-and-shoulders bust, and the half figure cut off below the waist or at the hips were all used in Italy during the Hellenistic period both for ex-votos and as decorative elements in architecture. Terracotta votive heads are too familiar and numerous to require extensive documentation. Giglioli illustrates several from Cerveteri and Civita Castellana.[82] Decorative heads ornament capitals,[83] the walls and ceilings of tombs,[84] ash urns,[85] antefixes,[86] architectural friezes,[87] and the frames of city gates.[88] The head-and-shoulders bust and the half figure were especially popular in Sicily, where they were used particularly to represent the great goddess of the island, the bust or half figure being appropriate to the epiphany of a chthonic divinity.[89]

But busts of the head-and-shoulders variety were also used, at least in Italy, for other divinities. Three small terracotta busts from Pompeii represent Minerva; a bust of Hermes comes from Canosa.[90] Antefixes in the form of a head-and-shoulders bust were found at Cosa, part of a late repair of the Temple of Jupiter on the Arx.[91] In the late Hellenistic period in Italy such busts, as well as half figures, were used for portraits, both funerary and votive, without any apparent chthonic overtone.[92] They were also used decoratively. There are, for example,

82. Giglioli pl. 419, fig. 1, 420, figs. 1–3.

83. Tomba Campanari, Vulci: Giglioli pl. 390, fig. 1.

84. Orvieto and Bolsena: Giglioli pl. 363.

85. Giglioli pl. 408, fig. 3, pl. 417, fig. 2.

86. See, among many others, Andrén 2: pls. 6, 9, 17–18 (Cerveteri), 27, 30 (Civita Castellana), 68 (Orvieto), 86 (Chiusi), 103 (Rome).

87. Giglioli pl. 384, fig. 1.

88. Volterra and Falerii Novi: Giglioli pl. 421. Perugia: Giglioli pl. 423, fig. 1.

89. R. Paribeni, *NSc* 1939, 378–79 and n. 1 on 379; O. Brendel, "Two Fortunae, Antium and Praeneste," *AJA* 64 (1960), 44–45.

90. A. Levi, *Le terracotte figurate del Museo Nazionale di Napoli* (Florence, 1926), 186–87 nos. 818, 819, fig. 141; 61 no. 260, fig. 59.

91. L. Richardson 1960, pl. 22, fig. 1.

92. Funerary: B. Schweitzer, *Die Bildniskunst der römischen Republik* (Leipzig/Weimar, 1948), 31, figs. 5–6, 8–10; West (note 1 above), pl. 12, fig. 47; R. Bianchi-Bandinelli, *Storicità dell'arte classica* 2 (Florence, 1950), nos. 130–31, pl. 64, no. 135, pl. 66; A. Giuliano, "Busti femminili da Palestrina," *RömMitt* 60 (1953), 172–83, pls. 69–73; G. Quattrocchi, *Il museo archeologico prenestino* (Rome, 1956), 19–20 nos. 11–15, figs. 5–6. Votive: Bianchi-Bandinelli (note 92 above), pl. 58, fig. 113; F. Poulsen, *Das Helbig Museum der Ny Carlsberg Glyptotek, Beschreibung der etruskischen Sammlung* (Copenhagen, 1927), 5–6 H8 and H9; *Bildertafeln der etruskischen Museums (Helbig Museum) der Ny Carlsberg Glyptotek* (Copenhagen, 1928), pl. 5; Giglioli pl. 420, fig. 4; West (note 1 above), 97, pl. 23, fig. 92; Levi (note 90 above), 151 no. 689, fig. 117.

busts that are clearly not portraits in the Tomb of the Volumnii at Perugia and half figures over the Porta Marzia in the same city.[93]

There is no way of telling whether our sadly fragmentary lady, I iii 1, was a bust rather than a half figure, although fragment k clearly indicates that she was one or the other, while the fragment of background plaque, l, and the strut, m, show that she was an attached decorative figure, rather than a freestanding ex-voto. The fact that she is modeled by hand of "architectural" clay, rather than in the fine dense clay of most ex-votos, would not rule out the possibility of her being a votive figure. Votive terracottas were sometimes made by hand of "architectural" clay and dedicated in the same sanctuaries as the commoner mold-made figures (page 167). But fragments l and m argue against any such interpretation here.

I iii 2. Sixteen fragments of a single fabric, highly characteristic and consistent, although possibly not all from a single figure. The single identifiable figure is a nude or half nude male cut off just below the hips and apparently attached to a heavy background plaque by means of struts.

Fabric. The clay has a bright orange-yellow outer layer, sometimes covered by a buff shell; the core is buff or gray. The grog is copious peppery sea sand mixed with coarsely ground red pozzolana, very noticeable on the surface of the pieces. The fragments are exceptionally thick-walled and heavy, with a relatively hard surface. The breaks are rough but not crumbly. As far as one can gather from the pieces preserved, the style of this figure was very like that of I iii 1; the treatment of the flames (?) of I iii 2e forms a close parallel to that of the hair in I iii 1a.

a (Pl. 169). Right hip of a nude male figure together with the upper thigh and the beginning of the curve of the belly. The figure was cut at the base of this fragment high on the thigh, where a part of the smooth finished base surface is preserved and can be observed in the plate.

Ht. 0.18 m; w. 0.175 m; max. th. 0.08 m.

b (Pl. 170). Fragment of drapery showing a broad triple fold. Across part of the central fold is a short horizontal groove, apparently deliberate, as in some of the drapery fragments of I iii 1 (cf. Pl. 164).

Ht. 0.09 m; w. 0.05 m; max. th. 0.045 m.

c (Pl. 171). Fragment showing a drop-shaped lappet with a shallow central groove.

L. 0.108 m; w. 0.07 m; max. th. 0.022 m.

d (Pl. 172). Heavy convex fragment, apparently an anatomical part covered with thin clinging drapery. A low forked ridge crosses it vertically. Above and to the left are five vertical crinkles.

L. 0.17 m; w. 0.105 m; max. th. 0.035 m.

e (Pl. 173). Fragment whose exposed surface is convex, covered with long

93. Giglioli pl. 415, fig. 2, pl. 416, fig. 2, pl. 423, fig. 1.

wavy flame-like strands, possibly hair, a lion's mane, a fleece, or perhaps most likely, the flame of a torch. The piece is finished along each long side and behind. The undersurface is smooth and slightly convex, quite evidently not intended to be seen.

L. 0.18 m; w. 0.11 m; max. th. 0.057 m.

f (*Pl. 174*). Fragment of a strut or support of half oval section, broken at either end. The element is bent at an obtuse angle; its upper surface is smooth and convex. The undersurfaces are flattened; one is packed hard, as though the object rested on it; the other is slightly concave. The part with concave back fans out and flattens more than the other, which is nearly semicircular in cross section.

L. 0.126 m; w. of broad end 0.095 m; w. of narrow end 0.06 m; th. of broad end 0.03 m; th. of narrow end 0.06 m.

g (*Pl. 175*). Fragment of a thin-walled, hollow, circular object. The lower edge of the wall is flat, as though it rested upon this. Along this edge on the vertical wall is an irregularly grooved fascia 0.03 m high, above which a near cyma reversa under a narrow bead supports the flaring upper wall of the object, which is broken.

Ht. 0.08 m; w. 0.058 m; max. th. 0.023 m.

h. Heavy fragment of a background plaque with one straight finished edge. The clay is wadded on its undersurface like that of the pedimental background plaques, and the upper surface is roughly scored with grooves made by the fingertips. Not only is the fabric of this fragment characteristic of the group under discussion, but it is too heavy and too densely packed to have been any part of the background of the pediment of this temple.

L. of finished edge 0.135 m; total l. 0.16 m; w. 0.11 m; th. 0.04 m.

i. Part of a heavy strut or interior support for a large figure. The fragment bends at a right angle; its surfaces are carelessly smoothed and show fingerprints.

L. 0.11 m; w. 0.10 m; max. th. 0.05 m.

In addition to these there are seven fragments of indeterminate character in the same fabric. Three are heavy-walled, slightly convex, smooth-surfaced pieces, perhaps parts of nude anatomy.

Although all these fragments are of a single fabric, it is not easy to assemble them into a single figure. The circular object, g (Pl. 175), is very thin-walled in comparison with the other pieces. It may be a completely separate object, an ex-voto of some kind, perhaps a round arula, but it is certainly not, as it may appear, a fragment of an amphora lip. The male figure, a (Pl. 169), which is cut off just below the hips and was probably attached to the background plaque h, may have worn the heavy cloak of which b (Pl. 170) seems to be part (cf. the Jupiter of the Porta Marzia at Perugia).[94] But the thin drapery and the drop-shaped lappet (c and d, Pls. 171, 172) would not suit such a figure. The flame-like fragment e (Pl. 173) may be from a torch carried by the male figure, like the

---

94. Giglioli pl. 423, fig. 1.

torch carried by the "Hymenaeus" of the Civita Alba pediment,[95] or those carried by various underworld demons on Etruscan sarcophagi and ash urns.[96]

I iii 3. Eleven fragments, nine showing parts of drapery or anatomy covered with drapery, one strut or interior support, and the curved end of a palm branch. There are no recognizable pieces of anatomy in this group, but the size of the folds of hanging drapery suggests a life-size figure, and the fragment c, showing thin crinkly cloth drawn taut, suggests that the figure was female. The drapery is livelier and more diversified than that of groups I iii 1 and I iii 2, the folds looser and more natural, their surfaces lightly retouched with a point.

Fabric. The clay is a pinkish buff in color, occasionally with a pale gray core. The grog is of finely ground red pozzolana used sparingly, mixed with occasional larger grains of pozzolana and grains of coarse black and white sand. The firing was at a relatively low temperature; the surface is tender and tends to weather; the breaks are crumbly.

a (Pl. 176). End of a hanging garment, a narrow rounded fold to the right, a rippled surface to the left.

Ht. 0.15 m; w. 0.068 m; max. th. 0.025 m.

b (Pl. 177). A broad shallow groove between two folds. The upper edge of this fragment, which slants up to the left, is rounded and finished, like the free edge of a strut or inner wall.

Ht. 0.15 m; w. 0.10 m; max. th. 0.03 m; l. of finished surface 0.05 m.

c (Pl. 178). Fragment with a smooth convex surface, lightly and irregularly retouched with a point. A thin, overlapping fold crosses the fragment in the middle. Possibly part of an arm in the sleeve of a thin chiton.

L. 0.09 m; w. 0.095 m; max. th. 0.032 m.

d. Part of an interior supporting wall, the sides streaked with the marks of fingertips, the unbroken edge roughly rounded.

L. 0.09 m; w. 0.08 m; max. th. 0.03 m.

Such supporting walls and struts are common, perhaps regular, in the interior of large terracotta statues (see, e.g., below, II i 1 i–j, II i 7, and II i 9). A number of such interior supports can be seen especially clearly in the lower section of a free-standing life-size female figure in the Vatican.[97] The feet are modeled on an irregular base. The clay is "architectural," the walls of the figure very thick, the interior supporting walls very heavy. These interior walls do not reach to the full height of the figure; they are not more than a foot high, irregular in shape, the upper section rounded off. Obviously they simply performed the function of an armature and supported the figure during modeling and firing.

e (Pl. 179). Tip of a palm branch, curling to the left. The center rib is set off by a

95. Andrén 2: pl. 98, fig. 356.
96. E.g., Giglioli pl. 396, fig. 2, pl. 397, fig. 1, pl. 412, fig. 2.

97. Vatican, Museo Etrusco Gregoriano, inv. no. 13916.

scored groove. The single row of leaves, to its right, flares toward the tips, the individual leaves separated by shallow angular grooves.

L. 0.13 m; w. 0.06 m; max. th. 0.03 m.

In addition to the above, there are two minor fragments of drapery and four inconsiderable fragments of indeterminate character.

There is nothing to show whether this was a freestanding figure or not, or whether it was a half figure or full length.

I iii 4. Eleven fragments, nine showing parts of drapery, one a smooth convex surface, one a chunk of wadding from the interior of a statue. The treatment of the drapery is very like that of I iii 3. It seems likely that these figures were a pair.

Fabric. The clay is fired to an even pinkish buff, distinctly pinker than I iii 3. The grog is of copious, rather coarsely ground red pozzolana mixed with a little coarse black and white sand. The surface is covered by a thin pinkish buff slip through which the grog shows clearly. The breaks are rough when fresh but tend to weather smooth.

a (Pl. 180). Large fragment showing part of the overfold of a peplos and the skirt below. Two double folds and part of the third of the overfold are preserved; they fan out irregularly toward the edge, which is rippled and flares. The folds of the skirt are straighter, shallower, and narrower.

Ht. 0.15 m; w. 0.17 m; max. th. 0.04 m.

b (Pl. 181). Fragment with a convex surface over which heavy drapery is pulled, making narrow rounded folds separated by broad smooth planes. One hooked fold crosses the center from upper right to left; another runs vertically on the right. Probably from the front of a thigh (cf. I i 18, Pl. 135).

Ht. 0.09 m; w. 0.066 m; max. th. 0.025 m.

c and d (Pls. 182, 183). Two fragments of a roll of heavy twisted drapery wound over a convex surface, perhaps parts of the rolled edge of a cloak.

c. Ht. 0.092 m; w. 0.07 m; max. th. 0.04 m.

d. Ht. 0.06 m; w. 0.035 m; max. th. 0.04 m.

e (Pl. 184). Fragment of a strap or loop of ribbon twisted around a narrow rod-like object. The edges of the ribbon are raised, its ends rounded, but perhaps not deliberately.

L. 0.05 m; w. 0.037 m; max. th. 0.022 m.

In addition to the above there are five more fragments of drapery and a shapeless chunk of wadding from the interior of a statue.

Like I iii 3, this may have been a full-length, freestanding statue. It was undoubtedly female, since the figure wears a peplos (fragment a, Pl. 180). She also seems to have worn some sort of cloak (fragments c and d, Pls. 182, 183), although usually in the Hellenistic period the heavy cloak worn by a female figure is drawn around the hips and covers the lower part of the body so that the overfold of the peplos cannot be seen. One of the fighting goddesses from the Civita Alba relief of the Gauls at Delphi wears a peplos and a cloak, but since the cloak floats out behind the figure the drapery is not twisted.[98] A figure on a terracotta relief from the Esquiline in Rome also wears a peplos and has a twisted scarf thrown over her left shoulder and carried diagonally across the front of the body.[99] And two of the Muses from Tivoli wear the peplos with cloaks wound in various ways around the shoulders or arms.[100] It is, of course, impossible to say exactly how the twisted drapery of our figure was arranged.

I iii 5. Eight fragments of a large-scale figure. Four are draped surfaces, one a smooth, slightly convex surface, one a convex surface with a central knob. Two seem to be bits of interior wadding.

Fabric. The clay is very close to that of the pedimental figures in color, grog, and treatment, but the heaviness of the pieces and the large scale of the drapery make it highly improbable that these pieces belong with the pedimental group.

a (Pl. 185). Long convex fragment against which a loose corner of drapery hangs. The material is fluted in shallow folds with sharp edges; the loose edge is folded back over itself twice. At the right of the fragment a broad, flat, finished edge indicates that this is part of a figure in high relief rather than in the round.

Ht. 0.22 m; w. 0.09 m; max. th. 0.06 m; w. of finished edge 0.03–0.04 m.

b (Pl. 186). Broad fragment showing parts of five wide, shallow folds with sharp edges, fanning out from a point above the break along the upper edge of the fragment. At the lower right the broad folds break into smaller fluttering folds in two horizontal steps.

Ht. 0.10 m; w. 0.065 m; max. th. 0.04 m.

c (Pl. 187). Convex fragment with straight sides and a roughly modeled square knob in the center. Beyond a shallow groove on the right is what looks like the beginning of a second fold of the same sort. What this fragment represents is unclear.

L. 0.06 m; w. 0.09 m; max. th. 0.028 m.

In addition to the above there are three other fragments of drapery, or possibly anatomy, and two wads of clay.

d (Pl. 188). Another fragment in the same fabric seems not to belong to a statue or relief. It is part of a heavy, solid, circular object with a flat base, low-profiled wall, broad flat rim, and countersunk top surface. It is clumsily modeled by hand; the undersurface shows crevices in the clay like those occurring on the back of some of the pediment plaques (page 168). Possibly this was part of a crude circular arula, although no parallel is known for this.

Ht. 0.07 m; w. 0.131 m; th. of base 0.038 m.

I iii 6. Three fragments seem to come from another large figure modeled against a background plaque. These are a fragment of drapery against a flat background, part of a heavy strut, and apparently part of a cornucopia.

---

98. Andrén 2: pl. 101, fig. 363 (no. II: 6).
99. Andrén 2: pl. 106, fig. 381.

100. Lippold (note 8 above), 3.1: 21 no. 499, pl. 4, 45 no. 511, pl. 7.

Fabric. The clay is fired to pinkish buff with a gray core, the surface shading from buff to pink. The grog is of coarse sand mixed with a small amount of finely ground red pozzolana. The fragments are heavy, the texture hard and somewhat porous. The breaks are rough but do not crumble.

a (Pl. 189). A tall conical object covered with large flattened beads of clay set together to make a mass, probably from a cornucopia. The object is modeled half round with an open back and roughly finished edges.

Ht. 0.13 m; w. 0.085 m; max. th. 0.03 m.

The identification of this fragment as part of a cornucopia depends on its similarity to the cornucopia carried by the male figure identified as the Genius Lunae in the Apollo pediment from Luni.[101] The surface of his cornucopia is covered with similar close-set flattened pellets, and a cornucopia carried by a Roman of the Trajanic period dressed as Mercury, now in the Vatican, has a similar beading decorating the upper part.[102]

b. Small fragment of drapery against a flat background.

Ht. 0.06 m; w. 0.075 m; max. th. 0.028 m.

c (Pl. 190). Strut or supporting wall. Both sides are irregularly grooved by the fingertips. At one edge is a concave cutting. Carefully finished and slipped.

L. 0.12 m; w. 0.14 m; max. th. 0.044 m; l. of finished edge 0.06 m.

It is hard to find a convincing interpretation for this assortment of scrappy fragments. They seem to belong to at least six separate figures. Four of these were modeled against background plaques (I iii 1 and 2, I iii 5 and 6). Two of these four, at least (I iii 1 and 2), were busts or half figures. These half figures, to judge from the style of the drapery, the treatment of the locks of hair, and the flames of the torch (?), made a pair. Figures I iii 3 and 4, which may have been freestanding and full length, probably made another pair, since the treatment of their drapery is so similar. Both were female figures, I iii 3 wearing a thin chiton (Pl. 178), I iii 4 a peplos (Pl. 180). I iii 3 may have been a figure of Victoria carrying a palm branch and I iii 4 possibly Athena, since the peplos is above all her costume. Still less can be said about figures I iii 5 and 6, except that I iii 6 seems to have carried a cornucopia. If this was a male figure it may well have represented the Genius Cosae, by analogy with the Genius Lunae from the Apollo pediment at Luni[103] and the Genius Populi Romani represented on coins of the first century B.C., nude except for his cloak and boots, beardless and curly haired, carrying the cornucopia, much as he appears, for example, on the Flavian reliefs from the Cancelleria.[104] If the figure was female, the best candidate for the republican period is Italia, again represented on coins of the first

---

101. Andrén 1: 284 A3, 2: pl. 93; Banti (note 64 above), 46, pl. 24.

102. Lippold (note 8 above), 3.1: 157 no. 561, pl. 56.

103. Andrén 1: 284 A3, 2: pl. 93.

104. H. A. Grueber, *Coins of the Roman Republic in the British Museum* (London, 1910), 1: 233–35 nos. 1704–24, 3, pl. 32, figs. 9–11 (c. 89 B.C.); 1: 406 nos. 3329–30, 3, pl. 42, fig. 23 (c. 74 B.C.); F. Magi, *I rilievi flavi del Palazzo della Cancelleria* (Vatican City, 1945), 24, 76, pls. 3 and 8. Cf. also S. Reinach, *Repertoire de la statuaire grecque et romaine* (Paris, 1897–98), 2.1: pls. 46–47.

century.[105] Concordia, Fortuna, and Pietas all carry the cornucopia on coins of the second triumvirate,[106] and the cornucopia continues to be an attribute of Concordia under the empire.[107] An inscription to Concordia of the republican period was found not far from Temple B, reused as part of the lining of a medieval grave (Pl. 31). It would be pleasant to attach the inscription to the temple and the "cornucopia" of I iii 6a to the temple's cult statue. But the scrappy figures I iii 5 and 6 make a pair, and were modeled against background plaques, and it is very hard indeed to see a cult image in either of them.

Where to put these figures on the temple, or in it, is another difficult problem. Conceivably those with background plaques could be put in the pediment, but not, of course, without removing entirely the entertaining mythological scene already there. Busts, or a single bust, do actually appear in a few representations of pediments in Hellenistic Italy. A single bust decorates the pediment of a model of a stage building in Naples,[108] and two busts, apparently portraits, flank a shield ornamented with a frontal face surrounded by a sunburst of petals in the pediment of the Tomb of the Volumnii at Perugia.[109] But nowhere is there a combination of life-size busts and half life-size full figures, let alone a combination of life-size busts and a mythological scene. And the fabric of the mythological figures and those of group I iii is too similar to let us imagine that these were made in a different shop or at a different time, that is to say, that the life-size figures and busts replaced the mythological scene in the pediment in a redecoration. Some other place must therefore be found for them.

It is quite possible to reconstruct a temple with a multitude of statues on the pitch of the roof, such as one sees on coins of Tiberius and Caligula representing the temples of Concordia and Divus Augustus at Rome.[110] But Temple B at Cosa seems too small to have had life-size statues on its roof, even as acroteria, and in any case such figures would presumably not have been modeled in relief against background plaques.

The enigmatic life-size half figure of a man, or Triton, modeled in high relief

105. Grueber (note 104 above), 1: 415–16 nos. 3358–63, 3, pl. 43, fig. 5 (c. 72 B.C.); M. Bieber, *Antike Kunst* 14 (1971), 111, pl. 36, fig. 7.

106. Concordia: Aureus with the head of Lepidus: Grueber (note 104 above), 1: 584 Type 3; M. Bahrfeldt, *Nachträge und Berichtigungen zur Munzkunde der römischen Republik* (Vienna, 1897), 15.8, pl. 1, fig. 16.

Fortuna: Denarius with the head of Mark Antony: Grueber (note 104 above), 1: 588 no. 4293, 3, pl. 58, fig. 17; E. A. Sydenham, *The Coins of the Roman Republic* (London, 1952), 186 no. 1144, pl. 29; denarius with the head of Octavian: Grueber (note 104 above), 1: 184 no. 1126, Pl. 28.

Pietas: Coins of Mark Antony struck in Gaul: Grueber (note 104 above), 2: 400–402 nos. 65–72, pl. 104, figs. 2–8.

107. Concordia: H. Mattingly, *Coins of the Roman Empire in the British Museum* 1 (London, 1923), 137 no. 116, pl. 24, fig. 14; E. Nash (note 31 above), 1: 294, fig. 347. Concordia and Fortuna (with Securitas): L. Breglia, *Roman Imperial Coins* (London, 1968), 44 no. 6; cf. also Reinach (note 104 above), 2.1: 247–51, 261–66.

108. Levi (note 90 above), 173–74 no. 773, fig. 134; M. Bieber, *The History of the Greek and Roman Theater* 2d ed. (Princeton, 1961), 130, fig. 480.

109. Giglioli pl. 415, figs. 1–2.

110. H. Mattingly (note 107 above), 1: 137 no. 116, pl. 24, fig. 14, 153 no. 41, pl. 28, fig. 6, 156 no. 59, pl. 28, fig. 9, 157 no. 69, pl. 29, fig. 14; A. M. Colini, "Indagini sui frontoni dei templi di Roma," *BullCom* 51 (1924), 336, fig. 8.

without a background plaque that was found on the Arx of Cosa and had apparently been part of the decoration of the Temple of Jupiter[111] must be considered in connection with these from Temple B, for it was nailed to some sort of wooden background. In the report on the temples of the Arx I suggested that it might have been one of a pair of acroteria representing Tritons, although I am not happy with the notion of acroteria modeled in the half round.

A suggestion of von Vacano in his recent study of the Talamone pediment seems well worth consideration. From his reconstruction of the pediment he removed the large winged figure previously set at the center of the composition for a number of reasons, the three most cogent being that the preserved side edges of its background plaque are straight and vertical, instead of undulant and interlocking like the edges of the other pediment plaques, that the figure is much larger than any other in the pedimental composition, all of which are otherwise at the same scale, and that there are fragments of at least one other large figure at the scale of the winged genius preserved among the fragments from Talamone in the Florence museum.[112] He concluded that these large relief figures, the genius and his counterpart, should be fastened to the outer walls of the cella and offered as a parallel the big relief figures carved on the façade of the cella of one of the second-century Doric temple tombs at Norchia.[113]

Perhaps, then, we can imagine figures I iii 5 and I iii 6, and possibly I iii 3 and I iii 4 as well, fastened to the outer wall of the cella on either side of the doorway, while the half figures I iii 1 and I iii 2 might have flanked the door at its upper corners, like the heads on either side of the arch of the Porta Marzia at Perugia, or those on an ash urn from Perugia, and another representing the Seven Against Thebes from Volterra.[114] Were the cella door lower in fact than it has been reconstructed, the half figures might have stood side by side above the cella door, in which case they would have looked rather like the half figures in the loggia above the Porta Marzia and not unlike the funerary reliefs with rows of busts dating from the late republic and early empire.[115]

If von Vacano's suggestion be accepted, I should like to suggest that the beautiful life-size terracotta relief figures from Tivoli may also have been designed to decorate the outer cella wall of a temple. Parts of five figures are preserved,[116] four with parts of their background plaques. In each case the plaque has straight sides slightly converging toward the top,[117] and the plinth of each figure seems to have been treated differently. Andrén's no. II: 1 stands on a

111. E. H. Richardson 1960, 319–20 B 5, fig. 9.

112. von Vacano (note 7 above), 44–49.

113. von Vacano (note 7 above), 48 and n. 126; G. Rossi, "Sepulchral Architecture as Illustrated in the Rock Façades of Central Etruria," *JRS* 15 (1925), 43–44 ("a procession of warriors").

114. Giglioli pl. 423, fig. 1, pl. 407, fig. 2, pl. 398, fig. 2.

115. Giglioli pl. 423, fig. 1; O. Vessberg, *Studien zur Kunstgeschichte der römischen Republik* (Lund/Leipzig, 1941), pl. 22, fig. 1, pl. 26, figs. 1–3; West (note 1 above), pl. 12, figs. 44–46, pl. 35, fig. 149.

116. Andrén 1: 370–72, 2: pl. 114, figs. 403–5.

117. This can be seen quite clearly in the photograph of the fragment II: 1 (Andrén 2: pl. 114, fig. 403).

rocky base, while the base of no. II: 2 is simply a flat fascia.[118] The plinth of II: 4 is restored.[119] Each figure was designed separately and meant to be fastened separately to its background. I earlier assumed that these were pedimental figures,[120] but they are all standing, all frontal, and could have been fastened to any flat surface. A position along the cella wall in the pronaos of the temple seems more appropriate for them than a place in the pediment.

I iv. Bases

A group of twenty-one fragments of terracotta are the remains of what seem most likely to have been bases or plinths, hollow rectangular boxes with flat bottom surfaces and figured vertical walls trimmed with moldings. There are also fragments of a number of interior walls and struts. What these boxes were used for is hard to see; a corner of one is preserved, but no fragment that might be part of a top surface. The interior struts imply that as bases they would have carried something relatively heavy, but the thickness of the bottom and side walls is considerably less than that of the pediment's background and the background plaques belonging to the large-scale relief figures of Group I iii. In one case the figured wall was pierced by a wide opening. In no case is a complete measurement—length, width, or height—preserved.

Fabric. The color and consistency of the fabric varies from fragment to fragment but resembles most closely and is probably related to the fragments of the large-scale relief figures I iii 1, 2, 4, and 5, although these fragments of bases are not usually so heavy walled as the fragments of the figures. The clay fires pinkish buff in color, usually with a gray core and a buff skin. In two cases this is covered by a hard white slip. The grog is of coarse sand mixed with finely ground red pozzolana, used sparingly. The firing was at a relatively high temperature; the pieces are hard, slightly porous; the breaks are rough and jagged and do not crumble.

I iv 1 (Pl. 191). Three large joining fragments forming part of the base and one vertical wall of one of these boxes. The clay of the base is packed hard, squeezed into craters and fissures like the back of some of the pediment background plaques and the fragment of background belonging to the large half figure I iii 2. The vertical wall is trimmed at the base with a heavy, irregular, raised fascia, above which the wall is stepped back and decorated with two undulating vine tendrils separating from a point at the left, the thinner one running across the front more or less horizontally, the thicker branching upward. These tendrils

---

118. Andrén 2: pl. 114, fig. 403.
119. Andrén 2: pl. 114, fig. 404.

120. E. H. Richardson 1960, 308.

have a rounded section; the thicker one is tripartite, a heavier central rib framed by narrow borders set off by sharp grooves. There is the stub of an interior strut at the right of the fragment.

L. 0.198 m; depth of base 0.126 m; ht. 0.145 m; max. th. of base 0.034 m; max. th. of vertical wall 0.03 m.

I iv 2 (Pl. 192). Small fragment of a vertical wall of a similar object crossed by an almost straight section of tripartite grooved tendril with a flattened central rib. A bit of what may have been a smaller tendril appears on a broken corner of the fragment.

Ht. 0.10 m; l. 0.059 m; max. th. 0.024 m.

I iv 3 (Pl. 193). Fragment of a similar vertical wall crossed by a curved section of tripartite grooved tendril. One edge of this fragment rolls under, as though it were the top or a corner of the piece. The opposite edge is a smooth finished curve roughly parallel to the curve of the tendril. The surface is covered with a hard white slip on which are traces of red paint.

L. 0.09 m; ht. 0.09 m; max. th. 0.03 m.

I iv 4. Three fragments of tripartite grooved tendrils broken from the wall of one of these or a similar piece.

a (Pl. 194). Curved section, the grooved tendril springing from, and pinched together at its joint with, a smooth knot or stem.

L. 0.12 m; max. w. 0.029 m; max. ht. 0.026 m.

b (Pl. 195). Straight section.

L. 0.068 m; w. 0.024 m; max. ht. 0.019 m.

c. Small straight section.

L. 0.045 m; w. 0.023 m; max. ht. 0.023 m.

I iv 5. Part of a base and the beginning of a vertical wall. The joint between the two is worked into a smooth curve. Possibly this is part of a side or back wall. The smooth rounded edge of I iv 3 is very similar.

L. 0.13 m; w. 0.185 m; ht. of wall 0.051 m; th. of base 0.033 m.

I iv 6. Similar fragment, the wall and a part of the underside of the base covered with a hard, greenish white slip.

L. 0.05 m; w. 0.095 m; ht. of wall 0.034 m; th. of base 0.021 m.

I iv 7. Part of a corner with a rounded joint like that of I iv 5.

Ht. 0.114 m; w. of left wall 0.059 m; w. of right wall 0.055 m; th. of walls 0.022–0.025 m.

In addition to the above there are five fragments of interior walls or struts and three shapeless fragments of the same fabric. There are also a few fragments with one flat surface covered with an elaborate design drawn with a blunt point. Whether these should be taken for the vertical walls of other bases with a different sort of decoration one cannot tell.

I iv 8. Three fragments of a flat plate showing a feather-like design on one surface. The parallel "feathers" are made of wavy grooves set in chevron pattern to a narrow raised central rib; between each pair of "feathers" is an incised groove.

a (*Pl. 196*). L. 0.115 m; w. 0.098 m; max. th. 0.027 m (the back of this fragment is broken, and to judge from the other fragments, it would originally have been much thicker).

b (*Pl. 197*). L. 0.037 m; w. 0.036 m; max. th. 0.06 m.

c. L. 0.047 m; w. 0.038 m; max. th. 0.06 m.

I iv 9. A fragment with an irregularly striated surface and a small section of smoothed surface at right angles to this.

L. 0.06 m; w. 0.06 m; max. th. 0.023 m.

It may be that these bases were some sort of acroterion support, like the two fragments found at Ardea decorated with a great palm spray in relief.[121] In this case perhaps the palm spray I iii 3e may belong to one of these, rather than to the relief figure of similar fabric with which it has been associated. It is also possible that these bases were plinths for the life-size statues of Group I iii, although it is not common to have bases and statues fired separately, and the walls of the bases are considerably thinner than those of most of the fragments of statuary.

II i. Ex-Votos, Red Group

Two further series of fragments of terracotta sculpture were found in the excavation of Temple B. Neither is connected in fabric or style with the pedimental and other decorative sculpture of the temple. The figures, to judge from the evidence available, were freestanding; they were life size, modeled by hand, and appear to have been votive statues. Of the Red Group fabric fifty pieces were found, a number of them made up of several joining fragments. They come from surface levels in the Comitium/Curia complex adjacent to Temple B on the NW, including the dump here of the clandestine excavators of Temple B.

Fabric. The clay is bright orange-pink in color, occasionally with a gray or brownish core, the surface a lighter pink shading to buff. The grog, of finely ground red pozzolana mixed with a little micaceous sand, is used sparingly. Rare small pearls of lime occasionally occur.

The figures were modeled by hand with relatively thin walls. Where the exterior is deeply convex the back is packed with extra wads of clay, and interior walls and struts gave added strength to the figure where it was needed. Four of the fragments of drapery (II i 4a–d) and one of the busts (II i 7) are pierced by nail holes; a lead rivet is preserved in one of the holes in the bust. They may have been intended to secure an interior support or armature of wood inside

---

121. A. Andrén, "Terrecotte decorative e figurate di Ardea," *BStM* 5 (1934), 26 no. 15, pl. 2, fig. 2.

the figure; possibly they were used to mend breaks in the figures, but unfortunately a break in the fragment invariably runs through the nail hole.

The firing was at high temperature; the pieces are very hard, with sharp breaks. The interior surfaces have a hard sandy texture on which the fingerprints of the modelers are often preserved. The backs of broad fragments in low relief are smoothed into parallel grooves with the fingertips. The outer surface, when not damaged by weathering, is very smooth and hard. No trace of paint is preserved. Many fragments have traces of mortar adhering; presumably they were used as rubble in later repairs and rebuildings of the temple and its precinct.[122]

Style. The modeling of the anatomical fragments is generally clumsy and inept. The hand (II i 1e, Pl. 202) and the curve of the upper arm (II i 1b and d, Pls. 199 and 201) show only the most perfunctory interest in anatomy; the fingers (II i 1f–h, Pls. 203–205) are merely roughed out. The drapery is elaborately varied, showing a nice distinction between a thin, clinging fabric and two heavier stuffs, but the treatment of the folds is repetitious. Smooth heavy folds hang straight or with the slightest curve, and thin fabric is drawn tight over the shoulder or arm (II i 1b, II i 2b), except where the sleeve buttons pull it into shallow grooved folds. Locks of hair (II i 2a, II i 3a–c) are designed in crisp wavy strands with grooving to give texture to the surface.

CATALOGUE

Fragments of at least three, and probably more, figures are preserved. These were life size, representing women in elaborate Hellenistic dress. One was a complete seated figure; two were busts or protomes cut off just below the breasts. Because of the homogeneity of the fabric, far greater than in any series of "architectural" terracottas, it is impossible to tell from the fabric alone which fragments belonged to which figure. In some cases the nature of the drapery or ornaments serves to show whether the fragment was part of a bust or of a complete figure.

II i 1. Ten fragments of a life-size seated female figure.

a (Pl. 198). Upper chest of a female figure wearing a heavy dress. The right breast and the base of the throat are preserved with part of the left breast. The swell of the breasts is very slight; they were apparently shaped by pushing out the already roughed out clay wall of the torso from behind. There are clusters of deep small fingerprints in the shallow concavities of the interior surface.

The dress is pulled down in broad shallow folds from the shoulders and was clearly held by a girdle just below the breasts. The straight edge at the neck falls in a loose V; a central lapping fold is turned to the figure's left.

---

122. Brown 1960, 128; L. Richardson 1960, 171.

Ht. 0.17 m; w. 0.175 m; max. th. 0.03 m.

b (Pl. 199). Fragment of an upper arm covered with a thin chiton with buttoned sleeves. Most of one button and the open loop of the edges of the sleeve between it and the next are preserved. The relief of the thin drapery is sharply and finely indicated.

Ht. 0.10 m; w. 0.06 m; max. th. 0.039 m.

c (Pl. 200). Fragment of an upper arm wearing a broad arm band set with a square jewel. The band has raised borders and a raised central rib. It is slightly crumpled, as though made of some soft material, perhaps ribbon or gold mesh. The jewel has a rectangular setting with a raised border; the jewel measures 0.025 m by 0.027 m; the width of the band is 0.024 m.

Ht. 0.061 m; w. 0.076 m; max. th. 0.028 m.

d (Pl. 201). Fragment of the same upper arm showing another part of the ribbon-like arm band.

Ht. 0.093 m; w. 0.065 m; max. th. 0.026 m.

e (Pl. 202). A fragmentary left hand, half closed. The ring finger, which is the only one preserved, wears a heavy ring with a rounded bezel, 0.018–0.02 in diameter. The back of the hand is smooth, without modeling. The sharply bent finger is left rough; the nail is not indicated.

Ht. 0.08 m; w. 0.085 m; max. th. 0.045 m.

f (Pl. 203). Middle finger, perhaps from a right hand, sharply bent like the ring finger of II i 1e. The surface is rough, the nail not indicated.

L. 0.06 m; max. w. 0.02 m; max. th. 0.018 m.

g (Pl. 204). Least finger, sharply bent, broken just below the second joint. The long narrow tip is bent up; a narrow nail is indicated by faint grooves at the sides and tip.

L. 0.043 m; max. w. 0.015 m; max. th. 0.017 m.

h (Pl. 205). Fragment of a ring finger, both tip and base missing. It is sharply bent, like II i 1e–g, and the surface is left rough.

L. 0.036 m; max. w. 0.018 m; max. th. 0.018 m.

i (Pl. 206). Six joining fragments forming a large piece of the upper rolled edge of a heavy cloak thrown across the lap of a seated female figure, with three stiff folds of her dress pulled down tight to the lap by the weight of the cloak. The folds of the rolled cloak are rounder than those of the dress, shallower, and more irregular; they twist spirally around the roll. The piece is heavily wadded in the interior, and part of an interior wall is preserved across the deep hollow made by the rolled cloak.

Ht. 0.22 m; w. 0.175 m; max. th. 0.048 m; max. w. of roll 0.133 m.

j. Large fragment of heavy drapery pulled smooth over a rounded projection, below which it fans out in shallow folds, perhaps drapery over the bent knee of a seated figure. An interior wall runs transversely across the hollow made by the bulge of the "knee."

Ht. 0.16 m; w. 0.165 m; max. th. 0.032 m; th. of interior wall 0.02–0.03 m.

It is fragment II i 1i (Pl. 206) that proves this to have been a seated figure; no other pose explains the twist of the cloak and the taut pull of the dress above it. The costume is the elaborate Hellenistic dress worn by the statues of the Muses Thalia and Klio from Tivoli, now in the Vatican,[123] a thin chiton with buttoned sleeves with, over it, a heavier sleeveless dress fastened on the shoulders and girt high under the breasts, and a heavy cloak. The ribbon-like arm band was worn only on the upper arm, sometimes a plain band, sometimes, as here, set with a jewel or a number of jewels. The dancing girl on a relief from Pergamum[124] wears such a band with a square jewel.

In Italy the double Hellenistic dress, chiton and peplos, although not common, appears occasionally. An alabaster urn from the Tomba Inghirami at Volterra, now in Florence, has on the lid the figure of a reclining woman wearing chiton and peplos with a ribbon bracelet on the upper arm.[125] The terracotta effigy of Larthia Seianti from Chiusi also wears a chiton and peplos.[126]

II i 2. Two fragments belonging to a life-size female figure or bust.

a (Pl. 207). Part of the back and right shoulder of a woman wearing a thin chiton with buttoned sleeves under a heavier sleeveless dress fastened on the shoulders and a heavy cloak drawn diagonally across the back and over the left shoulder. The narrow straight folds of the sleeveless dress are pulled forward, and over them falls a single long tendril of wavy hair that escapes the cloak where it brushed the nape of the neck. The back of the neck and the rest of the trailing hair that must have been gathered there and held by a ribbon or knot have been broken away.

Ht. 0.20 m; w. 0.27 m; max. th. 0.075 m.

b (Pl. 208). Fragment of an upper arm wearing a jeweled arm band similar to that worn by II i 1. The oval jewel, 0.02 m by 0.04 m, is set in a rectangular frame, 0.031 m by 0.025 m. The band, 0.028 m wide, has raised borders and a central rib set off by grooves.

Ht. 0.075 m; w. 0.06 m; max. th. 0.025 m.

In this figure the relationship of the three characteristic garments, chiton, peplos, and cloak, is clearer than in II i 1. The treatment of the thin chiton of II i 2a is shallower and less crisp than that in fragment II i 1b, for which reason the fragments are assigned to different figures. These are the only two figures in this group that definitely had arms.

II i 3. Three fragments showing locks of hair.

a (Pl. 209). Fragment preserving a deeply crinkled knot of hair bound by a round cord. From it hang the beginnings of three thick, wavy tresses retouched with a tool. The rounded surface of the chignon is crossed horizontally by three

123. Lippold (note 8 above), 3.1: 27 no. 503, pl. 4 no. 508; 34 no. 505, pl. 4; Bieber (note 16 above), 35, 60, pl. 34.

124. *Pergamum* 7.2, text 272–73 no. 344, pl. 38.

125. Florence, Museo Archeologico, inv. no. 78478: C. Laviosa, *Guida alle stele archaiche e al materiale volterrano, quinta settimana dei musei italiani, 25 marzo–1 aprile 1962* (Florence, 1962), 18.

126. Florence, Museo Archeologico: Giglioli pl. 394.

crisply waving strands of hair, unretouched. The piece has evidently been broken from the back of a head of a figure like II i 2, although it seems not to have belonged to that particular figure. Possibly it comes from II i 1, of whose back, however, we have no other fragment.

Ht. 0.19 m; w. 0.10 m; max. th. 0.075 m.

b and c. Two fragments, apparently roughly modeled locks of hair appliquéd to curved surfaces.

b. L. 0.08 m; w. 0.062 m; max. th. 0.027 m.

c. L. 0.07 m; w. 0.072 m; max. th. 0.039 m.

II i 4 (Pl. 210). Four fragments showing broad shallow triangular or rounded folds of drapery modeled on a slightly curving wall. Each preserves part of a nail hole along one broken edge. In one case (Pl. 210 lower right) the nail hole is driven through the wall of the fragment at an angle.

a. Ht. 0.107 m; w. 0.072 m; max. th. 0.028 m.

b. Ht. 0.112 m; w. 0.105 m; max. th. 0.03 m; diam. of nail hole 0.013 m.

c. Ht. 0.108 m; w. 0.083 m; max. th. 0.038 m; diam. of nail hole 0.013 m.

d. Ht. 0.075 m; w. 0.06 m; max. th. 0.03 m; diam. of nail hole 0.014 m.

The curved walls of these fragments cannot have been nailed to a flat wooden backing, as the flat pedimental background plaques were. The concave interior surface is pressed and smoothed by the fingertips like the interior surface of II i 1a. These fragments must come from the lower part of the skirt of a large statue that was reinforced in some way, perhaps by a wooden armature held in place by nails or rivets. Possibly this interior support was part of a wooden base on which the statue was mounted. These fragments are more heavily weathered than most of the others of this group; it may be that the statue from which they come stood in an exposed position and was broken in some way, and that these rivet holes are traces of a repair.

II i 5. Two fragments of smooth drapery modeled against a flat ground.

a (Pl. 211). Thick, straight border of a cloak or cover, decorated with irregular hooks and dashes cut in the surface with a broad pointed tool, apparently to represent braid or embroidery. The border, 0.043 m wide, is raised 0.001 m from the background, which seems to be the material of the main body of the garment, stretched flat on a flat surface.

Ht. 0.07 m; w. 0.08 m; max. th. 0.041 m.

b (Pl. 212). Corner of a thin cloak or scarf falling in a soft point, the right edge turned inward.

Ht. 0.069 m; w. 0.09 m; max. th. 0.034 m; w. of drapery 0.045 m.

In addition to the above fragments of drapery catalogued as II i 4 and 5, twenty-one others showing folds of drapery were recovered, all but two of which are modeled on curved surfaces.

II i 6 (Pl. 213). Three fragments of a garland or torus worked with a scale pattern of laurel leaves. Each leaf is outlined by a sharp cut and had a rib in relief down the center. The garland is convex and hollow, with rough packing in the interior, but its line is straight and it must have ornamented a flat surface, perhaps a statue base or an altar. Its fabric is evidence that whatever it decorated was part of Group II i and did not belong with the architectural decoration of Temple B. The leaves average 0.08 m long and 0.052 m wide.

    a. L. 0.113 m; w. 0.087 m; max. th. 0.02 m.

    b. L. 0.085 m; w. 0.06 m; max. th. 0.03 m.

    c. L. 0.061 m; w. 0.077 m; max. th. 0.027 m.

II i 7 (Pls. 214–216). Two joining fragments forming part of the lower section of a bust. The outer surface (Pl. 214) is worked to represent heavy drapery slanting up to the left in wide shallow folds, part of a cloak like that worn by II i 2 (Pl. 207). From the inner concave surface of this fragment a supporting wall projects at right angles (Pls. 215, 216). Its sloping upper surface is roughly rounded off; evidently like other interior walls (pages 197 and 199) this was a buttress, not a partition. The base is pierced by a nail hole, 0.013 m in diameter, in which a lead rivet is still fixed. Plate 215 shows the exterior best, Plate 216 the inner end of the rivet. The surfaces of the rivet head and the terracotta around it are badly chipped (Pl. 215), as though the rivet had been driven home after the piece was fired, but the nail hole was pierced for its insertion while the clay was still raw. The underside of the bust is carelessly flattened and given a rough texture with hatched scoring.

    W. 0.229 m; ht. 0.094 m; max. th. 0.045 m; th. of interior wall 0.02 m.

II i 8 (Pl. 217). Part of the base of a similar bust. Slanting up to the right over a plain convex surface are five roughly modeled tufts of hair or wool, probably the fringed edge of a cloak or shawl, but conceivably long locks of hair falling on the figure's shoulders. A sixth tuft has broken away at the lower left.

    W. 0.174 m; ht. 0.14 m; max. th. 0.045 m.

II i 9 (Pl. 218). Fragment of a base and support. The piece has a roughly flattened undersurface and one smooth straight edge. The top surface is very rough, and from it rises at right angles the broken stump of a curved supporting wall. On the outside of the curve and tangent to it the base is pierced by a nail hole, 0.02 m in diameter.

    L. 0.146 m; w. 0.11 m; max. ht. of finished edge 0.04 m; max. ht. of base and supporting wall 0.08 m; th. of supporting wall 0.018 m.

    Except for two shapeless fragments, these are all the pieces of this fabric found in and around Temple B. The seated figure II i 1 is certain, although perhaps not all of the fragments assigned to her are really hers, and probably a number of the unassigned fragments do belong to this figure. The two busts II i 7 and II i 8 are also certain. Whether the fragmentary figure II i 2 belongs to one of these busts, to yet another bust, or to a second full-length figure is unclear. The embroidered cloth II i 5 and the laurel garland II i 6 may have been parts of the decoration of the seated figure's seat and its base. II i 9 may have been part of its lower surface and interior support, in which case it is likely that it was nailed to a wooden statue base. The other fragments cannot be assigned.

By far the closest parallels to these Cosan terracottas, not only in costume (the elaborate Hellenistic dress of the Muses from Tivoli and Larthia Seianti), but also in type and workmanship, are a group of terracottas found at Ariccia in Latium in 1927, now in the Antiquarium of the Museo delle Terme.[127] They include two busts showing the head and shoulders of female figures, one of heroic size (inv. no. 112375, Paribeni Pl. 16), the other life size (inv. no. 112376), three seated figures at three-quarters life size (inv. nos. 112343, 112374, 112377, Paribeni Figs. 5–6), a half figure wearing a diadem ornamented with wheat ears (Paribeni Fig. 9 shows the head). The last is cut off a little below the waist and has her arms held close to her sides cut of at the same line.[128]

The seated figure (inv. no. 112343, Paribeni Fig. 6) wears a chiton with buttoned sleeves under a peplos. There is a jeweled ribbon on her upper right arm, and she wears a heavy cloak, one end of which covers her left shoulder, while the rest is gathered around her hips and covers the lower body, making a heavy roll across her lap and pulling the front of her dress into a fan of stiff straight folds, as in II i 1i (Pl. 206).

The seated figure inv. no. 112377 (not included in Paribeni's list) wears a large ring on the first finger of the left hand, as well as a ribbon bracelet on the upper arm and a chiton with buttoned sleeves. The third seated figure, inv. no. 112374 (Paribeni Fig. 5) is in a hard reddish clay very like that of the Cosan group. Her left hand, all of whose fingers are missing, is perfunctorily modeled like I i 1e (Pl. 202).

The life-size bust, inv. no. 112376, wears a cloak whose folds slant across the back and over the left shoulder, as in II i 2a (Pl. 207) and the bust II i 7 (Pl. 214). Her hair is caught by a ribbon at the nape of the neck and falls in three wavy tresses over the neck and shoulders. The hair of the other figures from Ariccia is elaborately looped in double Psyche knots with many loose tresses, a considerably more complicated arrangement than any we have evidence for at Cosa, but the treatment of the individual locks—long, wavy, crisply grooved—is much like that of the Cosan examples.

The two busts and the half figure from Ariccia are crowned with wheat ears; this, with the little pig that one of the seated figures holds in her hand, strongly indicates that they come from a shrine of Ceres and Proserpina. As observed above (page 186), such busts and half figures were used in Sicily especially to represent Demeter and Kore, these shapes being especially suitable to illustrate the epiphany of a chthonic goddess.[129] But since similar busts were used in

127. Paribeni (note 89 above), 370–80, pls. 16–17.

128. There are more statues now in the Museo delle Terme than in Paribeni's list. He mentions only two seated figures, whereas there are now three. And several of his fragmentary statues have had other fragments joined to them: the head illustrated on his plate 17 is now set on the life-size bust inv. no. 112376; the head on figure 9 has been joined to a half figure; the hand holding a small pig, figure 10, is the left hand of the seated figure inv. no. 112343 (fig. 6). In addition to these female figures, there is a standing figure of a togatus wearing a bulla about three-quarters life size (Paribeni fig. 7) with many added fragments.

129. Paribeni (note 89 above), 378–79 and n. 1 on 379; Brendel (note 89 above), 44–45. Cf. von Rohden and Winnefeld (note 14 above), 4.1: 4–7, 4.2: pl. 20.

Hellenistic Italy to represent other divinities, and even mortals, we cannot simply on this evidence assume that the Cosan busts and the seated figure were necessarily dedicated to Ceres and Proserpina, or Libera, as the wheat-wreathed examples from Ariccia must have been, although their many resemblances to the Ariccia terracottas make this an attractive possibility.

II ii. Ex-Votos, White Group

Thirty-three fragments in this fabric were recovered, of which three are made up of two or more joining fragments. They come from the surface levels of the excavations in and around Temple B, the surface level of the Comitium/Curia complex, and the dump in the Comitium made by the clandestine excavators of Temple B.

Fabric. The clay is greenish white to buff in color with a surface shading from pink through pinkish buff to greenish white. The grog is of fine sea sand, black, brown, and red. The fragments are thin-walled, fired at a relatively low temperature; the breaks have a fine, grainy texture and tend to crumble and weather. The surface was slipped; the slip is badly worn, and no trace of paint is preserved.

Style. The modeling of the anatomical fragments II ii 1d–f is perfunctory; the drapery is treated superficially and impressionistically, the folds of material indicated by rows of close shallow grooves that merge and divide irregularly. The slight crusts and ridges of clay left along the edges of the grooves by the working of the folds are not smoothed off (Pls. 219–221). The surface of the heavier drapery is rippled and varied by patches of roughly smoothed clay that clog and blur the folds (Pl. 221); apparently these parts were worked with a spatulate instrument. The inner surface of most of the fragments was packed and smoothed by hand; a few fragments have a smooth-finished inner surface. The pendants of the necklace and beads of the girdle (II ii 1a–c, Pls. 219, 221) were modeled separately and appliquéd to the surface; so were the eyes of the little boar II ii 2 (Pl. 225). The boar's head, although sketchily modeled, is surprisingly lively. Bits of lead, probably the remains of an armature, adhere to two fragments.[130]

CATALOGUE

These fragments, except the boar's head II ii 1, all belong to a single statue, the life-size figure of a woman wearing a chiton and a heavy cloak. Her girdle is a

---

130. Cf. E. H. Richardson 1960, 371 A2.

broad ribbon set with beads along each edge, and she wears a necklace of many small pendants. Probably she held the little figure of a boar in one hand. The upper parts of the figure were fired at a higher temperature than the lower parts; the surface of these fragments is pink, and the pieces are harder and less weathered than those from the skirt.

II ii 1. Thirty-two fragments of a life-size figure of a woman.

a (Pl. 219). Fragment from the front of the figure, showing the base of the neck, the necklace and the edge of the chiton. The necklace is made up of an apparently rigid curved band with raised edges, 0.01 m wide, set with two rows of small round beads, 0.015 m apart, on either side of the central groove; from this hang ten pendants, each made up of a round bead and an elongated pear-shaped drop. The pendants are 0.022 m long and lie in a shallow channel between the curved band of the necklace and the edge of the chiton.

The middle of the upper edge of this piece appears to be not broken but roughly finished; the clay was smoothed back over the edge by hand and overlaps the interior surface in a piecrust edge. This finished edge is only 0.06 m wide, not wide enough to permit the insertion of a head and neck made and fired separately. The figure must have been modeled in sections and the sections assembled before firing.

Ht. 0.107 m; w. 0.15 m; max. th. 0.022 m.

b (Pl. 220). A small part of the left arm and breast. The thin material of the chiton is pulled taut over the curve of the arm and crinkles in narrow irregular folds over the breast.

Ht. 0.08 m; w. 0.09 m; max. th. 0.028 m.

c 1 and 2 (Pl. 221). Two fragments showing part of the girdle and skirt of the figure together with part of the cloak.

1. Heavy drapery falling in straight narrow folds that fan a little from upper left to lower right. This crosses a horizontal band, 0.04 m wide, decorated along both edges with round beads. Below this band is a section of smooth drapery.

Ht. 0.14 m; w. 0.09 m; max. th. 0.03 m.

2. A section of the lower border of the girdle appears at the upper right, a raised border on which are set three round beads or studs and a central rib set off by furrows. Below the girdle the skirt hangs in shallow folds, the grooves between them scraped out with a rounded stick. The folds are irregular in direction and depth; three fade out toward the lower edge of the fragment, while at the left another begins, increasing in depth toward the lower edge of the fragment.

Ht. 0.148 m; w. 0.145 m; max. th. 0.025 m.

The pendant necklace of II ii 1a (Pl. 219) was fashionable in the Hellenistic period;[131] it is worn, for example, by the terracotta image of Larthia Seianti from

---

131. Bieber (note 16 above), pl. 38; Giglioli pl. 327, fig. 1, pl. 375, fig. 2, pl. 376, fig. 5.

Chiusi dated by recent studies to the third quarter of the second century B.C.[132] Larthia Seianti also wears a jeweled girdle not unlike the Cosan example (Pl. 221), as does, among many others, the reclining woman on the ash urn from the Tomba Inghirami of Volterra cited above.[133]

Twenty-five other fragments of this fabric come from parts of the skirt of the chiton or the cloak. Fifteen show the same sort of shallow, rippled, irregular folds as fragment II ii 1c 2 (Pl. 221); ten show the broader straight folds of the cloak of II ii 1c 1 (Pl. 221).

d (*Pl. 222*). Part of a forearm near the wrist, perfunctorily modeled.

L. 0.072 m; w. 0.055 m; max. th. 0.02 m.

e (*Pl. 223*). Part of the middle finger of the left hand, broken at the second knuckle. The nail is indicated by faint grooves at the base and sides.

L. 0.052 m; max. w. 0.018 m; max. th. 0.015 m.

f (*Pl. 224*). Turned up tip of a least finger of perfunctory modeling with no indication of the nail.

L. 0.028 m; max. w. 0.013 m; max. th. 0.01 m.

II ii 2 (*Pl. 225*). Most of the head of a small pig with a very long snout, presumably a boar. The snout has a broad lump near its base and narrows toward the tip, swelling just behind the nostrils. Nostrils and mouth are indicated by deep cuttings. The eyes are small flattened discs of clay added separately. The head is solid.

L. 0.084 m; ht. at break 0.058 m; w. at break 0.052 m.

These thirty-three pieces are the only ones in this fabric from the area of Temple B. For this reason one may presume that the boar's head II ii 2 was an integral part of the statue from which the thirty-two fragments of drapery and anatomy come. Probably it was held on the palm of one hand, like the little pig held by one of the seated statues from Ariccia (Museo delle Terme inv. no. 112343, Paribeni Fig. 10).

There is nothing to indicate whether this statue was seated or standing. It seems to have been modeled without interior walls or struts, but possibly there was a wooden armature fastened together with lead. There are no nail holes or rivet holes preserved, as there are in Group II i.

The fact that this figure seems to have held a pig, or at least was closely associated with a pig, suggests that this was an offering to Ceres and reinforces the impression already made by the seated figure and the busts of Group II i that the temple in whose vicinity these fragments were found was dedicated to that goddess. The evidence of the ex-votos suggests that it was a temple of Ceres, or perhaps Ceres with her daughter Proserpina, or with her Roman companions, Liber and Libera.

---

132. Giglioli pl. 394; J. Thimme, "Chiusinische Aschenkisten und Sarkophage der hellenistischen Zeit," *StEtr* 25 (1957), 117 and n. 18.

133. Florence, Museo Archeologico, inv. no. 78478; Laviosa (note 125 above), 18.

VIII. 150–140 B.C.

(Plan X; Figs. 59–75; Pls. 226–42)

Soon after the completion of Curia III and Temple B, the area stretching from the Comitium to the expanded NW Porticus (pages 135–38) was overlaid by a basilica twice as wide as the space between the Square and Street 7. The lower half covered Street 7 and the downward slope beyond. The plan of the building was clear and simple: a broad nave and surrounding ambulatory with a tribunal on the short axis. It was enclosed by walls on three sides and opened to the Square through a portico. The space occupied by the Basilica was a nearly rectangular plot, $121\frac{1}{4}$ p.R. by $91\frac{3}{8}$ p.R. (35.89 m by 27.05 m) covering 3280 p.R.^{2} (940.82 square meters), but the use of the walls of the annex of Atrium Building I at one end and the Comitium and Curia at the other made it a somewhat irregular trapezoid.

The architect, however, was free to lay out the front and rear lines parallel to the Square, making the measurement from the centers of the façade columns to the back wall 90 p.R. (26.64 m) and proportioning the whole depth to length as nearly 3:4. The terrain within this perimeter was traversed lengthwise by two older walls (pages 114 and 211). The first, 14.30–14.40 m back of the façade line, was the rough retaining wall for the leveled surface of the early forum. The second, 20.20–20.60 m back, was the boundary wall along the NE side of Street 7 (page 113). No evidence of other structures has been found, and our architect

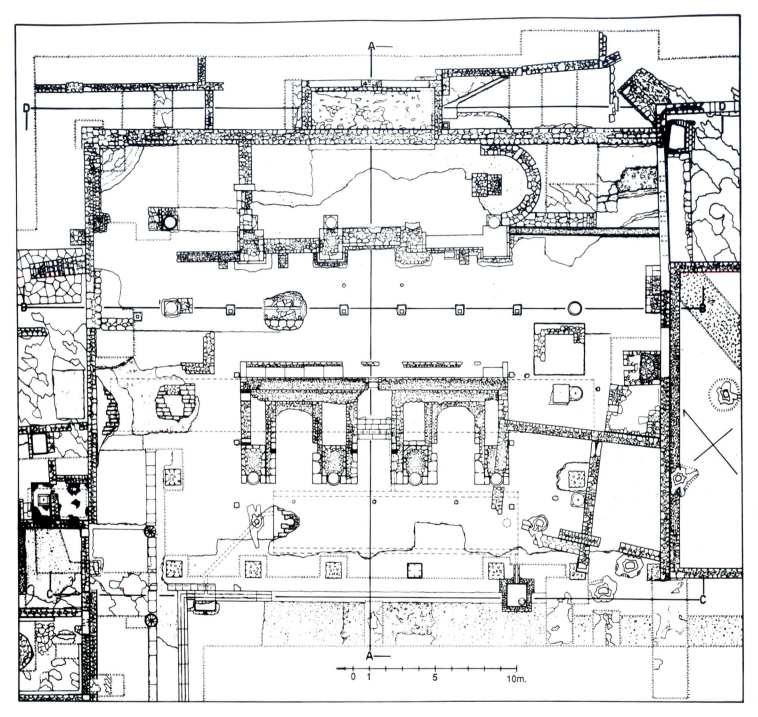

PLAN X.   Plan of Basilica

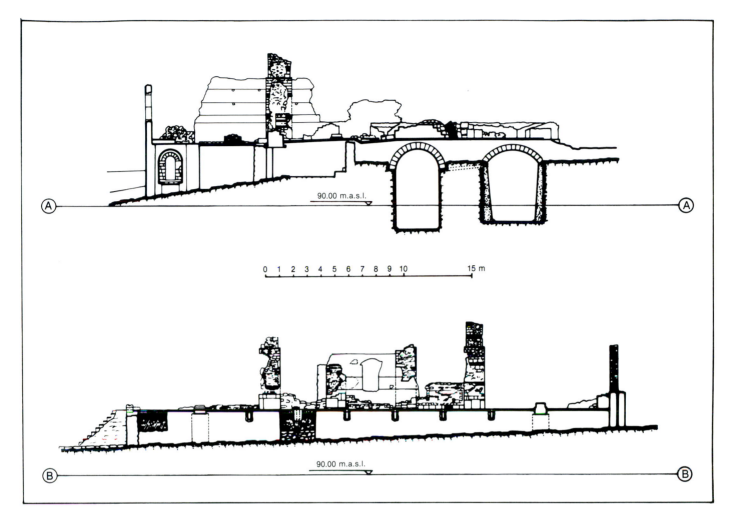

Fig. 59.   Basilica, sections as excavated, A and B

made use of both walls. The retaining wall was kept for support for the vault of a new cistern, while the boundary wall buttressed the NE line of columns of the nave. These older walls also sectioned the deep fills of the NE part of the new building, down to the heavy foundations at the back. The wall of the annex of AB I was likewise incorporated, providing spread footings 2 p.R. (0.59–0.60 m) thick on large, quarry-shaped blocks without prepared beddings. The rubblework above, $1\frac{11}{16}$ p.R. (0.50 m) thick, was of unsquared limestone blocks, diminishing in size from bottom to top, bonded and rendered with mortar (Pl. 100).

The massive foundations added on the NE and NW, rising 2.30–3.50 m above the rock, were on spread footings from 3 p.R. (0.89 m) to $4\frac{3}{8}$ p.R. (1.30 m) thick. The outer faces were of finished limestone masonry, evidently intended to be visible. The blocks were trim, rectangular or trapezoidal, dressed with a point and laid with fine joints neatly raked out. Their sizes are extremely variable,

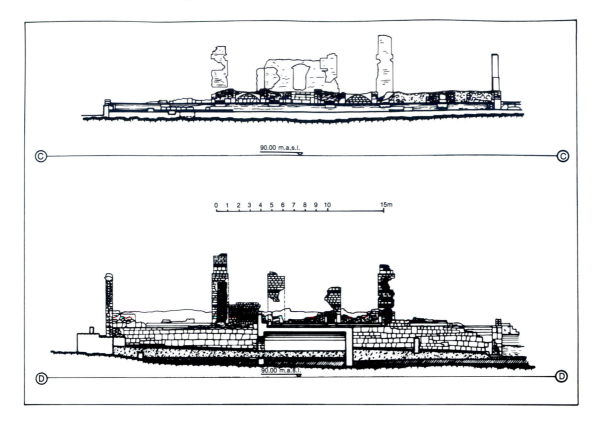

ranging from 0.30 m to 1.10 m in length and 0.20 m to 0.60 m in height, with an average surface of about 0.34 square meters (Fig. 60; Pl. 228). On the inner faces, not meant to be seen, the blocks of the upper $4\frac{1}{2}$–5 p.R. (1.33–1.45 m) were roughly squared off and fitted, snecked with chips and broken tile, and below these the rubble was smaller and unshaped, tailing into the fill behind. The SE foundations were both part of the Curia and adjacent to the Comitium. The Curia's NW cellar beneath the hall above had already been built overlapping the NE wall of the Comitium (page 139), and now was used for the Basilica. This wall of the cellar was 2 p.R. (0.592 m) thick and 2.06 m high, the height of the Comitium, above the other foundations of the Basilica (Fig. 5; Pl. 101). From its SW end the wall of the Basilica ran beside the wall of the Comitium to the Square.

The foundations of the tribunal, projecting 10 p.R. (2.96 m) on the length of 20 p.R. (8.58 m), abutted the NE foundation without bond, although its walls above, as shown by the remains of their S angle, were of one build with the rest of the building (Pl. 229). The foundations were of random rubblework, footed on the rock, 2 p.R. (0.592 m) thick at either end and $2\frac{1}{4}$ p.R. (0.666 m) on the NE, and were quoined at the exterior angles in four courses. These foundations were surmounted by a vault that supported the floor above and was made accessible by an arched door in the SE side. The vault, with a span of $5\frac{1}{2}$ p.R. (1.63 m), sprang from impost walls $1\frac{1}{8}$ p.R. (0.333 m) thick, with offsets at the footings. The rubblework was laid over wooden centering in a bed of mortar. The arched door, $2\frac{1}{4}$ p.R. (0.74 m) in span, had nine travertine voussoirs of equal size. It was not furnished with a threshold nor fitted for doors, and the vaulted space was left unplastered. Its floor was a fill of earth and broken stone. Any function other than support was clearly incidental.

The independent foundations for the system of internal supports of the Basilica within the outer ring were built up from the rock to an equal height. The foundations of the twelve columns of the two front rows, which rose 0.70 m to 1.25 m from the rock, were stout piers of heavy rubblework, a generous $3-3\frac{1}{2}$ p.R. (0.90–1.05 m) square. At either end of the outer row similar foundations, roughly $2\frac{1}{2}$ p.R. (0.74 m) by 3 p.R. (0.88 m), carried the responds. The foundation for the six columns of the rear row, which were built up 2.60 m to 2.90 m, was continuous and abutted the NE face of the boundary wall of Street 7. It has been examined in depth only at either end, but that it is continuous is apparent on the surface (Figs. 60, 61). The foundation at each end was a rough wall, 3 p.R. (0.89 m) thick, of large quarry-shaped limestone blocks compacted with smaller stones and mortared at the points of contact. It was finished off with a roughly stepped face $4\frac{1}{2}$ p.R. (1.32 m) beyond the center of either terminal column. At the NW the boundary wall was hacked off on this line, while at the SE it was left to extend into the outer foundation. The bases were capped across their full thickness beneath each column by a leveling slab, $\frac{5}{8}$ p.R. (0.185 m) thick, consisting of

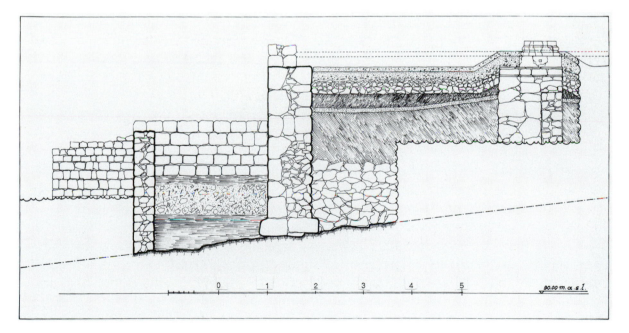

Fig. 60.   Basilica, N sounding, SE section

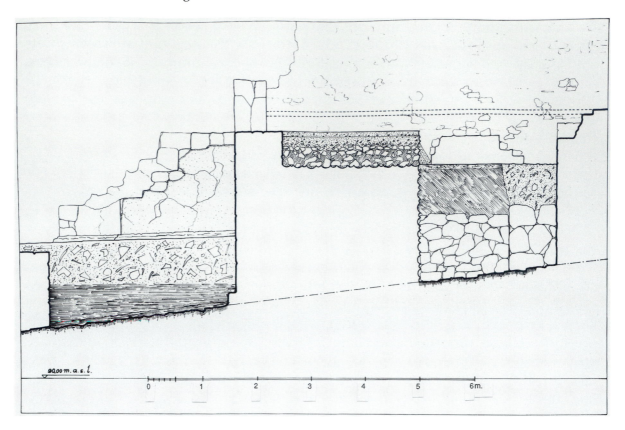

Fig. 61.   Basilica, E sounding, SE section

squared blocks of limestone between two courses of tile. Of the pairs of columns intervening at either end, those nearer the façade were footed on the extrados of the vault of the new main cistern on beds of rubblework. The foundations of the other two were not uncovered, but from their positions must have been seated on the SW crepido of Street 7.

Within these foundations two large rock-cut cisterns underlay the front half of the building. The one beneath the front aisle of the ambulatory had been in use from the beginning of the colony, first as an open tank and later as a vaulted cistern (pages 11 and 114; Fig. 42). It was 51 p.R. (15.10 m) long and 15 p.R. (4.44 m) deep, its floor about 20 p.R. (5.92 m) below the floor of the Basilica. The crown of the vault had been pierced by circular drawholes, $1\frac{3}{4}$ p.R. (0.52 m) in diameter, near either end. Now the SE drawshaft was plugged with a stopper of Vulci tufa just above the vault. The intake was likewise plugged with the same tufa at the outer end, and there was a longer stopper of rubblework just behind the impost. The NW drawshaft remained open. Parallel with the old cistern and almost twice as long, the new cistern ran $100\frac{3}{4}$ p.R. (29.82 m) from the NW inner foundations, beneath the nave, to within 3.87 m from the SE foundations (Pl. 230). Its depth below the line of the springing was $14\frac{1}{2}$ p.R. (4.29 m) but lay 22 p.R. (6.51 m) below floor level, because of the greater rise of its vault. The sides were vertical, $10\frac{3}{4}$ p.R. (3.18 m) apart, and lined with signinum, with cover-joints at the base. Its vault of seventeen limestone voussoirs, $1\frac{5}{8}$ p.R. (0.48 m) thick, was a bit angular in section but in design all but semicircular. The sole source of supply was an intake from the outer cistern at its midpoint, which entered on the line of the springing, 17.40 m from the NW end of the new cistern. A single draw-shaft, $1\frac{1}{2}$ p.R. (0.444 m) across, pierced the crown of the vault, $13\frac{7}{8}$ p.R. (4.11 m) from the NW end, close beside the foundation of a column. The capacity of the two cisterns was 634.76 cubic meters, some 167,705 gallons.

Within and between these substructures, as they rose, were laid the fills to support the pavement of the finished building. The wide strip along the Square above the old cistern had already been filled and terraced. It was necessary only to dig for the installation of the new cistern and the sixteen footings or piers for the columns. In the rear half of the building the whole area had to be filled. The grade of the rock from SW to NE is about 9° and from SE to NW about 2.5°. Two soundings, one at either end (Figs. 60, 61) showed the rock at 3.07–3.55 m below the floor. Here, between the NE wall and the foundation for the rear row of columns, a heavy packing of freshly broken limestone was laid directly on the rock, c. 1.00–1.48 m deep, overlaid by a series of trampled working floors about 0.184 m thick. Above these were strata of reddish ochre subsoil, yellowish and gray detritus, 0.11 m thick, and another working floor of spalls, 0.184 m thick. On these the floor, $1\frac{1}{2}$ p.R. (0.444 m) thick, was laid up to the bases of the columns, statumen, rudus, and nucleus clearly separate in cross section.

The foundations, except at the N corner, stand almost to their full height all about. Above them the NW and NE walls are reduced to disconnected stumps, while the rear wall of the tribunal still rises to within a few centimeters of its original height. The SE wall now mounts from 1.20 m at one end to 4.45 m at the other. With the exception of the party wall with the Curia, all were set flush with the outer face of the foundations. The NW and the freestanding length of the SE wall beside the Comitium were each $1\frac{3}{4}$ p.R. (0.518 m) thick. The long NE wall had the thickness of 2 p.R. (0.592 m), while the walls of the tribunal alcove measured $1\frac{1}{2}$ p.R. (0.444 m.). The party wall with the Curia was at its SW end $1\frac{3}{4}$ p.R. (0.518 m) wide, but had thinned at its NE end to $1\frac{1}{2}$ p.R. (0.444 m) and was set back $\frac{1}{4}$–$\frac{1}{2}$ p.R. (0.074–0.148 m) from the face of the foundation just above the joists of the floor of the Curia.

These walls were normally of random rubblework of unshaped blocks of limestone of fairly uniform size, $\frac{1}{2}$ p.R. (0.145 m) by $\frac{3}{4}$ p.R. (0.22 m). In the SE wall a number of squared blocks prepared for coursed rubblework were introduced sporadically in the party wall with the Curia and beyond it as a course intended to bring this stage of the work level with the top of the perimeter wall of the Comitium. The place of these blocks and their average size of 0.30 m by 0.17 m makes it likely that they came from the demolished and rebuilt NW wall of the Curia (Pl. 231). The SE wall was built up in continuous strips, each leveled off and mortared over the top. The bottom strip, of 2 p.R. (0.592 m), matched the thickness of the flooring of the Curia and brought the wall to the top of the perimeter wall of the Comitium. Above it three further strips of 3 p.R. (0.888 m) are discernible. These were laid from scaffolding, of which sporadic putlog holes remain visible on the interior. The NE wall of the tribunal was built in a similar way in strips 3 p.R. high, of which four and most of a fifth still stand (Pl. 232). The third and fourth were interrupted in the middle of the wall by an opening for a window, 4 p.R. (1.184 m) wide, spanned by a lintel and perhaps a relieving arch.

The columns of the façade and the piers of the interior were seated on square plinths of travertine set flush with the floor. Of the fifteen surviving plinths, six were covered by column bases and three were too battered to yield their fittings. The other six, one on the façade, two in the rear row, and three at the ends of the nave, all have cuttings for lifting tongs on the sides and pairs of pry notches on top. Otherwise they vary slightly in dimensions and design, depending, apparently, on the situations and stints of several masons (Fig. 62). The six Roman-Attic bases in place were worked in one piece with the beginning of their column shafts, depths of from 0.02 m to 0.19 m. They too were of travertine, as were the Hellenistic-Doric capitals surmounting the unfluted shafts of the columns. The lower diameters of the bases are $2\frac{5}{16}$ p.R. (0.684 m) and $1\frac{3}{4}$ p.R. (0.518 m), the upper $1\frac{3}{4}$ p.R. (0.518 m) and $1\frac{3}{8}$ p.R. (0.407 m) (Fig. 63). All surfaces of surviving members were finished with the same chisels and were covered by a shell-like coat of hard stucco, of which patches remain on some of the bases. The bottom and top joint beds of the bases had central roughly picked circular sinkings, $\frac{3}{8}$ and $\frac{1}{2}$ p.R. (0.11 and 0.15 m) in diameter and about 0.005 m in depth, while the top surfaces of the

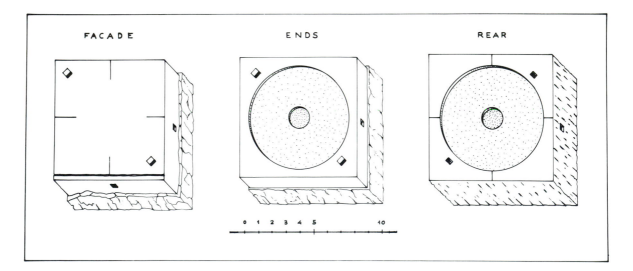

FIG. 62.   Basilica, plinths of columns of three types

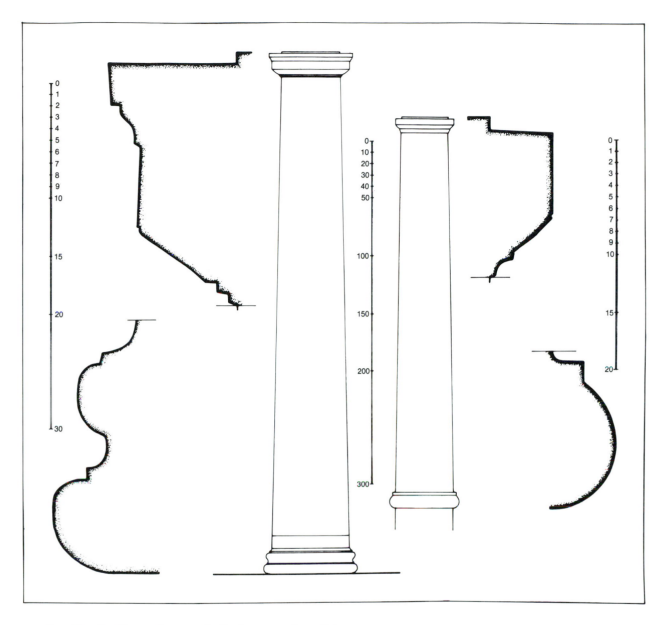

FIG. 63. Basilica, columns: shafts, bases, and capitals

abacuses of the capitals had discs about 0.011 m high and the same diameter as the upper diameters of the shafts, $1\frac{3}{4}$ p.R. (0.518 m).

Of the lower tier of columns the bases were low and of slight projection, $\frac{3}{4}$ p.R. (0.222m) high and $2\frac{13}{16}$ p.R. (0.822 m) in diameter, wider only $\frac{1}{4}$ p.R. (0.074 m) than the diameter of the columns (Pl. 233). They were pairs of somewhat angular tori, crowned with fillets, separated by a shallow scotia and finished with a quarter-round apophyge. The capitals were relatively prominent, equal to the bases in height (Pl. 234). Their visible height was divided in equal thirds between a flattened echinus over annulets, a low abacus, and a high cymatium of cyma reversa and fillet. The face of the abacus was plumb with the foot of the apophyge. Both bases and capitals were closely similar in design and workmanship to those of the second phase of Temple D on the Arx.[1] The foundations of the two responds at either end of the façade colonnade carried rectangular plinths of mortared limestone. At the NW this stood 2 p.R. (0.60 m) high from the floor of the earlier porticus now overlaid by the floor of the Basilica. Here, $2\frac{1}{2}$ p.R. by 2 p.R. (0.74 m by 0.592 m) in area, it supported the base of the respond, which would have brought its face into alignment with the inner face of the Basilica's NW wall. The bedding of the corresponding plinth against the SE wall, however, was $2\frac{11}{16}$ p.R. (0.80 m) wide, while the base would have stood out from the wall by the same amount, 0.518 m. On this reckoning the distance between bases of the responds was $115\frac{5}{8}$ p.R. (34.225 m), fifty column diameters.

The space bounded by the walls and colonnade of the façade was virtually a parallelogram. The columns within it made up the central nave, 82 p.R. by 50 p.R. (24.27 m by 14.80 m), three bays of 15 p.R. (4.44 m) by five of $14\frac{9}{16}$ p.R. (4.31 m), surrounded by the ambulatory, narrower across the ends and wider along the façade and rear. A columnar clerestory above the lower columns of the nave is attested to by a number of fragments that survived the collapse of the upper part of the building in Period II. All but one of them were reused in the fabric of the Odeum, erected immediately after (pages 241–44), and all were of travertine, finished with a toothed chisel of the gauge of that used for the lower columns. Of the two fragments of the bases, the larger piece is somewhat less than a quadrant of a torus and a bit of the shaft, 0.11 m high from the bottom. The other is a sliver of torus, having a chord of 0.17 m. They suffice to show that the diameter of the shaft was $1\frac{3}{4}$ p.R. (0.518 m), equal to the upper diameter of the columns of the lower tier, and that the base was a single heavy torus, crowned by a fillet of $\frac{1}{16}$ p.R. (0.0185 m) with a total projection of $\frac{3}{16}$ p.R. (0.055 m). A single fragment of shaft survives, the lower part of a bottom drum, 0.39 m long and 0.512 m in lower and 0.50 m in upper diameter. The bottom has a rough-picked central sinking, like those of the bases of the lower tier, 0.13 m in diameter, with a pricked center. An almost intact capital (Pl. 235), a fragment of somewhat more than a quadrant of another, and about an eighth of the bottom of a third with the attached portion of a shaft yield an upper diameter of $1\frac{3}{8}$ p.R. (0.407 m) and a complete profile, including a raised bearing disc. The overall height of the capital is 0.14 m. Below the disc is a plain abacus, $\frac{1}{4}$ p.R. (0.074 m) high; the rest of the $\frac{3}{16}$ p.R. (0.055 m) is equally divided between a low, slightly swelling echinus and a cavetto necking.

The exedra in the center at the rear of the building was 26 p.R. (7.70 m) wide and $10\frac{1}{2}$ p.R. (3.10 m) deep. It is probable that this tribunal was set off from the

1. Brown 1960, 111–14.

ambulatory by a low step and a pair of columns in the opening. A broad step at the foot of the seats of the Odeum of Period IX was made up of large slabs of Vulci tufa laid end to end, originally twelve in all, of which six were found in place (page 241; Pl. 236). They are $4\frac{1}{16}$ p.R. (1.2025 m) long and 1 p.R. (0.296 m) thick, designed to be laid side by side, and of two widths, four of $2\frac{1}{16}$ p.R. (0.611 m) and two of $2\frac{3}{8}$ p.R. (0.703 m). The top and front edges of the slabs have bands of anathyrosis about 0.07 m wide, and the front and top surfaces are dressed smooth, while the backs and bottoms are chisel-dressed (Fig. 64). One of the slabs of the lesser width was exceptional in having anathyrosis on only one side. On the front faces a line was lightly scribed, $\frac{5}{16}$ p.R. (0.092 m) from the top, above which the arrises were rounded by wear and below the faces were flecked with signinum. The back arrises were less deeply scuffed. This is evidence that the slabs were originally laid to project 0.092 m above a floor of signinum in front and about half as much behind. The surviving ragged edge of the flooring in front of the tribunal seems to mark the projection of such a step beyond the walls at either side, while the surviving floor of the tribunal shows that it was originally 0.04 m above the floor of the rest of the Basilica (page 219). Twice the number of slabs that have survived, eight of the lesser width and four of the

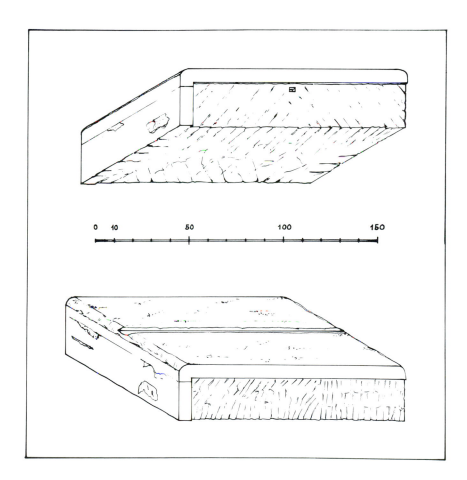

FIG. 64. Basilica, slabs Vulci tufa steps of two sizes

greater, would have exactly filled the opening with a step, of which two slabs having anathyrosis along only one side would have formed the two ends.

In the central section of the *scaenae frons* of the Odeum opposite the tribunal was found a small Ionic capital of Vulci tufa. While somewhat battered about the corners and edges, it was substantially complete in every detail (Fig. 65; Pl. 237). Carved together with a short length of shaft, $\frac{15}{16}$ p.R. (0.277 m) in lower diameter, the whole was 0.231 m high and 0.418 m wide on the abacus. The capital proper was four-sided, nearly $\frac{5}{8}$ p.R. (0.188 m) high, being stocky and of singularly provincial appearance.

It is entirely contained within the square of its abacus: the circumference of its volutes is within the circle of its echinus; the eyes of the volutes well within the upper diameter of the column. The volutes do not meet at the angles to swing diagonally outward, but are held apart by a swelling cushion-like triangle in the

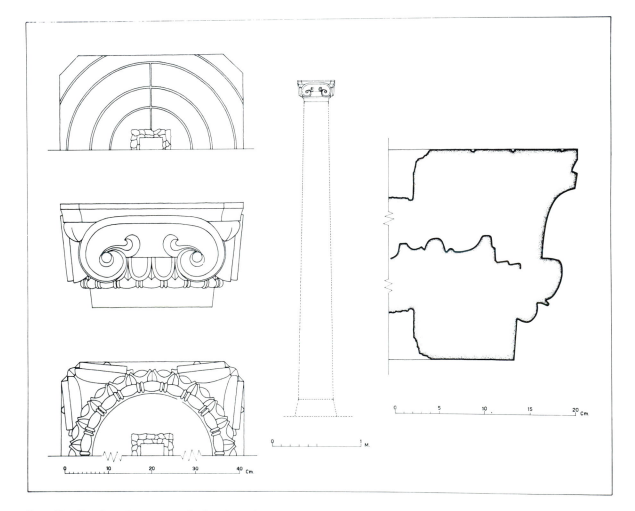

FIG. 65.   Basilica, Ionic capital of Vulci tufa

angle beneath the abacus. The lowest member is a heavy, elongated astragal of sixteen elements around. The echinus projects only half its height and is carved with an oblong egg-and-dart of twenty elements. The volutes have domical eyes centered on the level of the top of the echinus, and their flat bands unroll from a tight inner and open outer turn to join in a flattened convex arch above the tall concave canalis, which is partly filled by plump corner leaves.

All surfaces are finished smooth, and the carved faces appear to have been burnished. In the centers of the top and bottom are cubical sockets, $\frac{3}{16}$ p.R. (0.055 m) on a side, for mandrels when shaping the capital, and on the top surface are marked four deeply scribed concentric circles and a diameter. These, no doubt, were guides for carving. The diameter of the inner circle is 0.188 m, the height of the capital. The second is 0.277 m, the diameter of the shaft. The diameter of the third is 0.385 m, the extreme of the echinus, while the outer circle is $1\frac{9}{16}$ p.R. (0.4625 m), the circumference on which the eyes of the volutes lie. It may also have been the base diameter of the column.

The original floors of the building were of signinum, thicker where they rested on the deep fills of the rear half than where they were better supported. Except in the tribunal, they were laid on a level bed of clay of varying thickness over the construction floors (Figs. 60, 61). The statumen of broken stone was graduated from fist to egg size from bottom to top, 0.18 m to 0.25 m thick. The rudus of coarse gravel and finely broken tile in white lime mortar, 0.08–0.16 m thick, was topped with a nucleus, some 0.04 m thick, of crushed tile and potsherds in hard white mortar, polished smooth and made perfectly level.

Above the floor the original stucco of the interior was found in place in only a single strip, some 2.25 m long and 0.85 m high at the base of the middle of the SE wall of the building. Over a scratch coat, a heavy coat of lime, sand, and fine gravel was applied, 0.035 m thick. Over this came a coat, 0.005–0.01 m thick, of smooth texture and creamy color, composed of pulverized travertine and lime, which gave a hard, shell-like finish, showing not the slightest trace of color or relief. At the opposite end of the building were found two large fallen segments of the NW wall still covered with the same stucco with creamy finish. Outside, along the rear half of the NE wall in the levels associated with its collapse and inside in the repairs of Period IX at either end of the rear aisle were recovered more than two hundred fragments of the same distinctive stucco, variously colored. They represent a mural decoration of the Masonry Style consisting of orthostats in flat colors and marbling below a string-course adorned with a maeander, above which are simulated ashlar blocks with drafted margins, also rendered in both flat colors and marbling (Fig. 66). These data, taken together, seem to imply that only the rear aisle of the Basilica was decorated, while the other two sides were left plain creamy white.

Before the third column of the SE file from the corner a slab of travertine, $3\frac{3}{4}$ p.R. by $3\frac{1}{4}$ p.R. (1.11 m by 0.962 m), was found sunk with the first flooring and accurately fitted to the plinth of the column by a shallow rabbet. The surface had

F<small>IG</small>. 66.   Basilica, plaster of painted Masonry Style, restored

been dressed with the same toothed tool that was used for the plinths, and the sides had been left rough-pointed with the forward angles roughly chamfered (Pl. 238). The snug fit of the floor against these surfaces showed that the slab was set in place before the rudus and nucleus were laid down; later, when the thickness of the resurfaced floor came to a clean edge, it marked whatever stood on the slab. In front of the corresponding column at the opposite end of the nave, where only part of the second floor remained, it showed the negative imprint of the E corner of a similar slab. Both evidently supported bases or pedestals, presumably for statues. Three sizable fragments of a base molding of travertine, suitable for such a pedestal on a plinth of these dimensions, came to light (Fig. 67). One was built into the scaenae frons of the Odeum of Period IX. Another was found tumbled into the main cistern, and the third lay outside the NW wall in the debris of the Basilica. On the first the cyma recta molding had a projection of $\frac{5}{8}$ p.R. (0.185 m); on the second $\frac{3}{4}$ p.R. (0.222 m). The third was an angle of which one had the greater and the other the lesser projection. Set upon the embedded slabs with the wider projection in front and the lesser on the

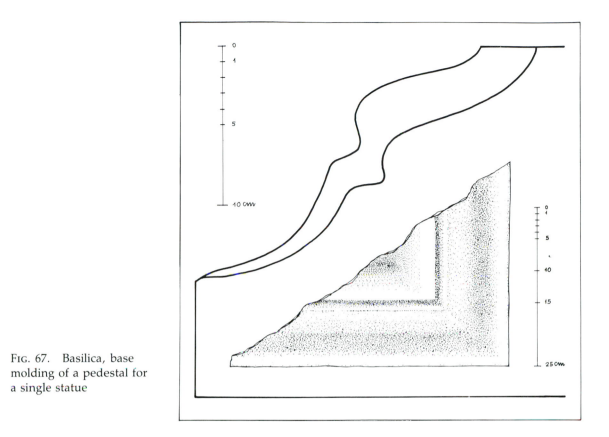

FIG. 67.   Basilica, base molding of a pedestal for a single statue

sides, the molding would converge from three sides to a bed, $2\frac{1}{2}$ p.R. (0.74 m) square, appropriate to the die of a pedestal for a single statue backed against a column.

Among the original fittings of the Basilica may be reckoned the well-curbs that stood over the two drawshafts in the SW aisle and the nave. Two joining fragments of one of them amount to about a quarter of the orifice of a plain and massive puteal of travertine, $1\frac{7}{8}$ p.R. (0.555 m) in bore (Fig. 68). The inner face is vertical; the outer tapers toward the crown 6.5°; and the inner edge is fluted with thirteen rope-worn grooves, testifying to its antiquity.

The roofing of the building at the time of its final collapse, between Periods IX and X, is attested to by the myriad fragments of fallen tiles that covered its floors. It is not unlikely that some of these were on the original roof, but under the circumstances it proved impossible to identify the original tiles with certainty. All the fragments, great and small, of which significant measurements could be obtained, appeared to be the same standard format: flanged tegulae 2 p.R. (0.592 m) long and $1\frac{1}{2}$ p.R. (0.444 m) wide designed to overlap and dovetail by $\frac{5}{16}$ p.R. (0.0925); semicylindrical tapered imbrices of the same length with an external diameter of $\frac{9}{16}$ p.R. (0.167 m) at one end and $\frac{11}{16}$ p.R. (0.204 m) at the other.

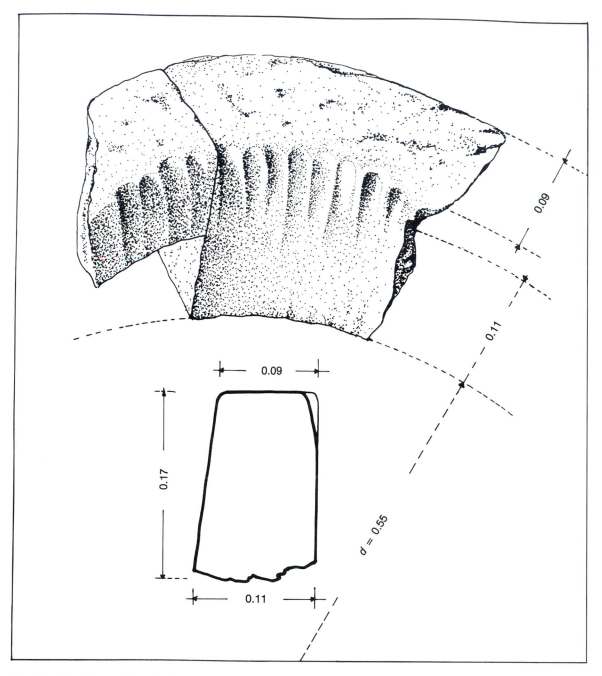

FIG. 68. Basilica, well-curb of cistern

Another sort of roofing was represented by scores of terracotta tesserae fallen all about the outside of the building, rarely within, in the levels of the collapse of Period IX. Many were found in compact groups of up to forty-five, and some eight hundred were catalogued for their completeness or significant stratification. In form rhombic prisms, they have tapered sides and angles of 60° and 120°. Mold-made, they average $\frac{1}{2}$ p.R. (0.148 m) on the upper long diagonal and 0.085 m on the short. The larger face is scraped flat, and the other arrises rounded. Traces of hard white mortar on the bottoms and sides indicate that they were laid with the smaller face down on a bed of signinum and filled between. They are clearly elements of a pavement that, from their provenience, must have covered the gallery over the ambulatory.[2]

The ground plan of the Basilica (Figs. 69, 70) was a compromise in which restricted length was compensated for by breadth and which allowed relatively large bays and columns. In second-century Cosa columns seem regularly to have risen about six and two-thirds bottom diameters (pages 99–100), and here the height of the lower columns would probably have been $15\frac{3}{8}$ to $15\frac{7}{16}$ p.R. (4.55–4.57 m) and the upper columns $11\frac{11}{16}$ p.R. (3.455 m). This is in accord with the preference for squarish units in spatial design manifested in temple architecture, in the Porticus, and in Vitruvius's rules of proportion for the "Tuscan" temple and the basilica itself.[3] Also the upper diameters of the lower columns are equal to the lower diameters of the upper columns, being three-fourths of the base diameter of the lower order. This equation, too, implies knowledge of the rules for Vitruvius's basilica.[4] The same rules in *De Architectura* also relate the height of the blind story between the lower and upper orders to the height of the latter. This pluteus, standing back of the gallery all around the building, was invisible to the normal throng within the Basilica, while the gallery provided an elevated position for observing the spectacles of the Forum. On the façade it was probably cantilevered out over the columns to form a *maenianum, quo ampliarentur superiora spectacula,*[5] having its floor pitched sufficiently to discharge rainwater through appropriate vents into the gutter beneath.

The sole information as to the dimensions of the timber roofing of the Basilica comes from the discs atop the capitals of the columns. The foundation of the pluteus was the timber architraves, $1\frac{3}{4}$ p.R. (0.518 m) wide, on the analogy of Vitruvius 5.1.8–9, *trabes compactiles* (double beams), and perhaps $1\frac{1}{2}$ p.R. (0.444 m) high. These carried the beams spanning the ceiling of the ambulatory and the floorboards on which the pavement was laid. The architrave of the upper order of the nave, upon which the main roof rested, would have been $1\frac{3}{8}$ p.R. (0.407 m) thick and was presumably a single beam not less than $1\frac{1}{2}$ p.R. (0.444 m) high. The clear span of the nave of over $53\frac{3}{8}$ p.R. (15.80 m) could only have been bridged by

2. Vitruvius 7.1.5, "*pavimenta sub diu*"; cf. Pliny, *NH* 36.25.62.

3. Brown 1960, 42, 44, 90–92, 94; Vitruvius 4.7.1–2, 5.1.5.

4. Vitruvius 5.1.3, 5.1.5; cf. 6.3.9.

5. Festus 120L; cf. Isidorus, *Etym.* 15.3.11; Vitruvius 5.1.2, 7.1.6.

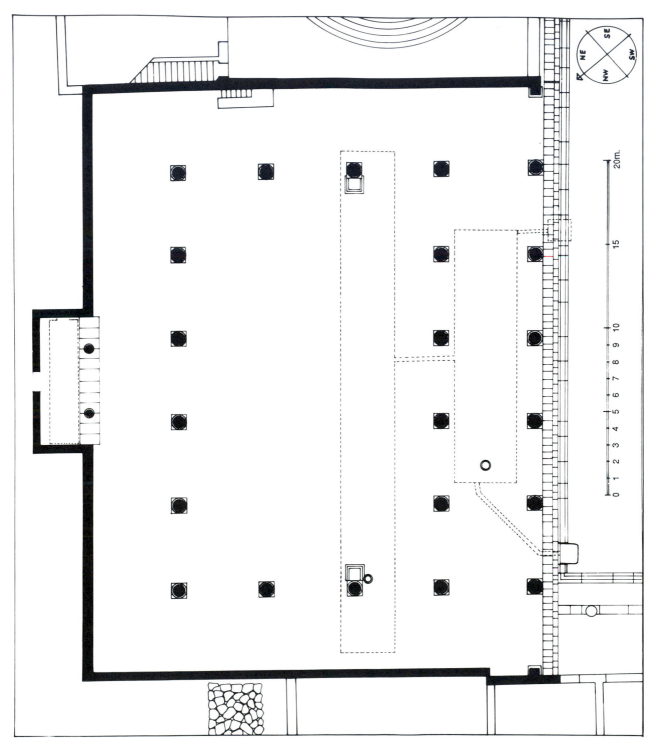

Fig. 69.   Basilica, restored plan

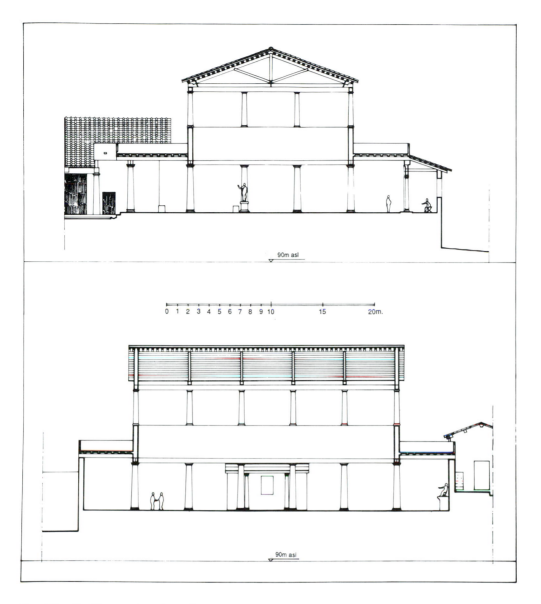

Fig. 70.   Basilica, restored sections

a truss. This is best restored as a kingpost design, the *transtra et capreoli* of Vitruvius that appeared in later basilical roofs of comparable span.[6] The extremely broad proportions of the nave and the spacing of the supports for the trusses make it plain that the roof was gable-ended rather than hipped. Moreover, since neither the well-preserved capital nor the bottom drum of the shaft shows any sign of abutment or attachment of a screen, the clerestory was evi-

6. Vitruvius 4.2.1, 5.1.9; Sackur, *Vitruv und die Poliorketiker* (Berlin, 1925), 123–43.

dently open, like the clerestory of the Basilica Aemilia at Rome of 179 B.C. as it may appear on a denarius of M. Aemilius Lepidus of 61 B.C.[7]

The tribunal's opening to the NE aisle was presumably spanned by a lintel at the height of the architraves of the aisle columns. The rear wall of the tribunal, standing $13\frac{3}{8}$ p.R. (3.96 m) above the floor, breaks off horizontally at what seems to be the bottom of the ceiling joists. The relation between this line and the calculated top of the architraves is an angle of 20°, indicating that the tribunal was covered by a sloping roof at a level below the gallery over the ambulatory. The lintel, spanning 26 p.R. (7.70 m), needed intermediate support, and the slabs and Ionic capital of Vulci tufa suggest themselves (pages 217–19). These columns, having a lower diameter of $1\frac{9}{16}$ p.R. (0.4625 m), would not have been more than 9 or 10 p.R. high, but the surface of the blocks of the stylobate gives no direct evidence of their emplacement. It may, however, be assumed that their two calculated widths were related to the setting of columns and that the columns, seen on the short axis of the Basilica and tribunal, were intended to appear framed between two columns of the ambulatory in front of them.

Our reconstruction shows the Basilica of Cosa to have been an airy structure, overtopping the neighboring buildings with pavilion-like lightness, and with its façade below seeming to continue the colonnaded enclosure of the NW end of the Square. Inside, the central volume was a light-bathed, spatial amplitude, articulated but not divided by its framing. Its height to the roof trusses was half its length. The high girdle of the blind story established its singleness and integrity as an interior, while it prevented the visual intrusion of extraneous activities. The circumambient aisles were scarcely partitioned from the nave by its wide-set columns and varied gradation of light. Only the alcove of the tribunal behind its step and columns and with its special source of light was set off from the common space and traffic as the seat of special activity. The added width of the aisle before it was no doubt designed to allow for congregation about this focal point. In a similar way the still wider aisle behind the façade provided for the reception of casual shelterers during bad weather. Its broad upper step made it also, on occasion, another platform from which to view events of public significance in the Square.

The building of the Basilica was the final step in the architectural enclosure of the Forum. Three coins give evidence that it was erected, at the latest, early in the third quarter of the second century B.C. The first, found in sectioning the NW end of the rear aisle of the ambulatory, embedded in the construction floor beneath the statumen of the pavement, was a somewhat worn sextantal as, struck around 210 B.C.[8] The second, found in sectioning the SE end of the rear aisle in the filling under the construction floor, was an almost new uncial quadrans, struck at the same time.[9] The third, found in the undisturbed bedding for the lower step before

7. *RömMitt* 63 (1956), Taf. 8; Crawford 1974, 419/3.
8. CD 910: Buttrey 1980, 32; Crawford 1974, 56/2.
9. CD 912: Buttrey 1980, 55; Crawford 1974, 56/5.

the façade, was a freshly minted denarius, anonymous and coined about 157/156 B.C.[10] This evidence is confirmed by the broken pottery from the floors of the Basilica and in the refuse pit of Area 16 of the annex of AB I, sealed by use as a lime kiln during the construction of the Basilica (page 137).[11] Three Rhodian amphora stamps (CE 917–919), extracted from the fallen section of the NW wall of the Basilica, bore names and eponyms that have been tentatively dated in the late second quarter of the second century B.C. (letter from V. R. Grace).[12]

The Basilica of Cosa was erected within a generation of the first great basilicas of Rome, and it is the oldest colonial or provincial basilica that has yet come to light. It corresponded in practically every feature to the type of building for which Vitruvius gave summary rules of proportion, while the inclusion of a *maenianum* related it specifically to the usages of the Roman Forum. Its prototype is to be sought among the early Roman basilicas, as yet scantily documented.[13] There had been only shops and offices of brokers in the Roman Forum in 210 B.C.,[14] and no basilica is mentioned in the chronicles until twenty-five years later, when Cato's basilica was built in his censorship and received his gentilicial name Porcia.[15] In 1946 to 1948 soundings were carried out in the E corner of the remodeled basilica of Augustan date in hope of finding some surviving trace of the original Basilica Fulvia-Aemilia of 179 B.C.[16] Three massive bases of columns together with their lower shafts did indeed come to light, but under its pavement the SE wall and three bases and column shafts of tufa of an earlier building emerged as well. This must have been the first basilica in Rome, the basilica without a name (Figs. 71, 72). About $24\frac{1}{3}$ p.R. of wall was uncovered, in which there was no opening. Behind it lay an alley, with a drain below pitching SW to the Cloaca Maxima, while on its other side the new bankers' offices faced the Forum. It appears that the façade of the basilica faced the other way, toward the NE, opening to the fish market. The spacing of the columns was $16\frac{3}{4}$ p.R. (4.96 m) on centers, and the SW aisle was about 9 p.R. (2.665 m) wide. The NE aisle was probably 14 p.R. (4.14 m) wide and the width of the nave only two bays, $30\frac{3}{4}$ p.R. (9.10 m). This first basilica must have been a sort of annex to the open *macellum* or *forum piscarium*, the basilica that Plautus knew.[17]

10. CD 1050: Buttrey 1980, 67; Crawford 1974, 197/1a.

11. Taylor 1957, 91–94, 105–7; Dyson 1976, 51–63.

12. The date of 150–120 B.C. proposed by G. Lugli, *La tecnica edilizia romana* (Rome, 1957), 39, 79, 115, 413, on the basis of the type of walling, was nearer the mark than his earlier conjecture of 120–100 B.C. in *AttiCStR* 8 (1956), 266. This had perhaps been influenced by the unverified opinion of A. von Gerkan, *RömQ* (1952), 130n. 5.

13. Vitruvius 5.1.4–5; K. Lehmann-Hartleben, *AJP* 59 (1938), 280–96; A. Boethius, *Eranos* 43 (1945), 89–110.

14. Livy 26.27.1–5, 27.11.16.

15. Livy 39.44.7; [Aurelius Victor], *De Vir. Ill.* 47.5.

16. *NSc* 73 (1948), 111–28; cf. *RömMitt* 63 (1956), 14–25.

17. Plautus, *Curc.* 472–74 and *Capt.* 813–15; G. E. Duckworth, *Ut Pictura Poesis, Studia Latina P. J. Enk Septuagenario Oblata* (Leiden, 1955), 58–65; L. Richardson, jr, *Studies in Classical Art and Archaeology, A Tribute to Peter Heinrich von Blanckenhagen* (Locust Valley, New York, 1979), 209–15; M. Gaggiotti, *Anal-Rom* 14 (1985), 53ff.

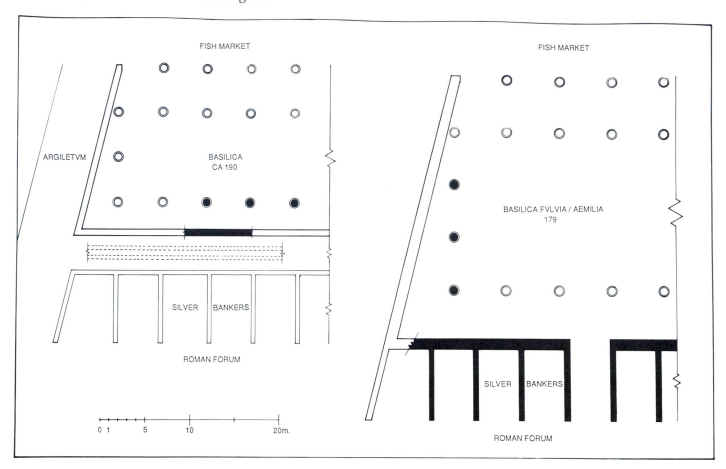

FIG. 71.   First basilica in Rome and Basilica Fulvia-Aemilia, partial plans, restored

After ten to fifteen years of use this first basilica was pulled down. Livy (40.51.5) again mentions that in 179 B.C. the censors Aemilius and Fulvius "contracted for a new basilica behind the new offices of the bankers and surrounded the fish market with shops that were for private use." This basilica was similar to the first but about one-third larger. It too faced on the fish market but backed directly on the bankers' offices, and there were one or two entrances from the Forum. But now the roofs of the rear aisle and the bankers' offices were treated as a special viewing platform, a *maenianum*. These new connections between the Forum and this basilica gave it a double function, but the vision of its lofty columned nave that stood some 20 m high and more than 112 m in length was also a new definition of Rome's civic center. Ten years later another basilica was erected on the opposite side of the Roman Forum, facing onto it. This, the Basilica Sempronia of 169 B.C., if it followed the design of the Basilica Fulvia-Aemilia, would also have anticipated the design of all the coming basilicas, Cosa's included.[18]

18. Livy 44.16.10–11.

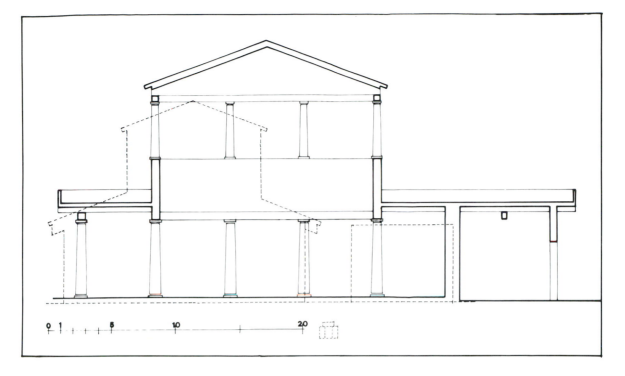

FIG. 72.   First basilica in Rome and Basilica Fulvia-Aemilia, sections, restored

The Basilica at Cosa had also, in some degree, transformed the NW and NE sides of the Forum, for its construction in the area between the Comitium/Curia complex and the N corner of the Forum entailed such extensive modification of the buildings flanking it as to amount to rebuilding. The walls of Curia III, it will be remembered, did not stand square (pages 139–40), but this was not the root of the trouble; it was rather that the architect of the Basilica wished to unify this side of the Forum and use the Comitium and Curia not only for space to arrange a stair to the gallery of the Basilica, but also as a rain catchment. This involved extensive alteration of the NW hall of the Curia and repavement of the Comitium.

In effect the NW wall of the Curia was demolished to bedrock and moved the amount of its thickness, 2 p.R. (0.59 m) to the NW to become a party wall with the SE aisle of the Basilica. Its line, curiously enough, does not seem to have been changed; at all events it was not straightened, so the SE wall of the Basilica is slightly bowed. The new masonry of the foundations is of random rubblework of unsquared limestone snecked with bits of tile and coarse pottery set in peppery, slightly friable mortar of sand and lime. There is a footing course, slightly spread, of large, quarry-shaped blocks laid on the rock without prepared bedding, and quoining in large dressed blocks at corners and openings. The wall is brought to a level top rendered with mortar at 96.01 m.a.s.l., above which are remains of six of an original series of eight joist holes, 0.25–0.30 m high, 0.22 m wide, and 0.33–0.43 m deep, to receive the floor joists, beams probably ideally 1 p.R. by $\frac{3}{4}$ p.R. Along the top of the joist holes is a setback in the wall of $\frac{1}{2}$ p.R. (0.14–0.15 m). One p.R. above the setback the wall was again brought to a level top; probably this represents the line of the pavement.

The sequence of work indicated by the evidence is the following: First a new wall was built tight against the NW flank of the Curia. This explains why there was no bond with it at the E corner of the Basilica and why in its construction the blocks of the old wall were not reused. It also explains, as nothing else will, why the new wall deviated from the square of the Forum just as the old one did, without apparently any attempt at correction. The suggestion is that the rooftree of the Curia projected, as the rooftree of a Tuscan temple did, and that in order to avoid having to dismantle the whole roof, the builders put up the new wall first, caught and supported the projecting ends of the heavy roof timbers on it, and then took down the old wall. The blocks of the old wall were then used in the continuation of the new one to the SW.

Along the upper part of the new wall on the Curia side climbed a stair, the print of four of whose steps, embedded at this end in the masonry, is very clear. Each step had a riser of 0.22–0.30 m and a tread of 0.37–0.38 m. The stair climbed from the level of the top of the Comitium steps to a landing supported on a rubblework vault, the broken haunch of which still survives. It would have consisted of fourteen steps with a total rise of 4.16 m. At the top one must have turned at right angles to go out to the terrace, or *basilicae contignatio*, covering the ambulatory around the Basilica. The foundation of the stair in the lower story, 22 p.R. (6.51 m) long and $4\frac{1}{2}$ p.R. (1.33 m) wide, is still reasonably well preserved. It consists of an L-shaped retaining wall of a single face of limestone boulders, set dry and without bond at either end, filled with earth and debris. The blocks show a tendency to increase in size toward the NE, where the base is deeper; the corner is quoined with larger blocks; and the wall is provided at the corner and short NE leg with a spread footing of 0.05–0.08 m. The wall is footed on bedrock without prepared bedding; presumably the earth floor of the existing cellar was dug out to build it.

Of the superstructure of the stair we may see the ruins in the mass of fallen stone that filled the cellar when it was excavated. Its supporting wall would have been built of random rubblework, and since no fragment that might have belonged to a stair block came to light, the stair itself would have been of wood or rubblework masonry faced with stucco, more probably the latter.

There are two niches cut in the wall under the stair and framed with small dressed blocks of limestone. That to the left stood c. 0.85 m above the pavement and 2.30–2.40 m from the line of the SW wall of the room. It would have been approximately 0.40–0.45 m square. Its companion, 0.85 m from it to the NE, would probably have been similar but is now badly ruined.

There is little trace of other change in the upper parts of the NW hall of the Curia at this time. The arrangement of the stair shows that it led outside, communicating with the Comitium, and if there was a door at its lower end, it must have opened outward. A thin curtain wall may have separated it from the rest of the room, but this has vanished. The gash where the bonded NW end of the SW wall has fallen out shows that it, too, was probably in part rebuilt, but this is of little help. The chunks of signinum pavement and large mosaic tesserae found in the debris filling the cellar of this hall are interpreted as remains of a pavement installed at this time or later, more likely at this time. It was relatively coarse, dark red signinum given a high surface finish and decorated at intervals, probably in lines, with mosaic tesserae. The fragments of signinum average c. 0.055 m thick; the tesserae average 0.02 m by 0.02 m by 0.016 m.

No plaster bearing recognizable decoration that could be assigned to a redecoration came to light. Either it disintegrated in the course of time, or else it was stripped from the walls for a subsequent redecoration with marble revetment. The latter, although possible, seems unlikely.

Thus the Curia remained in this period substantially the same as it had been before. The NW hall lost a narrow strip of space along its NW side but gained a bit in the N corner. The total loss was thus only a maximum of c. 4.60 square meters of floor space, and less, perhaps nothing, if space under the stair was accessible. Since we do not know the function of this hall, one cannot guess what difference the change would have made.

Since the changes in the NW hall of the Curia entailed dismantling of the N corner of the building, we may guess that it was at this time that the NE wall was torn out and rebuilt in masonry that matches that of the new NW wall for a distance of 9.20 m from the old N corner. At the same time the inner face of the rest of the NE wall of the podium of Curia II was dismantled and rebuilt in the new style. The alteration of the NE wall of the NW hall would have been dictated by necessity, that of the central hall by the wish to construct a cellar in the back half of its podium. The wall is normal in the stretch NW of the new doorway to the NW cellar. From this doorway to the doorway to the central cellar it is gradually thickened from 0.59 m to 0.79 m. Beyond the doorway to the center cellar it is simply a jamb for the doorway 0.80 m thick. The new inner face of the back wall of the podium attaches to this jamb and gradually widens a little to make a wall of a maximum thickness of 0.90 m. The thickening of the wall is clearly for the purpose of buttressing the heavy lateral walls in polygonal masonry of Curia II.

In the new NW cellar the little dry well for the drain of Comitium I and Curia III (pages 112–13) was no longer needed, since repavement of the Comitium now diverted the rain that collected there out toward the Forum. The pipe we have supposed carried the water the length of the room must now have been removed and the room refloored with beaten earth. Since the floor rose at least half a meter between its NE and SW ends, a space of only 8.58 m, it must have been either cut in shallow steps or very rude and steep. The fate of the dry well in this period is a mystery. Across its NW side was built a wall of limestone and mortar masonry, apparently to support the base of the NW wall of the Curia, although this was not necessary; its top must have been cut down, for only so can one account for the lack of intake and outlet channels; but it was not filled in. Perhaps it now served as a small reservoir, but it would have had to be filled by hand. The door to the new cellar shows some sign of being makeshift, despite the quoining of its jambs. It is 5 p.R. (1.48 m) wide, cut in two blocks of limestone. The outer sill, the thickness of the wall, stands 0.05–0.06 m above the inner. The inner is provided with square cuttings, c. 0.10 m on a side, for the metal shoes of the *cardines*, set just behind the jambs, and two *pessulus* notches, one tight against the outer sill just SE of center, the other 0.08 m behind the outer sill, 0.10 m NW of center.

Under the back half of the Curia proper a rough chamber was arranged by digging out part of the fill of its podium and fitting a door in the NE wall. The extent of this cellar could not be determined exactly in excavation, but certainly it did not pass the middle of the podium. The doorsill is cut in a great T-shaped block of coarse limestone that just fits in the opening, with smaller blocks fitted in around it. Like its companion to the NW it is 5 p.R. (1.48 m) wide, the raised outer sill $\frac{5}{8}$ p.R. (0.19 m) wide. The inner sill has a single cutting, roughly circular and 0.14 m in diameter, tight against the outer sill at its middle, but in the jamb on either side is a cutting for a metal fitting that has been removed. On the evidence this was a flattish rectangular bar, 0.03 m wide and more than 0.15 m long, with a short T-bar end set vertically that served to secure it. It is found in the top of the first course above the sill, only 0.23 m above the outer sill, so presumably it is one of a pair of hinges that stood near the top and bottom of the door. The door would have been of two leaves, one of which was secured by a bar that dropped into the central cutting in the sill. There is no evidence of change in the SE cellar of the Curia in this period.

The ground level along the NE side of the Curia in this period is shown by the sills of the doors, the occasional slight spread of the footing course, and the crests of bedrock. At the E corner of the building the footing of the building stood at 93.76 m.a.s.l.; at the door to the SE cellar the ground level was 94.25 m.a.s.l.; at the door to the center cellar it was 92.26 m.a.s.l. The fall of 1.99 m over a space of 15.20 m shows how steep and difficult any road along here must have been. In the absence of evidence, it has been presumed this was an unpaved footpath. No obvious use for these cellars presents itself.

At the other end of the Basilica, where the Porticus of the annex of Atrium Building I (page 138) had been covered by the NW aisle, this had also covered 13 p.R. (3.85 m) of the earlier Porticus of AB I and its terminal column. This in turn had blocked most of the broad opening of Taberna 5, leaving only a door, 4 p.R. (1.184 m) wide, just beyond the Basilica (Figs. 58, 69, 70), while the *maenianum* above overhung and intersected the sloping roof of the taberna. Furthermore the third and now last column of the Porticus stood 5 p.R. (1.48 m) from the *maenianum*. Having no further entablature to support its roof, the space between

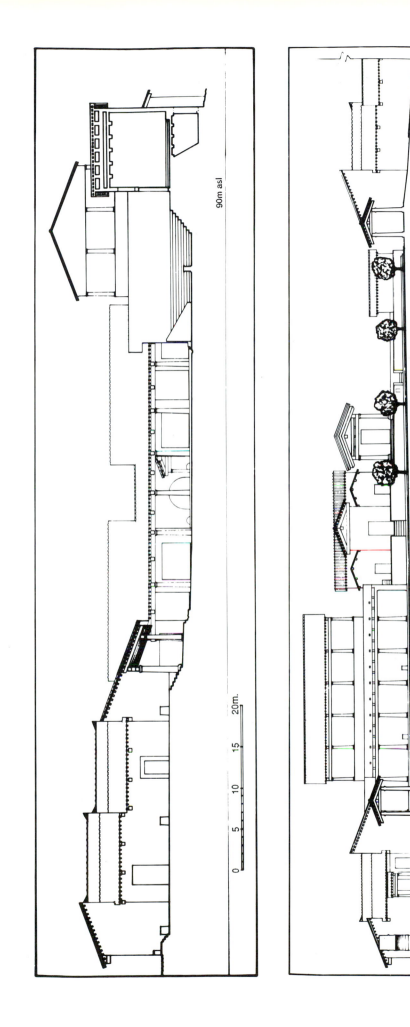

90m asl

0 5 10 15 20m.

90m asl

0 5 10 15 20m.

Fig. 73. Forum, as of 135 B.C., elevations and sections, NW/NE

was either left open to the sky, or the roof was raised to the height of the *maenianum* by a prop and an extension projected to the SW at the W corner of the gallery.

Another component of the Basilica, extending to the entire NE side of the Square from the NW ambulatory to the SE Porticus, was the steps rising beside the NE gutter (page 18). These obviously corresponded to the similar stairs of the SW Porticus of thirty years earlier (pages 121–22), where, beside the leveled Atrium Buildings and central Annex, the Porticus sloped downward with the SW gutter. On the NE side the remains of the gutter and some of the steps above have survived at both ends, lengths of 8.40 m near the upper end and 7.50 m near the lower (Pls. 241, 242), sufficient to show that the gutter declined northwestward, 0.74 m over $295\frac{1}{4}$ p.R. (87.40 m). At the NW end of the Basilica, from gutter to floor, there were two risers of 1 p.R. (0.296 m) and treads of 1 p.R. (0.296 m) and 2 p.R. (0.592 m). But having a level floor above, the lower step must have disappeared about three-fourths of the way along the front of the

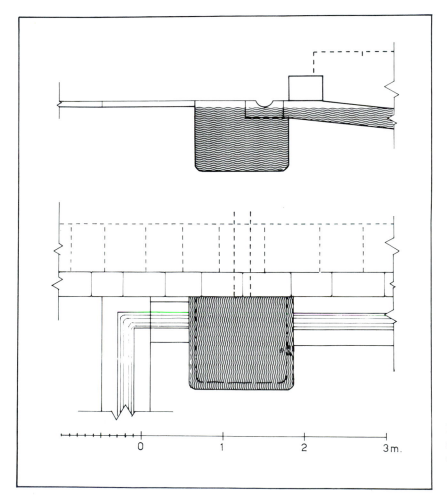

FIG. 74.   Basilica, new settling basin, N corner of square

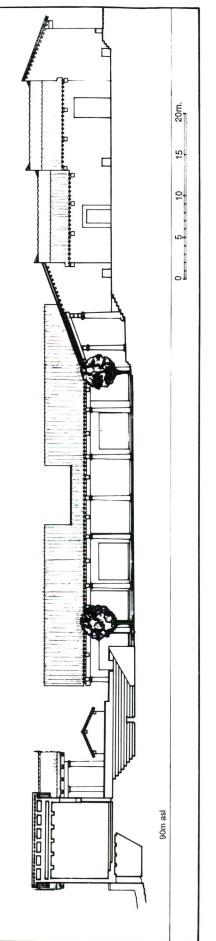

90m asl

Fig. 75.   Forum, as of 135 B.C., elevation and section looking SE

building because of the rising gutter, and at the SE end the upper step would have had a riser of only about 0.26 m. At the SE extremity of the Square, however, the gutter and steps were cut into the rock, all dropping down toward the Basilica, crossing the open portals of the forecourt of Temple B and the Comitium, where the base of the plastered wall had once been covered by the steps (page 16; Pl. 8). These steps on SW and NE, the sidewalks on the NW, and the sockets on the SE (pages 119–20) had finally framed the Square (Fig. 73).

The NE gutter now terminated in a new settling basin in the N corner of the Square (Fig. 74), almost twice the depth of the abandoned basin higher up to the SE (page 114; Fig. 42), to accommodate the increase in volume from a second gutter entering on the other side. This was the NW gutter, which had now changed grade. Inclined from W down to N beside the Porticus, AB II, the NW entranceway, and AB I, it augmented the supply to the cisterns of the Basilica. The present fourteen gutter blocks, together a length of 19.40 m, sloping at 0.0085 percent, had the same angle of declination as the NE gutter. These changes of the NW gutters (pages 114–15) appear to have followed on the discovery that the settling basin at the top of the NW entranceway had not functioned properly, while the basin in the W corner of the Square was sufficient to fill the Reservoir in the W corner of the Forum. Hence the NE and NW gutters came to supply the cisterns of the Basilica, which held 633 cubic meters or 167,000 gallons, and the SE and SW gutters supplied the Reservoir, which held 750 cubic meters or 198,150 gallons.

By this time the Cosans had built permanent houses with their own appropriate cisterns,[19] and at least two of the four reservoirs that had once provided water for domestic use were reserved for special purposes. Among these will likely have been the provision for a bath building built directly across Street O from the Reservoir at the W corner of the Forum. While the bath has not been excavated, it is the sort of public amenity that came into use at this time and should be considered as part of the overall development of the Forum that had now been realized.[20] The Forum was not to undergo significant change again until the end of the republican era.

19. Brown 1980, 63–66, and *Cosa IV, The Houses.*   20. Brown 1951, 82–84.

IX. 40/30 B.C.–A.D. 265/275

(Figs. 76–78; Pls. 243–58)

Those that lived within the walls of Cosa at the time of the sack of the city in 70 B.C. would have been some 1,000 to 1,200, and in the territory of the colony, including Old Cosa (Orbetello), about 8,000 more. These latter do not seem to have been attacked, but the Cosans of Ansedonia who did not escape were undoubtedly killed or enslaved. Ever since the Julian law of 90 B.C. wealthy Romans had been buying farms from impoverished colonists. Such were L. Domitius Ahenobarbus and L. or P. Sestius[1] and others, unknown except for their now ruined villas.[2] In accounts of later years of colonizing by Pompey, Caesar, and Octavian we find in the *Naturalis Historia* of Pliny mention of "Cosa of the Volcientes, founded by the Roman people, also Giglio and Giannutri . . . both opposite the coast of Cosa."[3] This tells of only the first colony of Cosa of 273 B.C. and the second of 197 B.C., no other. It shows that it was Cosans out in the territory or in Old Cosa that returned and settled in the plundered

1. L. Domitius Ahenobarbus: Cicero, *ad Att*. 9.9.3; Caesar, *Bell. Civ.* 1.34.2. L. or P. Sestius: F. Munzer, "P. Sestius," *RE* 24 (1923), 1886–90; T. R. S. Broughton, *The Magistrates of the Roman Republic* (New York, 1962), 2.168, 202, 264, 278; Cicero, *pro Sestio* 3.7.71; *ad Att*. 15.27.1.
2. L. Quilici and S. Quilici Gigli, "Ville dell'agro cosano con fronte a torrette," *RivIstArch* (1978), 11–64; A. Carandini and S. Settis, *Schiavi e padroni nell'Etruria romano* (Bari, 1979); Brown 1980, 70–71.
3. Pliny, *NH* 3.51 and 81: *Cosa Volcientium a populo Romano deducta* and *item Igilium et Dianum . . . ambae contra Cosanum litus*.

and empty site. The period of barrenness is shown by the new ceramics that appeared when the new settlers arrived. Black-glaze pottery had gone and Arretine was at hand. Thin-wall pottery was now lacquered and glazed, black or orange, while Aco and Cusonius were about. Deep saucepans had come, and wheel-thrown lamps were no more.[4]

Those who had come back or offered themselves as settlers were not, however, as many as before. In the excavated residential area in the NW part of the town (Plan I) eight dwellings had been burned down, never to rise again, along Streets L and M and Street 5, while only two above on Street N had been refurbished for use. In fact, the remains of the town as a whole give a picture of buildings restored unevenly in the center, the work concentrated around the Forum and the Arx, while a broad sweep up to the crumbling fortifications on the E, N, and W was probably converted to agricultural use.

The population of the first colony and republican municipium had for two hundred years lost coins that reappeared in the excavations, to a number of 393, which would have been at a rate of about two each year. The second imperial municipium of some three hundred years also dropped coins, but not more than about two hundred, or at a rate of two each three years. This would imply a population of only about 740 and 205 plots for the period between Hadrian and Commodus. The coins on the hill give the same picture as do the amphoras from the port, of which about two thousand have been found. The amphoras of the first period of the Portus Cosanus, 170–70 B.C., were 60 percent of the total. After the sack and the long period of disuse of the Portus Cosanus, it had silted up and Portus Herculis was the only harbor. The amphoras from 40/30 B.C. to the end of the first century after Christ make up 26 percent of the whole, while those of the second are but 14 percent.

In the Forum the Atrium Buildings on the Square lost all their tabernae but one. Two, AB VII and VIII, were not rebuilt, but VII became a farm or farms and VIII a stoneyard, while AB VI appears to have been a barnyard. AB I, AB II, AB III, AB IV, and AB V became houses with tabernae in the rear on Streets O, 5, and 7. These were inherently ready to become houses, and AB I was the largest. In its atrium there had been only one cubiculum (18) and two alae, but now two larger rooms were arranged on the SE side. These had been Entryway 4 and Taberna 5, which now had added an exterior blind wall on the Forum side and a new wall between the two new rooms. The floors of these had been brought down to the level of the floors of the atrium, 0.78 m below the portico. Corridor 12 beside Room 18 made it possible to add more rooms northeastwards: a large kitchen and stove (11), a bathroom (6) and closet (14), a workroom (21), and a shed for storage (16).

Apart from the house there were four tabernae on Street O in function again,

---

4. *MAAR* 32 (1973), 93–149, 34 (1980), 239–78;
Dyson 1976, 115–19; *Scientific American* 247 (1982), 148–58.

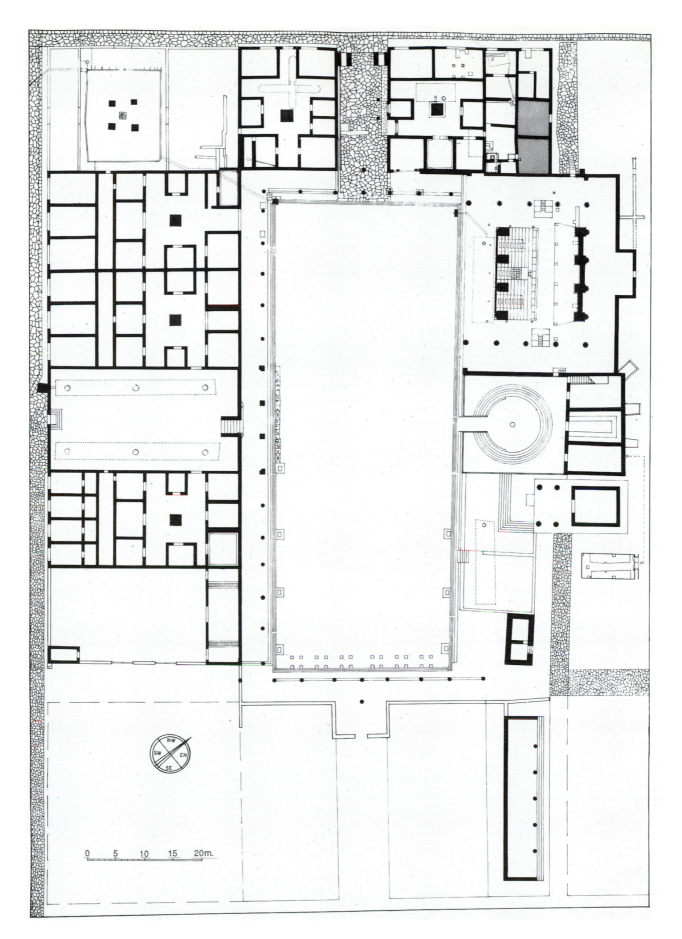

Fig. 76. Forum, restored plan, 40/30 B.C.–A.D. 265/275

one (13–19) architecturally unchanged (page 74), while the other three (15, 26/24, and 25) had counters built at their doors. In 15 was found a little baldachin with supports at the four corners set against the middle of the back wall, raised on various blocks of travertine and two capitals, one Doric and one Ionic. Another taberna (22) was opened on Street 7 by blocking the door from the Storage Shed 16. The shop sold hardware and ceramics. The office with entrance porch on the NW entranceway near the magistrate's platform (pages 132–35) was open again, and so was Taberna 2. Since there was now no other taberna facing the Square, this one may well have been used as the office of the aedile of the Forum.

The original AB II was the mirror image of AB I, but the two openings on the NW entranceway had long been closed up (pages 77–78 and 115). When it was made a house the entrances to the two tabernae and the fauces on the Square were blocked up, while tabernae and an entrance from Street O must have been opened. The regular corridor to the back, like Corridor 12 of AB I, here opening on the SW, was probably in use, because of the remains of an arrangement of basins just outside, probably belonging to the house. All but three of the rooms, eight in all, opened on the atrium. One, the SW taberna on the Square, had to be shored up with two parallel walls, making one large room and one narrow one. In the E corner of the larger room rainwater was piped down from the eaves and into the narrow room, perhaps to make a kitchen or bathroom.

The three houses along the SW side of the Square, Atrium Buildings III–V, were backed by a row of tabernae opening along Street 5 (pages 89–97). AB III was now the only one with entry from the Square. The NW taberna there had fallen in ruins, and the new owner pushed the new NW wall outside the old foundations. This made a new room, $21\frac{1}{2}$ p.R. wide and $11\frac{1}{2}$ p.R. deep (6.37 m by 3.30 m), entered by a slightly shorter corridor, 5 p.R. wide (1.48 m). The room was paved with a signinum floor with cover-joints around the edge, probably a bathroom, somewhat like the remodeling of the SW taberna of AB II. The rest of the rooms around the atrium were probably six, three of them on the SW side making a bank of rooms with a tablinum on the axis of the entrance; behind them was the long passageway that once had given access to the cellar tabernae below those on Street 5. The doors of these cellar tabernae were blocked up and the shops filled in, leaving the passageway an alley behind the house with access to the W Reservoir outside.

The tabernae and vestibula of AB IV and V had been closed toward the Square and each opened on the SW Annex, where the two cisterns could be drawn on for water. In the vestibulum room of AB IV the NW wall and in that of AB V the SE wall had been shored up with a second wall (Pl. 243), as in AB II. A thick signinum paving was laid in the taberna of AB IV to raise the floor level (Pl. 244), while the SE taberna of AB V received a fine mosaic floor (Pl. 245). From what is known of these rooms it may be assumed that atria and storerooms would have been modified as well.

The party wall between AB V and AB VI had collapsed sometime after 70 B.C. along a line about 0.50 m above the old floor. When that wall was rebuilt, AB V was a house, but the other a yard for grazing (Pl. 246), except for buildings at its NE end and S corner. The doors of the two tabernae and the fauces on the Square had been blocked up and the interior walls torn down, making a single long room of these (Pl. 247), crossed by the remains of two structures of masonry, low and thick, symmetrically located near the ends of the room. One higher than the other showed the bottom of a thick signinum-lined channel. They thus appear to have been troughs or mangers for cattle.

The Basilica had stood since the reoccupation of the site, apparently molder-ing, until the central part of the NW wall collapsed outward, falling into Rooms 16 and 22 of AB I (pages 135–37), filling them with its mass of stone and terracotta. In the depths of Taberna 22 were found two fine Tiberian asses, one of A.D. 15–16 and the other of A.D. 34–37.[5] Within a decade what was left of the upper part of the Basilica was demolished and an odeum was rising from a new floor of signinum (Fig. 77). In the nave the inner eight lower columns in the middle were backed by and engaged in stout rectangular piers measuring $6\frac{1}{6}$ p.R. (1.84 m) by 5 p.R. (1.48 m) of blocks of limestone with brick bonding at intervals between courses to a height of $15\frac{1}{6}$ p.R. (4.45 m). Where the blind story and upper columns had been, archivolts crossed from pier to pier across the nave. Springing from the piers they measured $5\frac{1}{4}$ p.R. by 4 p.R. (1.55 m by 1.184 m) with a crown on the radius of $19\frac{1}{8}$ p.R. (5.67 m) about $34\frac{3}{16}$ p.R. (10.20 m) from the floor, support-ing the roof to an overall height of about $55\frac{3}{4}$ p.R. (16.50 m) above floor level.

Sometime between A.D. 500 and 1000 all but one of these piers, the E one, had split and fallen northward, perhaps shaken in an earthquake (Pl. 249). They were found lying in the earth about a meter above the floor of the Odeum.

The piers also bolstered the substructures of the rectangular, ascending bank of seats and of the raised stage and scenery. The tiers of seats, about $1\frac{1}{2}$ p.R. (0.44 m) high and 2 p.R. (0.592 m) wide, rose to the top of the columns on walls 2 p.R. (0.592 m) and $2\frac{3}{8}$ p.R. (0.70 m) thick running alongside the piers. The walls supported ramped vaults bearing the seats, the central vault interrupted halfway down by a passage through from a flight of seven steps rising from behind. At the bottom, facing the stage, two wider steps rose from the floor $3\frac{1}{4}$ p.R. (0.962 m) and $2\frac{1}{2}$ p.R. (0.74 m) wide; on these the bisellia of the *decuriones* would have been placed. The Odeum, not being semicircular, still located its tribunalia between the block of seats and the stage, set back on either side. These were $10\frac{1}{2}$ p.R. (3.10 m) square, and although only their foundations remain (Pls. 226, 236), they were probably raised above the stage, like other tribunalia. Each would have required a stair of access and a platform for at least eight curule chairs for magistrates.

Across the floor from the seats the evidence for the wooden stage is six framed sockets of travertine, $\frac{3}{4}$ p.R. (0.22 m) square, in a row 12 p.R. (3.55 m) apart, the row

5. Buttrey 1980, CE 1201 and CE 1050.

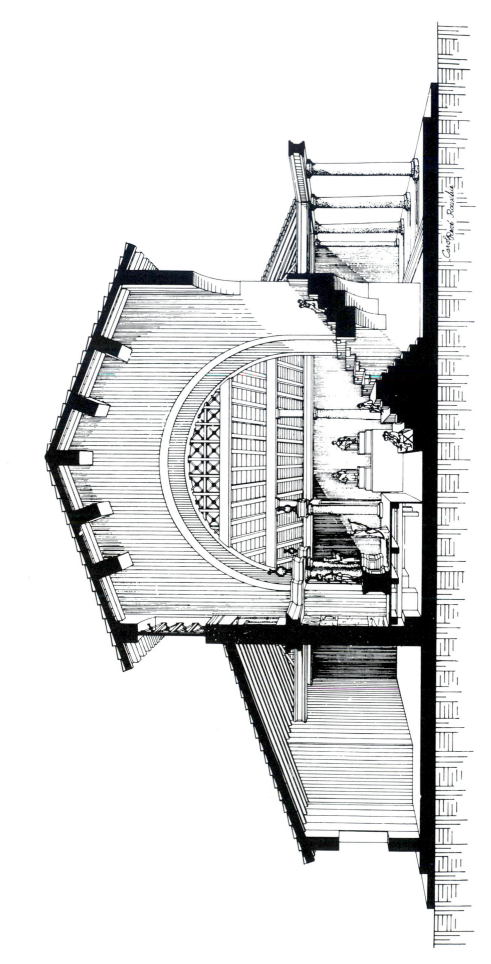

Fig. 77. Odeum, restored section (G. C. Izenour)

$60\frac{1}{2}$ p.R. (17.90 m) long and 12 p.R. (3.55 m) from the NE piers. To the bases of these piers had been added stone curbs along the inner faces and sides, and between them the three walls of the scaena were set back from the SW face 3 p.R. (0.90 m) in the middle and 2 p.R. (0.60 m) in the others, where beneath the stage two buttresses had been added. The highest part of the scaena (Pl. 251) shows a groove $\frac{1}{8}$ p.R. (0.037) deep and $4\frac{1}{2}$ p.R. (1.33 m) above the Odeum floor, surely for the insertion of the wooden floor of the stage, and as high as Vitruvius prescribes (5.6.2). The stage itself with its supporting posts, beams, and joists of wood had, in due course, naturally disintegrated.

The edge of the stage was tangent to the two columns beyond on either side, and before each is a travertine square, $1\frac{1}{16}$ p.R. (0.555 m) on a side, embedded in the new floor. Like the earlier bases for statues (pages 219–21), these would have honored those responsible for the Odeum. The same columns might have been used for rigging a curtain for the stage. Since the drapery would have been unframed and extended about 84 p.R. (24.86 m) from column to column, it would have had to be taut. Near the NW column is a square travertine block, $1\frac{1}{2}$ p.R. (0.45 m) on a side, level with the floor and centered with a square socket, $\frac{1}{2}$ p.R. (0.15 m) on a side. Fitted with a block of wood with a sheave or winch, it may have served to raise and lower the curtain for the performance.

On the floor and in the earth above (page 241) were found nineteen fragments of inscriptions on marble, seven and three of which could be recomposed into two groups. Both were found in the SE nave of the Odeum, were 0.02 m thick, and preserved remains of four lines: 0.028, 0.039, 0.039, and 0.062 m high with interspaces of 0.028, 0.028, and 0.03 m. The bottom line would have been about $4\frac{1}{2}$ p.R. (1.34 m) long and the overall height 0.292 m. As recomposed the two parts of the inscription record a restoration (Pl. 252).

nero.CaesaR.TI(beri)

claudI.CaesariS.AUG(usti)

gerMANICi.p(ecunia)p(ublica)F(ecit)

odeum sua PEcunIA.RESTITuit

Most of the first line had suffered in the *damnatio memoriae* of Nero, but the inscription is essentially clear: Nero Caesar, son of Tiberius Claudius Augustus Germanicus. The public money had built the Basilica; his money had rebuilt it as an Odeum.

These titles were used only from A.D. 50 until Claudius's death in A.D. 54. This marble plaque probably was affixed to the SE pillar about halfway above the stage and later fell or was torn down (Pl. 251). Nero's connection with Cosa is not strange. His natural father was Cn. Domitius Ahenobarbus, his mother Julia Agrippina. When after nine years Domitius died, Julia Agrippina added to her property all his possessions around Cosa, Monte Argentario, and the lagoon of

Orbetello. Her boy had surely contemplated Cosa and its Basilica, and when Claudius married Agrippina and adopted Nero, he might well have given his new son the opportunity to create the Odeum of Cosa, where he could devote himself to his singing at liberty.

A door, about $3\frac{1}{2}$ p.R. (1.04 m) wide, was opened at either end of the Odeum at different times. The first was from the Comitium, using the steps of the SE *suggestus* of the Basilica (Fig. 69; Pls. 231 and 226). It was cut at the time of the building of the Odeum, when the surbase was removed, broken up, and used as rubble in the tribunal, to widen the steps for the decuriones coming from the Curia to their places in the Odeum. On the opposite side the second door stood above a narrow solid stair from Street 7, 2.47 m high with ten treads and nine risers, a platform and a doorsill (Pl. 253). On the surfaces of the treads broken tegulae had been sunk into the mortar, flanges down, except for one bearing a stamp of the time of Hadrian (CD 1039 = *CIL* 15.298). This part of Street 7 (cf. Plan I) was in reality simply an alley, and the stair and door appear to have served as a stage door for the performers and stagehands.

The Curia and the NW Hall had somehow been shaken and shifted a bit, as appears from the layers of fill under the Curia. So three buttresses of stone were built against the NE wall for reinforcement, one placed diagonally against the N corner, about 3.00 m long and 2.30 m wide (Pl. 255), the other two at the ends of the long sides of the Curia, (a) 2.50 m long and 1.75–1.90 m wide (Pl. 103) and (b) probably 2.20 m long and 1.35–1.55 m wide, as though these walls had begun to slip over the slope of the rock to the N. The SE Hall and basement, however, seem not to have been affected.

About the middle of the second century after Christ this cellar became a humble Mithraeum, an artificial grotto with an earth floor. Parallel to the long cellar walls were built curbs of unmortared fieldstone, within which platforms of earth made places for banquet couches that could have provided space for about thirty devotees. In the middle of these platforms against the walls, but off-center toward the door, stand the two square bases that normally appear for the attendants of Mithras, Cautes and Cautopates; and a little beyond toward the back each platform has the usual "ritual" niche (Pl. 256). At the end of the grotto is a square pillar, centered, partly tumbled, 2 p.R. (0.60 m) on a side and at least 4 p.R. (1.20 m) high, made of tiles and blocks, standing 0.74 m from the back wall (Pl. 257) with a ritual well hollowed out under it from the front and lined with mortar. There are two other bases, both rectangular, one 0.70 m by 0.40 m at the end of the SE platform, and the other 0.50 m by 0.30 m in the W corner.

Two of these bases were large enough to support life-size sculptures, and part of a leg was found of white marble from mid-calf to ankle, rough finished with a strut behind, which might well have been a Mithras from the base at the end of the SE curb (Pl. 258). Behind the tall pillar Mithras might have been shown slaying the bull in a mural painting.

Some five bronze coins were found in or on the earth floor.[6] Three of them showed only the slightest wear and two wear only in minor details. They covered seventy-five years from Lucius Verus to Gordian III, from A.D. 164 to A.D. 241. Eleven terracotta lamps were found on the floor still whole or crushed; these were types that were in use up to about A.D. 400, undoubtedly the last days of the Mithraeum.[7]

Temple B and its forecourt seem not to have changed in this period, except that at some point a wall divided the sanctuary from the lesser forecourt. The Carcer (pages 38–41) went on to be a cabin, but the Colonnade beyond was in use only up to the third century after Christ, when an exedra was built across the SE entranceway with an opening $7\frac{1}{8}$ p.R. (2.11 m) wide. It was obvious that the municipium of Cosa was declining and that Old Cosa (Orbetello on the peninsula in the lagoon) and Cosa on the hill were alike gradually fading away.

Five emperors over sixty years attempted to give assistance to these towns without positive result. In A.D. 213 at least three inscriptions had been set up on the Arx (CB 715, CB 576/900, CC 701–703) and three in Old Cosa (*CIL* 11.2633a, 2633b, and one in the Antiquarium of Orbetello). It can be determined that two of these were from a generous emperor, Caracalla, and two were from the devoted *municipes*. The fulsome language would be explained by remission of taxes for the imperial fiscus. In A.D. 236 the *Curam Agens* of the municipium noted that the Porticus in the Forum, the houses there and the Odeum were in decay, and he was allowed by the Imperator Maximinus to take the public money necessary for renewing these buildings.[8] Five years later *pecunia publica* was given by Gordian III (A.D. 241), and the Cosans zealously lauded his divinity and majesty.[9] Trajan Decius (A.D. 251) gave money for a builder to make Cosa "holy and free" again.[10] And finally Aurelian (A.D. 271?) tried to help one or the other of these towns.[11] After six hundred years the Res Publica Cosanorum was dying. The last Cosans had probably already left their houses and farms on the summit, gradually settling in the rich plain below to the east, naming it Succosa, i.e., Sub Cosa (Fig. 78),[12] where they were nearer the Via Aurelia at one end and the lagoon and the sea at the other.

6. Buttrey 1980, CG 405, 407, 409, 410, 417.

7. See C. R. Fitch and N. W. Goldman, *Cosa: The Lamps* (forthcoming).

8. *Chiron* 11 (1981), 309–14.

9. *CIL* 11.2634.

10. *AJP* 83 (1962), 147–58.

11. *CIL* 11.2635, 2636.

12. *Ravennatis Anonymi Cosmographia* 4.32 and 5.2; *Tabula Peutingeriana* 99–100 and Pl. Bc 3.2.

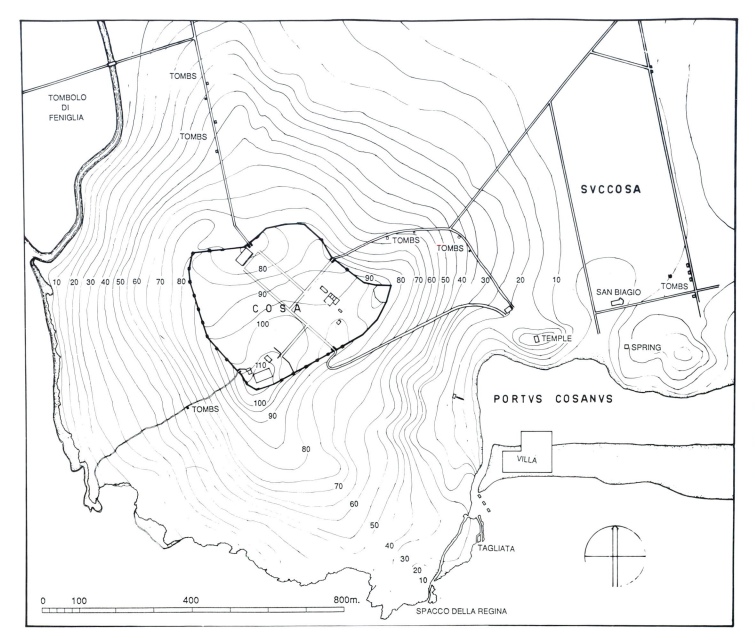

FIG. 78. Cosa and Succosa

X. A.D. 330–415

(Fig. 79; Pls. 259–68)

Cosa was still a place and a name but never again a municipium. From about A.D. 270 it was desolate and devastated for sixty years or so. The old buildings of the Forum along the SW and NW sides had collapsed or been demolished, and the Odeum and Comitium/Curia were in ruins. Only the walls of the Fornices, Temple B, and the Carcer still stood. Only eight coins were dropped in the Forum in those years. But then around A.D. 330 the NE part of the Forum underwent rebuilding as a marketplace for a village of farmers and herdsmen settled within the ancient walls of the old town, a *latifundium,* it seems, with an overseer, a *magister.* This estate seems to have been a hive of activity over some seventy years; the number of bronze coins that strayed increased from Constantine I to Valentinian II, when they came to an abrupt end.

Two boundaries of the old Forum were still Street 5 and Street O with its two entrances there, but they were now roads or paths of trodden earth, well above the ancient paving stones, like those of the first husbandmen who used the surveyors' grids for their pathways and farmyards. Now, however, the old Forum had been more or less evenly divided lengthwise through the Square from NW to SE. The NE portion was the new Forum, parceled out among religion, industry, trade, dwellings, and the office of the administrator. The SW portion

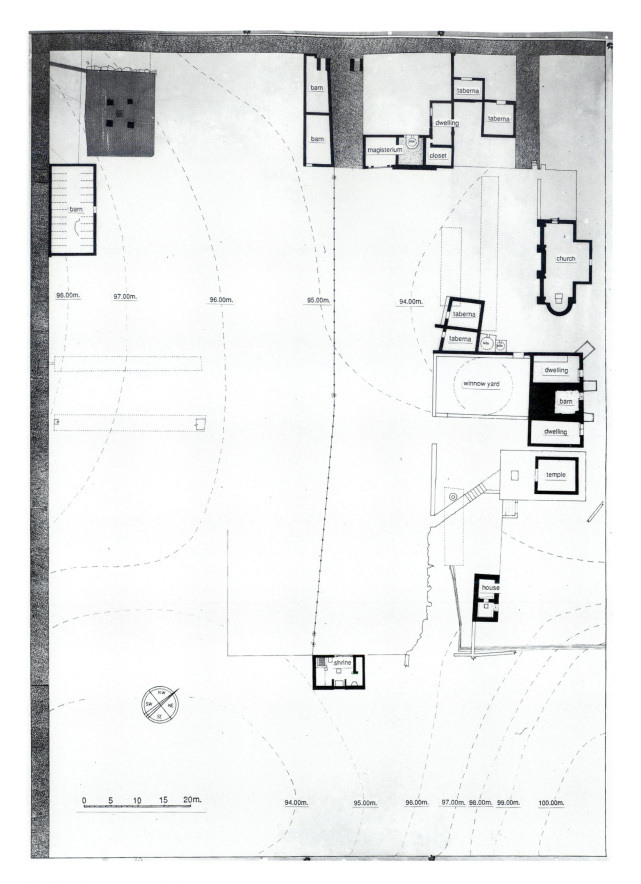

Fig. 79. Forum, restored plan, A.D. 330–415

up to Street 5 was evidently a tract of pasture for domestic animals. The partition through the old Square appears to have been marked by a line of fence posts, of which four postholes were found at each end and at the middle. Moreover, at the W end were a cistern, a reservoir, and three new barn-like buildings. The largest of these, near the Reservoir, had once been a row of three or four tabernae behind Atrium Building III (Plan VII). They had been demolished, but the outer walls had then been rebuilt above them (page 91; Fig. 33; Pl. 66). This building, $60\frac{1}{2}$ p.R. by $30\frac{1}{2}$ p.R. (17.80 m by 9.00 m), was most likely a stable for cattle and horses. Flocks of sheep and goats would have grazed on the pastures until the newborn lambs and kids needed to be put in their barns. These were surely the two new buildings built together over the NE side of Atrium Building II and the SW side of the NW entranceway (Plan V). Presumably the SE barn was for the sheep, adjacent to the pasture. The goats, using the SW archway of the Fornices as a door and emerging onto the upper Street O, would have preferred the wooded glades and underbrush.

On the NW side of the Forum six rooms were linked in a chain among the open spaces near the lower Street O and the two passageways leading to the Square and Church. One of these rooms had been a taberna facing the Square like the others (pages 70–73; Pl. 38), but when these were gone (page 240) this became the *Aedilitas*, from which the supervision of the Square, the markets, and the games had gone on, and finally the *Magisterium* where the manager took care of the estate.

The other rooms turned to the road and passageways, and three of them had certainly been a pottery. In the doorway of that adjacent to the *Magisterium*, but facing NW, a kiln $7\frac{3}{4}$ p.R. (2.30 m) in diameter had been installed (Pl. 259), while the two side rooms next to this on the NE were connected. Behind the kiln were broken mortars, bowls, pitchers, cups, and lids. Some were found in the smaller side room and a few in the larger room. It all fits together: kiln for the firing, supplies in the closet, and workshop. The wall of the NE side of these side rooms ran down to the road, and on the other side were two more rooms between this and Street 7. They had been tabernae earlier (pages 135–37 and 240) and had now been rebuilt, while all the others had been leveled. Open to the road with space in front of them, they may have been the only tabernae in the village.

Within another generation the ruined buildings along the NE side of the Forum had been partly rebuilt, but for different uses, with one exception. In the Basilica/Odeum the underlying floors and bank of seating had been covered by fallen building material and earth, out of which still rose the NE piers, the scaena (pages 241–43), and the tribunal (page 241). These remains became a small church, $62\frac{1}{2}$ p.R. long and $23\frac{5}{8}$ to 33 p.R. wide (18.50 m by 7.00–9.75 m). The sides were existing remains of the Basilica/Odeum, while the ends were new, an apse to the SE and a NW wall and entranceway. In the center of the apse were a step and the altar, while before the doorway was an open court and what was left of the flight of steps down to Street 7 for those coming from NW or NE.

Where the S corner of the Basilica/Odeum had been, two other ovens and two tabernae were now built (Pls. 226, 262). The ovens and one of the tabernae had been backed against the SE wall of the Basilica, which still stood and on the other side of which a fill about 1.40 m deep above the floor of the Comitium (Pl. 11) was put down, contained by a new wall on the line of the SE side of the podium of the Curia, 11.65 m long (Pls. 10, 264). The surface of the fill sloped from the top to the center, a tamped and leathery floor, while two openings to the area led from the S corner out to the Square and from the N corner down beside the new ovens. These units were connected and appear to have been the bakery of the village. In the yard the chaff would be winnowed from the grain. In the tabernae the grain would be ground and the dough kneaded, while the ovens baked the bread.

At the end of the base of the wall between the two tabernae were found two headless marble statues, life-size, draped figures of a man and a woman (Pls. 265, 266). Evidently they had come from the Basilica/Odeum, and the bakers, who were pagan, brought them here and kept them. The Curia and the Halls on either side having collapsed, the three basement cellars were roofed and used as dwellings, sheds, or barns in connection with the fields below.

Temple B survived through the first quarter of the fourth century after Christ; it then collapsed. One of the capitals (Pl. 108) fell into the Comitium before it was converted to use as a threshing floor. Certainly capitals and columns of slabs of sandstone must have fallen together, dragging down the roof of the pronaos. When the temple was rebuilt, it was confined to the cella. At that time the blocks of the steps from the forecourt had evidently been extracted for use in other buildings and places (Fig. 56), but the devout still made their way to the altar. The ancient jail nearby had become a dwelling, perhaps for the priest or sacristan. Below and between the temple and dwelling the old cistern was still in use, and beyond there were a number of partition walls marking out fields.

The ruined exedra at the center of the SE end of the Forum (page 121) was now remodeled as a shrine, a temple of Bacchus or Liber Pater.[1] The exedra had been 30 p.R. (8.89 m) long and 20 p.R. (5.92 m) wide, but the Shrine was divided across the front, having a square middle, 18 p.R. (5.33 m) on a side, and flanked by two rectangles with widths of 6 p.R. (1.77 m). Its walls were partly of the demolished Atrium Buildings VII and VIII and partly the back of the exedra, whose opening to the SE entranceway had to be closed. The other walls of the Shrine were uneven in texture, being both reused stones and bricks in coarse mortar.

The single doorway from the Square to the central room with its earth floor was a portal some $9\frac{1}{2}$ p.R. (2.81 m) wide with cuttings for the door frame and two doors, not centered because of a rubblework pedestal to the SW. In the center of the room a solitary cubical altar was found, also of rubblework, and at the back a

---

1. J. Collins-Clinton, *A Late Antique Shrine of Liber Pater at Cosa* (Études préliminaires aux religions   orientales dans l'empire romain 64 [Leiden, 1977]).

larger base. This was $4\frac{7}{8}$ p.R. by $3\frac{1}{2}$ p.R. (1.45 m by 1.03 m) and originally would have stood higher than its present height of 0.43 m (Pl. 267). Beside it lay a broken and headless statue of the young Bacchus (Pl. 268). Five other pieces of carved marble found here had presumably been taken from the ruins of the houses of the old town, all being first or second century in date, with even a dedication to Liber by a certain Zoe Mater. Partition walls from the back, about $4\frac{1}{2}$ p.R. (1.33 m) long, closely flanked the base on either side; they may have supported a baldachin over the standing Bacchus or perhaps were shelves for candles or lamps at night.

The lateral rectangles of the Shrine occupied the remaining signinum floor of the exedra, about 0.20–0.30 m above the central room. One-half of the NE side was covered and probably was a closet for supplies of food and drink and perhaps a dressing room, and at the outside corner a shaft of travertine on which to set one of the ornaments was found. Beyond, at the SE end, was a crude semicircular base, 4 p.R. (1.18 m) wide. The SW lateral rectangle was open to the center and arranged in thirds. Above the signinum floor at the SE end was a low wall, 0.50 m thick and about $1\frac{1}{4}$ p.R. (0.37 m) high. Behind it a mass of stone and clay stretched to the SW wall of the building. The top surface of this was nowhere found, but it would have been in area about 3.50 m by 1.77 m. Its general form suggests a banquet couch for six recumbent priests at a sacred meal. At its NW end was another square shaft on which a "Doric" capital, taken from the SE Porticus of the old Square, had been placed; on this probably stood the money jar for the Shrine, to judge by the number of coins found on the floor around it. The rest of the NW end of the SW side suggests a lustral basin, whose floor was the signinum pavement and whose sides rose to a height of 0.55 m or more.

The cults of the Temple, Shrine, and Church were all active in the Cosan village when Emperor Constantius II (A.D. 337–361) forbade the observance of pagan cults, first in A.D. 340 and again in A.D. 346.[2] Forty-four years later Valentinian II (A.D. 375–392) enforced the same law in A.D. 390,[3] and paganism vanished. The ruined Shrine, the broken effigies, and the one hundred fifteen coins on the floor exposed what Christianity could do about A.D. 400. The old Temple B must also have been destroyed, but then it came to life anew some five hundred years later as a church.

The Christians then could not have known that they would presently die or flee. When young Rutilius Claudius Namatianus passed a night at Portus Herculis in A.D. 416,[4] the people there told him that Cosa across the bay was desolate, because of a plague of mice. Rutilius thought this ridiculous, but the sailors would have had no doubts about this plague, the rat fleas, and rat-bite fever. So the Cosani passed away, and Cosa became Ansedonia.

2. Cod. Theod. 16.1.2 and 16.10.4.
3. Cod. Theod. 16.10.12.
4. E. H. Keene and C. F. Savage-Armstrong,

Rutili Namatiani de Reditu Suo (London, 1907), 54–55, 103, 132–33, 200; Ernst Doblhofer, ed., *De Reditu Suo* (Heidelberg, 1972), 1: 33–38, 108; 2: 138–42.

APPENDIXES

Appendix 1.   Paestum, "Teatro Circolare"

(Figs. 80–83)

On the N side of the Forum of Paestum, just E of the short axis of the Forum, lies the ruin of a building variously known and referred to in guide books as the Teatro Greco, Teatro Circolare, Bouleuterion, and Ecclesiasterion.[1] This was originally very similar to the Comitium/Curia complex of Cosa. It was excavated with funds furnished by the Enti della Provincia di Salerno during the superintendency of A. Maiuri, about 1934, but no report of the findings is known, and the journal of the excavations cannot be located. Therefore, with the permission of P. C. Sestieri, then superintendent of antiquities, in the spring of 1955 the American Academy in Rome examined, cleaned, and photographed the remains, ran a basic survey of them, and dug soundings in the fills and footing trenches. The work has permitted a reconstruction of the original complex and an outline of its history through antiquity.

The original complex was a rectangle of 170 p.R. by 140 p.R. (50.32 m by 41.44

---

1. E. Greco and D. Theodorescu, *Poseidonia/Paestum III: Forum Nord* (Collection de l'École Française de Rome 42 [Rome, 1987]), 27–29 and figs. 18–42.

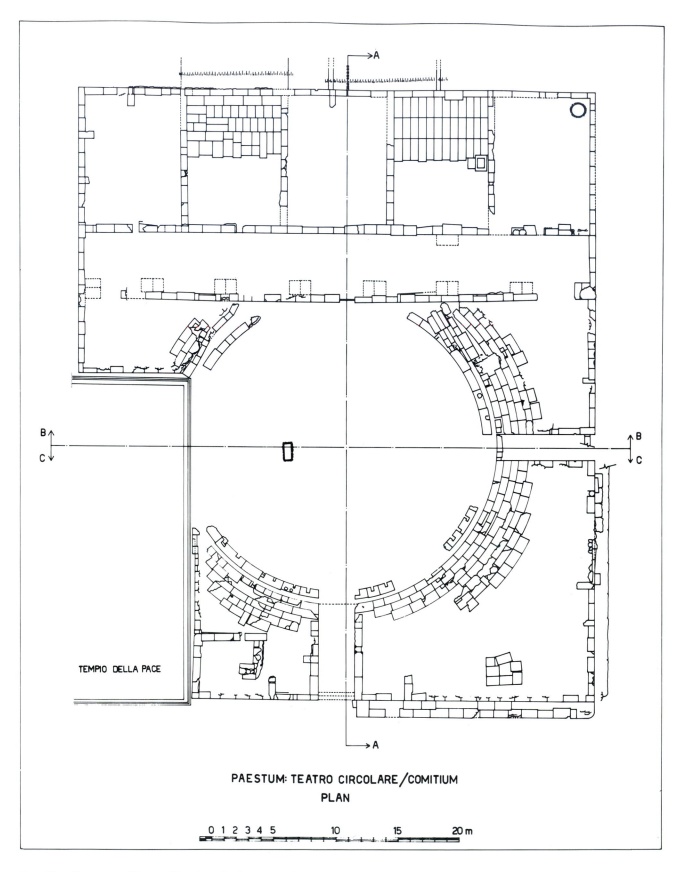

PAESTUM: TEATRO CIRCOLARE/COMITIUM
PLAN

TEMPIO DELLA PACE

0 1 2 3 4 5   10   15   20 m

Fɪɢ. 80. Paestum, "Teatro Circolare," plan, actual state

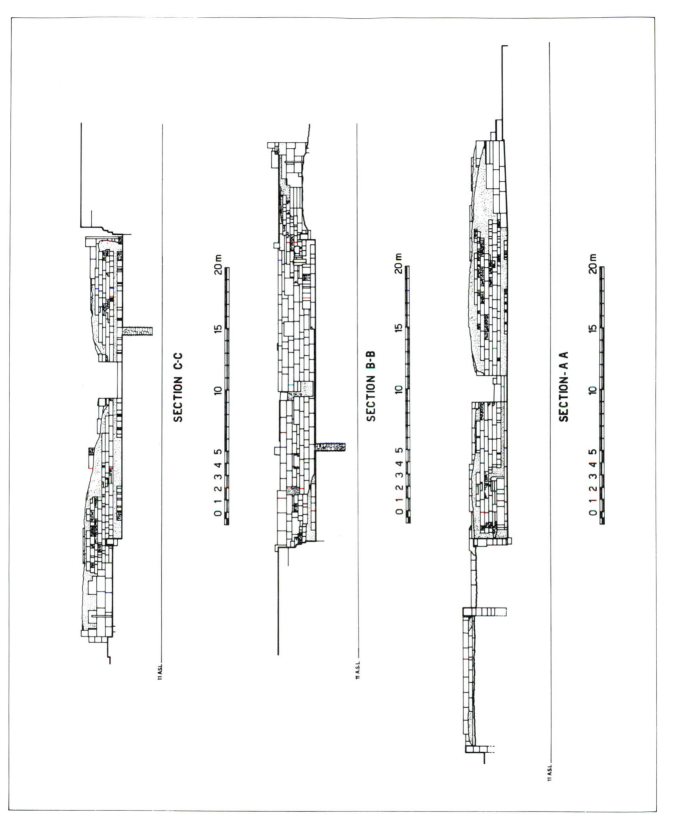

SECTION C-C

0 1 2 3 4 5 10 15 20 m

SECTION B-B

0 1 2 3 4 5 10 15 20 m

SECTION-A A

0 1 2 3 4 5 10 15 20 m

11 A.S.L.

11 A.S.L.

11 A.S.L.

Fig. 81.   Paestum, "Teatro Circolare," sections, actual state

m) laid out to the E of the broad street entering the Forum from the N on its short axis. The street, or the project for the street, and the layout of the open square of the Forum would have preceded it, but all other neighboring work seems to have been subsequent. On the W it is grazed by the street; on the S it is preceded by a broad (27 p.R., 9.99 m) portico that ran along the whole of this long side of the Forum. On the E is a narrow, paved alley from the Forum that provided communication to the E entrance of the new building and probably originally ran the whole length of this side of the complex. Later this was blocked on the N by the construction of the amphitheater and became little more than an angiportus, but in the beginning it was probably a proper street. On the N lay a great open square almost completely free of permanent structures. In other words, the complex was bounded along its two sides by streets and front and back by public squares. It would appear that the Latin colonists of 273 B.C. found a great agora-like plaza midway between the Tempio di Nettuno and the Tempio di Cerere and organized it into fora by dividing it into two long, narrow halves by a row of buildings set down the middle from E to W. That to the S then became the forum proper, the center of public buildings, civic life, and business; that to the N must have been reserved for a town market. The "Teatro Circolare" was set between the two, just E of the axial street that connected them; it would probably have been part of the original scheme and one of the earliest of the new buildings.

It was deeply bitten into subsequently by the construction of the Tempio della Pace, at which time a piece at the SW corner c. 26.55 m long and c. 9.20 m wide was subtracted from it and demolished to make room for the new temple, and it was further extensively damaged by rebuilding in the imperial period. Still, the essentials of the ground plan remain and permit a reasonable comprehension of the building and the function of its various parts.

The stone used throughout is the gray, deeply pitted, and fissured limestone native to Paestum, the stone used for everything but the elaborately carved moldings and metopes of the great temples and also used for the city's fortifications. Travertine-like in its surface, but coarser, it apparently lent itself fairly readily to sawing, but because of its pitting and irregularity could not be produced easily in blocks and slabs of standard dimensions. Consequently, the coursing is everywhere broken, and step cutting is fairly common. There is occasional snecking with small blocks, apparently where a fault in a large block had to be mended; in such cases the cut is rectangular. In all heavy walls that had to retain earth fill the blocks are large but not massive. The greatest length is 2.51 m, the greatest width 0.89 m, the greatest height 1.30 m. The usual block measures 1.15–1.25 m by 0.45–0.60 m by 0.30–0.40 m. Commonly only the exposed faces and joints are squared, the interior face being left quarry-dressed or irregularly sawn. The masonry is laid dry throughout and without anathyrosis. There is some evidence of quoining in somewhat larger blocks at wall junctures and corners, but it is not consistent practice. Corners and wall junctures are bonded on a rough header and stretcher system, and very occasionally a block elsewhere is laid header and tailed into the earth fill. There is great irregularity in the wall footing; occasionally it projects 0.10–0.15 m beyond the face of the wall at floor level; more commonly the face drops flush.

The area was divided into two discrete but intimately connected parts. That toward the Forum was entered by a broad throat on the major axis, 10 p.R. (2.93–2.96 m) wide, and by a narrower throat, 7 p.R. (2.07–2.10 m) wide, to the alley on the E. Presumably there was a third entrance to balance this on the W that was destroyed when the Tempio della Pace was built. The Forum entrance seems to have had no closure; the E entrance is provided with a sill block 0.42 m wide and 0.40 m inside the façade, and cuttings, presumably for a light gate, 0.68 m inside the sill block. The cuttings are shallow rectangular slots in the sides of the passage, 0.05 m deep, 0.12 m wide, and c. 1.37 m high.

The entrance throats ran 30 p.R. (8.88–9.00 m) sloping gently down, and brought one to a large circular floor 80 p.R. (23.68 m) in diameter. The maximum difference between the floor level on the exterior and interior is c. 0.66 m, so the slope was not more than 7.5 percent. In the S entrance were found remains of a soft signinum pavement, and it is presumed that such a pavement covered the whole of the floor, although no further remains of it could be located.

On all sides of the central floor, except dead ahead on the main axis where a cross wall ran tangent to the base circle, and except where interrupted by the entrance passages, rose concentric rings of steps. Parts of four remain in the NW sector, parts of six in the SW, parts of seven in the NE, and parts of eight in the SE. Weathering lines where blocks of the step above overlapped and protected the surface appear everywhere but in the blocks of the topmost step in the SE sector. Since the second step was everywhere robbed out in a later period but its place is clear, we may presume that originally there were nine steps in all four sectors. The steps are uniformly 1 p.R. (0.30 m) high and 2 p.R. (0.59–0.60 m) wide, but the blocks of which they are built are far from uniform in length and width. Each, however, is carefully cut to the curve on both faces. The longest interior chord is 2.75 m, in a block of the base step; the shortest that is clearly not a repair is 0.81 m, in a block of the sixth step. The width of the blocks that appear original varies from 0.70 m to 0.95 m. The usual block has an interior chord of 1.40–1.70 m and is 0.75 m wide.

Since steps of risers of 0.30 m are difficult to negotiate, radial stairs like those of a theater cavea were arranged by cutting an extra step 3 p.R. (0.88–0.90 m) broad, c. 0.25 m deep with a riser of 0.15 m into each of the larger steps except the base step. Parts of such a stair survive in the three better preserved sectors, and so one can be presumed for the fourth. These are not centered on the diagonal axes but seem to have been related to constructions beyond the rings of steps. That in the NE sector has one face, its only radial face, on a line drawn from the center of the circular floor to the intersection of the line of the tangent wall of the complex. Clearly this was to facilitate access to the long platform of which the tangent wall is the front. Presumably the stair in the NW sector, of which there are no remains, was symmetrically placed. That in the SE sector has its radial face on a line drawn apparently from the center of the circular floor to the center of a rectangular base of large blocks, 2.87 m by 2.35 m, perhaps ideally 10 p.R. by 8 p.R., embedded in the fill behind the steps. It is uncertain what this base held and why it should be located where it is, but it seems related rather to the open area of the Forum than to the stepped circle. Because of the rebuilding of the SW sector at the time of the construction of the Tempio della Pace, it is uncertain whether its stair is now in its original position; slight irregularities in the line make it seem unlikely. If it is, it lay abnormally close to the S entrance and must have served as access to a small squarish chamber or platform, c. 2.80 m by c. 2.60 m in interior dimension, built above the steps adjacent to the S entrance. The architecture of this structure is too uncertain to permit speculation about its function, but it is hardly likely to have been a speaker's platform. It was balanced by a somewhat later, but generally similar, structure on the SE side of the entrance, c. 3.40 m (11 p.R.?) square in interior dimensions, to which no direct access was arranged.

Most other interior arrangements of which there are traces are clearly of later date. There was no rail or parapet guarding the steps along the entrances; there was apparently originally no awning. Excavation in search of traces of an altar in the center of the circular floor proved fruitless. A narrow, roughly rectangular pit, 1.32 m by 0.55 m and 2.32 m deep, set without relation to other features c. 3.70 m W of the center of the circular floor, is almost certainly modern. It is lined with shaped stone and fieldstone, some large but for the most part small, carefully fitted in roughly coursed dry masonry. Exploration of its bottom produced no evidence at all, only soft, sandy loam. And ancient or modern, it is clearly a dry well to take care of surface drainage.

Beyond this amphitheatral complex, in development on the major axis, elevated to dominate it and give the whole focus, rose a high platform, and beyond that a series of buildings. The platform is defined by a wall run tangent to the base circle and another ideally 18 p.R. (5.30 m, the depth of the nine steps) to the N, parallel to the first. The front wall, of masonry a little more regularly coursed than that of the perimeter wall, is not bonded with the perimeter wall at its ends; instead it peters out some 2.85 m inside on the W, some 4.07 m on the E. This leads to the suspicion that it represents a later modification, the completed ring of steps originally giving access to the buildings beyond, as they must have in the Comitium of Cosa. But the quality of the fill and the material it contained, sampled in a trench through the middle of this platform, was identical with that found in parts that must be original. It therefore seems likely that at most we have to deal with a modification of the plan made during the construction of the building. And it may be that because there was no special point in bonding this wall at its ends, since the steps on either side would buttress it and the fills of platform and steps be very little different in height, the architect had never intended bonding it at all. The dressed S face of the wall behind cannot be called in evidence to support the notion of a change in plans, since it would in either case have been covered by an earth fill.

The platform was found in parlous state. Blocks from the upper parts of the front wall were toppled to either side and irregular pits and trenches scarred its interior. As far as could be determined, these were all the work of comparatively recent time, or the excavations of fifty years ago. Originally, the front wall seems to have continued, diminishing in depth with the rise of the steps, and run as a step or kerb a single block deep across the fill behind the steps to abut the perimeter wall; its lack of deep footing invited its destruction in these portions, but traces of it survive at the E end. The whole was filled with an unstratified mass of earth and debris brought to a level and rammed at the height of the top of the fill behind the steps, then paved with blocks of limestone of which only two survive in place. The surface of the pavement seems to have stood c. 2.90 m above that of the circular floor, 1 p.R. above the topmost step. A limestone column base that lay in the ruin of the front wall seems to be the only surviving element of the superstructure of this platform. A series of eight footings in large blocks abutting the front wall of the platform, each c. 1.05–1.30 m by 1.70–1.80 m, and a single footing against the back wall responding to the third footing from the E show that a columnar porch covered the whole.

Behind this platform and evidently fronting on it rose a series of three small buildings, one in the center on the principal axis and one at either extremity. These were apparently uniform in size, measuring ideally 30 p.R. (8.88 m) for the two at either end, $30\frac{1}{2}$ p.R. (9.03 m) for that in the center, in width overall, by 40 p.R. (11.84 m) in depth. They were separated by spaces, or courtyards, ideally 25 p.R. (7.40–7.70 m) wide. The whole series of buildings and intervening courtyards is intricately connected. The existing walls are all in bond with one another at both ends, and the lateral walls are simply extensions of the E and W perimeter walls of the complex. The masonry is everywhere uniform in character. Of the superstructure only a wall base of two courses survives in a few places; since the top course is not accurately leveled we must presume a third course, or capping, has been lost, but the rest may well have been of sun-dried brick. In the N half of each of the intervening courtyards are substantial remains of a pavement in large blocks of limestone, and in that E of the central building is a basin cut in a single block of limestone centered against the E wall and sunk in the floor. In outside dimensions this is 1.30 m long, 0.92 m wide, and 0.23 m deep. There is no indication of how this was filled or emptied.

The reconstruction of the amphitheatral portion of the building presents a number of minor difficulties, but no major one. There is every indication that originally the ring of nine steps was complete in each sector and rose to a surrounding level platform. There would have been three entrances, the major one to the Forum on the S, the minor ones to the streets on E and W. The minor entrances may have been provided with gates; the major one stood permanently open. The major entrance was flanked by small platforms, or chambers, set above the steps. The purpose and architecture of these is uncertain and their explanation is complicated by the fact that they were not perfectly symmetrical.

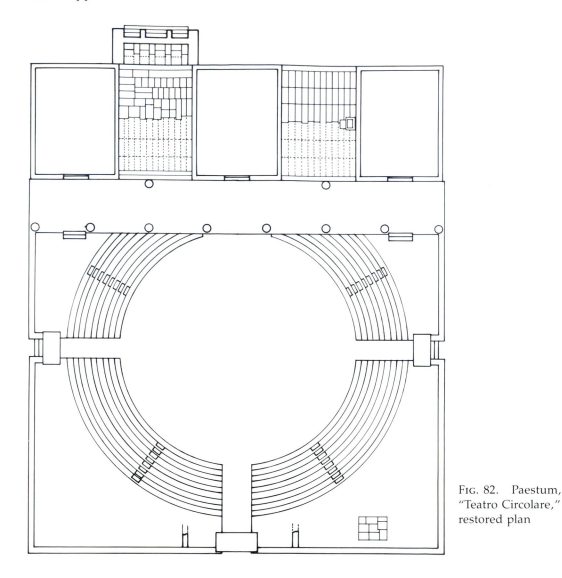

Fig. 82.   Paestum, "Teatro Circolare," restored plan

They were probably not for dedications of honorary statuary, since they are bonded into the perimeter walls; nor do they seem to have been speaker's platforms. Perhaps one might think of them as the remains of small shrines, *faute de mieux*. The other base in the SE sector would more likely have held a statue than anything else. There is nothing to suggest that any part of this area was in any way roofed at this period.

The platform at the N end was roofed, the roof supported on eight columns equally spaced along its front edge, raised a step above the top of the amphitheater. Probably it had a molding along its front edge and possibly a fence ran between the columns.

The three little buildings behind have been reconstructed in accordance with what we know of central Italian public architecture of this period, mainly on the

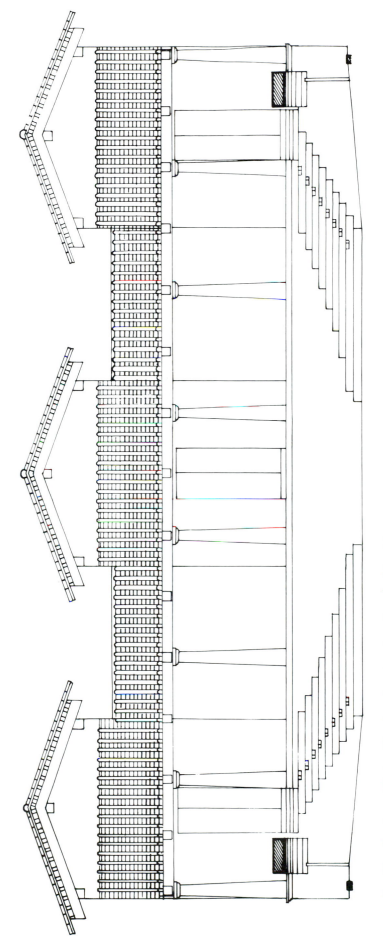

Fig. 83. Paestum, "Teatro Circolare," restored section, looking N

evidence of Cosa. They have been provided with gables run N and S, the height of the room envisaged as being equal to its width. The roofs have been restored on a system suitable for the roofing of small temples.

The evidence for the date of the building is especially material found in a sealed and undisturbed level of the footing trench explored along the E side of the building at the SE corner in an excavation 0.50–0.75 m wide and 2.00 m long (pages 264–66), and also material recovered from exploration of the fills of the platform (page 264) and the central building of the N series (page 264). Other soundings proved sterile or inconclusive.

In the footing trench the first 50 cm contained an abundance of sherds of pottery in large fragments. The datable wares ranged from the first century B.C. ("Samian" ware) to the third century (early Late Roman B ware and Ribbed Ware); there was also a coin of Nero and a fragment of a lion's head spout from the sima of the Tempio della Pace. The material bears witness to the successive repavements of the street. Toward the bottom of this layer the finds diminished sharply in quantity and a shallow level of rammed black earth was encountered. This overlay a thin stratum of soft yellowish calcareous sandstone formed after the building had been erected, presumably by the action of rainwater on the chips and masons' debris that lay about the base of the wall. Under this seal lay a third level of dark earth, evidently deliberate fill about the wall footing. From this were extracted five sherds and from the working level beneath it another, all of early, locally manufactured black-glaze ware. This is a variant of Lamboglia's "Campana A" with which it shares shapes and details.[2] The biscuit is light red and sandy, the glaze a deep black spotted with patches of iridescence. The shapes were libation cups, small bowls, saucers, and the like; there are no stamps. This has been designated "Paestan A." The picture here is remarkably clear and strongly indicates a date in the third century, probably its latter half.

In the soundings made in the fills of the platform and central building the evidence was less impressive, since the deposits were not so clearly sealed, but it points in the same direction. These fills were a mass of earth and debris brought presumably from somewhere where there was sacred material deposited. It contained fragments of votive figurines and a considerable amount of early pottery—sherds of Ionian, Corinthian, and early Attic wares, but no Black or Red Figure and no Lucanian—together with sherds of two identifiable local wares. One of these is Paestan A; the other, far rarer, is a painted ware in which the biscuit is yellowish and the surface is decorated with bands of silvery black glaze and red lines. In this fabric were recognizable fragments of a beaker and a tall narrow vessel. This has been designated "Paestan Painted Ware."

The amphitheater is clearly a place of assembly, and the dimensions of the

---

2. Lamboglia 1952, 163–96; cf. below, Appendix 2.

steps, 1 p.R. high and 2 p.R. wide, suggest that it was for assembly in which the people stood. If the capacity be calculated on the modulus of $1\frac{1}{2}$ p.R. per place, the steps alone would have accommodated roughly twelve hundred persons. Others may have stood in the space behind the steps or in the central circle. The radial stairs would have facilitated people's access to their places; they may also have served as boundaries of sectors. And they certainly served to bring people to the top of the cavea and the enigmatic constructions there at the S end.

The long platform at the N end was approached at its extremities from the cavea and provided access to the three little buildings that fronted on it. But it clearly was more than simply an approach, for it is 18 p.R. broad and so arranged as to provide the focus of, and dominate, the amphitheater just above the top-most step. There can be no doubt that it was the stage on which the drama of these assemblies unfolded, but it cannot very well be a theater stage, given its height and the absence of any arrangement for curtain or scenery. The pattern is clearly that of the Comitium of Cosa with slight modifications, notably a clearer focus and an increase in emphasis on the broad, high platform in development of the main axis. This must be the speaker's platform, the *suggestus*, the rostrum on which the magistrates sat and honorary statues might be set up. A triple stair installed leading up from the N Forum to the courtyard W of the Curia was greater than the width of the courtyard by about the thickness of the walls to either side, 8.68 m overall, but despite its size, it seems to have had no monumental character or ceremonial function. Rather, it was simply to facilitate approach to the Curia and to provide a fourth entrance to the Comitium. The date of its construction must remain vague.

And as at Cosa and Rome the three little buildings behind the *suggestus* must be the Curia and its adjuncts. The central hall would have been the Curia proper, the others those additional halls of Curia III at Cosa, perhaps the equivalent of the tabularium of Rome. Their uniformity in size and shape with the Curia, their tight architectural organization and bond in the complex is reflected on the one hand in the later enlargement of the Cosan Curia and on the other in the grandiose triad at the S end of the Forum of Pompeii.

In the early part of the present decade, 1981–84, an archaeological team under the direction of E. Greco and D. Theodorescu examined the Comitium/Curia complex of Paestum as part of a project to clean and publish as well as possible under the circumstances the unpublished excavations of Paestum. They were entirely unaware of the work of the American Academy in Rome in 1955. Consequently, while they have produced an admirable survey and a very complete set of drawings for the complex,[3] their lack of certain vital information led them into several important errors. Since they did not know that the fills in the *suggestus* and Curia complex were completely consistent, they assumed the lack of bond in

3. Greco and Theodorescu, note 1 above.

the front wall of the *suggestus* meant that it was a later modification, to which they arbitrarily gave an imperial date. They therefore reconstructed the Curia as a long, low transverse building with an E/W gable and a single door on the main axis of the Comitium. Their conception of the interior arrangements of this is not clear. To make a speaker's platform in the Comitium they hypothesized there might have been a small platform in front of the Curia door, although in that case how one might have reached this from the Comitium is not at all clear. They also created a second speaker's platform over the vaulted S entrance from the Forum, the usefulness of which it is hard to see.

Moreover, while they correctly observed the evidence for vaulting over the S entrance, they failed to note a springer block still in place at the E entrance and so restored this and the W entrance as unroofed corridors. Nor did they appreciate the nature of the column footings in the interior of the *suggestus* added in front of the Curia; consequently, they reconstructed this as simply an unroofed platform. To understand the architecture properly, it is necessary to correct these errors.

Appendix 2. The Pottery Evidence from the "Teatro Circolare," Paestum, 1955

(Figs. 84–87)

There are three main deposits of material containing potsherds: (1) the material collected while cleaning the surface of the Comitium arena, including the steps and the entrances; (2) the material from the trench dug along the exterior face of the SE corner of the Comitium down to hardpan; and (3) the material from the fills behind the apron wall (*rostra*) and in the SW corner of the central room of the Curia building. The material from the rostra fill and the center room is essentially the same (see the Cipriani/Avagliano catalogue, below). It dates from the mid-sixth century to the mid-third. One fragment of Corinthian ware, Cipriani/Avagliano 49, pl. 269.2, is dated 580–570 B.C.; this is the earliest datable sherd from the complex.

Material from the Surface Areas, Comitium Arena

It contains sherds of all periods represented; the earliest is a fragment of the ware Cipriani/Avagliano calls *Coloniale, di tradizione ionica*, datable to the second half of the sixth century. The latest datable fragment is part of a Late Roman B bowl with collared rim (type 883), a type dated by Waage, *Antioch*, to the early phase of Late

Roman B, before the introduction of Late Roman C, although the Paestan example is not exactly like any of Waage's type 883 profiles, and the shape is one that appears later.

Material from the Trench along the Exterior Face of the SE Corner, First 90 Centimeters

The material is apparently all of a single period, dated by three fragments of Late Roman B bowls. The shapes are early Late Roman B, second and third centuries A.C. (Waage, *Antioch* 44, figs. 26 and 27). With these were fragments of Ribbed Ware, found together with Late Roman B at Cosa, and heavy cooking pans with red- and brown-glazed interiors, also found with Late Roman B at Cosa.

Material from the Trench along the Exterior Face of the SE Corner, Construction Level

In addition to a few sherds of miscellaneous unidentifiable glazes and buff domestic wares, there are five fragments of Black-Glaze, including the foot of a cup, a saucer rim, part of a heavy-walled unguentarium (cf. Cipriani/Avagliano 11, Fig. 84.11), and a unique angular kylix handle like those of the kylices illustrated by Trendall, *Paestan Pottery* (1936), pls. 20c, 35d, fig. 58, but more clumsily shaped. The evidence indicates a date for this deposit in the second quarter of the third century B.C.

Material from the Trench along the Exterior Face of the SE Corner, Lowest Stratum (Footing)

Three very small sherds of Black-Glaze, of different fabrics, one of them a rim with the beginning of a design executed in white paint that touches the lower furrow (cf. Pl. 276, Cipriani/Avagliano's *Ceramica di fabbrica pestana a vernice nera con decorazione sovraddipinta*). There is also one fragment of a scyphoid cup in fine, hard buff clay with gray core and thin, greenish varnish (cf. Cipriani/Avagliano 21, 22, Pl. 273.3, mid-sixth century B.C.).

The material from the fills includes pieces of votive terracottas and loom-weights and is apparently debris discarded from a sanctuary. None of the Black-Glaze from the Teatro Circolare, from either surface areas or fills, is stamped, although the Paestan museum contains many handsomely stamped fragments of Black-Glaze. Perhaps these were not dedicated in sanctuaries, but rather reserved for funerary use.

Emeline Hill Richardson

INDEX TO THE CATALOGUE OF CIPRIANI AND AVAGLIANO

Trench in the SW Corner of the Center Room of the Curia Building, First Level

1. Corinthian, second half of the sixth century, B.C.   Pl. 269.5
2. Colonial, second half of the sixth century B.C.   Fig. 84.2
3. Black-Glaze, second half of the fifth century B.C.   Fig. 84.3
4. Paestan Red Figure, second half of the fourth century B.C.
5. Paestan Black-Glaze with added paint, second half of the fourth century B.C.
    Pl. 271.3; Fig. 84.5
6. Paestan Black-Glaze with added paint, end of the fourth century B.C.
    Pl. 271.2; Fig. 84.6
7. Paestan Black-Glaze, second half of the fourth century B.C.   Fig. 84.7
8. Paestan Black-Glaze, last third of the fourth century B.C.   Fig. 84.8
9. Paestan Black-Glaze, first half of the third century B.C.   Fig. 84.90
10. Paestan Black-Glaze, first half of the third century B.C.   Fig. 84.10
11. Paestan Black-Glaze, beginning of the third century B.C.   Fig. 84.11
12. Cooking ware, fourth century B.C. and later.   Fig. 84.12
13. Cooking ware, end of the fourth century B.C. and beginning of the third.
    Fig. 84.13
14. Cooking ware, end of the fourth century B.C. and beginning of the third.
    Fig. 84.14
15. Cooking ware, beginning of the third century B.C.   Fig. 84.15
16. Terracotta figurine, third century B.C.   Pl. 272

Trench in the SW Corner of the Center Room of the Curia Building, Second Level

17. Corinthian, second half of the sixth century B.C.   Pl. 269.1
18. Attic Black Figure, second half of the sixth century B.C.   Pl. 269.10
19. Colonial in the Ionic tradition, second half of the sixth century B.C.
    Fig. 85.19
20. Colonial in the Ionic tradition, second half of the sixth century B.C.
    Fig. 85.20

21. Colonial in the Ionic tradition, mid-sixth century B.C.   Pl. 273.3
22. Colonial in the Ionic tradition, mid-sixth century B.C.   Pl. 273.5
23. Colonial in the Ionic tradition, end of the sixth century B.C.   Fig. 85.23
24. Colonial in the Ionic tradition, end of the sixth century B.C.   Fig. 85.24
25. Black-Glaze, fifth century B.C.   Fig. 85.25
26. Black-Glaze, 500 B.C. or later.   Fig. 85.26
27. Black-Glaze, 500 B.C. or later.   Pl. 275.6; Fig. 85.27
28. Paestan Red Figure, second half of the fourth century B.C.   Pl. 274.1
29. Paestan Black-Glaze with added paint, first half of the third century B.C.
    Pl. 276.5
30. Paestan Black-Glaze with added paint, end of the fourth century B.C.
    Pl. 276.4
31. Paestan Black-Glaze with added paint, c. 320–270 B.C.   Fig. 85.31
32. Paestan Black-Glaze with added paint, first half of the third century B.C.
    Fig. 85.32
33. Paestan Black-Glaze with added paint, first half of the third century B.C.
    Fig. 85.33
34. Paestan Black-Glaze with added paint, third century B.C.   Fig. 85.34
35. Paestan Acroma Depurata, third century B.C.   Fig. 85.35
36. Cooking ware, end of the fourth century B.C. and later.   Fig. 85.36
37. Cooking ware, end of the fourth century B.C. and later.   Fig. 86.37
38. Cooking ware, end of the fourth century B.C. and later.   Fig. 86.38
39. Cooking ware, fourth–third century B.C.   Pl. 277.3 and 6
40. Cooking ware, fourth century B.C.   Fig. 86.40
41. Cooking ware, fourth century B.C.   Fig. 86.41
42. Cooking ware, handle of lid, fourth–third century B.C.
43. Amphorae, end of the fourth century, beginning of the third century B.C.
    Fig. 86.43
44. Terracotta figurine, last decades of the fourth century B.C.   Pl. 278.1

Apron Wall (Rostra) Fill

45. Corinthian, mid-sixth century B.C.   Pl. 269.9
46. Corinthian, beginning of the fifth century B.C.   Pl. 279.3
47. Corinthian, mid-sixth century B.C.   Pl. 269.4
48. Corinthian, second quarter of the sixth century B.C.   Pl. 269.7
49. Corinthian, 580–570 B.C.   Pl. 269.2
50. Corinthian, sixth century B.C.   Pl. 269.3
51. Attic, second half of the fifth century B.C.   Pl. 280.3
52. Attic, fifth century B.C.   Pl. 280.2
53. Colonial in the Ionic tradition, second half of the sixth century B.C.
    Fig. 86.53

54. Colonial in the Ionic tradition, second half of the sixth century B.C. Fig. 86.54
55. Colonial in the Ionic tradition, second half of the sixth century B.C. Fig. 86.55
56. Colonial in the Ionic tradition, mid-sixth century B.C.   Pl. 282.1; Fig. 86.56
57. Colonial in the Ionic tradition, second half of the sixth century B.C. Fig. 86.57
58. Colonial in the Ionic tradition, second half of the sixth century B.C. Fig. 86.58
59. Colonial in the Ionic tradition, end of the sixth century B.C.   Fig. 86.59
60. Colonial in the Ionic tradition, end of the sixth century B.C.   Fig. 86.60
61. Colonial in the Ionic tradition, end of the sixth century B.C.   Fig. 86.61
62. Colonial in the Ionic tradition, end of the sixth century B.C.   Fig. 86.62
63. Colonial in the Ionic tradition, end of the sixth century B.C.   Fig. 86.63
64. Colonial in the Ionic tradition, end of the sixth century B.C.   Fig. 86.64
65. Colonial in the Ionic tradition, second half of the sixth century B.C. to first half of the fifth.   Fig. 86.65
66. Colonial in the Ionic tradition, second half of the sixth century B.C. to the first half of the fifth.   Fig. 87.66
67. Black-Glaze, first half of the fifth century B.C.   Pl. 271.4
68. Black-Glaze, c. mid-fifth century B.C.   Pl. 281
69. Paestan Red Figure, second half of the fourth century B.C.   Pl. 279.4
70. Paestan Black-Glaze with added paint, end of the fourth century B.C. or beginning of the third.   Pl. 276.8; Fig. 87.70
71. Paestan Black-Glaze with added paint, c. 300 B.C.   Pl. 276.6; Fig. 87.71
72. Paestan Black-Glaze with added paint, 300 B.C.   Pl. 276.7
73. Paestan Black-Glaze with added paint, first half of the third century B.C. Pl. 276.3
74. Paestan Black-Glaze with added paint, first half of the third century B.C. Pl. 276.1
75. Paestan Black-Glaze, mid-fourth century B.C.   Fig. 87.75
76. Paestan Black-Glaze, last quarter of the fourth century B.C.   Fig. 87.76
77. Paestan Black-Glaze, c. 320–270 B.C.   Fig. 87.77
78. Paestan Black-Glaze, last decades of the fourth century B.C.   Fig. 87.78
79. Paestan Black-Glaze, fourth century B.C.   Fig. 87.79
80. Paestan Black-Glaze, beginning of the third century B.C.   Fig. 87.80
81. Paestan Black-Glaze, end of the fourth century B.C. to first half of the third. Fig. 87.81
82. Paestan Black-Glaze, end of the fourth century B.C. to first half of the third. Fig. 87.82
83. Paestan Black-Glaze, third century B.C.   Fig. 87.83
84. Paestan Black-Glaze, third century B.C.   Fig. 87.84
85. Paestan Black-Glaze, third century B.C.   Fig. 87.85

86. Paestan Black-Glaze, first quarter of the third century B.C.   Fig. 87.86
87. Paestan Black-Glaze, first decades of the third century B.C.   Fig. 87.87
88. Paestan Black-Glaze a Fasce, end of the fourth century B.C.   Pl. 270.2
89. Paestan Miniature, sixth to fourth century B.C. (?)   Pl. 283.1
90. Cooking ware, last third of the fourth century B.C.   Fig. 87.90
91. Cooking ware, end of the fourth century B.C. and later.   Fig. 87.91
92. Cooking ware, end of the fourth century B.C. and later.   Fig. 87.92
93. Cooking ware, end of the fourth century B.C. and later.   Fig. 87.93
94. Cooking ware, fourth century B.C. to third.   Fig. 87.94
95. Cooking ware, fourth century B.C. to third.   Fig. 87.95
96. Cooking ware, fourth century B.C. to third.   Fig. 87.96
97. Cooking ware, fourth century B.C. to third.   Fig. 87.97

CATALOGUE

Trench in SW Corner of the Center Room of the Curia Building, First Level ($\pi\alpha$)

I. CERAMICA

A. CERAMICA CORINZIA

1.   Fr. di *kotyle* (Pl. 269.5). Argilla giallina compatta, vernice bruna, sovraddipintura paonazza. Si conserva parte del largo piede ad echino su cui si innesta un breve tratto di parete obliqua. Decorazione: interno verniciato; sulla parete esterna trattini radiali collegati in basso da una linea orizzontale; fascia paonazza lungo il profilo esterno del piede; sotto, linea e coppia di fasce concentriche verniciate.

Alt. cm. 1, 8; diam. ricostruibile cm. 6

Cfr. Payne, *Necrocorinthia,* pp. 309–310, fig. 151; *Corinth* XIII, pp. 106 e 208, 240–242, tav. 92.

Seconda metà del VI sec.a.C.

B. CERAMICA DI FABRICA COLONIALE

Di tradizione ionica

2.   Fr. di coppa di tipo B2 (Fig. 84.2). Argilla arancio rosato compatta; v.n. a riflessi metallici. Si conservano un tratto dell'orlo e della vasca.

Alt. cm. 2, 8; lungh. cm. 5, 8.

Oltre alla bibliografia tradizionale costituita dai sempre citati F. Villard–G. Vallet, *Lampes du VIIe siècle et chronologie des coupes ioniennes,* in *MEFR* LXVII, 1955, p. 7 ss., in cui cfr. in particolare, pp. 21–23, tav. VI, 1–3, il contributo fondamentale sulla spinosa problematica relativa alle fabbriche ed alla cronologia inferiore della produzione rimane quello di P. G. Guzzo, *Excursus II: Coppe così dette*

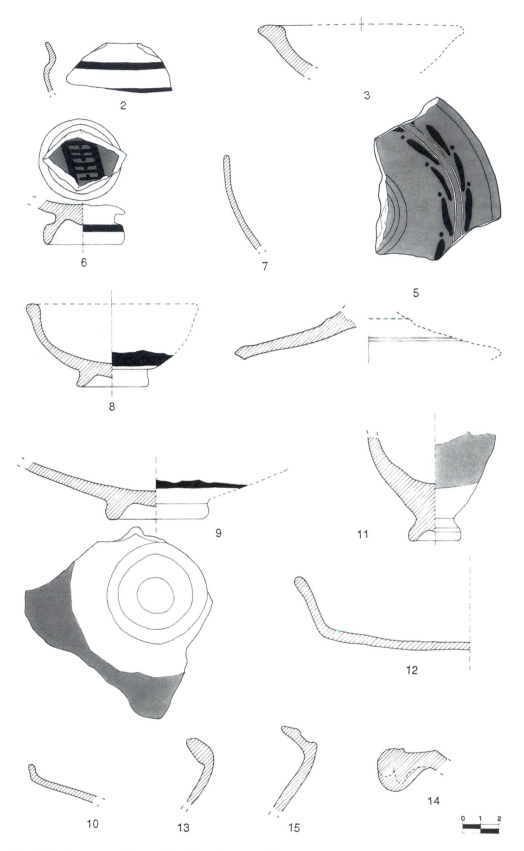

Fig. 84. Paestum, "Teatro Circolare," pottery from trench in SW corner, center room of Curia building, first level

ioniche, in AA.VV., *Les Céramiques de la Grèce de l'Est et leur diffusion en Occident*, Naples, 1978, pp. 123–24. Per alcuni degli esemplari rinvenuti a Poseidonia, ormai sufficientemente numerosi da rendere necessaria una classificazione sistematica, cfr. E. Greco, in AA.VV., *Il commercio greco nel Tirreno in età arcaica*, Salerno, 1981, p. 58 ss. e *Poseidonia-Paestum* II, p. 87, k1–k2, p. 141, n. 273, fig. 68. Seconda metà del VI sec.a.C.

A vernice nera

3. Fr. di coppetta (Fig. 84.3). Argilla nocciola, v.n. a riflessi metallici. Orlo ingrossato, estroflesso ed appiattito nella parte superiore; vasca a pareti convesse.

   Alt. cm. 3, 4; lungh. cm. 9, 3.

   Il pezzo si ispira a forme di produzione attica della seconda metà del V sec.a.C., per le quali cfr. *Agora* XII, pp. 133 e 296, n. 847, fig. 9. Seconda metà del V sec.a.C.

C. CERAMICA DI FABRICA PESTANA

A figure rosse

4. Fr. di bottiglia (Pl. 270.2). Argilla arancio rosato, v.n. opaca. È pertinente alla zona inferiore della parete, prima del piede. Decorazione: motivo ad onde correnti destrorse risparmiate.

   Alt. cm. 2, 9; largh. cm. 3, 5.

   Seconda metà del IV sec.a.C.

A vernice nera con decorazione sovraddipinta

5. Fr. di coperchio (Fig. 84.5; Pl. 271.3). Argilla arancio rossastro, v.n. opaca, sovraddipinture evanide. Bordo obliquo formante un angolo ottuso all'attacco con la parete tesa; la zona centrale di innesto del pomello di presa è rilevata e circondata da un anello in rilievo. Decorazione: tralcio circolare formato da una coppia di linee concentriche graffite da cui si dipartono foglie di ulivo destrorse e bacche.

   Lungh. cm. 7, 4; largh. cm. 7, 5.

   Il motivo decorativo è ampiamente diffuso nella produzione pestana, specie su bordi di *skyphoi* a corpo ovoide di medie dimensioni, presenti in contesti tombali databili dalla metà del IV sec.a.C., inediti.

   Seconda metà del IV sec.a.C.

6. Fondo di coppa (Fig. 84.6; Pl. 271.2). Per argilla e vernice simile al pezzo precedente, sovraddipinture evanide. Piede ad anello con cavità interna tronco-conica ed ombelico centrale, raccordato alla vasca da un brevissimo fusto cilindrico. Decorazione: risparmiati il fusto e l'interno del piede; al centro della vasca tracce di un motivo a scala con fila centrale di punti allineati in fila verticale.

   Alt. cm. 2; diam. piede cm. 4, 5.

   L'esemplare è pertinente ad un tipo di coppa emisferica con piede ad anello, talvolta modanato, solitamente decorato all'interno con teste femminili, volatili, motivi floreali, stellari e, assai più frequentemente, con delfini e/o seppie, ben rappresentato a Paestum in contesti urbani databili tra la fine del IV e la prima metà del III sec.a.C., per cui cfr. *Poseidonia-Paestum* II, pp. 101–103, nn. 80–88 e p. 106.

Prima metà del III sec.a.C.

A vernice nera

7.   Fr. di *skyphos* (Fig. 84.7). Argilla arancio vivo, v.n. metallica. Orlo arrotondato, rientrante e distinto da un gradino nel punto di incontro con l'interno della parete, accentuatamente convessa nella parte conservata.

Alt. cm. 5, 5; largh. cm. 4, 1.

Assimilabile alla serie Morel 4311 e, in particolare, ai tipi 4311a1 e 4311a2, per cui cfr. Morel 1981, p. 304, tav. 126. Per la forma cfr. anche P. G. Guzzo, in *NSc* 1972, p. 545, fig. 13, nn. 2–10.

Seconda metà del IV sec.a.C.

8.   Fr. di coppetta monoansata (Fig. 84.8). Argilla arancio rosato, v.n. opaca. Orlo ingrossato, lievemente estroflesso ed arrotondato superiormente; bordo verticale che si arrotonda nel punto di attacco con la vasca profonda. Piede echiniforme irregolare collegato alla vasca da un sottile gradino rilevato. Decorazione: verniciati l'interno e l'esterno eccettuati la parte inferiore della vasca ed il piede.

Alt. cm. 4, 4; diam. piede cm. 4, 2.

Assimilabile alla serie Morel 6231 prodotta in Italia Meridionale e, in particolare, al tipo 6231a1, cfr. Morel 1981, p. 395, tav. 194.

Ultimo terzo del IV sec.a.C.

9.   Fondo di coppa (Fig. 84.9). Argilla arancio rosato, v.n. opaca. Pareti oblique, piede ad anello. Decorazione: risparmiati il tratto inferiore della parete esterna ed il piede.

Alt. cm. 3, 1; diam. piede cm. 5, 5.

Riconducibile alla forma Lamboglia 27, cfr. Lamboglia *C.P.*, pp. 176–177, ed alla serie Morel 2784 con particolare riferimento al tipo 2784a1, cfr. Morel 1981, p. 224, tav. 73. Per altre attestazioni della forma nello ambito della produzione pestana della prima metà del III sec.a.C., cfr. *Poseidonia-Paestum* II, p. 108, fig. 60, n. 110, e *Poseidonia-Paestum* III, p. 149, nn. 748–749, fig. 93.

Prima metà del III sec.a.C.

10.   Fr. di piatto (Fig. 84.10). Argilla arancio rosato, v. bruno-rossiccia. Breve bordo verticale arrotondato nella parte superiore, parete tesa, quasi orizzontale, più spessa verso il centro della vasca. Decorazione: risparmiato il tratto inferiore della parete esterna.

Lungh. cm. 6, 2; largh. cm. 3, 5.

Simile all'esemplare precedente, ma di minori dimensioni.

Prima metà del III sec.a.C.

11.   Fondo di unguentario (Fig. 84.11). Argilla arancio, v.n. a riflessi metallici. Corpo ovoide a pareti molto spesse; alto piede ad echino con cavità interna troncoconica ed ombelico centrale.

Alt. cm. 5, 8; diam. piede cm. 2, 9.

Cfr. per la forma L. Forti, *Unguentari del primo periodo ellenistico*, in *RAAN*, 37, 1962, p. 151, tav. VII, XI (III sec.a.C.); E. Greco–D. Theodorescu, *Il Foro di Paestum. Relazione preliminare delle campagne di scavo 1981–1983*, in *AION ArchStAnt* VI, 1984, fig. 46, l. Un pezzo analogo, ma di più piccole dimensioni (n.i.26865) è presente in un contesto del III secolo iniziale costituito dalla tomba 47 della necropoli pestana di Spinazzo (scavo 1972, inedita) in significativa associazione con un altro unguentario a v.n.con anse, un terzo unguentario piriforme decorato a fasce ed uno *skyphos* a v.n. con decorazione sovraddipinta.

Inizi del III sec.a.C.

Ceramica da cucina

12.   Fr. di pentola (Fig. 84.12). Argilla arancio con grossi inclusi litici marroni e neri. Orlo lievemente ingrossato, arrotondato superiormente ed estroflesso, bordo verticale innestato obliquamente sul fondo concavo indifferenziato.

Alt. cm. 4, 5; diam. ricostruibile cm. 15, 7.

Rientra nella tradizione delle pentole basse con fondo leggermente concavo e breve parete verticale documentato in ambito greco fra V e IV sec.a.C., cfr. *Agora* XII, p. 227, tav. 95, 1974–76. È verosimile comunque, trattandosi di una forma d'uso, che questa tipologia abbia continuato senza sostanziali trasformazioni anche dopo il IV sec.a.C.

Dal IV sec.a.C.

13.   Fr. di olla (Fig. 84.13). Argilla nocciola con inclusi litici marroni e neri. Orlo estroflesso con alto bordo verticale innestato obliquamente sulla parete e distinto da questa mediante una scanalatura.

Alt. cm. 3, 8; lungh. cm. 7, 4

Per la forma cfr. Bailo Modesti 1984, fig. 30, 1, che presenta alcuni esemplari analoghi rinvenuti nell'abitato antico di Pontecagnano, in un contesto databile alla fine del IV-inizi del III sec.a.C. Altri pezzi assimilabili sono documentati in alcuni corredi tombali pestani inediti, databili dalla fine del IV ai decenni iniziali del III sec.a.C. A quest'epoca si può riferire ad esempio l'olletta n.i.22948a dalla tomba 33 della necropoli della Licinella, scavo 1969.

Fine del IV–inizi del III sec.a.C.

14.   Fr. di pentola (Fig. 84.14). Argilla arancio, porosa. Orlo sagomato per l'allettamento del coperchio; alto bordo verticale cui è saldata un'ansa a bastoncello impostata orizzontalmente.

Lungh. cm. 9, 5.

Cfr. *Poseidonia-Paestum* III, pp. 141–142, n. 724, fig. 94 (l'esemplare presenta un'impressione digitale al centro dell'ansa).

Fine del IV–inizi del III sec.a.C.

15.   Idem (Fig. 84.15). Argilla analoga a quella del pezzo precedente. Orlo estroflesso, appiattito superiormente e sagomato all'interno per l'allettamento del coperchio; breve tratto di parete obliqua.

Alt. cm. 5; largh. cm. 6, 5.

Il profilo dell'orlo è del tutto analogo a quello della pentola n.i.40162 proveniente dallo scavo del *dromos* della tomba 117 della necropoli pestana di Spinazzo (scavo 1972, inedita) contenente materiale degli inizi del III sec.a.C.

II. TERRECOTTE FIGURATE

A. PICCOLA PLASTICA

16.   Fr. di statuetta (Pl. 272). Argilla nocciola con tracce di latte di calce in superficie. È pertinente al corpo di una figura femminile panneggiata di tipo tanagrino. Si conservano la parte centrale del bacino e la gamba destra leggermente flessa al ginocchio e portata di lato, ricoperte dal chitone a fitte piegoline verticali e dall'*himation* dispostovi sopra orizzontalmente, dal bacino al ginocchio.

Alt. cm. 11; largh. cm. 4.

III sec.a.C.

Trench in SW Corner of the Center Room of the Curia Building, Second Level ($\pi\beta$)

I. CERAMICA

A. CERAMICA CORINZIA

17.   Fr. di *microkotyle* (Pl. 269.1). Argilla nocciola chiaro, v.n. opaca, sovraddipintura paonazza. Si conserva un breve tratto del fondo piano con piede ad echino. Decorazione: interno verniciato; fascia paonazza lungo il profilo interno del piede; sul fondo esterno traccia di una sottile banda circolare.

Lungh. cm. 3; largh. cm. 3, 2.

Cfr. n. 1, p. 269.

Seconda metà del VI sec.a.C.

B. CERAMICA ATTICA

A figure nere

18.   Fr. di vaso di forma aperta (Pl. 269.10). Argilla beige, v.n. opaca, sovraddipinture bianche e paonazze. Si conserva il tratto inferiore della parete. Decorazione: interno verniciato; all'esterno dall'alto, tracce illeggibili della scena figurata su coppia di bande paonazza e bianca; sotto altre bande verniciate e sovraddipinte di diverso spessore inquadrano una fascia risparmiata.

Alt. cm. 7, 4; largh. cm. 5, 2.

Seconda metà del VI sec.a.C.

C. CERAMICA DI FABRICA COLONIALE
Di tradizione ionica

19.   Fr. di coppa di tipo B2 (Fig. 85.19). Argilla arancio con nucleo grigio, v. rossastra. Comprende parte dell'orlo e della vasca.
Alt. cm. 5, 2; largh. cm. 5, 7.
Cfr. n. 2, p. 269.
Seconda metà del VI sec.a.C.

20.   Idem (Fig. 85.20). Argilla arancio chiaro, v.n. diluita a riflessi metallici. Comprende parte dell'orlo e della vasca.
Alt. cm. 3; largh. cm. 4.
Cfr. n. 2, p. 269.
Seconda metà del VI sec.a.C.

21.   Fr. di coppa *skyphoide* (Pl. 273.3). Argilla arancio chiaro, v.n. poco lucente. Orlo estroflesso, arrotondato con bordo verticale e breve tratto di parete quasi rettilinea. Decorazione: interno verniciato con fascia risparmiata sull'orlo; sulla parete esterna, verniciata, ampia fascia risparmiata all'attacco tra il bordo e la zona superiore della vasca.
Alt. cm. 4, 8; largh. cm. 7, 3.
Assimilabile alla c.d. *"ionische Becherschale"* del Neutsch per cui cfr. *Palinuro* 2, p. 109, tav. 33, 2, 8, 9; de la Genière 1968, p. 197, tav. 18, 3, 1–2; cfr. anche A. Bedini, in *NSc* 1972 (III suppl.), pp. 262 e 265, nn. 170 e 172, fig. 275. Per gli esemplari provenienti da Poseidonia cfr. *Poseidonia-Paestum* II, p. 106, n. 99, fig. 60 e 142 n. 284, fig. 68.
Metà del VI sec.a.C.

22.   Idem (Pl. 273.5). Argilla nocciola, v. grigiastra, lucente. Per forma e decorazione è analogo al pezzo precedente.
Alt. cm. 4, 6; largh. cm. 4.
Metà del VI sec.a.C.

23.   Fr. di coppetta monoansata (Fig. 85.23). Argilla arancio chiaro, v. rossastra, opaca. Comprende l'orlo arrotondato, leggermente rientrante ed un breve tratto della vasca a profilo continuo con tracce dell'attacco dell'ansa. Decorazione: interno verniciato; all'esterno sull'orlo sottile fascia verniciata; larga banda verniciata nella zona centrale della parete.
Alt. cm. 2; largh. cm. 5, 3.
Questa tipologia con le sue numerose varianti, che differiscono essenzialmente nello schema della decorazione dipinta, è ampiamente rappresentata in tutti i livelli di vita di età tardoarcaica e classica indagati a Poseidonia, raggiungendo anche, in alcuni casi, la prima metà del IV sec.a.C. Tralasciando gli innumerevoli confronti da tutta l'Italia Meridionale e limitandosi ad una prima disamina degli esemplari di provenienza poseidoniate, la gran parte dei quali è di produzione locale, si cfr. *Poseidonia-Paestum* II, pp. 88–89, k12–13, fig. 59; pp. 106–107, nn. 100–102, figg. 60 e 64; p. 142, nn. 285–286, fig. 67, p. 159, n. 451,

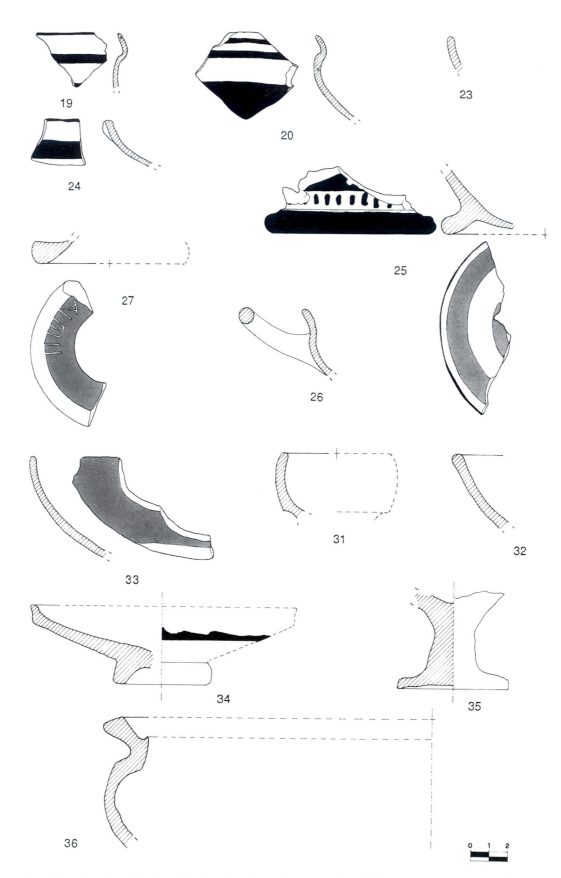

Fig. 85. Paestum, "Teatro Circolare," pottery from trench in SW corner, center room of Curia building, second level

fig. 85; *Poseidonia-Paestum* III, pp. 117–118, nn. 472, 124, 531, 477, 440, 689, 445, 463, 777, figg. 88 e 103.

Dalla fine del VI sec.a.C.

24.   Idem (Fig. 85.24). Per argilla e vernice è analogo al pezzo precedente. Comprende l'orlo rientrante, lievemente appiattito nella parte superiore, il breve bordo verticale con tracce dell'attacco dell'ansa e parte della vasca poco profonda a profilo continuo con fondo piano indifferenziato. Decorazioni: interno verniciato con tondo centrale risparmiato; all'esterno sull'orlo linea orizzontale verniciata e fascia, pure verniciata, nella parte centrale della vasca.

Alt. cm. 3, 4; diam. base cm. 3, 5.

Cfr. il pezzo precedente.

Dalla fine del VI sec.a.C.

A vernice nera

25.   Fr. di grande *skyphos* (Fig. 85.25; Pl. 274.3). Argilla arancio con nucleo beige, v.n. abbastanza lucente, sovraddipintura paonazza. Comprende un breve tratto di parete obliqua con gradino irregolarmente rilevato nel punto di attacco con il piede ad anello. Decorazione: nella parte inferiore del corpo, prima del piede, fascia risparmiata decorata con bastoncelli verticali e delimitata in basso da linea paonazza; piano d'appoggio risparmiato; profilo interno del piede verniciato; sul fondo esterno tracce di un anello verniciato.

Alt. cm. 3, 5; largh. cm. 9, 4.

Per il profilo del piede si rifà ad alcuni *cups-skyphoi* attici (Agora III, pp. 83–84, n. 333, fig. 4) di cui costituisce una elaborazione prodotta in qualche centro greco dell'Italia Meridionale, anche per l'inserzione, nella zona risparmiata alla base della vasca, di bastoncelli verticali. Prodotti simili sono attestati anche dagli scavi dell'abitato arcaico di Pontecagnano, cfr. Bailo Modesti 1984, p. 235, fig. 33, ultima fila in basso, al centro.

V sec.a.C.

26.   Fr. di *kylix* di tipo C (Fig. 85.26). Argilla nocciola, v.n. lucente. Orlo estroflesso arrotondato superiormente con bordo obliquo distinto da un gradino all'interno della vasca. Ansa a bastoncello a maniglia incurvata verso l'alto ed impostata orizzontalmente nel punto di attacco della vasca. Decorazione: risparmiati l'interno dell'ansa e la zona fra gli attacchi.

Alt. cm. 4; largh. cm. 6, 5.

È riferibile alla forma *Kleine Schale* C del Bloesch (H. Bloesch, *Formen attischer Schalen*, Bern 1940, p. 119 ss. e tav. 33) che trova corrispondenza nel tipo C *concave lip* dell'Agora, cfr. *Agora* XII, p. 91 ss., fig. 4, tav. 19, e, in particolare per l'articolazione di orlo e ansa, figg. 4, 413. Per le *kylikes* di tipo C di produzione e/o di trovamento poseidoniate, cfr. *Poseidonia-Paestum* II, p. 141, nn. 276–278, fig. 68, e *Poseidonia-Paestum* III, pp. 120–122, fig. 89, nn. 685 e 687.

Dal 500 a.C.

27.   Idem (Fig. 85.27; Pl. 275.6). Argilla arancio chiaro, v.n. opaca con chiazze metalliche, sovraddipintura paonazza. Comprende parte del piede ad anello decorato con banda paonazza all'attacco del fusto; profilo esterno e piano d'appoggio sono risparmiati. Sotto il piede sono graffiti i segni: A I ⋔ I I

Alt. cm. 1, 5; largh. cm. 8.

Per la forma cfr. il pezzo precedente ed anche *Agora* xii, fig. 4, 415.

Dal 500 a.C.

D. CERAMICA DI FABBRICA PESTANA

A figure rosse

28.   Fr. di vaso di forma chiusa (*lebes*?) (Pl. 274.1). Argilla arancio rosato, v.n. opaca, sovraddipintura evanida. Comprende parte di spalla e parete. Decorazione: sulla spalla risparmiata fila orizzontale di bolli verniciati; sulla parete parte di foglia d'edera con contorno sovraddipinto.

Alt. cm. 2, 8; Largh. cm. 2, 4.

Seconda metà del IV sec.a.C.

A vernice nera con decorazione sovraddipinta

29.   Fr. di coppetta (Pl. 276.5). Argilla arancio rosato, v.n. a riflessi metallici. Comprende parte della vasca. Decorazione: all'interno entro coppia di linee concentriche sovraddipinte in bianco, seppia; all'esterno zona risparmiata.

Alt. cm. 3, 4; largh. cm. 5, 8.

Per la discussione sulla forma cfr. il n. 6. Decorazione simile in *Poseidonia-Paestum* ii, pp. 101–102, n. 81, fig. 75.

Prima metà III sec.a.C.

30.   Fr. di bottiglia (Pl. 276.4). Per l'argilla e la vernice è analogo al pezzo precedente. Comprende un breve tratto di parete su cui resta traccia di una capigliatura stretta da nastri, verosimilmente pertinente ad una testa femminile di profilo a sinistra.

Alt. cm. 3, 8; largh. cm. 3, 3.

La parte superstite della decorazione rimanda ad uno schema abbastanza diffuso come la testa femminile di profilo, nella produzione di Gnathia, cfr. J. R. Green, *Some Painters of Gnathia Vases*, in *BICS* 15, 1968, 34–50, p. 44, tav. ixd, ed in quella pestana dove il motivo è presente soprattutto sul ventre di bottiglie e su pareti di *skyphoi*. I confronti in ambito locale si possono istituire con materiali di provenienza tombale (bottiglia n.i.26877 dalla tomba 52 della necropoli di Spinazzo, inedita) databili tra la fine del IV sec.a.C. e i decenni iniziali del secolo successivo. Un'esemplificazione dello stesso tema decorativo è anche in *Poseidonia-Paestum* II, p. 103, n. 93, fig. 74.

Fine del IV–decenni iniziali del III sec.a.C.

A vernice nera

31.   Fr. di coppetta (Fig. 85.31). Argilla arancio, v.n. poco lucente. Alto bordo convesso con orlo rientrante, arrotondato, gradino tra il bordo e l'attacco del fusto del piede.

Alt. 3, 8; largh. cm. 5, 8.

Assimilabile alla serie Morel 2424, cfr. Morel 1981, p. 169, tav. 49. Innumerevoli sono i confronti in tutta l'Italia Meridionale e specialmente da contesti databili fra gli ultimi decenni del IV ed il primo quarto del III sec.a.C., cfr. Morel 1970, p. 101, fig. 24, 13. Cfr. anche *Poseidonia-Paestum* I, p. 19, nota 7, fig. 42, 39; *Poseidonia-Paestum* II, p. 111, n. 135, fig. 60 e *Poseidonia-Paestum* III, p. 136, nn. 657b, nn. 528, 483, fig. 93.

320–270 a.C.circa.

32.   Fr. di coppa (Fig. 85.32). Argilla arancio vivo, v.n. lucente. Orlo leggermente ingrossato con la parte superiore tagliata obliquamente verso l'interno; bordo a profilo obliquo sottolineato all'esterno, nel punto di attacco della vasca da una solcatura.

Alt. cm. 4, 7; largh. cm. 7, 1.

Assimilabile alla serie Morel 2587, cfr. Morel 1981, pp. 188–189, tav. 58.

Prima metà del III sec.a.C.

33.   Fr. di coppa (Fig. 85.33). Argilla arancio cupo, v.n. metallica. Orlo assottigliato rientrante e distinto all'interno da una rigatura in rilievo; vasca emisferica a profilo continuo. Decorazione: all'esterno, ampia zona risparmiata nella parte inferiore della vasca.

Alt. cm. 8; largh. cm. 6.

Per la discussione sulla forma cfr. n. 9, p. 272.

Prima metà del III sec.a.C.

34.   Piattino (Fig. 85.34). Argilla nocciola chiaro, v.n. a riflessi metallici. Orlo estroflesso arrotondato nella parte superiore con breve bordo verticale che forma un angolo con la vasca a parete obliqua, tesa; piede ad anello. Al centro sul fondo foro passante praticato intenzionalmente. Decorazione: la zona inferiore esterna della vasca ed il piede sono risparmiati.

Alt. cm. 4; largh. cm. 9, 5; diam. piede cm. 5, 5.

Simile alla forma Lamboglia 27C per cui cfr. Lamboglia, *C.P.*, pp. 176–177; per altri esemplari di Paestum cfr. *Poseidonia-Paestum* I, p. 118, n. 6, fig. 38, 26–28 e *Poseidonia-Paestum* II, p. 110, n. 128, figg. 64, 77.

III sec.a.C.

Acroma depurata

35.   Fr. di piattello su piede (Fig. 85.35). Argilla beige chiarissimo. Comprende il fondo della vasca raccordata senza soluzione di continuità all'alto fusto cilindrico; piede a disco con fondo piano.

Alt. cm. 6; diam. piede cm. 6, 1.

Il pezzo è pertinente ad un tipo di piattello su piede che in ambito pestano ha la più ricca documentazione in due contesti, sostanzialmente inediti, lo scarico del santuario extraurbano di Fonte, per ciò che attiene ai livelli di età ellenistica, ed il santuario suburbano della località Lupata-Torre, dove proviene da contesti databili nell'ambito del III sec.a.C. È verosimile dunque ipotizzare che questa forma, probabilmente un *thymiaterion*, abbia un uso ed una funzione relativi alla sfera del sacro ed alle manifestazioni del culto. Per i santuari citati cfr. *Paestum* 1987, pp. 30–31 (M. Cipriani) e pp. 44–45 (G. Avagliano).

III sec.a.C.

Da cucina

36.   Fr. di pentola (Fig. 85.36). Argilla arancio scuro ricca di inclusi litici neri. Orlo estroflesso nettamente tagliato nella parte superiore; bordo obliquo, parete fortemente convessa; all'interno dell'orlo dente per l'allettamente del coperchio.

Alt. cm. 7; largh. cm. 14, 5.

Cfr. Morel 1970, pp. 104–105, fig. 28; *Sibari* III, p. 206, n. 49, fig. 208 e 255; *Poseidonia-Paestum* I, p. 18, n. 6, fig. 39, 18; *Poseidonia-Paestum* II, p. 197, fig. 66, n. 185; *Poseidonia-Paestum* III, p. 146, fig. 94, n. 634. Per una disamina di alcuni tipi di pentole della fine del IV sec.a.C. e, più in generale, per una presentazione della ceramica da cucina e da fuoco proveniente da un contesto di V–IV sec.a.C., cfr. Cipriani 1988, p. 71 ss. e, in particolare, pp. 82–84.

Dalla fine del IV sec.a.C.

37.   Idem (Fig. 86.37). Argilla arancio scuro, stracotta. Simile per forma al pezzo precedente.

Alt. cm. 6, 5; largh. cm. 8, 8.

Cfr. il n. 36.

Dalla fine del IV sec.a.C.

38.   Idem (Fig. 86.38). Argilla mattone con nucleo grigio. Orlo estroflesso delimitato alla base da un gradino rilevato; bordo obliquo che all'esterno si innesta senza soluzione di continuità nella parete ed all'interno presenta alla base un altro gradino in rilievo.

Alt. cm. 3, 5; largh. cm. 7, 8.

Cfr. i nn. 36–37.

Dalla fine del IV sec.a.C.

39.   2 frr. (a–b) di pentola (Pl. 277.3 e 6). Argilla arancio vivo con ingubbiatura grigia e sovraddipintura bianca. Si conservano due tratti di parete decorati: (a) con un elemento vegetale stilizzato, (b) con un motivo a zig-zag compreso tra fasce.

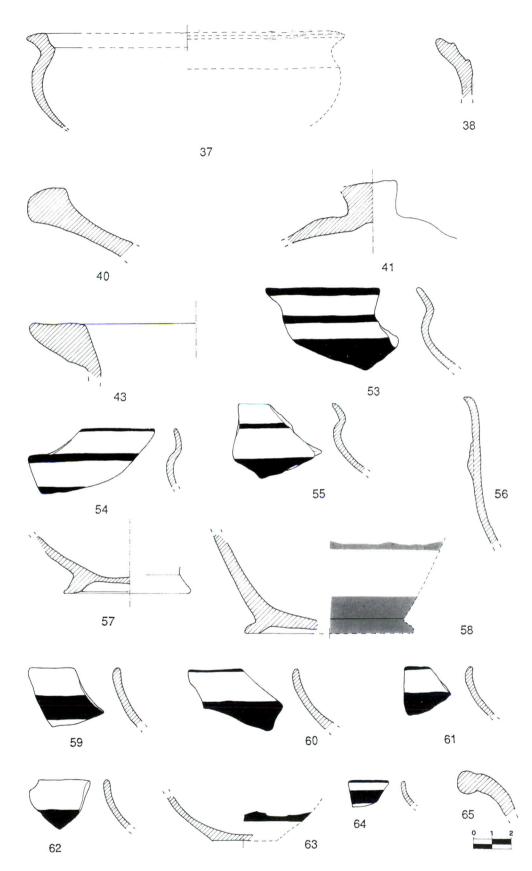

FIG. 86.   Paestum, "Teatro Circolare," pottery from trench in SW corner, center room of
Curia building, second level (nos. 37–43) and apron wall (rostra) fill (nos. 53–65)

(a): alt. cm. 7, 7; largh. cm. 7, 7.

(b): alt. cm. 8, 5; largh. cm. 6, 4.

Cfr. *Poseidonia-Paestum* II, p. 116, nn. 179–180, fig. 78.

IV–III sec.a.C.

40. Fr. di bacino (Fig. 86.40). Argilla arancio rossastro con tracce di ingubbiatura bianca. Comprende parte dell'orlo ingrossato, estroflesso e appiattito nella parte superiore con un breve tratto di vasca a parete obliqua.

Alt. cm. 6; largh. cm. 9.

La forma, che rientra nella classe dei bacini in argilla grezza diffusa in territorio greco ed indigeno sin dal VI sec.a.C., non subisce sostanziali variazioni nel tempo se non piccole trasformazioni nella sagoma dell'orlo. Un inquadramento generale della classe per l'età arcaica è in G. Bailo Modesti, *Cairano nell'età arcaica. L'abitato e la necropoli*, Napoli 1980, p. 76, tav. 86, 89. Per una disamina di bacili simili dal territorio pestano cfr. Cipriani 1988, pp. 70–71.

IV sec.a.C.

41.   Coperchio (Fig. 86.41). Argilla nocciola, rossastra in superficie. Pomello di presa troncoconico; pareti a profilo convesso.

Alt. cm. 4; largh. cm. 9, 5.

Per una tipologia dei coperchi da contesti stratigrafici di V e IV sec.a.C. dal territorio pestano cfr. Cipriani 1988, pp. 86–90.

IV sec.a.C.

42. Pomello di presa di coperchio. Argilla arancio. A bottone con fusto cilindrico.

Alt. cm. 2, 8; diam. cm. 3, 7.

IV–III sec.a.C.

E. ANFORE DA TRASPORTO

43.   Fr. di orlo di anfora (Fig. 86.43). Argilla arancio scuro con nucleo grigio; ingubbiatura rosata. Orlo a sezione triangolare orizzontale nella parte superiore, sottolineato da una gola nel punto di attacco con il collo.

Alt. cm. 3; lungh. cm. 11, 2.

Rientra nella diffusissima tipologia delle anfore con orlo piatto sporgente a sezione triangolare, databile dagli ultimi decenni del IV sec.a.C. e per cui cfr. N. Lamboglia, in *RStLig* 18, 1952, p. 162, fig. 20; P. Orlandini, in *NSc* 1956, p. 355; *Sibari* II, p. 143, n. 195, figg. 135, 198.

Fine IV–inizi III sec.a.C.

II. TERRECOTTE FIGURATE

A. *Piccola plastica*

44.   Fr. di statuetta di galletto (Pl. 278.1). Argilla arancio scuro con tracce di ingubbiatura biancastra. Ricavato da due matrici, cavo. Comprende la testa dell'animale.

Alt. cm. 6, 3.

Il frammento è pertinente ad una di quelle statuette di animali, galletti ma anche cagnolini e porcellini, che a Paestum sovente accompagnano le deposizioni infantili della fine del IV sec.a.C. Si ricordino, tra i numerosi possibili confronti, le statuette presenti nelle tombe 1 e 2 della necropoli di Tempa del Prete (scavo 1953, esposte in Museo) dove queste sono in associazione, fra gli altri materiali, con alcuni vasi a figure rosse della produzione pestana dell'ultimo quarto del IV sec.a.C. Per questi cfr. Trendall 1987, pp. 328, 544, tav. 215d, 549 e 550 tav. 216b.

Ultimi decenni del IV sec.a.C.

Apron Wall (Rostra) Fill (ππ)

I. CERAMICA

A. CERAMICA CORINZIA

45.   Fr. di *kotyle* (Pl. 269.9). Argilla grigio chiaro, vernice bruna. Piede ad echino, distinto dalla parete da una sottile scanalatura. Decorazione: nella zona inferiore della parete raggi; alla base di questa e sul profilo esterno del piede sottili fasce verniciate; il profilo interno del piede è decorato da due sottili bande verniciate.

Alt. cm. 2, 5; largh. cm. 7, 7.

Per la forma e la decorazione cfr. *Corinth* XIII, pp. 106–107 e 186, n. 160–3, tav. 24.

Metà del VI sec.a.C.

46.   Idem (Pl. 279.3). Argilla arancio chiaro con nucleo grigio, vernice nera opaca. Parete obliqua, piede ad echino. Decorazione: interno verniciato; sulla parete esterna raggi raccordati in basso da una fascia a v.n. che copre la parte superiore del piede. Profilo interno del piede sottolineato da una fascia verniciata; resti di una fascia analoga sul fondo.

Alt. cm. 3, 4; largh. cm. 5, 5.

Per una simile decorazione a raggi cfr. *Corinth* XIII, p. 217, n. 265–1, tav. 37, 265–1 (con bibliografia e confronti).

Inizi del V sec.a.C.

47.   Fr. di parete di vaso aperto (*kotyle*?) (Pl. 269.4). Argilla giallina; vernice nero-bruna, sovraddipintura paonazza; dettagli graffiti. Sulla parete esterna parte di decorazione figurata rappresentante volatile a destra.

Alt. cm. 3, 5; largh. cm. 5, 2.

Cfr. *Corinth* XIII, p. 176, 147–1, tav. 21.

Metà del VI sec.a.C.

48.   Fr. di pisside globulare (Pl. 269.7). Argilla giallina, vernice nera opaca, sovraddipinture bianche e paonazze; graffiti. Decorazione: dall'alto, tre sottili fasce concentriche su finta baccellatura con linguette alternativamente bianche, nere e paonazze; sotto, tra due coppie di sottili fasce orizzontali doppia fila di puntini disposti a scacchiera. In basso tracce della scena figurata.

Alt. cm. 4, 8; largh. cm. 3, 2.

Per la forma cfr. Payne, *Necrocorinthia*, pp. 322–323; *Corinth* XIII, p. 180, n. 155c, tav. 22.

Secondo quarto del VI sec.a.C.

49.   Fr. di *oinochoe* (Pl. 269.2). Argilla beige-rosato, vernice bruna, sovraddipintura paonazza, dettagli graffiti. Su serie di linee verniciate e sovraddipinte zampa di felino a sinistra e in basso a destra riempitivo floreale.

Alt. cm. 5, 6; largh. 2, 7.

Cfr. *Corinth* XIII, p. 179, n. 155, 6 e p. 182, 157f, tavv. 22 e 23.

580–570 a.C.

50.   Fr. di *lekythos* (Pl. 269.3). Argilla giallina, vernice nera opaca, sovraddipintura paonazza. Decorazione: dall'alto, due coppie di linee orizzontali paonazze, seguono due fasce di diverso spessore, l'una paonazza, l'altra verniciata.

Alt. cm. 5, 3; largh. cm. 4.

VI sec.a.C.

B. CERAMICA ATTICA

51.   Fr. di coppetta (Pl. 280.3). Argilla arancio, con ingubbiatura rossiccia, vernice nera molto lucente con riflessi metallici. Comprende breve tratto del piede cilindrico svasato alla base; fondo piano con tracce della fossetta centrale. Decorazione: piano di posa risparmiato.

Alt. cm. 1, 3; largh. 6, 5.

Cfr. *Agora* XII, pp. 130–131, pp. 294–295, nn. 816–823, fig. 8, tav. 32.

Seconda metà del V sec.a.C.

52.   Fr. di vaso di forma aperta (Pl. 280.2). Argilla arancio, vernice nera lucente, sovraddipintura paonazza. Comprende parte del piede ad echino cavo con breve fusto cilindrico. Decorazione: sul fusto linea paonazza; lungo il profilo interno del piede fascia verniciata.

Alt. cm. 1, 8; largh. cm. 8.

V sec.a.C.

C. CERAMICA DI FABBRICA COLONIALE
Di tradizione ionica

53.   Fr. di coppa di tipo B2 (Fig. 86.53). Argilla rosata con nucleo grigio; vernice rossastra.

Alt. cm. 5; largh. cm. 6, 5.

Cir. il n. 2, p. 269.

Seconda metà del VI sec.a.C.

54.   Idem (Fig. 86.54). Argilla arancio rosato, vernice nero-bruna, arrossata all'interno.

Alt. cm. 3, 4; largh. cm. 7.

Cfr. il n. 2, p. 269.

Seconda metà del VI sec.a.C.

55.   Idem (Fig. 86.55). Argilla arancio chiaro, vernice nera a riflessi metallici.

Alt. cm. 4, 2; lungh. 4, 6.

Cfr. il n. 2, p. 269

Seconda metà del VI sec.a.C.

56.   Fr. di coppa *skyphoide* (Fig. 86.56; Pl. 282.1). Argilla arancio, vernice nera a riflessi metallici. Orlo estroflesso, bordo verticale, parete convessa. Decorazione: all'interno sotto l'orlo risparmiato larga banda verniciata; all'esterno fascia risparmiata all'altezza dell'ansa.

Alt. cm. 8, 3; largh. cm. 3, 1.

Cfr. il n. 21, p. 275

Metà del VI sec.a.C.

57.   Fondo di coppa *skyphoide* (Fig. 86.57). Argilla arancio rosato, vernice bruna opaca. Piede ad echino. Decorazione: interno verniciato con tracce del tondo di impilamento; sul piede fascia verniciata.

Alt. cm. 3; diam. piede cm. 6, 8.

Il pezzo si inserisce nell'ambito della produzione poseidoniate della seconda metà del VI sec. a.C. e trova stretto riscontro, se non per la forma, del resto non precisabile nella sua interezza, per le caratteristiche dell'argilla e della vernice in alcune coppe di provenienza tombale, quali la n.i.21890 della tomba 89 e la n.i. 21918 della tomba 113 della necropoli del laghetto, inedite. Per una disamina delle fasci di questa necropoli, cfr. da ultimo M. Cipriani, in *Paestum* 1987, pp. 37, 38.

Seconda metà del VI sec. a.C.

58.   Fr. idem (Fig. 86.58). Argilla arancio rosato con nucleo grigio; vernice nera poco lucente diluita. Decorazione: interno verniciato; all'esterno fascia risparmiata nella zona inferiore della parete.

Alt. cm. 10, 5; largh. cm. 8, 2.

Cfr. il n. 57.

Seconda metà del VI sec. a.C.

59.   Fr. di coppetta monoansata (Fig. 86.59). Argilla beige, vernice rossastra. Orlo arrotondato, leggermente rientrante, tratto di parete convessa. Decorazione: interno verniciato, all'esterno fascia orizzontale verniciata.

Alt. cm. 3, 3; largh. 3, 7.

Cfr. i nn. 23–24, pp. 275–77.

Dalla fine del VI sec. a.C.

60.   Idem (Fig. 86.60). Argilla arancio, vernice nera a riflessi metallici. Simile per forma e decorazione all'esemplare precedente.

Alt. cm. 4; largh. cm. 5, 5.

Dalla fine del VI sec. a.C.

61.   Idem (Fig. 86.61). Argilla arancio, vernice nera lucente, a riflessi metallici, a tratti diluita. Simile per forma e decorazione all'esemplare precedente.

Alt. cm. 3; largh. cm. 2, 7.

Dalla fine del VI sec. a.C.

62.   Idem (Fig. 86.62). Argilla nocciola chiaro, vernice nera opaca. Simile per forma e decorazione agli esemplari precedenti.

Alt. cm. 3, 2; largh. 3, 5.

Dalla fine del VI sec. a.C.

63.   Idem (Fig. 86.63). Argilla arancio, vernice nera poco lucente, diluita. Decorazione: interno verniciato con cerchio risparmiato al centro, sul fondo della vasca. All'esterno parte di fascia verniciata.

Alt. cm. 2, 5; largh. 5, 2.

Dalla fine del VI sec. a.C.

64.   Idem (Fig. 86.64). Simile agli esemplari precedenti, ma di tipo miniaturistico. Argilla arancio, vernice nera lucente a riflessi metallici.

Alt. cm. 1, 9; largh. 2, 5.

Cfr. i nn. 59–63.

Dalla fine del VI sec. a.C.

65.   Fr. di *hydria* (Fig. 86.65). Argilla nocciola, vernice bruna. Orlo distinto arrotondato estroflesso, con breve tratto del collo a tromba. Decorazione: fascia verniciata sul labbro.

Alt. cm. 4; largh. cm. 8.

È pertinente ad un tipo di *hydria* con decorazione a fasce prodotto a Poseidonia dalla seconda metà del VI sec. a.C. e almeno fino alla metà del secolo successivo. Esso costituisce una variante locale di gruppi di materiali, prevalentemente *hydriai*, ma anche anfore ed *olpai*, fabbricati nelle colonie greche dell'Italia Meridionale imitando modelli greco-orientali, cfr. *Poseidonia-Paestum* i, pp. 19–20, fig. 41; *Poseidonia-Paestum* ii, pp. 90–91, nn. K26–K28 (con bibliografia), fig. 59, p.142, n. 287, p.159, n. 452, fig. 85; *Poseidonia-Paestum* iii, pp. 139–141, fig. 105, n. 563.

Dalla seconda metà del VI sec. a.C. alla prima metà del V sec.a.C.

66.   Idem (Fig. 87.66). Argilla arancione con nucleo grigio, vernice bruna, opaca, Comprende il piede ad echino con un breve tratto di parete obliqua, distinta da una scanalatura all'attacco del piede. Decorazione: fascia verniciata alla base della parete e sul piede.

Alt. cm. 3, 7; largh. 9, 4.

Cfr. il n. 65.

Dalla seconda metà del VI alla prima metà del V sec. a.C.

A vernice nera

67.   Fr. di *skyphos* (Pl. 271.4). Argilla arancio rosato, vernice nera opaca, sovraddipintura paonazza. Orlo assottigliato, leggermente rientrante, indistinto dalla parete a profilo convesso; ansa orizzontale a bastoncello a maniglia, impostata subito sotto l'orlo. Decorazione: risparmiati l'interno dell'ansa e la zona fra gli attacchi; coppia di linee paonazze sotto l'ansa.

Alt. cm. 3, 9; largh. cm. 6, 4.

Costituisce un'imitazione locale, poseidoniate, di modelli attici della prima metà del V sec. a.C., cfr. *Agora* xiii, pp. 81–83, p. 257, tav. 14, 313.

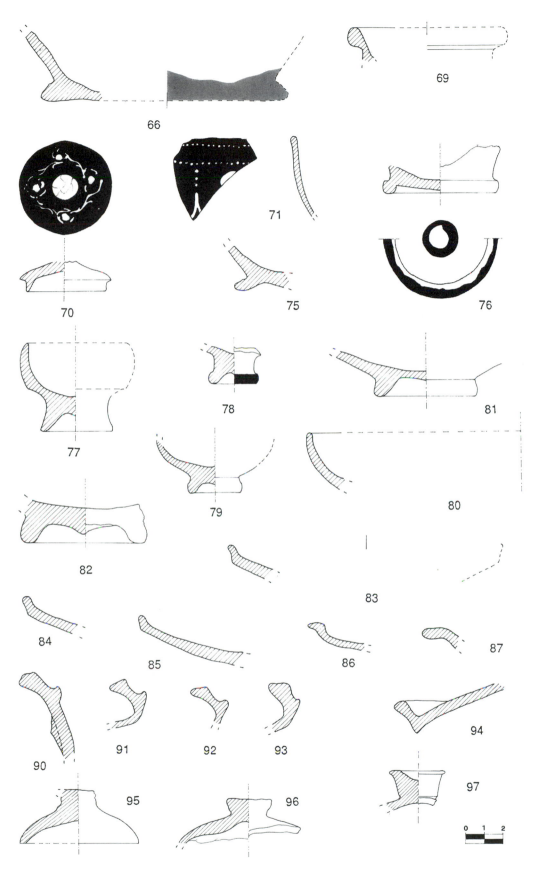

FIG. 87. Paestum, "Teatro Circolare," pottery from apron wall (rostra) fill

Prima metà del V sec. a.C.

68.   Fondo di *cup-skyphos* (Pl. 281). Argilla arancione con nucleo grigio, vernice nera poco lucente, a tratti diluita ed arrossata. Pareti fortemente convesse, piede toriforme. Decorazione: piede risparmiato con profilo interno sottolineato da una fascia a v.n. Sul fondo esterno, al centro, anello verniciato. Ricomposto e lacunoso.

Alt. cm. 6, 9; diam. piede cm. 9, 5.

Di officina probabilmente poseidoniate, si confronta per il piede toriforme e la decorazione con *Agora* XII, p. 259, n. 338, tav. 16.

Intorno alla metà del V sec. a.C.

D. CERAMICA DI FABRICA PESTANA

A figure rosse

69.   Piccolo coperchio (Pl. 279.4). Argilla arancio chiaro con ingubbiatura nocciola, vernice nera lucente a riflessi metallici. Breve tratto del fusto del pomello, parete obliqua, orlo arrotondato e bordo verticale. Decorazione: fascia verniciata alla base del pomello; sulla parete, tra due linee concentriche verniciate fascia ad onde correnti destrorse.

Alt. cm. 2, 2; diam. 6, 3.

Seconda metà del IV sec. a.C.

A vernice nera con decorazione sovraddipinta

70.   Piccolo coperchio (Fig. 87.70; Pl. 276.8). Argilla arancio, vernice nera opaca, sovraddipinture in bianco, giallo e paonazzo. Parete convessa con orlo nettamente tagliato ad angolo retto; bordo pendulo verticale. Decorazione: sulla spalla quattro bolli paonazzi collegati da tralci in bianco e giallo.

Alt. cm. 2; diam. cm. 5, 2.

Il pezzo, che originariamente doveva essere completo di presa ad ombrello, è pertinente ad una forma tipica della produzione pestana sovraddipinta e cioè la piccola *neck-amphora* con coperchio, per cui cfr. Forti 1965, pp. 71–72, tav. XXVa. Un esemplare simile per forma è in *Poseidonia-Paestum* II, p. 103, n. 94, fig. 74, con diversa decorazione.

Fine del IV–inizi del III sec. a.C.

71.   Fr. di *skyphos* (Fig. 87.71; Pl. 276.6). Argilla arancio, vernice nera opaca, sovraddipinture in bianco. Orlo assottigliato, leggermente estroflesso, bordo verticale, parete convessa. Decorazione: sul bordo doppia fila orizzontale di puntini; da quella inferiore si diparte una fila verticale di tre puntini desinente con nappina; nel campo così determinato resta parte di un elemento illeggibile (grappolo d'uva?)

Alt. cm. 4, 5; largh. cm. 4, 5.

Per il tipo cfr. Forti 1965, p. 74, fig. 21. La forma è assimilabile a quella del tipo Morel 4131a1, per cui cfr. Morel 1981, p. 292, tav. 118. Un esemplare del tutto analogo è in *Poseidonia-Paestum* III, p. 130, n. 494, figg. 93, 104.

300 a.C. circa.

72.   Idem (Pl. 276.7). Argilla arancione, vernice nera lucente a riflessi metallici, sovraddipinture in bianco. Simile per la forma dell'orlo al pezzo precedente. Tracce dell'attacco di un'ansa. Decorazione: sul bordo esterno parte di una fila orizzontale di bolli in bianco, interrotta in corrispondenza dell'ansa.

Alt. cm. 2, 5; largh. cm. 3, 5.

Analogo per forma al n. 71; la decorazione, simile, è però composta da bolli di maggiori dimensioni.

300 a.C.

73.   Fr. di coppa (Pl. 276.3). Argilla arancione, vernice nera a riflessi metallici, sovraddipinture in bianco e paonazzo. Decorazione: all'esterno parte di fascia orizzontale in bianco; all'interno, dall'alto, fascia ondulata paonazza; sotto fra due coppie di fasce accostate rispettivamente bianca e paonazza, fila di *chevrons* in bianco.

Alt. cm. 3; largh. cm. 3, 5.

Per la discussione sulla forma e la decorazione cfr. quanto detto a proposito dei nn. 6 e 29. Lo stesso motivo decorativo è presente sul coperchio di *skyphos* n.i.49618 della tomba 44 della necropoli pestana di Arcioni, databile agli inizi del III sec. a.C., inedita.

Prima metà del III sec. a.C.

74.   Idem (Pl. 276.1). Argilla arancio scuro, vernice nera a riflessi metallici; sovraddipinture in bianco, giallo e paonazzo. Decorazione: dall'alto tratti di linee orizzontali rispettivamente paonazza, bianca e paonazza; sotto tralcio di foglioline d'edera cuoriformi in bianco e giallo collegate da una linea orizzontale paonazza.

Alt. cm. 2, 9; largh. cm. 2, 7.

Cfr. il n. 73.

Prima metà del III sec. a.C.

A vernice nera

75.   Fr. di fondo di *skyphos* (Fig. 87.75). Argilla arancio, vernice nera poco lucente. Breve tratto di parete obliqua, piede a disco. Fascia risparmiata nella zona inferiore della parete; lungo il bordo ed il profilo del piede fasce verniciate.

Alt. cm. 2, 6; largh. cm. 5, 5.

Per la forma cfr. A. Bottini–E. Greco, *Tomba a camera dal territorio pestano: alcune considerazioni sulla condizione della donna*, in *DialArch* 8, 2, 1975, pp. 231–274, tav. D,2; *Poseidonia-Paestum* II, p. 146, nn. 330, 332–333, fig. 69.

Metà del IV sec. a.C.

76.   Fondo di *skyphos* (Fig. 87.76). Argilla arancio, vernice nera metallica. Breve tratto di parete fortemente rastremata in basso; piede ad anello. Piano di posa verniciato; sul fondo esterno, al centro, anello verniciato.

Alt. cm. 2, 9; diam. piede cm. 6, 2.

Assimilabile alla serie Morel 4373, tipica delle produzioni apule, per cui cfr. Morel 1981, p. 311, tav. 131 ed in particolare il tipo 4373 b1 e b2, da Ordona.

Ultimo quarto del IV sec. a.C.

77.   Coppetta (Fig. 87.77). Argilla arancio, più scuro in frattura, vernice nera lucente a riflessi metallici. Alto bordo convesso con orlo assottigliato, rientrante; alto piede cilindrico nettamente svasato alla base con cavità interna troncoconica ed ombelico inserito. Lacunosa.

Alt. cm. 4, 7; diam. piede cm. 4.

Cfr. il n. 31.

320–270 a.C. circa.

78.   Piede di vasca di *lekane* (Fig. 87.78). Argilla arancio, vernice nera poco lucente, a tratti diluita. Fusto cilindrico, piede ad anello, con cavità interna troncoconica ed ombelico.

Alt. cm. 2, 1; diam. piede cm. 2, 9.

Ultimi decenni–fine del IV sec. a.C.

79.   Fondo di coppetta (Fig. 87.79). Argilla arancio, vernice nera poco lucente. Tratto di vasca a pareti convesse fortemente rastremate all'attacco con il piede ad echino, con cavità interna troncoconica, ombelicata al centro. Piede irregolarmente verniciato sul fondo esterno.

Alt. cm. 2, 8; diam. piede cm. 3.

IV sec. a.C.

80.   Fr. di coppa (Fig. 87.80). Argilla arancio, vernice nera metallica. Orlo rientrante lievemente assottigliato, vasca a pareti fortemente convesse a profilo continuo.

Alt. cm. 3, 5; largh. cm. 9, 2.

Forma tipica della produzione pestana della prima età ellenistica, per cui cfr. *Poseidonia-Paestum* ii, p. 108, fig. 60 (con bibliografia).

Inizi del III sec. a.C.

81.   Fondo di patera (Fig. 87.81). Argilla arancione, vernice nera a riflessi metallici. Tratto di vasca rettilineo impostato obliquamente all'attacco con il piede ad anello, cavo, ombelicato sul fondo esterno. All'esterno la parte inferiore della parete ed il piede sono risparmiati.

Alt. cm. 2, 5; diam. piede cm. 5, 8.

Cfr. *Poseidonia-Paestum* ii, p. 111, n. 133, fig. 62.

Fine IV–prima metà III sec. a.C.

82.   Idem (Fig. 87.82). Simile al precedente. Argilla arancio scuro, vernice nera a riflessi metallici. Piede ad echino. Decorazione simile al precedente.

Alt. cm. 2, 8; diam. piede cm. 6, 7.

Cfr. il numero precedente.

Fine IV–prima metà III sec. a.C.

83.   Fr. di piattino (Fig. 87.83). Argilla nocciola, vernice nera lucente a riflessi metallici. Si conserva l'orlo lievemente estroflesso con bordo verticale a profilo leggermente concavo, formante un angolo ottuso con la vasca a pareti tese.

Lungh. cm. 8, 3; largh. cm. 2, 8.

Cfr., anche per la datazione, il n. 34, p. 279.

III sec. a.C.

84. Idem (Fig. 87.84). Argilla arancio, vernice nera poco lucente. La forma è del tutto simile a quella del pezzo precedente. Qui resta traccia all'esterno della parete della fascia risparmiata nella parte inferiore della vasca.

Lungh. cm. 8; largh. cm. 3, 5.

III sec. a.C.

85. Idem (Fig. 87.85). Argilla arancio chiarissimo con ingubbiatura rosata, vernice nera opaca. Per la forma e la decorazione è simile ai due esemplari precedenti.

Lungh. cm. 7, 2; largh. cm. 6, 1.

III sec. a.C.

86. Idem (Fig. 87.86). Argilla arancio, vernice nera opaca. Orlo estroflesso, appiattito superiormente, bordo verticale formante un angolo ottuso con la vasca a parete tesa.

Lungh. 4, 5; largh. cm. 3, 7.

Assimilabile alla serie Morel 1514: cfr. Morel 1981, p. 118, in particolare il tipo 1514 gl, tav. 20, da Paestum.

Primo quarto del III sec.a.C.

87. Fr. di piatto (Fig. 87.87). Argilla e vernice simili al pezzo precedente. Orlo appiattito, nettamente estroflesso, sottolineato all'esterno, all'attacco con il bordo verticale, da una scanalatura.

Lungh. cm. 3; largh. cm. 3, 1.

Cfr. *Poseidonia-Paestum* i, p. 19 nota 7, n. 43, fig. 42. Per la forma dell'orlo si avvicina ai pezzi della serie Morel 1315 ed in particolare al tipo 1315 c1, cfr. Morel 1981, p. 104, tav. 13.

Primi decenni del III sec. a.C.

A fasce

88. Fr. di coperchio (Pl. 270.5). Argilla arancio ricca di inclusi; vernice nero-bruna, diluita, a riflessi metallici. Comprende un tratto di parete decorato da una fascia tra due linee concentriche verniciate.

Lungh. 6, 8; largh. 5, 4.

La forma, un coperchio di grande *lekane,* e la decorazione, fasce concentriche di vario spessore in vernice bruno-rossiccia, sono tipiche della produzione pestana della fine del IV sec. a.C., come documenta, tra i numerosi possibili confronti, la *lekane* n. i. 27024 della tomba n. 76 della necropoli di Spinazzo, in associazione con una pisside a f.r. del Pittore di Spinazzo, la cui produzione può fissarsi intorno al 300 a.C., cfr. Trendall 1987, pp. 349–350. Per esemplari analoghi da contesti di abitato, cfr. *Poseidonia-Paestum* ii, pp. 100–101, n. 76, fig. 74.

Fine del IV sec.a.C.

Miniaturistica

89.   *Oinochoe* a bocca trilobata (Pl. 283.1). Argilla arancio. Orlo estroflesso, collo cilindrico svasato alla base; ansa verticale a nastro, impostata su labbro e ventre.

Alt. cm. 7, 5; diam. piede cm. 2, 6.

L'esemplare trova numerosi confronti tra il materiale votivo miniaturistico dei santuari di Paestum e Foce Sele, distribuito tra VI e IV sec. a.C., senza sostanziali variazioni morfologiche. La forma non è comunque tra le più diffuse, che restano l'*hydriska* ed il *krateriskos*.

VI–IV sec.a.C.?

Da cucina

90.   Fr. di pentola (Fig. 87.90). Argilla arancio vivo. Orlo estroflesso ripiegato verso l'esterno e segnato alla base da un gradino rilevato; bordo obliquo all'interno, sagomato per l'allettamento del coperchio, breve tratto di parete obliqua con tracce dell'attacco di un'ansa.

Alt. cm. 5, 1; largh. cm. 9.

Cfr. *Sibari* III, p. 206, 49, figg. 208, 255; *Meligunis Lipara*, tav. g, n. 10, t. 273 (ultimo terzo del IV sec.a.C.); *NSc* 1955, p. 324, fig. 36, t. 113 da Leontini; *NSc* 1958, p. 325, figg. 28–30, da Manfria.

91.   Idem (Fig. 87.91). Argilla arancione. Orlo estroflesso, appiattito superiormente e leggermente inclinato verso l'esterno; bordo verticale a profilo concavo internamente sagomato alla base per l'allettamento del coperchio; breve tratto di parete fortemente convessa.

Alt. cm. 2, 4; largh. cm. 12, 6.

Per la forma cfr. quanto detto a proposito del n. 36, p. 280.

Dalla fine del IV sec. a.C.

92.   Idem (Fig. 87.92). Argilla nocciola. Forma simile a quella dell'ex. precedente.

Alt. cm. 2, 5; lungh. cm. 8, 1.

Dalla fine del IV sec. a.C.

93.   Idem (Fig. 87.93). Argilla arancione. Forma simile a quella degli exx. precedenti ma con parete di maggior spessore.

Alt. cm. 2, 6; lungh. cm. 9, 2.

Dalla fine del IV sec.a.C.

94.   Fr. di coperchio (Fig. 87.94). Argilla grigia. Orlo arrotondato con bordo pendulo, obliquo, a profilo concavo ed estremità ingrossata e squadrata; tratto di parete rettilinea.

Alt. cm. 6; largh. cm. 8, 7.

Cfr. AA. VV., *Locri Epizefiri. Ricerche archeologiche su un abitato della Magna Grecia*, Mostra documentaria, Locri, ottobre 1983, tav. X, 5, in basso.

IV–III sec. a.C.

95.   Piccolo coperchio (Fig. 87.95). Argilla arancione con ingubbiatura grigiastra. Presa cilindrica, spalla fortemente emisferica con orlo tagliato orizzontalmente.
   Alt. cm. 3, 2; diam. cm. 6, 4.
   IV–III sec. a.C.

96.   Fr. di coperchio (Fig. 87.96). Argilla grigiastra. Pomello di presa troncoconico, spalla convessa.
   Alt. cm. 2, 2; largh. cm. 6, 7.
   IV–III sec. a.C.

97.   Pomello di coperchio (Fig. 87.97). Argilla arancio con nucleo grigio. Troncoconico con fossetta troncoconica nella parte superiore; scanalatura all'attacco con la spalla.
   Alt. cm. 2, 2; diam. cm. 3, 1.
   IV–III sec.a.C.

Paestum, 19 luglio 1988   Marina Cipriani
                                                            Giovanni Avagliano
                                            Soprintendenza Archeologica di Salerno.

Abbreviations to Appendix 2

Agora XII	B. A. Sparkes and L. Talcott, *The Athenian Agora XII: Black and Plain Pottery of the 6th, 5th and 4th Centuries* B.C. Princeton, 1970.
Bailo Modesti 1984	G. Bailo Modesti, *Lo scavo nell'abitato antico di Pontecagnano e la coppa con l'iscrizione AMINA[----]*, in *AION ArchStAnt* VI (1984).
Bloesch 1940	H. Bloesch, *Formen Attischer Schalen—von Exekias bis zum Ende des Strengen Stils*. Bern, 1940.
Cipriani 1988	Marina Cipriani, *S. Nicola di Albanella: Scavo di un santuario campestre nel territorio di Poseidonia-Paestum*. Rome, 1988.
Corinth XIII	C. W. Blegen, H. Palmer, and R. S. Young, *Corinth* XIII: *The North Cemetery*. Princeton, 1964.
Forti 1965	L. Forti, *La ceramica di Gnathia*. Naples, 1965.
Lamboglia *C.P.*	N. Lamboglia, *Per una classificazione preliminare della ceramica campana*, in *Atti del I Congresso Internazionale di Studi Liguri* (*Bordighera 1950*), pp. 139–206. Bordighera, 1952.
Meligunìs-Lipara II	L. Bernabò-Brea and M. Cavalier, *Melingunìs-Lipara II: La*

	necropoli greca e romana nella contrada Diana. Palermo, 1965.
Morel 1970	J. P. Morel, *"Fouilles à Cozzo Presepe, près de Métaponte,"* MEFR, 81 (1970), I: 73–116.
Morel 1981	J. P. Morel, *Céramique campanienne:les formes.* Rome, 1981.
Paestum 1987	G. Avagliano, M. Cipriani, et al., *Paestum (Città e Territorio nelle colonie greche d'Occidente I).* Naples, 1987.
Palinuro 2	R. Naumann and B. Neutsch, *Palinuro, Ergebnisse der Ausgrabungen II: Nekropole Terassenzone und Einzelfunde, Viertes Ergänzungsheft der Mitteilungen des Deutschen Archaeologischen Instituts Rom.* Heidelberg, 1960.
Payne, *Necrocorinthia*	H. Payne, *Necrocorinthia.* Oxford, 1931.
Poseidonia-Paestum I	E. Greco and D. Theodorescu, *Poseidonia-Paestum* I: *La "Curia."* Rome, 1980.
Poseidonia-Paestum II	E. Greco and D. Theodorescu in collaborazione con M. Cipriani et al. *Poseidonia-Paestum* II: *L'Agora.* Rome, 1983.
Poseidonia-Paestum III	E. Greco D. Theodorescu in collaborazione con A. Rouveret et al., *Poseidonia-Paestum* III: *Forum Nord.* Rome, 1987.
Sibari II	AA. VV., *Sibari: Scavi al Parco del Cavallo (1960–1962; 1969–1970) e agli Stombi (1969–1970)* in NSc 24 (1970), supplement 3.
Sibari III	AA. VV., *Sibari III: Rapporto preliminare della campagna di scavo: Stombi, Casa Bianca, Parco del Cavallo, San Mauro (1971),* in NSc 26 (1972), supplement.
Trendall 1987	A. D. Trendall, *The Red-Figured Vases of Paestum* (The British School at Rome). Hertford, 1987.

ABBREVIATIONS OF MEASUREMENTS

Alt.	=	Altezza
Cfr.	=	Confronta
Ex./exx.	=	Esemplare, esemplari
Fig.	=	Figura
F. n.	=	Figure nere
F. r.	=	Figure rosse
Fr./frr.	=	Frammento/frammenti
Largh.	=	Larghezza
Lungh.	=	Lunghezza
N. i.	=	Numero d'inventario
P./pp.	=	Pagina/pagine

V. n.   = Vernice nera
Diam.   = Diametro

Appendix 3. Faunal Material from Forum SW/SE Cistern

The human skeletal remains and animal bones come from one of a pair of vaulted cisterns in the Forum extension, Southwest Annex, that lies at right angles to the long southwest side of the Forum proper and on the axis of the approach to it from the Arx. It communicated with the Forum through a gate flanked by columns and terminated on the SW at a stair leading up to the Streets 5 and P, the latter of which continued SW to the entrance to the Arx.

The size of the cisterns has prevented their being systematically and completely emptied; they measure nearly 30.00 m in length. The bones were found in a sounding, 3.10 m by 1.50 m, made to the floor of the SE cistern at its E end. They were recovered at a depth of 2.00 m below the spring of the vault, mixed with debris from its collapse. The depth of the cistern at its E end is c. 3.10 m from the spring of the vault to the signinum floor. The accumulated fill beneath the vault in part represents refuse from the late antique settlement that grew up in and around the Forum from the third century after Christ on (pages 247–51).

Some specimens of pottery were closely datable to the fourth century A.C.,[1] but in addition to the pottery and bones, the fill also contained substantial building debris, which suggests that it was put down deliberately at one time. When that was cannot be determined, but the working hypothesis that the skeletal remains were fourth century or later in date seems confirmed by the analyses made by Ms. Gruspier and Dr. Scali. Their results may indeed carry one forward in time to the end of the castle period of medieval Ansedonia in 1329.[2] The limited extent of excavation in the cistern and the composition of the fill mean, of course, that the sample is far from complete.

Human Skeletal Material

Kathy Gruspier (M.A., Sheffield University)

C69—Skeleton No. 1: The remains of one of three individuals, Skeleton No. 1 is an adult male, approximately twenty-five years old. The skeleton is fairly complete, but lacks the skull and pelvis. Physically this individual was just as robust as modern European man, but not quite as tall (167.28 cm).

Pathology includes fractured rib, surrounded by penostitis, which is extensive

1. Dyson 1976, 160.   2. Brown 1951, 21–23.

and spreads onto the rib below. The fracture, because it is unhealed and has jagged edges, is most probably pathologic in origin. Fractures of this type are caused by localized infections in the surrounding tissue, which in this case would be the lungs. The cause, or type, of the infection cannot be determined.

Spinal pathology includes Schmorl's nodes on both aspects of all the thoracic and lumbar vertebrae. The cause of these nodes has not yet been determined; traits of human variation, stress, and trauma to the spine have been suggested. The third and fourth lumbar vertebrae exhibit localized degenerative changes on the anterior-superior borders. As with the rib, this change is most likely due to an infection in the overlying muscle or organs, in this case the psoas muscle, large intestine, and sigmoid colon.

Most interesting is the trauma to the second cervical vertebra (the axis). The dens epistrophei and both articular facets have been cleanly cut through. The individual was decapitated by a sharp axe or sword, wielded by a person standing to the right of the victim. The specific area of the cut and the fact that it was one clean blow could suggest that it was done by a professional executioner. Although the wound may have occurred right after death, it is quite feasible that decapitation was the cause of death. There are no other signs of violence or previous trauma of any sort on this otherwise healthy individual.

C69—Skeleton No. 2: Remains of a second individual, approximately half of a skeleton of a young male, twenty to twenty-three years of age. The aging can be done very accurately by epiphyseal union and one pubic symphysis. Physically he was a large, robust, tall individual (178.43 cm) who had not reached his full height as the time of death.

There are no signs of pathology or nutritionally induced stress. The cause of death is not certain. He was definitely not decapitated, as was Skeleton No. 1. The one remaining femur exhibits a large bony exostitis on the greater trochanter. This is due to muscle strain and is most often found in individuals who rode horseback frequently.

C69—Skeleton No. 3: Midshaft femur of a third individual.

Animal Bones from Forum SW/SE Cistern
Dr. Salvatore Scali (Museo dell'Arte Orientale, Rome)

I resti del cane meritano una trattazione particolare, primo perchè hanno una diversa provenienza, secondo perchè interessano solo il cranio e le mandibole, pur presentando un ottimo stato di conservazione, ci si chiede perchè non sono presenti gli altri resti dell'animale. Tenuto conto che durante lo scavo di Ansedonia si sono trovati anche dei resti umani non si può escludere che questi fossero associati ad una delle sepolture tardive rinvenute in una cisterna (Forum SW/SE Cistern).

Lo studio dei resti del cane, vista la buona conservazione del cranio e delle mandibole che con certezza appartengono ad uno stesso individuo, ha interessato principalmente un lavoro osteometrico, onde poter confrontare le misure prese con altri resti di varie razze (vedi tab. comparative allegate). Questo è servito per inquadrare, quanto possibile, la razza di appartenenza. Dai confronti metrici si può dedurre che si tratta di un individuo adulto e molto vicino, dalla dimensione della testa, al pastore tedesco come taglia.

I resti di animali selvatici, trovati nel campione di Ansedonia, sono testimoniati da due soli frammenti provenienti dalla cisterna del foro; un cranio di arvicola e un frammento di carapace di tartaruga. Entrambi si possono considerare intrusi nel contesto faunistico, in quanto l'arvicola ha nella cisterna una sua nicchia ecologica e la tartaruga può essere stata attratta, in quel luogo, per vari motivi come umidità o la ricerca di cibo.

Tabella Comparativa delle Misure del Cranio del *Canis Familiaris* di Ansedonia

	Canis f.	Dingo	Setter	Past. ted.	Lupo
Lunghezza assoluta	18,4	18,5–20,2	18,5–21,9	19,4–23,4	23,5–28,3
Lunghezza palato	9,4	8,9–9,7	8,9–11,0	9,2–11,7	11,3–13,4
Lunghezza muso	8,4	8,0–8,6	7,7–9,7	8,1–10,4	10,5–12,6
Minima distanza interorbitale	3,7	3,2–4,0	3,4–4,9	3,4–4,9	3,7–5,4
Minima larghezza del palato (dietro P1)	2,7	2,9–3,4	3,0–4,0	3,1–4,1	3,7–5,3
Max. larghezza del palato (dietro P4)	5,5	5,5–6,8	6,0–7,4	6,3–7,7	7,3–9,1
Max. altezza post.	5,4	4,5–5,1	4,6–5,8	4,5–5,6	5,4–7,0
Max. altezza orbita	3,0	3,0–3,5	3,0–3,7	3,0–3,7	3,4–4,2

Tabella Comparativa delle Misure della Mandibola del *Canis Familiaris* di Ansedonia

	Canis f.	Dingo	Setter	Past. ted.	Lupo
Lunghezza mandibola	14,3	13,5–14,7	13,5–17,3	14,3–17,4	17,5–20,2
Altezza ramo verticale	5,5	4,9–5,6	5,0–6,6	5,0–6,9	6,6–8,3

Tabella Comparativa delle Misure dei Denti Superiori del *Canis* di Ansedonia

	Canis f.	Dingo	Setter	Past. ted.	Lupo
Altezza C	1,9	1,7–2,2	1,8–2,4	1,9–2,3	2,5–3,1
P4	1,8	2,0–2,1	1,8–2,0	1,8–2,3	2,3–2,9
M1	1,2	1,3–1,4	1,2–1,5	1,3–1,5	1,6–2,0
M2	0,6	0,7–0,9	0,8–0,9	0,7–0,9	0,9–1,1

Tabella Comparativa delle Misure dei Denti Inferiori del *Canis* di Ansedonia

	Canis f.	Dingo	Setter	Past. ted.	Lupo
Altezza C	2,0	1,8–2,1	1,6–2,2	1,7–2,3	2,4–2,8
P2	0,9	0,8–1,0	0,9–1,0	0,8–1,1	1,2–1,5
P3	1,0	1,0–1,1	1,0–1,2	1,1–1,3	1,4–1,7
P4	1,2	1,2–1,3	1,1–1,3	1,2–1,5	1,5–1,9
M2	0,9	0,5–0,6	0,4–0,7	0,5–0,7	1,1–1,4

PLATES

PLATE 1.   SE cistern on NE side

PLATE 2.   NW cistern on SW side

PLATE 3.   Planting pit #0

PLATE 4.   Comitium and Curia, air view

PLATE 5. Comitium, NE retaining wall, exterior

PLATE 6. Unfinished planting pit, #4

PLATE 7. Comitium, NE retaining wall, exterior plaster

PLATE 8.   Comitium, SW retaining wall, exterior plaster

PLATE 9.   Comitium, amphitheater center, circle step, and drain

Plate 10.   Comitium, SE steps

Plate 11.   Comitium, NW retaining wall/Basilica SE wall

PLATE 12. Comitium, sounding in N corner

PLATE 13. Curia, floor and base of pillar

PLATE 14.   Curia, fragments of wall decoration

PLATE 15.   Comitium, sounding in NE quadrant

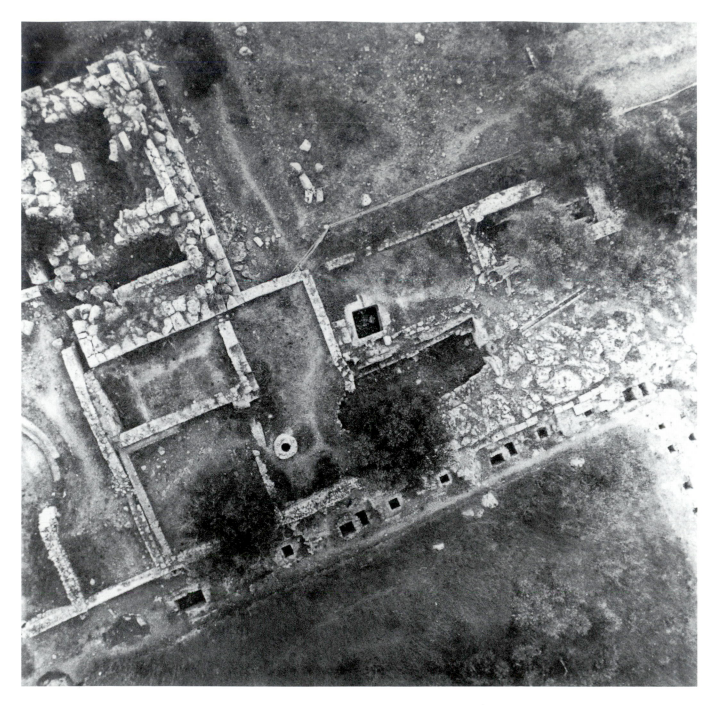

PLATE 16.   Forum, E corner, air view

PLATE 17.   E corner enclosure, silting tank, reveal block, looking SW

PLATE 18.   Cistern enclosure, sounding in N corner

PLATE 19.   Precinct and Carcer, looking SE

PLATE 20.   Carcer, looking N

Plate 21.   Carcer, cross wall

Plate 22.   Carcer, doorway,
looking NE

Plate 23.   Forum Square,
planting pits and post holes,
NE side

Plate 24. Forum Square, Post Hole #5, NE side

Plate 25. Cistern enclosure, stair to Comitium

PLATE 26.   Cistern enclosure, floor and immured drum, looking E

PLATE 27.   Forum Square, NE retaining wall, looking E

Plate 28.   Templum Beta, dry-laid NW wall

Plate 29.   Templum Beta, NE wall, exterior

Plate 30.   Templum Beta, NE wall, interior

Plate 31. Inscription, C72.129

Plate 32. Forum, SE cistern, SE end

Plate 33. Forum, SE cistern, NW end

PLATE 34. Forum, E corner, Street Q, open drain

PLATE 35. Templum Beta, forecourt, E corner

PLATE 36.   Templum Beta, forecourt, pavement covering the abandoned silting tank

PLATE 37.   Forum Square, E corner, looking N

Plate 38.   AB I, balloon
photograph (Whittlesey)

Plate 39.   AB I, looking E

PLATE 40.   AB I, Impluvium, cistern
vault and drains, looking E

PLATE 41.   AB I, Atrium, cistern drawshaft

PLATE 42.   AB I, Room 18,
doorsill

Plate 43.   AB I, Room 7, looking NE

Plate 44.   AB I, Entryway 1, looking NE

PLATE 45.   AB I, Entryway 12, looking SW

PLATE 46.   AB I, Entryway 4, looking E

PLATE 47.   AB I, Taberna 2, doorsill, reused

PLATE 48.   AB I, Taberna 2, Entryway 1, Room 7, looking SE

PLATE 49. AB I, Taberna 5,
E corner

PLATE 50. AB I, Taberna 19,
soak-away pit vault

PLATE 51. AB I, Taberna 15,
looking NE

Plate 52.   AB II, NE façade (between and beneath late walls), looking S

Plate 53.   AB II, SE façade and sounding (SW wall of entryway and blocked opening of SW taberna), looking W

Plate 54.   AB VII, NE façade and partition walls of Spaces 10, 8, and 6, looking NW

Plate 55.   AB VII, SW wall of Taberna 3, looking NW

Plate 56.   AB VII, Impluvium in 12, drain and cistern, looking N

PLATE 57.   AB VII, cistern in 12, looking NE

PLATE 58.   AB VII, gutter and steps of passageway, looking N

PLATE 59.   SE entranceway (Shrine of Liber Pater), "Tuscan" capital

PLATE 60.   Square, AB III/IV, Annex, AB V/VI, balloon photograph (Whittlesey)

PLATE 61. AB III and II, juncture corners, looking W

PLATE 62. AB III/IV, party wall and quoins, looking NW

PLATE 63. AB III, NW façade and Reservoir, looking SW

PLATE 64.   AB III, NW wall, reveal, and doorsill in partition wall, looking NW

PLATE 65.   AB III, NW wall and opening to Reservoir, sounding with passageway and pier, looking SW

PLATE 66.   AB III, SE party wall, SW end and sounding, looking S

PLATE 67.   AB V, NE façade and portico, looking W

PLATE 68.   AB VI, sounding, NW taberna, looking NW

Plate 69.   AB V/VI, SW wall and S corner on Streets 5 and Q, looking NW

Plate 70.   AB VI, SE wall, engaged half-column, looking SE

PLATE 71. Forum Annex, SE column base, looking E

PLATE 72. Forum Annex, SW end, stairs and exedrae, looking W

PLATE 73. N corner plot, Taberna 25, looking S

PLATE 74. N corner plot, Taberna 24/26, looking S

PLATE 75. Street O, sidewalk before Taberna 26, "Tuscan" capital

PLATE 76.   Curia, SE side of podium, looking SW

PLATE 77.   Curia, N corner, basin and vault, looking NE

PLATE 78.   Forum Square, double trench, central, looking NE

PLATE 79.   Forum SW Porticus, looking SE

PLATE 80.   Forum gutter and W
settling basin, looking NW

PLATE 81. Forum Reservoir, looking E

PLATE 82.   Forum Reservoir, looking N

PLATE 83.   Forum Reservoir, central pier
and sounding, looking N

PLATE 84.   Forum Square, SE end, post holes of one square, looking SE

PLATE 85.   Forum Square, SE end, post hole with lid and ring

PLATE 86.   Forum Square, SE end, post hole, eccentric

PLATE 87.   Streets O and 6, looking NE

PLATE 88.   Street 5, sewer,
looking SE

PLATE 89.   SE entranceway, sounding, looking W

PLATE 90.   NW Porticus and entranceway, looking SW

PLATE 91. NW Porticus, drum and column, looking S

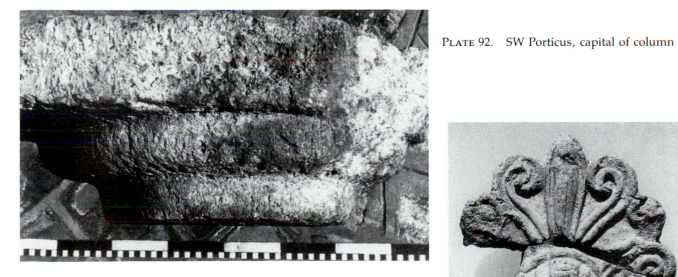

PLATE 92. SW Porticus, capital of column

PLATE 93. Antefix with head of goddess (C69.203)

PLATE 94. Fornices, looking S

PLATE 95. Fornices, SW unit, looking SW

PLATE 96. Fornices, NE unit, looking NE

Plate 97.   Forum Square, SW center, apron of slabs and sockets, looking SE

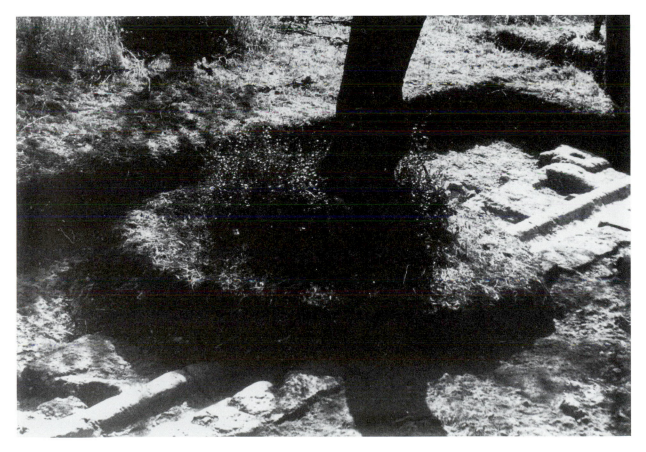

Plate 98.   Forum Square, SW center, apron of slabs and sockets, looking E

PLATE 99.   NW entranceway, centered remains of *suggestus,* looking SE

PLATE 100.   NW end of SW retaining wall along Street 7, looking SE

Plate 101.   Curia III, NW wall as later rebuilt, interior

Plate 102.   Curia III, SE wall, interior of upper part

PLATE 103.   Curia III, NE wall with buttresses, view looking NW

PLATE 104.   Temple B, NE wall

PLATE 105.   Temple B,
SE flank

PLATE 106.   Temple B, N corner and
passage between Temple B and Curia III

PLATE 107. Temple B, cella, interior with pit of clandestine diggers

PLATE 108. Temple B, column capital found in Comitium

PLATE 109.   Temple B, shell antefix with a head of Silenus

PLATE 110. Temple B, shell antefix with the head of a maenad (head)

PLATE 111. Temple B, shell antefix with the head of a maenad (shell)

PLATE 112.   Temple B, raking cornice

PLATE 113.   Temple B, tile for the setting of the raking cornice

Plate 114.   Temple B, open cresting A

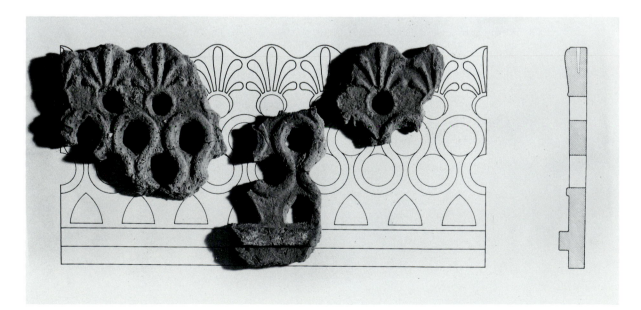

Plate 115.   Temple B, open cresting B

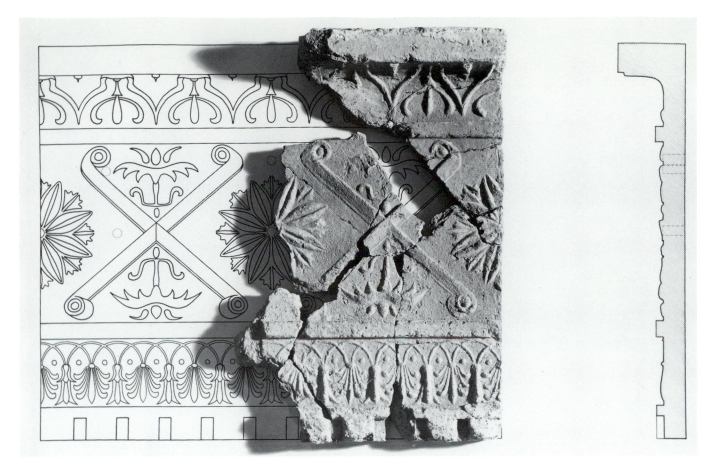

PLATE 116.   Temple B, revetment plaque with a design of crossed ribbons

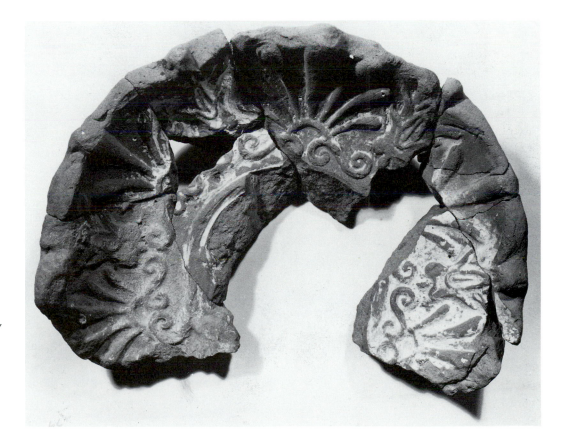

PLATE 117.   Temple B, repair of the decoration, antefix shell

PLATE 118.   Temple B, repair of the decoration, open cresting

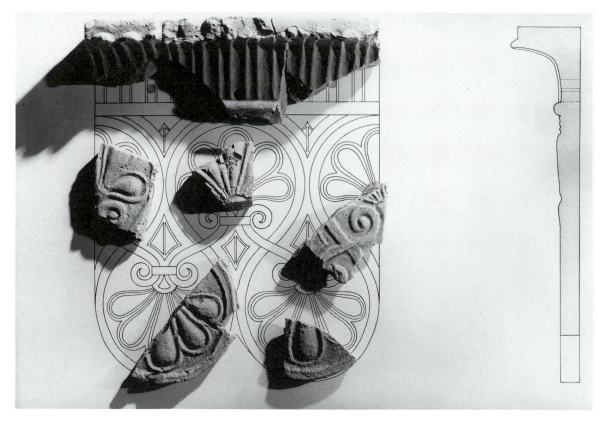

PLATE 119.   Temple B, repair of the decoration, revetment plaque of serpentine design

PLATE 120.   Temple B, pedimental sculpture I i 1

PLATE 121.   Temple B, pedimental sculpture I i 2

PLATE 122. Temple B, pedimental sculpture I i 13a, profile to right

PLATE 123. Temple B, pedimental sculpture I i 13a, full face

PLATE 124. Temple B, pedimental sculpture I i 13a, three-quarters view

PLATE 126.   Temple B, pedimental sculpture I i 13c

PLATE 125.   Temple B, .pedimental sculpture I i 13b

PLATE 127.   Temple B, pedimental sculpture I i 14a

PLATE 128.   Temple B, pedimental sculpture I i 14b

PLATE 130.   Temple B, pedimental sculpture I i 15b

PLATE 129.   Temple B, pedimental sculpture I i 15a

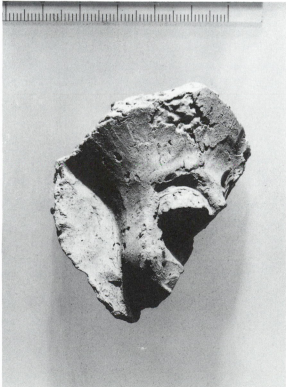

PLATE 131.   Temple B, pedimental sculpture I i 15c

PLATE 132.   Temple B, pedimental sculpture I i 16a

PLATE 133.   Temple B, pedimental sculpture I i 16b

PLATE 134.   Temple B,
pedimental sculpture I i 17

PLATE 135. Temple B, pedimental
sculpture I i 18

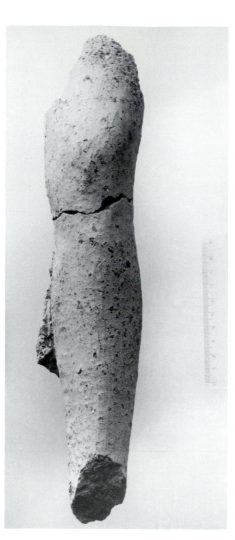

PLATE 136. Temple B, pedimental
sculpture I i 19, front view

PLATE 137. Temple B, pedimental
sculpture I i 19, side view

PLATE 138.   Temple B, pedimental sculpture I i 20

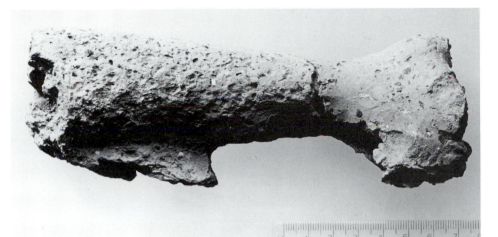

PLATE 139.   Temple B, pedimental
sculpture I i 21

PLATE 140.   Temple B, pedimental sculpture I i 22,
interior of arm

PLATE 141.   Temple B, pedimental sculpture I i 22,
exterior of arm

PLATE 142.   Temple B,
pedimental sculpture I i 23

PLATE 143.   Temple B, pedimental
sculpture I i 24a

PLATE 144.   Temple B, pedimental
sculpture I i 24c

PLATE 145.   Temple B, pedimental sculpture I i 25

PLATE 146.   Temple B,
pedimental sculpture I i 26

PLATE 147.   Temple B,
pedimental sculpture I i 27

PLATE 148.   Temple B, pedimental sculpture I i 28

Plate 149.   Etruscan ash-urn, Volterra, Museo Guarnacci, no. 223

Plate 150.   Etruscan ash-urn, Volterra, Museo Guarnacci, no. 221

PLATE 151.   Etruscan ash-urn, Paris, Bibliothèque Nationale

PLATE 152.   Etruscan ash-urn, Volterra, Museo Guarnacci, no. 238

PLATE 153.   Etruscan ash-urn, Volterra, Museo Guarnacci, no. 236

PLATE 154.   Etruscan ash-urn, Volterra, Tomba Inghirami

PLATE 155. Temple B, frieze I ii 1

PLATE 156. Temple B, frieze I ii 2

PLATE 157. Temple B, frieze I ii 3

PLATE 158. Temple B, frieze I ii 4

PLATE 160. Temple B, frieze I ii 6

PLATE 159. Temple B, frieze I ii 5

PLATE 161. Temple B, frieze I ii 7

PLATE 162. Temple B, fragments of life-size statuary I iii 1a

PLATE 163. Temple B, fragments of life-size statuary I iii 1b

PLATE 164. Temple B, fragments of life-size statuary I iii 1c

PLATE 165. Temple B, fragments of life-size statuary I iii 1d

PLATE 166. Temple B, fragments of life-size statuary I iii 1e

PLATE 167. Temple B, fragments of life-size statuary I iii 1l

PLATE 168. Temple B, fragments of life-size statuary I iii 1m

PLATE 169. Temple B, fragments of
life-size statuary I iii 2a

PLATE 170. Temple B, fragments of life-size statuary I iii 2b

PLATE 171. Temple B, fragments of life-size statuary I iii 2c

PLATE 172. Temple B, fragments of life-size statuary I iii 2d

Plate 173. Temple B, fragments of life-size statuary I iii 2e

Plate 174. Temple B, fragments of life-size statuary I iii 2f

Plate 175. Temple B, fragments of life-size statuary I iii 2g

PLATE 176.   Temple B, fragments of
life-size statuary I iii 3a

PLATE 177.   Temple B, fragments of life-size
statuary I iii 3b

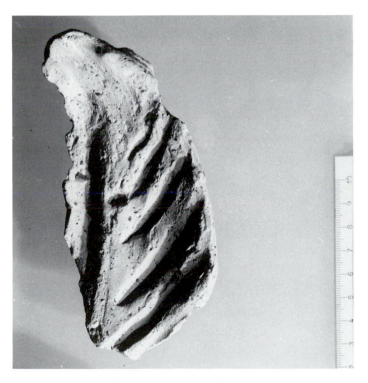

PLATE 178.   Temple B, fragments of life-size
statuary I iii 3c

PLATE 179.   Temple B, fragments of life-size statuary I iii 3e

Plate 180.   Temple B, fragments of life-size statuary I iii 4a

Plate 181.   Temple B, fragments of life-size statuary I iii 4b

Plate 182.   Temple B, fragments of life-size statuary I iii 4c

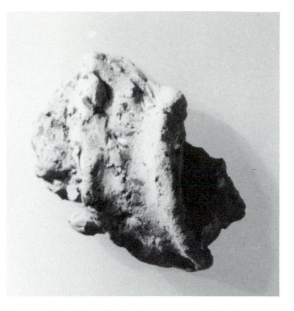

PLATE 183.   Temple B,
fragments of life-size
statuary I iii 4d

PLATE 184.   Temple B, fragments of life-size
statuary I iii 4e

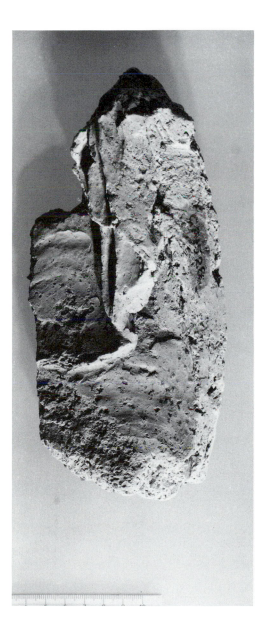

PLATE 185.   Temple B, fragments of life-size statuary I iii 5a

PLATE 187.   Temple B, fragments of life-size statuary I iii 5c

PLATE 186.   Temple B, fragments of life-size statuary I iii 5b

PLATE 188.   Temple B, fragments of life-size statuary I iii 5d

PLATE 189.   Temple B, fragments of life-size statuary I iii 6a

PLATE 190.   Temple B, fragments of life-size statuary I iii 6c

PLATE 191. Temple B,
bases I iv 1

PLATE 192. Temple B, bases I iv 2

PLATE 193. Temple B, bases I iv 3

PLATE 194.   Temple B, bases I iv 4a

PLATE 195.   Temple B, bases I iv 4b

PLATE 196.   Temple B, bases I iv 8a

PLATE 197.   Temple B, bases I iv 8b

PLATE 198.   Temple B, ex-votos,
Red Group II i 1a

PLATE 199.   Temple B, ex-votos, Red Group II i 1b

PLATE 200.   Temple B, ex-votos, Red Group II i 1c

PLATE 201.   Temple B, ex-votos, Red Group
II i 1d

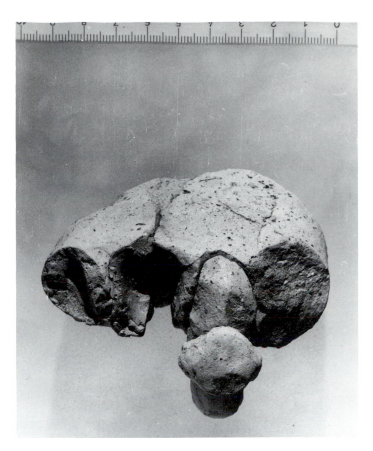

PLATE 202.   Temple B, ex-votos, Red Group II i 1e

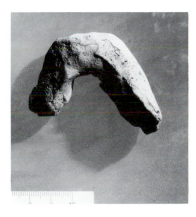

PLATE 203.   Temple B, ex-
votos, Red Group II i 1f

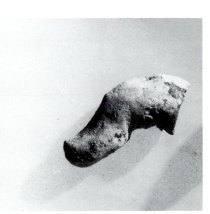

PLATE 204.   Temple B, ex-votos,
Red Group II i 1g

PLATE 205.   Temple B, ex-votos,
Red Group II i 1h

Plate 206.   Temple B, ex-votos, Red Group II i 1i

Plate 207.   Temple B, ex-votos, Red Group II i 2a

PLATE 208. Temple B, ex-votos, Red Group II i 2b

PLATE 209. Temple B, ex-votos, Red Group II i 3a

PLATE 210. Temple B, ex-votos, Red Group II i 4

PLATE 212.   Temple B, ex-votos, Red Group II i 5b

PLATE 211.   Temple B, ex-votos, Red Group II i 5a

PLATE 213.   Temple B, ex-votos, Red Group II i 6

PLATE 214. Temple B, ex-votos, Red Group II i 7,
front

PLATE 215. Temple B, ex-votos, Red Group II i 7, side

PLATE 216. Temple B, ex-votos, Red Group II i 7, back

PLATE 217. Temple B, ex-votos, Red Group II i 8

PLATE 218. Temple B, ex-votos, Red Group II i 9   PLATE 219. Temple B, ex-votos, White Group II ii 1a

PLATE 220. Temple B, ex-votos, White Group   PLATE 221. Temple B, ex-votos, White Group II ii 1c
II ii 1b

PLATE 222.   Temple B, ex-votos, White Group II ii 1d

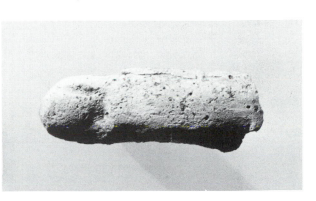

PLATE 223.   Temple B, ex-votos, White Group II ii 1e

PLATE 224.   Temple B, ex-votos, White Group II ii 1f

PLATE 225.   Temple B, ex-votos, White Group II ii 2

PLATE 226.   Basilica and surroundings, balloon photograph (Whittlesey)

PLATE 227.   Basilica and surroundings, looking E

Plate 228.   Basilica, NE foundations and tribunal, looking S

Plate 229.   Basilica, tribunal and vault, looking WNW

Plate 230.   Basilica, second cistern, looking SE

PLATE 231.   Basilica, SE wall with putlog holes, looking ESE

PLATE 232.   Basilica, NE wall of tribunal with window, looking N

PLATE 233.   Basilica, column base of
lower tier

PLATE 234.   Basilica, column capital of
lower tier

PLATE 235.   Basilica, column capital of
upper tier

PLATE 236. Basilica, slabs of Vulci tufa, reused

PLATE 237. Basilica, Ionic capital of Vulci tufa, reused

PLATE 238. Basilica, block of travertine fitted to a plinth of a column

PLATE 239.   Basilica, stair to the platform above the ambulatory, base in the NW cellar of the Curia

PLATE 240.   Basilica, stair to the platform above the ambulatory, print on the NW wall of Curia III

PLATE 241.   Steps along the NE side of the Square, SE section, looking NW

PLATE 242.   Steps along the NE side of the Square, NW section, looking E

PLATE 243.   AB IV, house, once taberna on Square, doubled walls

PLATE 244.   AB IV, house, once taberna on Square, raised floor

PLATE 245.   AB V, house, once taberna on Square, mosaic floor

PLATE 246.   AB VI, barnyard, SE wall

PLATE 247.   AB VI, barnyard, mangers

PLATE 248.   Basilica, collapsed NW wall

PLATE 249.   Odeum, fallen pillars beside standing one

PLATE 250. Odeum, remaining piers, ramped vaults, and steps, looking NE

PLATE 251. Odeum, pillar and floor of scaena

PLATE 252. Odeum, inscription of Nero and Claudius

PLATE 253. Odeum, stair from
Street 7

Plate 254.   Comitium, remains of second flooring, looking E

Plate 255.   Curia, NW buttress

PLATE 256. Curia, SE
basement, Mithraeum,
looking NE

PLATE 257. Curia, SE
basement, Mithraeum, parts
of square pillar

PLATE 258. Curia, SE
basement, Mithraeum, marble
leg with strut

PLATE 259.   Base of kiln for firing earthen vessels

PLATE 260.   Basilica, church in NE aisle, NW court and entrance

PLATE 261.   Basilica, church in NE aisle, SE apse and altar

PLATE 262.   Basilica, taberna with two ovens in S corner, looking S

PLATE 263.   Basilica, second taberna in S corner, looking S

PLATE 264.   Comitium, late wall and new threshing floor, looking S

PLATE 265.   Basilica, tabernae in S corner, statue built into party wall

PLATE 266.   Basilica, tabernae in S corner, statues extracted and mounted

PLATE 267.   Shrine of Liber Pater, central room, looking SE

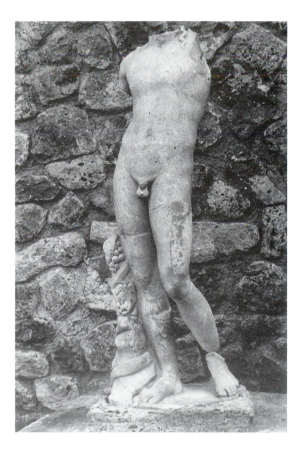

PLATE 268.   Shrine of Liber Pater, statue of Bacchus

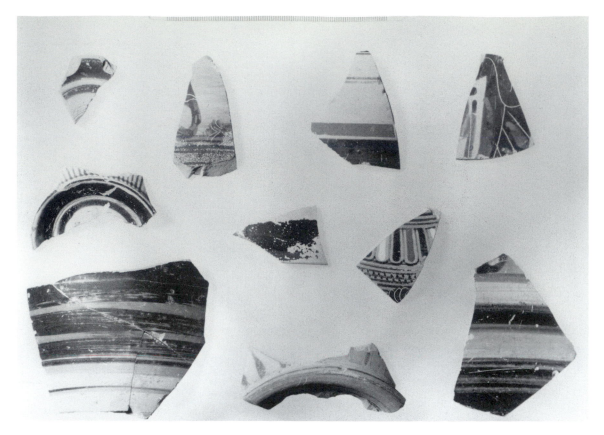

PLATE 269. Paestum, "Teatro Circolare," imported pottery, second half of the sixth century B.C.: Corinthian: Cipriani/Avagliano 1, 17, 45, 47, 48, 49, 50; Attic Black Figure: Cipriani/Avagliano 18

PLATE 270. Paestum, "Teatro Circolare," Paestan Red Figure and Black-Glaze, late fourth century: Cipriani/Avagliano 4, 88

PLATE 271.   Paestum, "Teatro Circolare," Paestan Black-Glaze with superimposed color, second half of the fourth century: Cipriani/Avagliano 5, 6; Black-Glaze, first half of the fifth century: Cipriani/Avagliano 67

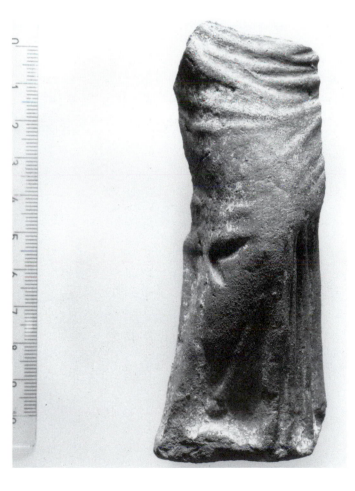

PLATE 272.   Paestum, "Teatro Circolare," headless terracotta figurine, third century B.C.: Cipriani/Avagliano 16

Plate 273. Paestum, "Teatro Circolare," fabbrica coloniale di tradizione Ionica, mid-sixth century: Cipriani/Avagliano 21, 22

Plate 274. Paestum, "Teatro Circolare," Black-Glaze, fifth century B.C.: Cipriani/Avagliano 25; Paestan Red Figure, second half of the fourth century B.C.: Cipriani/Avagliano 28

PLATE 275. Paestum, "Teatro Circolare," Black-Glaze, fifth century B.C.: Cipriani/Avagliano 27

PLATE 276. Paestum, "Teatro Circolare," Paestan Black-Glaze with superimposed color, end of the fourth and early third century B.C.: Cipriani/Avagliano 29, 30, 70, 71, 72, 73, 74

PLATE 277. Paestum, "Teatro Circolare," gray cooking ware with white decoration, fourth to third century B.C.: Cipriani/Avagliano 39a and b

PLATE 278. Paestum, "Teatro Circolare," fragments of terracotta figurines, last decades of the fourth century B.C.: Cipriani/Avagliano 44

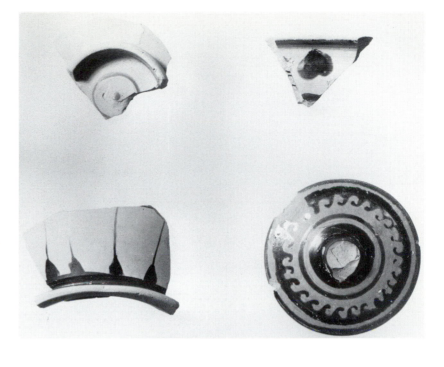

PLATE 279.   Paestum, "Teatro Circolare," miscellaneous pottery: Corinthian, beginning of the fifth century B.C.: Cipriani/Avagliano 46; Paestan Red Figure, second half of the fourth century B.C.: Cipriani/Avagliano 69

PLATE 280.   Paestum, "Teatro Circolare," Attic pottery, fifth century B.C.: Cipriani/Avagliano 51, 52

PLATE 281.   Paestum, "Teatro Circolare," Black-Glaze pottery, probably Paestan, mid-fifth century B.C.: Cipriani/Avagliano 68

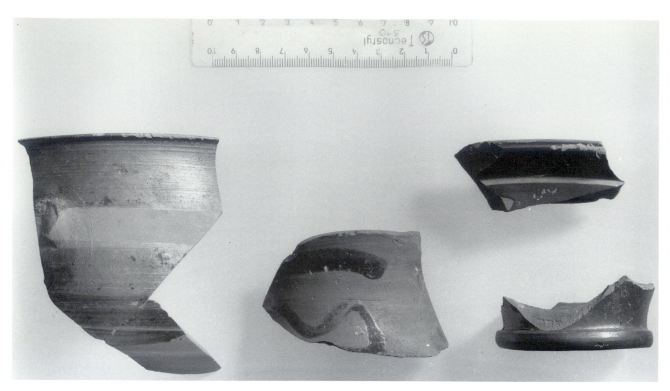

PLATE 282. Paestum, "Teatro Circolare," miscellaneous pottery: coloniale di tradizione Ionica, mid-sixth century B.C.: Cipriani/Avagliano 56

PLATE 283. Paestum, "Teatro Circolare," miscellaneous finds: Paestan miniature oenochoe, sixth to fourth century B.C. (?): Cipriani/Avagliano 89; Loomweights; fragment of a bronze pin

THE AMERICAN ACADEMY IN ROME is a center for the fine arts and for advanced research in the humanities. Founded in 1894, the Academy was chartered by an act of Congress as a private institution in 1905 in recognition of its singular contribution to America's cultural and intellectual life. The Academy's central purpose is its fellowship program. Each year, through a national competition, the Academy awards approximately thirty Rome Prize Fellowships in architecture, design arts, landscape architecture, literature, musical composition, painting, sculpture, visual arts, classical studies, archaeology, history of art, modern Italian studies, and postclassical humanistic studies. These fellowships provide the Rome Prize winners with a stipend, travel funds, room and board, and a study or studio in which to pursue independent work for six months to two years at the Academy's eleven-acre site on the Janiculum Hill. Distinguished professionals are also invited to live and work at the Academy as Residents. Since its founding, the Academy has awarded approximately one thousand fellowships and residencies. The Academy also maintains a research library with 110,000 volumes, representing one of the world's principal scholarly resources in classical archaeology and Roman topography. The Academy sponsors two series of publications, the *Memoirs* and *Papers and Monographs.* Exhibitions, concerts, lectures, and symposia given by Fellows, Residents, and invited guests draw international audiences to the Academy, strengthening ties between the American, Italian, and other European cultural and scholarly communities. The Academy is supported by gifts and grants from individuals, colleges and universities, foundations, corporations, and the National Endowments for the Arts and the Humanities.